TONI MORRISON

TONI MORRISON

Memory and Meaning

Edited by
Adrienne Lanier Seward and Justine Tally

University Press of Mississippi / Jackson

www.upress.state.ms.us

The University Press of Mississippi is a member
of the Association of American University Presses.

"The Buckeye" originally appeared in *Prairie Schooner* 62, no. 1 (Spring 1988).
Copyright © 1988 by Rita Dove. Reprinted by permission of the author.

"Aaayeee Babo, Aaayeee Babo, Aaayeee Babo" was originally
written for this volume. Copyright © 2011 by Sonia Sanchez.

The excerpt from Lucille Clifton's poem "i am accused of tending to the past" in Ann
Hostetler's essay "Resurrecting the Dead Girl" is taken from *The Collected Poems of
Lucille Clifton*. Copyright © 1987 by Lucille Clifton. Reprinted with the permission of
The Permissions Company Inc. on behalf of BOA Editions Ltd., www.boaeditions.org.

Portions of "'And the Greatest of These': Toni Morrison, The Bible, Love," by Katherine
Clay Bassard, are taken from chap. 6 of her book *Transforming Scriptures: African
American Women and the Bible* (Athens: University of Georgia Press, 2010), 93–105.

Claudine Raynaud's "The Pursuit of Memory" is an abridged and reworked version of an essay
originally published as "Toni Morrison: Le lieu et la mémoire," in *Etudes de poétique*, ed. Josiane
Paccaud-Huguet et Michèle Rivoire (Lyon: Presses Universitaires de Lyon, 2001), 45–63.

Copyright © 2014 by University Press of Mississippi
All rights reserved
Manufactured in the United States of America

First printing 2014
∞
Library of Congress Cataloging-in-Publication Data

Toni Morrison : memory and meaning / edited by Adrienne Lanier
Seward, Justine Tally ; foreword by Carolyn C. Denard.
  pages cm
Includes bibliographical references and index.
ISBN 978-1-62846-019-3 (hardback) — ISBN 978-1-62846-020-9
(ebook) 1. Morrison, Toni—Criticism and interpretation. I. Seward,
Adrienne Lanier, 1945– editor of compilation. II. Tally, Justine, editor of
compilation.
  PS3563.O8749Z9137 2014
813'.54—dc23   2014005688

British Library Cataloging-in-Publication Data available

CONTENTS

ix   Acknowledgments

xi   Foreword
         CAROLYN C. DENARD

xv   Introduction

3   The Buckeye
         RITA DOVE

Part I. "This is where I belong"

7   "Dangerously Free": Morrison's Unspeakable Territory
         PHILIP WEINSTEIN

19   Modernity and the Homeless: Toni Morrison and the Fictions of Modernism
         MARC C. CONNER

33   Resurrecting the Dead Girl: Modernism and the Problem of History in *Beloved*, *Jazz*, and *Paradise*
         ANN HOSTETLER

42   To Make a Humanist Black: Toni Wofford's Howard Years
         DANA A. WILLIAMS

Part II. "Regrets, excuses, righteousness, false memory and future plans mixed together or stood like soldiers in line"

53   Trying to Get Home: Place and Memory in Toni Morrison's Fiction
CHERYL A. WALL

66   The Pursuit of Memory
CLAUDINE RAYNAUD

80   Personal and Cultural Memory in *A Mercy*
EVELYN JAFFE SCHREIBER

93   *Love*: An Elegy for the African American Community, or The Unintended Consequences of Desegregation/Integration
LUCILLE P. FULTZ

Part III. "Her garden was not Eden; it was so much more than that"

107   From Eden to Paradise: A Pilgrimage through Toni Morrison's Trilogy
SHIRLEY A. STAVE

119   "And the Greatest of These": Toni Morrison, the Bible, Love
KATHERINE CLAY BASSARD

132   Palimpsest: Reading John Winthrop through the Morrison Trilogy
JUSTINE TALLY

144   Magically Flying with Toni Morrison: Mexico, Gabriel García Márquez, *Song of Solomon*, and *Sula*
DAVÍD CARRASCO

Part IV. "Now it seemed both fresh and ancient, safe and demanding"

159   Property and American Identity in Toni Morrison's *Beloved*
LOVALERIE KING

172   Aeschylus, Euripides, and Toni Morrison: *Miasma*, Revenge, and Atonement
TESSA ROYNON

185	Toni Morrison's Performance of the Word in *Song of Solomon*: The Folkloric, the Fantastic, and "Some Old Folk's Lie" ALMA JEAN BILLINGSLEA BROWN
194	"A Kind of Restoration": Psychogeographies of Healing in Toni Morrison's *Home* VALORIE THOMAS

Part V. "You can keep on writing but I think you ought to know what's true"

207	Aesthetic Activity CLAUDIA BRODSKY
218	"'There is the Power,' he thought, 'right there'": Dramatizing Entropy in *Tar Baby* and *Paradise* HERMAN BEAVERS
231	Telling Stories: Evolving Narrative Identity in Toni Morrison's *Home* JAN FURMAN
243	"Newness trembles me"? Representations of White Masculinity in Toni Morrison's *A Mercy* MAR GALLEGO-DURÁN
255	The Sound of Change: A Musical Transit through the Wounded Modernity of *Desdemona* LENORE KITTS
269	Aaayeee Babo, Aaayeee Babo, Aaayeee Babo SONIA SANCHEZ
273	Contributors
279	Index

ACKNOWLEDGMENTS

Many people were instrumental in bringing this project to fruition. The support of members and friends of the Toni Morrison Society, under whose auspices the concept of the book was initiated, was unfailing. For expert and often solicited backup at the "midnight hour" for solving formatting and other technical problems, we are grateful to Michael Acosta and Paula Pyne. We would also like to extend our gratitude to William Henry, Georg Bauer, and the staff at the University Press of Mississippi for their help and guidance through various stages of this project.

We wish to thank our contributors, of course, for their dedication and hard work in revising and cheerfully working to tight deadlines, and most especially for the depth of their grasp of the Morrison canon—as these essays demonstrate.

FOREWORD

In the summer of 1969, I was a hardworking and supremely happy rising high school junior, who had remained in the all-black high school despite the "freedom-of-choice" options offered to us in the late '60s. That summer, I was waiting for the start of my junior year to reap the "golden girl" benefits of a high school life well lived: district Tri Hi-Y president, class officer, prom committee, drum majorette, mixed octet...and then my high school closed. Closed—doors locked, lights out, no more, finished—almost overnight, it seemed, and without warning or time to prepare for where we were going or think about what we were leaving. I had said goodbye to school friends in May 1969 fully expecting to see them in place in September in our familiar roles. Some of them, in the aftermath of the abrupt closing of our school that summer, I never saw again. Closing the black high school in my neighborhood, as it did in so many black neighborhoods in the South, atomized the community. The notice of the decision was just a brief article in the newspaper that summer. The court's decision in the Desegregation Now case (*Alexander v. Holmes County Board of Education*) seemed to have come without warning, without time for us to prepare for where we were going or to gather up the affective cultural "belongings" that we had so quickly to leave behind. Football and basketball games—over; holiday and spring choir concerts—silenced; teachers as revered community leaders—gone; classmates whose names I knew and watched grow on the stage, on the court, and in the classroom—scattered to other schools and other places. The deep ache of that loss—what to do with it, what to think about it, how to recover from it—was just a big hole in my heart. Until I read *Sula*.

Its opening line resonated deeply within me: "In that place where they tore nightshade and blackberry patches from their roots to make room for the Medallion City Golf Course, there was once a neighborhood." Those lines gave me a way to frame, "to see," a shattered moment in my own life through a clearer, more affirming lens. I read about the people from Medallion as if they were my own. No laments here from Toni Morrison—just the loving eye of a narrator who knew them and loved them, without an outsider's unknowing, pathetic, overwrought gaze. When I first read *Sula* as a student in John McCluskey's class in African American Literature at Indiana University in the summer of 1976, the fullness of my memory, of what was good and sustaining about that community that had changed in 1969, was restored. As the post-*Brown* generation growing up in the South, we had generally accepted that integration was good, historic—so the shock and sadness of the sudden and irretrievable change in my community had been silenced in all of us in the early '70s for something greater than ourselves. We moved forward without much open reflection. History called, and we, like so many brave students before us, answered. Not many had been reflective enough to think about what we were losing or even how to describe it if we had. We had just carried around a silent aching in our hearts over the memory of the kind of community life that had shaped our values and worldview, unsure if it was even right to see its passing as a kind of loss, unsure if we should question any of the triumphs of the long-awaited goal of integration. Through the rich joy and sadness of *Sula*, I began to see my own neighborhood differently—the good and the bad. I was given an example in the novel of how to cull meaning from that memory, how to honor it as I moved forward.

And over the years, through graduate coursework, dissertation, writing, teaching, and, yes, in the work of the Toni Morrison Society, I have tried to affirm, again and again, what I remember most about the community that shaped me: a legacy of excellence—in language, in education, in music, in presentation, in food, in laughter, in music, in spirituality, in generosity. It was a memory that the novel brought me back to, and in sustaining and culturally affirming ways. *Sula* showed me how to appreciate the fullness of the culture of the community I grew up in, to see its integrity, and to insist on its value at a time when it was under siege. Reading *Sula* at that impressionable moment in my life shaped me personally and also shaped my work as a scholar, for the overarching goal in my work has been to glean from Morrison's novels the African American cultural values deeply embedded in them.

Personal and empowering recollections leading to and existing alongside committed and clarifying scholarship have become distinctive of the best critical engagement in Morrison's work and, as well, became the fertile ground for the emergence of the Toni Morrison Society. Founded on May 28, 1993, at the annual meeting of the American Literature Association in Baltimore, the society quickly attracted national and international scholars and readers of Morrison's work. Four months after the society's founding, Toni Morrison was awarded the Nobel Prize for Literature. Now, twenty years later, we simultaneously cherish both achievements—through personal memory and the continuation of a record of excellent scholarship.

It is those two distinctions—personal memory and scholarly meaning—that the society wanted to capture in the essays and tributes that we presented to Ms. Morrison on the occasion of her eightieth birthday. The result was a remarkable and riveting collection of scholarly essays, personal reflections, poems, and tributes titled *Memory and Meaning*. "Memory" to capture the poignant reflections of the impact of Toni Morrison's life on so many who knew her personally, and "meaning" for the ways in which her writings have helped to shape the contours of American literary criticism for the past forty years.

This volume grows out of that collection. While the essays here are now largely scholarly, focusing on the critical meanings in Morrison's fiction, the collection also includes essays that derive their power from unstated transformative and instructive personal experiences that some of contributors have had with Toni Morrison. The society's members have richly appreciated the impact of these personal encounters. She has always been an honored guest at society conferences, and by being there, listening to scholars discuss her work and often engaging with us in that discussion, she has given us more than her writings; she has also given us her presence.

The essays here are important testaments to the legacy of the personal memory and scholarly engagement that so many of us have experienced with Toni Morrison and her works. Sometimes she is a part of that memory; other times she is a conduit that brings our own personal memories forward. As she told Paula Giddings in an interview in 1977: "I'm fascinated by what it means to make somebody remember what I don't even know."

Indeed, it was the clarifying quality of Toni Morrison's work that helped me to restore my memory of, and see with new eyes the values of, the black community that I grew up in before the atomizing the changes wrought by the U.S. Supreme Court's desegregation order in 1969. And the impact of that restoration has shaped the course of my scholarship and my career. This volume acknowledges and has come into being as a tribute to the generative power of memories of and through Toni Morrison and her critical achievement as a literary artist of the first order.

Carolyn C. Denard
Founder
Toni Morrison Society
April 28, 2013
New London, Connecticut

INTRODUCTION

Toni Morrison writes "with a prose so precise, so faithful to speech, and so charged with pain and wonder that the novel becomes poetry." These words are as appropriate today as they were in John Leonard's 1970 *New York Times* review of her first novel, *The Bluest Eye*. Nine novels later this remarkable author continues to be an imposing presence in world literature and to wield an almost uncanny influence on scholars, and on serious readers beyond those professionally committed to literary studies. Witness, for example, the ease with which Morrison converted a socially and culturally diverse audience into an "amen corner" on *Oprah*.

With the understanding that the personal is political, Morrison creates stories sent with her own postage stamp, stories that open our consciousness to realities that many have willfully refused entry. Exhorting social changes that need addressing, she refocuses our perceptions through the eyes of those who have paid dearly, too dearly, as victims of individual and social neglect and abuse. For over forty years, she has astounded us with the beauty of her words as intensely as she has impressed us with the urgency of her concerns. As humanist, author-scribe, literary critic, editor, playwright, and librettist, and as a friend of our minds, she has revealed herself as a woman so comfortable in her own skin that she author-izes us to be our "own best thing."

Political, yes, but the writing by her own standards must be "irrevocably beautiful" ("Rootedness," 345). Her fictions are so well-crafted that her characters have become part of our lives; her words, to paraphrase David Carrasco, enable us to "fly magically" through worlds we never knew. With Morrison we have learned to read beyond the page, to evoke memories and experiences that we have never had. With her we have learned to be free to soar, free to imagine, like Pilate, free to know more people and to love them all, free to revel in, as Piedade inspires us to do, "the unambivalent bliss of going home to be at home" (*Paradise*, 318).

This volume is simultaneously commemorative and celebratory, acknowledging the fortieth anniversary of the publication of her first novel, the twentieth anniversary of the awarding of the Nobel Prize for Literature (1993), and the twentieth anniversary of the founding of the Toni Morrison Society. Its title, *Toni Morrison: Memory and Meaning*, connotes Morrison's concern with the role of memory (and disremembering) in coming to terms with the difficult and violent past of African Americans in the United States. Memories are themselves, as she has so effectively shown us, meaningful, so "meaning" is meant to encompass not only scholarly explications of her work but equally the personal significance that her stories have for her readers.

But to speak of the "meaning" of her work is only to scratch the surface of the "Morrison phenomenon." Thomas Kuhn's articulation of "paradigm shifts," in ways initiated by her texts, permeates the essays. They consistently reflect, in approach and interpretation, the revolutionary change in the study of American literature, inaugurated by *Playing in the Dark*, by focusing on the interior lives of enslaved Africans and their descendants, thereby generating readings that challenge and subdue previously held, universally accepted, and, for many, ideologically and politically irresistible assumptions. But what these essays do *assume* is black subjectivity. Rather than simply arguing for it, they commandeer it to reread and revise the nature of slavery and its consequences for slave and master into our time. The analyses collected in this volume attest to a broad range of interdisciplinary specializations and interests; not only do they enhance the breadth and depth of Morrison studies, but they also work to shift the paradigms for scholarship in religion, history, classical mythology, psychology, folklore, law, and philosophy. If it is true, as M. M. Bakhtin postulates, that "collective memory" resides in the linguistic forms and expressions shared by a community, even when the signifiers have been divorced from their signifieds, then Morrison's additions to that memory have enriched us almost beyond human comprehension, extending a "Morrison community" around the world. No matter where we are, in real space or in cyberspace, no matter where we "hail from," these expressions inspire recognition, as we for once all speak in the same tongue. It is the language of "re-memory," "dis-remembering," "quiet as it's kept," "Baby Suggs, holy," "the Thursday man," "circles of sorrow," "the white girl," "a bench by the road," "my telling cannot hurt you," "Not Doctor Street"—the list is endless—not to mention that wonderful outlaw cry "Hey Celestial!" To these we must now add Cee, "the original caring-for," and Desdemona, who dreams she would "compete with the

Amazons," as we struggle to come to terms with the demands these newest works make on us.

In *Home* we find a reworking of many of the tropes and themes that run throughout Morrison's fiction. Frank's "footprints left in the snow" (11) as he escapes from the mental institution remind us of Violet's footprints in *Jazz*. The biting cold and his need for *shoes*, as well as his memories of his family's forced exodus from Texas when "the sole of my shoe flapped until Pap tied it up with his own shoelace" (42), echo Florens's obsession with fancy footwear and soles (souls). Frank's last name, Money, revisits Deacon and Stuart Morgan in *Paradise*, whose original surname was "Moyne," an anagram of "money." The sweet bay tree also signals the close association of Pecola with the marigolds and the earth in *The Bluest Eye*, while in *Home* "the sweet bay tree split down the middle, beheaded, undead" (144), describes Frank, whose "roots resisted disturbance and fought back." This metaphor no less applies to Cee, "Hurt right down the middle / But alive and well" at the end of the novel (147).

It is particularly notable that on the first page of the narrator's story, when Frank attempts to concentrate on a "single neutral object" (7) so that he can lie completely still, thereby simulating a deep morphine-induced semicoma, all his first choices conjure up major metaphors of earlier novels:

Breathing. How to do it so no one would know he was awake. (7)

    Ice, he thought, a cube of it, an icicle, an ice-encrusted pond, or frosted landscape. (7)

    Fire, then? Never, Too active. (7)

Here we have air (*Song of Solomon*), water/ice (*Beloved*), and fire (*Sula*), which, together with the dominant motif of the flowering or barren earth (*The Bluest Eye*), represent the four cardinal elements of life. These he consciously identifies a page later but dismisses in favor of train tracks ("endless, endless tracks" [8]), extending another major Morrison trope to include not only the forced exodus from the South (as in *Jazz*) but the return *home*.

In *Home* Morrison's exploration of the meaning of home to her characters by extension implicates her readers in their own understanding and recalls Robert Frost's "Death of the Hired Man": "Home is the place where, when you have to go there, / They have to take you in," a place where, no matter what happens, you belong. Having fled "the worst place on earth," Frank's fraught return to Lotus is the only possible destination in his desperate attempt to save Cee. Turning her over to Miss Ethel, who "loved mean," Frank is banished from the healing, giving him time to discover the type of love that can turn Miss Ethel's garden into "something more than Eden" (130).

In fact, perhaps the most dominant link among all the novels, and one that is central to *Home*, is Morrison's abiding concern with the nature of love. At one point in his challenge to the narrator, Frank admonishes, "You don't know anything about love. Or me" (69). While our logical first reading of this statement is that the narrator does not know about Frank, it might also be that Frank means "Me neither." Love is something Frank and Cee must learn. Frank never clearly uses the word "love" in his relationship with his homeboys or in his caring for Cee, yet we would infer this love from all his concern for them, and his willingness to sacrifice his own well-being on their behalf. But actually Frank depends on his friends' "knowing" him (e.g., "Afterward, for months on end, Frank kept thinking, 'But I know them. I know them and they know me'" [99]) and on Cee's heroic picture of him for his sense of identity: "Deep inside her lived my secret picture of myself—a strong good me" (104). This "love," however, cannot hold until Frank learns to love himself through acceptance and atonement, for, to paraphrase Baby Suggs, the only love he can have begins with the love he imagines for himself.

These many links have inspired our decision to use quotes from Morrison's tenth novel as headings for the five parts of this book, grouping the essays as they relate to or engage themes also prevalent in *Home*. Like the novel itself, our volume is also framed by poetry: "The Buckeye" by Rita Dove and "Aaayeee Babo, Aaayeee Babo, Aaayeee Babo" by Sonia Sanchez. These outstanding poems not only pay homage to the author but also appropriately bookend this volume commemorating her work.

Part I: "This is where I belong"

The nature of belonging that permeates Morrison's fiction is the subject of the four essays of part 1. Each of these contributions configures this notion differently, moving in ever-widening concentric circles from the author's fictional examination of what it means to belong (or not) to a people, to a country, to modernity, to history, and to humanity.

Morrison's admission of her personal vulnerability to "romanticizing blackness" leads Philip Weinstein to look at the strategies she uses to avoid such romanticism, at the "risky business" of her "willingness to probe racial experiences that are painful to the touch," and at her willingness to enter her "own territory" with the same unflinching eye that she turns on the territories of others. Weinstein explores the "reflexive light" that Morrison sheds on the people to whom she belongs even as she explores the extremes of "white-conditioned black distress" that cause a pervasive and persistent sense of unbelonging.

This unbelonging is a trope that Marc Conner expands to a pervasive sense of "homelessness," which for Morrison is "the crisis of modernity." Noting that her response to this "radical condition" is "at odds with the dominant discourses of postmodern and postcolonial theory," he argues that in her work it is "both unremittingly embodied and resolutely religious in its nature." It is Morrison's "ontological impulse" through her storytelling that teaches us about and revises modernity itself.

For Ann Hostetler the trope of the dead girl in Morrison's trilogy marks the "space of 'unbeing,'" the unbelonging to a historical sphere. In Hostetler's reading, it is the dead girl ("the silence at [the novels'] center") that disrupts the narrative paradigm and strives to heal "the ruptures of historical discontinuity." As stories of resurrections, the novels are also reclamations of "discarded narrative alternatives," which invite us to "an ongoing dialogue with a past" of exclusion.

Dana Williams's essay extends the theme of belonging (and exclusion) to Morrison's professional work as an accomplished editor. In acknowledging editors as "curators of culture," Williams highlights Morrison's instrumental role in shaping "the representation of African American culture in printed texts in the years immediately following the decline of the Black Arts Movement." She argues for Morrison's "unabashedly methodical" representation of blackness "as a distinct cultural reality" by closely examining the author's years at Howard University to answer the question of how Morrison came to develop that concept of blackness.

Part II: "Regrets, excuses, righteousness, false memory and future plans mixed together or stood like soldiers in line"

Belonging, identity formation, and the importance of place and home all come to the forefront once again in part 2, but here these themes are all filtered through the crucial play of memory and re-membering. Indeed, the sites of memory conjure up both positive and negative connotations and crucially influence (and sometimes impede) both the integrity and the integration of the individual in his or her society.

"Place and displacement, home and homelessness, belonging and exile, memory and loss" infuse the analysis of Cheryl Wall as she explores the primary sites of memory in Morrison's novels, with particular emphasis on *The Bluest Eye* and *Paradise*. She asks, What makes these detailed physical locations at once destructive and inviting? Extending her considerations in a concluding critical commentary on *Home*, Wall argues that it is through an "act of moral imagination" that Frank comes to embrace the place he so desperately tried to leave behind to become a soldier.

Using a psychoanalytic framework, Claudine Raynaud draws on memory as "the return of the repressed" in *Beloved*. Whether bumping into a rememory that belongs to someone else, or the haunting of a house by a phantasm that re-presents the traumatic (or catatonic) memory of the infanticide, Raynaud links the "geological metaphor" (of literary archaeology) of a spatially oriented "myth of memory" to "the metaphoric process at work in black American literature."

Personal and cultural memory are both at work in Evelyn Jaffe Schreiber's essay, which centers on *A Mercy*. Drawing on "neuroscience and social theories of memory and trauma," Schreiber alleges that "attaining a positive sense of self occurs when personal memories can sustain subjectivity." According to this critic, characters can escape neither their inherited cultural expectations nor their bodily stored memory. Bodily performed cultural ritual clashes at times with demands of the new environs and creates conflict, but personal memory "maintains dominion of the self, despite the pressures of the greater culture."

Though sharing a collective memory and experience of slavery and segregation, the African American community, as Lucille Fultz argues, watched as integration uprooted and at times destroyed the "rootedness" of that community and its actual geographic place. Different attitudes, reactions, and levels of participation in many cases produced an ambivalence of a goal that had long given meaning to the historical struggle. Morrison's *Love* is a meaningful discussion of the losses and gains of the civil rights community and takes up differences incurred by both class and gender.

Part III: "Her garden was not Eden; it was so much more than that"

Morrison has long acknowledged, and her critics have repeatedly signaled, her indebtedness to the Bible and other religious texts not only in her extensive use of names taken from this omnipresent ur-text but in her undeniable concern with the meaning(s) of love and the relevance of human compassion for the survival of the black community in the face of life-threatening chaos.

This is hardly to say that the author imbues her narrative with an uncritical acceptance of the God of the Old Testament. On the contrary, Shirley A. (Holly) Stave argues that Morrison actively sustains a religious critique of Christianity in her trilogy while exploring alternative theologies "more capable of providing wounded souls the healing and refuge they require." For Stave, Sweet Home is a riff on the Garden of Eden with its "lush pastoral setting" that is far from innocent. She then engages both *Jazz* and *Paradise* as a "startling critique of the Judeo-Christian God," positing salvation not as religious reward but as the "result of human forgiveness and connectedness."

Katherine Clay Bassard also examines Morrison's meditations on love in her novels in light of her readings and (re)readings of the Bible. She goes on to examine how Morrison seeks to reclaim love (as agape, eros, and philos) as "an ethical mandate to break the cycle of racism, sexism, and other oppressions" while concluding that in the author's artistic vision, "Eros (sexual love) and agape (divine, self-sacrificial love) are either mobilized or disallowed by the presence or absence of philos (brotherly, communal love)."

The crucial foundation of both love and mercy is emphasized in Justine Tally's exploration of John Winthrop's famous sermon on the *Arbella* in 1630 as a mediation between biblical texts and Morrison's trilogy, a palimpsest for intertextual referencing. For Winthrop, "whether governed by the Law of Nature or the Law of the Gospel, the Law of Mercy lies incumbent on each of the members of the community, also instructed in Romans 1:31." And what makes the act of mercy possible is its foundation in love. The trilogy, in fact, takes on maternal love, romantic love, and love of ideology, interrogating them in their extreme manifestations as the annihilation of any sense of self, and positing the healing of individual characters through the abiding strength, compassion, and support of the community.

Davíd Carrasco continues the exploration of religious themes in his reflection on Morrison's "language of catching, of doing, and of togetherness" through an analysis of *Song of Solomon*'s interpretation of magical flight and *Sula*'s emphasis on sacred place. Drawing on his conversations with the author, Carrasco characterizes the various ways that the sacred appears in Morrison's texts as traditional Christian ritual and symbols, African-influenced themes and characters, and what Morrison calls "Strange Stuff." As portrayed in many religious traditions, magical flight is the "search for a 'spiritual ally,' often in the form of a bird, who enables the seeker in the face of some profound challenge to change 'place.'"

Part IV: "Now it seemed both fresh and ancient, safe and demanding"

Morrison is inspired by, and engaged with, properties of the ancient texts, at once infusing them with a sense of newness while exploding any security we may falsely have entertained. The four essays in this part examine the formation of identity and the search for integrity in Morrison's characters in decidedly different yet enriching ways. Using classical mythology, African-derived philosophy and spiritual systems, folklore, and legal history, these readings examine the ways in which Morrison both locates the protagonists in their historical moment and provides them with a usable past from which to move forward into a viable future.

Lovalerie King takes a legal analysis to shape her discussion about what it has meant to be a black slave caught between the American ideas of identity and property. How can you belong to a place that denies you the "rights, protections, and privileges associated with citizenship"? Centering her discussion on *Beloved*, King explores the implications of a system in which "an essential aspect of American identity is the right to claim ownership of tangible and intangible property," foregrounding the denial of these rights that made black people "acutely aware" of the terms of their unbelonging, so masterly materialized in the figure of Beloved herself.

Tessa Roynon reaches back into the literary past of Greek tragedy to explore the consequences of crime and atonement, revenge and reconciliation, as reflected in four of Morrison's novels (*Song of Solomon*, *Beloved*, *Jazz*, and *Love*). Although African Americans have traditionally been alienated from the American judicial system through lack of protection and willful blindness, Morrison's novels "suggest alternative means to atonement," and hence to greater integrity, breaking the criminal cycle and eschewing both the legal system and the "infinite violence of revenge."

While Milkman's journey in *Song of Solomon* is also geographical as well as psychic, Alma Jean Billingslea Brown employs the idea of "participatory relationship" among performers, readers, and writers, so characteristic of Morrison's writing, to elucidate an understanding of performance as "'make-belief,' which worries the line between reality and performativity." The trope of flying frames the protagonist's search for identity, ultimately located through his rootedness to his past in Shalimar, Virginia, and through folklore to his African legacy.

Valorie Thomas introduces her own concept of African diasporic vertigo as a method of healing and "decolonizing" the psyche. Drawing on ancient African traditions and motifs of the trickster and the liminal space of the crossroads, Thomas argues that Morrison's strategy in *Home* eschews the "quest for purification and redemption" in favor of a "restorative" narrative that "prioritize[s] the black subject's ability to embody psychic balance and cultural equilibrium over the quest for purification and redemption."

Part V: "You can keep on writing but I think you ought to know what's true"

Aside from the "irrevocable beauty" of her work, Morrison's writing is nothing if not provocative in its relentless search for truth, and the book's final part responds to those challenges in multiple ways.

Claudia Brodsky examines Morrison's writing as a challenge to Walter Benjamin's assertion that "the aestheticization of politics" (in fascism) is answered by "the politicization of art" (in communism). She describes the author's aesthetic activity as "the experience, identification, and fabrication of beauty," which is *always* political, because what could be more irrefutably beautiful (and irrefutably political) than "seeing beauty ... where nothing had been seen at all"?

Herman Beavers continues to interrogate the intersections of aesthetics and the politics of race, gender, and class in his challenge to early oppositional readings of *Tar Baby*, in which Jadine rejects the "ancient properties" of black communality represented by Son, privileging a fixation on a "racially inflected drama" rather than on a critique of black nationalism. By incorporating the male violence toward females so overt in Morrison's seventh novel, Beavers engages *Paradise* and *Tar Baby* in a "coherent conversation" that reassesses "our assumptions about change and affiliation, suggesting that they can only be enjoyed via a propensity to create systems open to the many forms alterity can assume."

The elusiveness of "truth" is explored in Jan Furman's innovative reading of Morrison's tenth novel, *Home*, by tracing Frank Money's struggle for psychic coherence through dealing both with his past in Lotus, Georgia, and post-traumatic stress from his years in the Korean War. Taking her cue from the author that "structure is meaning," and borrowing from studies in psychology and human development, Furman "links the structural dimension of Frank's first-person perspective to his evolving narrative identity." The exploration of Frank's "dynamic narrative" in his geographical as well as psychological journey home reveals the novel's "significant concerns with the moral and metaphysical transformation of human life," which represents a move toward self-acceptance and maturity.

Mar Gallego-Durán steps into this conversation in her analysis of *A Mercy* as an "interrogation of the internal workings of racial but also class and gender politics" of the seventeenth century, which positions the novel as a challenge to the foundational impositions of white patriarchy. In her reading, the characters "test the limits of hegemonic masculinity by transgressing social and sexual boundaries," thereby signaling "the threats posed by an increasingly sexist, racist, and class-conscious value system." Such a reading also challenges the unexamined myth of the founding of the country as "of the people, by the people, for the people," given that "people" were obviously defined as "white, heterosexual, and male."

Racial, class, and gender politics expectedly pervade Morrison's reimagining of Shakespeare's *Othello* and the tragedy of his character Desdemona. Lenore Kitts anchors her examination of these themes in the stage production of *Desdemona* in another recurring element in Morrison's work: the "persistence of the past into the present through song." In what Kitts calls a "provocative experiment," she argues that Morrison's lyrics challenge audiences "to reevaluate the actions of Shakespeare's characters, particularly the women," and, equally important, that Morrison "modernizes the ambiguities about Africa in Shakespeare's play with the aid of [the Malian composer Rokia] Traoré's socially charged music."

Kitts's essay and the volume end on this note as a reminder of the world in which we live: the world Morrison continually and imaginatively rewrites illuminates the blindness produced by uncritical acceptance of our myths, modern and ancient, and the perniciousness of losing our language, our voice, our story. Morrison's work is now instrumental to our understanding of the world that she continues to expand beyond our wildest dreams, the world of her boundless imagination. We must take the visions she has granted us and leave the easy, protected confines of our self-satisfied paradigms and belief systems; we must go on, like Denver, out into the world . . . and if happiness or love is not possible or even relevant, commitment is.

Works Cited

Bakhtin, M. M. *The Dialogic Imagination*. Trans. Michael Holquist. Austin: University of Texas, 1988.

Frost, Robert. "Death of the Hired Man." In *The Poetry of Robert Frost: The Collected Poems, Complete and Unabridged*, ed. Edward Connery Lathem, 34–39. New York: Henry Holt, 1969.

Kuhn, Thomas. *The Structure of Scientific Revolutions*. 2nd ed. Chicago: University of Chicago Press, 1970.

Leonard, John. "Books of the Times." Review of *The Bluest Eye*. *New York Times*, November 13, 1970.

Morrison, Toni. *Beloved*. New York: Knopf, 1987.

———. *The Bluest Eye*. New York: Vintage, 2007.

———. *Desdemona*. Lyrics by Rokia Traoré. London: Oberon Books, 2012.

———. *Home*. New York: Knopf, 2012.
———. *Jazz*. New York: Vintage, 2004.
———. *Love*. New York: Vintage, 2005.
———. *A Mercy*. New York: Alfred A. Knopf, 2008.
———. *Paradise*. New York: Knopf, 1998.
———. "Rootedness: The Ancestor as Foundation." In *Black Women Writers (1950–1980): A Critical Evaluation*, ed. Mari Evans, 339–45. New York: Anchor Books, 1984.
———. *Song of Solomon*. New York: Knopf, 1997.
———. *Sula*. New York: Knopf, 1973.
———. *Tar Baby*. New York: Knopf, 1981.

TONI MORRISON

THE BUCKEYE

RITA DOVE

We learned about the state tree
in school—its fruit
so useless, so ugly

no one bothered to
commend the smudged trunk
nor the slim leaves shifting

over our heads. Yet
they were a good thing to kick
along gutters

on the way home,
though they stank like
a drunk's piss in the roads

where cars had smashed
them. And in autumn
when the spiny helmets split

open,
there was the bald
seed with its wheat-

colored eye.
We loved
the modest countenance beneath

that leathery cap.
We, too, did not want to leave
our mothers.

We piled them up
for ammunition.
We lay down

with them
among the bruised leaves
so that we could

rise, shining.

PART I

"This is where I belong"

"DANGEROUSLY FREE"

Morrison's Unspeakable Territory

PHILIP WEINSTEIN

> Only a musician would sense, know... that Cholly was free. Dangerously free.
> —*The Bluest Eye*

In an interview on *Fresh Air* (September 9, 2010), Terry Gross asked Jonathan Franzen how he could tell when his writing of *Freedom* was going well. His answer (paraphrased) was that it was going well when it hurt to do it. The writing of his that mattered (in both *Freedom* and *The Corrections*) did so because it cut close to the bone. It mattered because it made its way past his defenses and said something disturbing—and painful to say—about his sense of himself in the world. Franzen added that, for him, such moments were never directly political, since in proclaiming his political views he could remain well defended, sure that he was right. To go deeper was to lose the certainty of being right.

In this essay I want to testify to Toni Morrison's willingness to probe racial experiences that are painful to the touch—and would remain unspeakable without her having found (as she put it in *Playing in the Dark*) "the words to say it" (13). *Playing in the Dark* emerged in 1992 as a stunning argument about how white writers "play" black materials to produce white identities. It was about the undeclared literary politics involved in writing "the other." Again and again those essays hit home, showing the implicit symbiotic relations that white authors sustain with an abiding "Africanist persona" (17). Poe,

Cather, and Hemingway will never look the same again. Yet *Playing in the Dark* gives voice as well to a more intimately self-reflexive, potentially self-exposing drama at work in Morrison's own writing. "My vulnerability would lie in romanticizing blackness" (xi), Morrison recognizes. Yes, black life must be given its positive cultural weight as no white writer has known how to do, but its troubled side must also be written with undeviating candor. As a novelist, she must enter her "own" territory with the same self-risking dedication that she draws on when entering "other" territory. "Imagining is not merely looking or looking at," she writes; "nor is it taking oneself intact into the other. It is, for the purposes of the work, *becoming*" (4).

A becoming in which one's prior identity does not remain intact poses the question: what are the risks of becoming what one writes about? What in such moments of becoming does one see in new ways that the "intact" writer could not earlier see? What happens to the faculty of judgment in these moments, especially when the character that the writer has become approaches the monstrous? I want to examine not the white others Morrison has created but rather the reflexive light she has shed on her own people as she explores extremes of white-conditioned black distress. That reflexive light differs utterly from the pitiless beam of light trained by drunken white hunters on an exposed Cholly Breedlove, caught lying in the grass with his almost-lover Darlene: "The flashlight wormed its way into his guts and turned the sweet taste of muscadine into rotten fetid bile" (148). Cholly and Darlene's impetuous lovemaking is here interrupted and denatured into sadistic white spectacle. The penetration being described is not the intimate one between lovers but the deforming and public one of the white flashlight into Cholly's guts. "Sullen, irritable, he cultivated his hatred of Darlene. Never did he once consider directing his hatred toward the [white] hunters. Such an emotion would have destroyed him" (150).[1]

Morrison follows the white-damaged, enraged Cholly Breedlove—and his release of that rage on his "own"—with unjudging attention. She narrates the wounds Cholly has incurred: his orphaning, his emotional undoing, his soiling himself "like a baby" (157) and weeping, and finally—in a futile and terrifying act of male assertion—his raping his daughter Pecola. Rather than judge him, Morrison imaginatively enters him. "Only a musician would sense, know . . . that Cholly was free. Dangerously free. Free to feel whatever he felt—fear, guilt, shame, love, grief, pity" (159). Having become Cholly Breedlove during this sequence that builds from wound to wound to scandal, Morrison grants him the unforeclosed energy she herself possesses as his creator. Imagining her way into his situation, she sees that—though arrested on every scale of normative judgment a reader might impose—Cholly is free to turn his jail into his opportunity. The damage done to him is at the same time the condition of the freedom available to him. Cholly can become free only insofar as he relinquishes the (white) frame of norms that he has failed—and that has judged him to be a failure. It is as though, placing herself *inside* Cholly's dilemma, Morrison grasps that this too is a life situation, one full of peril, but not an automatic death sentence. In a patriarchal model of discipline, labor, legitimacy, and power, she might have pondered, Cholly Breedlove is obviously a disaster. But that's his white-imposed condition, not his fate—his past, not his future. What will he do *now*?

More broadly, Morrison seems to glimpse, at this crucial moment in *The Bluest Eye*, that the damage done to her people—damage rooted in their history of enslavement—is at the same time the condition of their radical freedom. However hedged in and beset with liabilities, they are never not free—never not "dangerously" free. Morrison's subsequent novels work out how black freedom involves something radically different from the white fantasy of freedom-as-unconfinement—fantasy born of innocence and false to the impediments of creaturely life itself. Rather, the freedom open to her people strenuously engages every obstacle in their path, taking on, as Morrison puts it later in *Song of Solomon*, "the condition our condition is in" (222).

Sula (1974) is the first novel to begin to carry out Morrison's determination to imagine her way into the heart of racial trauma—into it, through it, and beyond it. Shadrack inaugurates the project. Undone by his immersion in the violence of World War I, he finds himself first in a hospital for the shell-shocked, and thereafter wandering on the road:

> Twenty-two years old, weak, hot, frightened, not daring to acknowledge the fact that he didn't even know who or what he was . . . with no past, no language, no tribe, no source, no address book, no comb, no pencil, no clock, no pocket handkerchief, no rug, no bed, no can opener, no faded postcard, no soap, no key, no tobacco pouch, no soiled underwear and nothing nothing nothing to do . . . he was sure of one thing only: the unchecked monstrosity of his hands. (12)

The passage registers an ecstasy of cultural unfurnishing.[2] Since, at this juncture in Morrison's career, nothing inherited or inheritable can do any good for her "natally" alienated black characters, she *begins* by dispossessing them.[3] Even as the slaves are "born dead"—slavery impacted, starting at zero—so her characters start to compel her attention in the measure that their stories unfold on the far side of that foreclosure. The unfurnished Cholly leads to the unfurnished Shadrack, and he prepares us for the centrally unfurnished Sula. Cholly had to soil himself before grasping the dimensions of his disinheritance, and Shadrack first recognized his own face by seeing it imaged in a hospital toilet bowl. No less, Eva Peace only arrives at her determination to survive by engaging the shit-filled prison of her life. Clearing Plum's tortured body of its pebbly turds, absorbing the stench all about her in the outhouse, Eva reaches the bottom and thinks: "Uh uh. Nooo" (34).

Until such degradation is confronted and taken on, no surmounting is possible. Sula emerges as the character whose lack of cultural furnishing registers as dangerous promise, not deprivation. Nel thinks of the insufferable coolness of Sula's nonrelational life as "aesthetic," a term that fits the way that Sula had earlier watched her mother Hanna burn, "not because she was paralyzed, but because she was interested" (78). Sula takes all inherited modes of social behavior to be contaminating. If others figure for her as compromise or impediment, she bars them from her own passional center. "I want to make myself," not babies, she informs her grandmother Eva. When Eva threatens her with hellfire, Sula retorts: "Whatever's burning in me is mine!" (93). She blinks at nothing, sentimentalizes nothing, founds her "experimental" life on nothing but her own sensuous resources. "Aesthetic": a virtually Nietzschean stance toward the world, beyond inherited terms of good and evil, measuring her scene instead, coolly, as the value-neutral realm she finds herself in.[4]

The experiment is short-lived—Sula is dead by her early thirties—and it is also hemmed in by omissions, penetrated by absent or abandoned others. We know little of Sula's post-Medallion life, and we see the prominent events of her childhood—her burgeoning intimacy with Nel, her accidental drowning of Chicken Little—as shadows that ineradicably stain her project of pristine self-birthing. But to judge this novel in such ethical terms is to miss so much of its risk taking. In *Sula* Morrison breaks free of conventional coordinates: we simply do not know in advance what these characters may do. The death scenes that punctuate the novel serenely escape judgment, never falling into the territories of blame or praise. Likewise, the narrative voice neither condemns nor attacks Sula—allowing Morrison instead to articulate what a life might look like (in its beauty and its meanness) outside the communal coordinates that make up black norms. Sula is "experimental" as the unforgettable figures in García Márquez's *One Hundred Years of Solitude* are. Like them, she embodies a metaphoric stance toward life itself—a striking *gesture* beyond good and evil, success or failure—that no repertory of conventional roles can provide.[5]

Song of Solomon pursues such "dangerous freedom" in a range of ways. First, it develops—in the character of Pilate—the premise of radical unconventionality first broached in Sula. Navelless, Pilate's very body bespeaks a self-birthing. Yet unlike Sula, she seeks to join that freedom with an intricate set of chosen immersions. She wears her father's legacy (and memory) dangling from her ear, she appropriates the roles of both mother and grandmother, she lives in the middle of the city, she ends her life wishing "I'd a knowed more people. I would of loved 'em all" (336).

At a riskier level, this novel explores, in the character of Guitar, how far racial anguish might actually take a sensitive and determined male. It is standard for critics to subject Guitar to ethical censure and to note the fatal implications of his devotion to the Seven Days. But judging Guitar is as shortsighted as judging Sula. In *becoming* Guitar, Morrison imagines her way into his deepest promise and threat—and this outside the terms of right or wrong, should or shouldn't. Orphaned by the casual slaying of his father and humiliated by his mother's fawning acceptance of this event, Guitar embodies Morrison's *gesture* of where a resourceful black man might go with such anger. It is not simply anger. Guitar insists on love, invoking the passion that drives Jews who hunt down Nazis: "What I'm doing ain't about hating white people. It's about loving us. About loving you. My whole life is love" (159). Moreover, the stance he embodies constitutes a vision no one else is positioned to grasp, allowing Morrison to give Guitar perhaps the most haunting lines in the novel: "It's the condition our condition is in. Everybody wants the life of a black man.... What good is a man's life if he can't even choose what to die for? ... It *is* about love. What else but love?" (222, 223). Guitar has immersed himself in ultimate territory—who lives, who dies—and he insists on love of his own murdered people as the emotion inexhaustibly animating him. Everything in us (as readers) that wants to judge—to achieve distance by inserting a moral boundary between ourselves and the character we are reading about—recoils from the extreme consequences of Guitar's stance.[6] We do not want to go where Morrison is taking us, and if we have to go there, we want assurance that Guitar is mistaken.

It is easy enough to see that his lines are ringed with irony. Guitar will kill one of his own people, Pilate (even though "we don't off Negroes" [161]), and will also attempt to kill Milkman, despite his life being "about loving you." Morrison has distanced herself from Guitar as well, in remarks made outside the novel, even as she has provided us (in *Playing in the Dark*) with an unsurpassable statement about a writer's complex relation to his or her characters: "An author is not personally accountable for the acts of his fictive creatures," she writes, "although he is responsible for them" (86). I take this last clause to align with Morrison's creative act of *becoming* Guitar. He is indispensable to what she is able to see in *Song of Solomon*. It is *as* Guitar that she sees these things—Guitar who brings Montgomery, Alabama, and Emmett Till into the novel, who changes the pertinent pronoun from "I" to "we." The irony at play does not serve to provide the distancing veil of judgment but rather leads us into deepening mystery. Guitar means exactly what he says, and such is the condition his condition is in—the confinements and injustices he finds himself immersed in—that his love undoes him, taking him into murder. "Gimme hate, Lord!" a drunken Porter had begged earlier (26). If you would fight against the injustices done to your people, hate is easier to carry, more useful; gorged on polarizing judgment, hate slips the knife in without remorse. By contrast, Morrison has dared to imagine a man's love for his race under ultimate pressure. She is not accountable for Guitar, but her imaginative becoming makes her responsible for him. *Song of Solomon* does not disown his dangerous freedom.

The third locus of risk taking involves Morrison's *structural* moves in *Song of Solomon*. To explore what it means to be a young black man in the urban world of mid-twentieth-century America, Morrison needs Milkman *and* Guitar. This vision of male possibility is both twinned and embattled. When Morrison imagines her world most compellingly, it is dialogic, not dialectic—nourished more by tension than by resolution.[7] If she possessed the key to racial damage in America, if she envisaged the calm that will follow this many-centuried storm, she would not need to write novels. Her ("aesthetic") business is to see what she can see—to *become* others and imagine as her own their ways of engaging their conditions—and *Song of Solomon* neither blinks at what it sees nor pretends to see more than it does.

Let me put some flesh on those conceptual claims. The novel "knows" that contemporary urban conditions are intolerable, yet that disfigurement attends every male attempt at avenging or escaping those conditions. It "knows" that Macon Dead Jr. is both faithful to his father and deformed by that faithfulness, that Pilate's home is both a den of security and a place where Hagar weakens and dies, that Milkman and Guitar are twins who cannot bond but are destined (in the novel's final image) to enter each other's "killing arms" (337). The novel's conclusion—Milkman in sheer flight, heading toward his enemy/lover Guitar—is (though endlessly debated) utterly right, for there is no knowable resolution on the other side of this moment of encounter, no urban denouement waiting in the wings. Pressing black suffering, dysfunction, and shame as far as she can press them, Morrison concludes *Song of Solomon* in an unresolved leap: a gesture of courage, not purporting to be anything more than courage.

I take *Beloved* to be Morrison's supremely risk-taking novel. Shortly after the novel appeared in the late 1980s, Morrison was asked, in a TV interview, what the act of writing had required of her. Her answer (paraphrased) was "courage." And she added that if the slaves possessed the resourcefulness required to survive slavery, she should be able to summon the courage to write about it. I want to explore in three ways the kinds of "dangerous freedom" Morrison creates in *Beloved*—freedom on the far side of most normative ideas about it.

My brief for freedom does not scant the murderous pressure exerted by white abuse in the novel: the rape of Sethe that leaves the watching but hemmed-in Halle crazed and unmanned (milky clabber running down his face); the unnegotiable violence of Sethe toward her children that overwhelms even Baby Suggs's resources for survival. Perhaps the consequence of such unrelenting violation of fundamental bodily pieties is epitomized in Paul D's remembering "a witless coloredwoman jailed and hanged for stealing ducks she believed were her own babies" (78). Under the accumulation of such routine violations, the mind finally snaps, its defenses shattered.

Yet in the characters of Sixo and Stamp Paid, Morrison reveals free will operating within the inescapable conditions of slavery itself. Sixo, though never emancipated, never seen outside the confines of slavery, remains free—free to steal shoats and then banter with their owner, free to fall in love (with a slave girl many miles away), free to arrange a love nest with her and impregnate her (thus ensuring his racial lineage), free to choreograph his own execution. No less, Stamp Paid is free—though his enactment of freedom is etched in even deeper pain. When his wife—who had been taken from him and sexually exploited for over a year—is finally returned to him, he focuses silently on her neck: "She had a real small neck. I decided to break it. You know, like a twig—just snap it" (275), he tells Paul D. Instead of doing this, he changes his name—ceasing to be Joshua and becoming Stamp Paid. He sees himself as having fully (and then some) paid the price of the stamp—he no longer owes anyone anything. More intricately, rather than venting on his returned wife the outrage of his impotence, he directs that anger inwardly, takes his wound into himself. Like Eva deliberately relinquishing her leg in *Sula* as the self-inflicted wound required to regain agency, Stamp Paid conceives and performs his own symbolic castration, accepting, accommodating, and redirecting the wound pressed on him by white patriarchal power. Pushed to the wall, he becomes other, reconfigures his life situation, and is free again. At an appalling price, but free.

The most appalling price paid for freedom is, of course, Sethe's murder of her infant child. Like other acts of violence in Morrison's novels, this one has been endlessly subjected to ethical scrutiny. As readers, we do not want to encounter this event shorn of our ethical orientations: we insist on the furnishing needed to moralize the deed. Thus Sethe's killing of Beloved has been read as the twisted and sinful consequence of the pressures slavery enforced on her, as heroic resistance to that pressure (a sort of jamming of its machinery), as a moment of unthinking violence (nearer to manslaughter than to premeditated murder), and as many other things, as well. We seem to need a closure on this event that the novel itself does not provide. I believe that Morrison's not providing such closure—like her refusal to provide it in *Song of Solomon*, but more painfully missing here—is exactly right. Sethe is—perhaps more at this moment than anyone else in Morrison's fictional world—dangerously free. She kills that child freely—swiftly but not irrationally. It is her chosen act. It is at the same time a chosen act she cannot live with, one whose traumatic reverberations haunt her thereafter. In killing Beloved she has closed down her own sensorium, put herself on automatic pilot, sought henceforth just to survive: "Working dough. Working, working dough. Nothing better than that to start the day's serious work of beating back the past" (86). Free to kill Beloved, Sethe is not free to avoid continuously suffering from having done so. Freedom is real, even as the desire to escape its consequences is driven by fantasy. Once again, Morrison's novel explores intolerable emotional territory, showing us what no one wants to know: that in the condition the slaves' condition was in, no good moves existed. All of Sethe's options were bad; she went with the one she felt she had to. To judge her for this—either to blame or to clear her—is not so much irrelevant as impossible. Morrison's imaginative act of becoming Sethe at her crisis burrows into this ordeal at a level too profound for judgment.

Finally, there is in this novel a structural move that likewise goes beyond the judgment-infused norms of Western fiction: Morrison's invention of the character Beloved. Not a ghost like revenants in Western literature (figures typically shrouded, demonized, baleful), Beloved is at once a crazed young woman walking down the road near Cincinnati, the returned dead daughter of Sethe (mentally aged two, but physically embodying the nineteen years of her natural/unnatural life), and the fleshed-out epitome of all the abandoned children on all the slave ships that left West Africa for the New World during some three centuries. Beloved can comprise all of these because Morrison is writing beyond the Western notion of unitary character itself: our demand that the characters we encounter reflect something of that deep and coherent (even if conflicted) psychology we imagine ourselves to possess. The figure of Beloved—neither sentimentalized nor demonized, impossible to judge—allows Morrison to limn a canvas beyond the ken of realism (a realism always answerable to what might "statistically" take place). Put otherwise, Morrison deploys Beloved in such a way as to let us glimpse, stereoscopically, the entire drama (in space and time) of black suffering and abandonment that makes up the reality of New World slavery.

I opened this essay with Jonathan Franzen's sense that if his writing did not hurt—if it did not penetrate his own defenses—it could say nothing necessary. I suggest that Toni Morrison's achievement rests likewise on her willingness to push beyond all comfort zones. However, the ones she gets beyond are less personal like Franzen's (so much, still, the territory of embattled individuality) than racial. She has chosen to enter the unspeakable territory of black trauma and dysfunction, and she has traced this wound to its origin: the slave trade, the Middle Passage, natal alienation and longing, the shamefulness of this history, the pain of taking it on.

It is not accidental that Morrison's risk differs so much from Franzen's. As a white male writer, Franzen understands his challenge as, at heart, an individual one: will he have the courage to confront his personal demons, to penetrate the defenses he requires to sustain his sense of identity? He would never dream of a larger role—of being (or being taken as) a spokesperson for his race. By contrast, the pervasive shame and dysfunction that Morrison must encounter, as a twentieth-century black American woman, are a legacy bequeathed by her race's four-hundred-year history in the New World. The damage of this legacy is by no means all that she finds in it, but that damage remains unavoidably before her, demanding that she take it on. How to do so without casting blame (there is plenty to go around, and it's not hard to pinpoint who, how, when, and where)? Put in other terms, Morrison has had to forge a writerly career inescapably rooted in national (never just personal) experiences in which her people have been right and wronged. No less, hers is a career in which—beyond all choice—she will be read as (and in a measure will read herself as) a spokesperson for her race.

Let us return now to the issue of writerly risk. I believe a considerable risk inheres in Morrison's situation, and it has little to do with personal self-esteem. Morrison writes under an incessant (though unspoken) pressure to make a case to and for her own people—a pressure that has only intensified since she won the Nobel Prize in 1993. If you will, she suffers under the writerly limitation of already being in the right, of knowing too well the injustice inflicted on her people. In lawyerly terms, racial experience takes too readily the shape of a case, and she is already familiar with the brief. It is a persuasive brief. In literary terms, Morrison is therefore abidingly at risk of writing the melodrama of good being abused by evil and nevertheless surviving that abuse.

It is plausible to suggest that Morrison's career reveals a determination (conscious or not) to avoid writing such melodramas—to find her way into black experience outside the shaping stances of right and wrong. *The Bluest Eye* took her near the pitfall of these stances, and I have been following in this essay the ways in which the subsequent novels "push back," seek breathing room outside this brittle and foreknown ethical binary. My essay focuses on her career through the writing of *Beloved*, but it is not hard to see that *Jazz* centers on a race's living resources rather than its outwardly imposed harms. No less, *Paradise* probes the kinds of hubris that a too-successful racial bid for survival and progress might engender. "No room at the inn"—the West's perennial story of abjecting its unwanted other—sounds at once the Christ drama of two thousand years ago and the bass note of a Ruby that insists on disowning its own. And Morrison's ninth novel, *A Mercy*, opens up the melodrama of abandonment and orphanhood—the moral high ground that was earlier the preserve of slavery—as more broadly foundational in the seventeenth-century New World. Native Americans, indentured servants, and women of all stripes are hurled into this uncivil and unmapped colonial territory. *A Mercy* conveys vividly just how much unfreedom coexisted on these shores before the Declaration of Independence.

Compelling as her later novels can be, *Beloved* still seems to me to take the greatest risks. There, returning to the melodrama of slavery, she engages the moral urgency that gives melodrama its abiding appeal, yet strips that urgency of its familiar binary coding. *Beloved* immerses us in the presence of acts that we have to judge but cannot judge. In that novel, Morrison manages—all but impossibly—to be both the spokesperson of her race and the speaker of experiential truths that are impossible to "ethicalize," to "group-locate" in a satisfying binary. As a white reader, I find myself moved in so many ways: shame for what whites have done, admiration for what blacks have survived, but finally something closer to Aristotelian pity and terror in the face of an experience so appallingly real. Reading *Beloved*, I become aware of the primal privilege offered by narrative itself: an imaginative sharing of something that would be unbearable if you had to live through it. And I feel gratitude toward Morrison for showing how, all so quietly and devastatingly, it was lived through.

In sum, she means most to this white reader because, in reflecting on what is darkest in her race's inheritance, she has trusted her dangerously free imagination, seeing what it sees, refusing to say more than it sees. Such work eschews the security of any lawyer's brief, the foreknowing of what is right and what is wrong. She has gone to the source of racial pain and explored that pain in ways that therefore move not just her people but any people who read her—ways outside the framework of praise and blame. Beyond political consolation, lodged in a territory of fully human distress, her best work shows that even when most caught, we are also free—and this freedom is as terrifying as it is noninnocent. "An innocent man is a sin before God," she writes in *Tar Baby*: "Innocent and therefore unworthy. No man should live without absorbing the sins of his kind, the foul air of his innocence" (243). Perhaps only a black woman writer could know—and find "the words to say it"—that innocence is the garb we wear whenever we refuse to take responsibility for our frightening and inalienable freedom. No writer in our time has shown more powerfully the pitfalls of innocence and, beyond such innocence, the contours of the condition our condition is in.

Notes

1. I have developed this argument more fully in my *What Else But Love?* (109–31).

2. One wonders if Morrison has in mind Henry James's famous litany (in his study of Hawthorne) of cultural materials available to British writers but not to American ones: "No State, in the European sense of the word, and indeed barely a specific national name. No sovereign, no court, no personal loyalty, no aristocracy, no church, no clergy, no army, no diplomatic service, no country gentlemen, no palaces, no castles, nor manors, nor old country-houses, nor parsonages, nor thatched cottages, nor ivied ruins; no cathedrals, nor abbeys, nor little Norman churches; no great Universities nor public schools—no Oxford, nor Eton, nor Harrow; no literature, no novels, no museums, no pictures, no political society, no sporting class—no Epsom nor Ascot!" (34).

I suspect that, given her M.A. in English and her wide reading in the Western canon, Morrison was familiar with this celebrated passage. If so, it is not random that in *Playing in the Dark* we encounter a kindred cultural summary, this time keyed not to Jamesian manners and the picturesque but to the constitutive activities of nineteenth-century American life that simply mandated white familiarity with blacks: "How could one speak of profit, economy, labor, progress, suffragism, Christianity, the frontier, the formation of new states, the acquisition of new lands, education, transportation (freight and passengers), neighborhoods, the military—of almost anything a country concerns itself with—without having as a referent, at the heart of the discourse, at the heart of the definition, the presence of Africans and their descendants?" (50).

In the interest of keeping this note manageable, I do not cite, but refer the reader to, two bravura passages of lack in *Song of Solomon*: Railway Tommy's lyrical summary of all that Guitar and Milkman—as black men—will never have (60), and Porter's equally lyrical summary to First Corinthians of what she too will forever be deprived of (200).

3. "Natal alienation" is Orlando Patterson's memorable phrase for the plight of slaves who are born as others' property—that is, born othered (alien). See his magisterial *Slavery and Social Death*, chap. 1.

4. Barbara Johnson's well-known essay "'Aesthetic' and 'Rapport' in Toni Morrison's *Sula*" opens up the resonance of this unemphasized term in the novel. Johnson does not enlist Nietzsche in her argument, but his recurrent claim that the world can be justified only aesthetically—not morally—aligns with Morrison's practice in *Sula*.

5. For further development of this stance in García Márquez's work, see my *Unknowing: The Work of Modernist Fiction*, 237–43.

6. For a brilliant meditation on the ways in which great novels resist closure (endgame) and explore alternative pathways (gambits), see Sacvan Bercovitch's "Culture in a Faulknerian Context," 284–310.

7. Mikhail Bakhtin has explored extensively (in *The Dialogic Imagination*) the ways in which novels operate dialogically, not dialectically. Rather than impose a unifying master view (identifiable as the author's stance), great fiction gives full range to the conflicting voices that speak a culture's living debates. "Take a dialogue," Bakhtin later writes, "and remove the voices . . . remove the intonations . . . carve out abstract concepts and judgments from living words and responses, cram everything into one abstract consciousness—and that's how you get dialectics" (*Speech Genres*, 147).

Works Cited

Bakhtin, Mikhail. *The Dialogic Imagination*. Ed. Michael Holquist. Trans. Caryl Emerson and Michael Holquist. Austin: University of Texas Press, 1981.

———. *Speech Genres and Other Late Essays*. Ed. Caryl Emerson and Michael Holquist. Trans. Vern W. McGee. Austin: University of Texas Press, 1986.

Bercovitch, Sacvan. "Culture in a Faulknerian Context." In *Faulkner in Cultural Context: Faulkner and Yoknapatawpha*, ed. Donald M. Kartiganer and Ann J. Abadie, 284–310. Jackson: University Press of Mississippi, 1995.

James, Henry. *Hawthorne*. 1879. Ithaca: Cornell University Press, 1963.

Johnson, Barbara. "'Aesthetic' and 'Rapport' in Toni Morrison's *Sula*." *Textual Practice* 7, no. 2 (1993): 163–72.

Morrison, Toni. *Beloved*. 1987. New York: Vintage International, 2004.

———. *Playing in the Dark*. New York: Vintage, 1992.

———. *Song of Solomon*. 1977. New York: Penguin, 1987.

———. *Sula*. 1973. New York: New American Library, 1983.

———. *The Bluest Eye*. 1970. New York: Penguin, 1994.

Patterson, Orlando. *Slavery and Social Death: A Comparative Study*. Cambridge: Harvard University Press, 1985.

Weinstein, Philip. *Unknowing: The Work of Modernist Fiction*. Ithaca: Cornell University Press, 2005.

———. *What Else But Love? The Ordeal of Race in Faulkner and Morrison*. New York: Columbia University Press, 1996.

MODERNITY AND THE HOMELESS

Toni Morrison and the Fictions of Modernism

MARC C. CONNER

It is both dangerous and irresistible to discuss Toni Morrison in relation to other writers. Despite her famous denials of influence—"I am not *like* James Joyce; I am not *like* Thomas Hardy, I am not *like* Faulkner" (McKay, 152)—Morrison is one of the most widely and deeply read of writers, and her fiction, even if it resists the conscious influence of other writers, certainly participates in their broader cultural dialogue. Morrison's work especially involves itself in the dialogue about modernity. Her work emerges from and points us toward modernity, provoking two central questions: What is modernity? And what does Toni Morrison teach us about modernity? Two quotations by major modernist thinkers get at the heart of these two questions: first, from Ralph Ellison, writing about the death of his father when Ellison was only three years old, in his highly personal essay of 1965, "Tell It Like It Is, Baby": "*But what quality of love sustains us in our orphan's loneliness, and how much is thus required of fatherly love to give us strength for all our life thereafter?*" (35). The second, from Martin Heidegger: "It is proper to every gathering that the gatherers assemble to coordinate their efforts to the sheltering; only when they have gathered together with that end in view do they begin to gather" (*Writings*, ix). These utterances are essential entries into the thought of Toni Morrison and how Morrison conceives of our historical moment of the late twentieth century and the early twenty-first: our orphan's loneliness, which for Ellison meant not just his own suffering but the essential human condition; and the need to gather the orphans together—and to Morrison, we are all orphans—with their sheltering in view. To gather, Heidegger asserts, is meaningless unless we gather to give shelter.

How does Toni Morrison address these ideas of *the orphan* and *the sheltering*? How is this paradigmatic of the modern condition, and how do her novels express this condition? Again—what is modernity, and what does Morrison tell us about it? These two questions are not easily separable. In our historical moment, our conception of modernism and our conception of Morrison blend. To begin, Morrison points us to the fact that there are many modernisms: for the literature scholar, "modernism" typically means that period of the early twentieth century, connected to the First World War, taking in the new theories of Freud and impressionism, and centering on literary figures such as Joyce, Woolf, Hemingway, Pound, Proust, Stein, Hughes, and many others. This is the modernism that Morrison encountered as a young graduate student at Cornell in the early 1950s, when she wrote her master's thesis on Woolf and Faulkner. Here she states that "alienation is a definition of this century"—her own first definition of modernity: to be modern is to be alienated ("Thesis," 1–2). Her novels give eloquent and heartrending representations of this alienation, what she poignantly terms in *The Bluest Eye* "being put outdoors"—"the real terror of life" (17). The figure of the outcast, the exile, the preterite, dominates Morrison's fiction as it dominates modernity; she rightly perceives that the crisis of modernity is *homelessness*, in its most far-reaching sense, what Lukács calls our "transcendental homelessness" (41).

Here we see that Morrison recognizes a broader scope to modernity: like the political theorists and the philosophers, she locates modernism earlier in history, around the mid-seventeenth century, concomitant with the rise of science, the effect of the Reformation, the growth of skepticism, and the early theories of the secular nation-state. These are, of course, the roots of literary modernism, passing through the Enlightenment and German phenomenology, with a selective reading of Nietzsche mixed in, to get us to the Armory Show of 1913. But we would do well to look closely at those roots, for certainly Morrison has examined them keenly—her sense of the world changes that brought us to the twentieth century is precise, and indeed as her thought has developed from the late 1960s to this moment, her conception of the modern has broadened and deepened, going far beyond Faulkner and Woolf and the period between the wars, for few writers are more sensitive to roots, ancestors, and genealogies, whether familial, cultural, or intellectual. In fact, the seventeenth century has much to say about Morrison's concept of modernity as alienation. When Descartes in 1641 reaches beyond absolute doubt in his *Meditations* and asserts that, if nothing else, the thinking self exists, he voices the definitive modern impulse: the self exists, I exist, but in radical separation and isolation from the rest of the creation: a philosophical version of what Ellison terms "our orphan's loneliness."

Morrison is one of the great portraitists of the orphan in world literature: her first outcast child, Pecola, left homeless and mad on the periphery of her community; Sula, the charismatic, willed outcast, or Shadrack, so baffled by his encounter with modernity in the trenches of World War I that he calls the community to its own death; Macon Dead, whose ruthless ethic of owning things and owning people is a logical extension of modernity's principle of isolation; Jadine, having lost her ancient properties in the modern world of the commodity and appearance; Sethe, alienated from her community when they refrained from sounding the alarm as schoolteacher approached, and who refuses to return to that community until, perhaps, the novel's end; Wild, an extension of Beloved, who lives on the very border of nature and civilization; the Convent women, willed outcasts from the modern world who seek an alternative ethos away from modernity's categories of sexuality, gender, race, and power; the shattered childhood love of Heed and Christine, and the plight of Junior, described at the end of *Love* as the "little rudderless, homeless thing" (198); Florens in *A Mercy*, abandoned by her mother and rejected by the Smith, left scratching her story on the floor and walls of her dead master's unfinished house; and Frank Money, the wandering, battle-scarred, "tilted man" (80) in *Home*. These are isolates all, embodiments of modern Western culture's drive toward the self in isolation, a drive that forms in the matrix of modernism in the early seventeenth century.

But that seventeenth century proffers another view of the human condition, a response to, and even a rejection of, this inexorable isolation and homelessness. John Milton, in 1674, produces his great epic *Paradise Lost* as a long narrative that explains, according to Milton, the how and the why of this homelessness. Milton grounds our "transcendental homelessness" in our desire for knowledge, our will to know—a motif that is at the very heart of Morrison's most recent work, particularly the novels that follow *Beloved*. From this urge to know comes humanity's exile from paradise into the mortal world of alienation. But Milton closes his epic with a much-expanded vision of verse 17 of Genesis 3, when God clothes Adam and Eve after casting them out, offering a gesture of *shelter* in recompense for their new homelessness. This gesture of tender mercy on the heels of stern justice becomes two entire books at the end of Milton's epic, in which a different knowledge is imparted, a knowledge that enables Adam and Eve to live within the broken world. And Milton concludes the poem with the image of the pair walking away from Eden in somber companionship: "The world was all before them, where to choose / Their place of rest, and Providence their guide: / They hand in hand with wand'ring steps and slow, / Through Eden took their solitary way" (XII:646–49). Adam and Eve prefigure the litany of outcasts that dominate the Bible—Cain, Ishmael, Jacob, Joseph, Moses, David, and especially Christ, who states, "But the Son of man hath not where to lay his head" (Luke 9:58)—but they also offer a model of how to exist within this condition: this image of "hand in hand," wandering in a world of alienation, but finding one's shelter not in a human or a divine abode but in the companionship of another, in love. Shelter is ultimately not a place, not a thing or an object; it is a verb, the action of love. And Morrison has famously stated that "all the time that I write, I'm writing about love or its absence" (Bakerman, 40).

This moment at the end of *Paradise Lost* has long been a meditation for Morrison. *Paradise*, after all, is hardly her first investigation into the concept of paradise and its loss. Milton's final image of "hand in hand" surfaces in multiple forms throughout Morrison's oeuvre: the hands at the end of *Jazz*, Paul D's placing of his hands on Sethe's breasts, Sula's dismembering of her own hand as a child (a dismembering that foretells her later sundering from her girlhood friend, the one hand to which she needed to cling), Frank and Cee in *Home*, who, "like some forgotten Hansel and Gretel, locked hands as they navigated the silence and tried to imagine a future" (53), and especially the hands holding the bird in the Nobel speech, those hands that may hold life or death, and about which the wise old woman states, "What I do know is that it is in your hands. It is in your hands" (7). This is an author for whom the laying on of hands is an essential concept in her craft. Hands, the taking of hands, the holding of hands, the supplication of hands, constitute Morrison's narrative theology of shelter, which is precisely her response to the homelessness of modernity.

Does Morrison have Milton in mind at times in her work? Does she consciously draw on Descartes in her narratives? These questions are irresolvable. But careful readers know that Morrison has read more widely and deeply than nearly any other author—among the modernist fiction writers, perhaps only Joyce and Ellison are her equals in this regard. If we think there is an allusion or influence lurking somewhere in her work, it's probably there, and in a more complex form than we imagine. Indeed, Morrison employs allusion in a more complex way than most modernists—writers, texts, and influences are *layered* in her work, not obvious on the surface, but leavened into the prose at the level of word and voice, in the very rhythm of the language.

This context of the seventeenth century, of Descartes and Milton and the advent of modernity, of radical isolation and the sheltering comfort of hands, opens all sorts of doors into Morrison's worlds, particularly her relation to modernity. And Morrison pushes this connection further. In this seventeenth century, the European empires truly begin, and the African slave trade shifts from a minor commodity market to the engine that will drive these empires all the way to the First World War—the war that marks the end of this particular age of empire and to which many would point as the culmination of Enlightenment thought and the definitive event in modernity—what Benedict Anderson refers to as "the modern darkness" produced by "the century of Enlightenment" (19). In her essay "Home," Morrison states: "The overweening, defining event of the modern world is the mass movement of raced populations, beginning with the largest forced transfer of people in the history of the world: slavery" (10). Morrison marks the genesis of modernity in the advent of slavery on its massive, technological, rational, and transcontinental form that begins in this same period of Descartes and Milton. We might well locate this historical genesis in 1621 when the Dutch West India Company was organized with an initial monopoly on the African slave trade and access to the New World ports. As John Hope Franklin has chronicled, it was in the seventeenth and eighteenth centuries that "the trade in humans developed into such a big business" (40). Morrison's modernity arises squarely in the midst of this phenomenon, emphasizing therefore modernity's origin in the displacement and alienation—the *making homeless*—of entire gatherings of people. Consequently *A Mercy* is set in the heart of this period of crucial historical transition, the late seventeenth century. As Morrison has stated, "I was looking for a period before racism was inextricably related to slavery. The only place was this period before a race hierarchy was established legally and later culturally in the states" (Brophy-Warren, W5).

The postcolonial theorist Homi Bhabha has focused on Morrison as the epitome of the postnational, postcolonial ethnic writer. In a series of writings, Bhabha has looked to Morrison as a defining figure in his complex articulations of the alienation that results from the wreckage of modernity. For Bhabha, "Toni Morrison's rememory of the 'global' history of slavery at the end of *Beloved*" (*Postmodernism*, 444) is paradigmatic of the late-twentieth-century rejection of the hegemonic discourses of first-world post-Enlightenment thought. Bhabha's contribution to modernist theory is the way he has brought together the discourses of modernism and postcolonialism, how he—along with Edward Said, Gayatri Spivak, and Benedict Anderson, among others—has revealed the essential underpinnings of empire in the tangled discourses of race and conquest in the twentieth century. Drawing on the writings of Franz Fanon, Bhabha investigates "what it means to be . . . a member of the marginalized, the displaced, the diasporic." He argues that Fanon goes beyond merely "the historicity of the black man" and focuses on "the temporality of modernity," a time concept that "makes the question of ontology inappropriate for black identity" and "impossible for the very understanding of humanity in the world of modernity." Fanon, like Bhabha and like Morrison, rejects the notion of the black person's belatedness—that she can enter the pantheon of white European triumph, given enough time. Rather, each writer seeks "another time, another space," and, Bhabha argues, in that seeking they succeed "in destroying the 'ontology of man'" (*Location*, 236–38). This certainly seems appealing in its opposition to first-world domination; and yet something in this response to modernity is troubling—troubling to Morrison, on some level. By "destroying the 'ontology of man,'" with what is Fanon or Bhabha left? Each fails to destroy merely "the white man's ontology," but rather, like Marx or Nietzsche or the other grand levelers of modernity, he destroys ontology altogether. Bhabha's is a wholly material critique, asserting that "for Morrison, it is precisely the historical and discursive boundaries of slavery that are the issue" ("The World," 377). Well, yes, of course—but not *only* that, and even, ultimately, not *primarily* that. Here Morrison's work parts company with the great postmodern critiques of modernity, precisely in Bhabha's rejection of ontology, his discrediting of the religious sphere. Such a rejection means he must reject the worldviews held by the overwhelming majority of the planet as misinformed or immature or insufficiently educated or undeveloped or some other condescending, pitying dismissal—a gesture that is profoundly problematic, and that is hard to find in Toni Morrison's fiction.

Modernity—or at least the theorists of modernity—errs most grievously in its insistence on the secular, its rejection of ontology. Modernity seems to view the work of art as the new location of the sacred—we think of Stephen Dedalus shifting from a worship of God to a worship of art—but Morrison is not satisfied with this. She insists we must locate the sacred *in the world*, in our ministry to the homeless. We must offer shelter, a "small bench by the road" (Denard, 44). Thus her fascination with Catholicism, that most sacramental of religions, to which she converted when she was twelve (Als, 64). Hers is in some complex way a didactic art.

If the crisis of modernity is homelessness, a rupture between our desire for shelter and the world's refusal to bequeath to us a sense of place, what causes this crisis? Whence comes our homelessness, what Heidegger terms "the absence of the ground" (*Poetry*, 92)? Another theorist of modernity, Jürgen Habermas, has explored the connections between modernity and time, between the empirical and the eternal. Habermas argues that the modern impulse away from the past, toward the present, away from authority and precedent and toward radical subjectivity, undermines the unity of the religious impulse and the human drive toward understanding: "The principle of subjectivity is not powerful enough to regenerate the unifying power of religion in the medium of reason. . . . [Thus] the demotion of religion leads to a split between faith and knowledge which the Enlightenment cannot overcome by its own power." As a result, he concludes, "the spirit has estranged itself," and "the dialectic of the Enlightenment . . . is exhausted" (Habermas, 20–21). And it is precisely here that we see Morrison making her most radical and transformative intervention in the discourses of modernity. She is not content with this "demotion of religion," the abandonment of the life of the spirit for the merely material world. Through a range of narrative strategies, particularly her complex explorations of Gnostic principles, Morrison seeks to reconcile faith and wisdom and thereby resurrect the spirit in the twenty-first century.

Now, Toni Morrison is not a theorist of modernity, or a philosopher, a cultural critic, or a literary critic. She is a great modern novelist who is profoundly uncomfortable in her role and in her time. She immerses herself in modernist aesthetics only to reject much of that tradition; she produces strikingly complex modern novels that finally are rejections of the modern novel; she crafts a compellingly avant-garde modernist narrative style only to insist on her connections to the past, the ancient ways, the traditional craft of the timeless storyteller. These would seem to be paradoxes, but Morrison resolves them by that most unmodernist of moves: an insistence on the ethical and theological function of her writing. If modernity rejects anything, it rejects didacticism, the notion that art exists to teach us something about our social, ethical, or religious lives. Not so Morrison—through her commitment to a complex mode of storytelling, and through her conception of theological narration, she seeks to minister to her historical moment, to help her audience to see better, or, to invoke one of her favorite metaphors, to clear cataracts in our eyes. Her aim here is unmistakably aesthetic, resolutely ethical, and radically religious.

The modern thinker who is most helpful in understanding Morrison's stance toward modernity may well be Walter Benjamin, that perceptive, non-systematic, gentle, and tragic figure who perceived so much of our plight in the twentieth century. In his luminous essay "The Storyteller," Benjamin argues that in the twentieth century, the art of storytelling is vanishing. He links this to the fragmentation of culture that follows World War I, but also to the more general dissolution of tradition, continuity, community, and connection to the landscape and the rhythms of nature—a sundering of traditional life that begins in the seventeenth-century movement from the countryside to the cities, from the homestead to the hinterlands of empire, a part of the general rupture of human life engendered by the Enlightenment and modernity.[1] Through the loss of our ability to convey experience through story, we lose the oral tradition and the involvement with others, as human experience becomes increasingly isolated—what Heidegger, Sartre, and the Christian existentialists call an alienated existence, what Morrison calls the definition of the century. Benjamin's concept of the storyteller foretells Morrison's own craft.

"Every real story," Benjamin writes, offers "something useful.... The storyteller ... has counsel for his readers ... not for a few situations, as the proverb does, but for many, like the sage." This counsel or wisdom reveals the central role of the storyteller within the tribe: "A man listening to a story is in the company of the storyteller.... A great storyteller will always be rooted in the people" (Benjamin, 86, 100). Thus the crucial element in the story is precisely *memory*. In storytelling, nature and the cosmos are not indifferent but "still concerned with the fate of men" (108)—in short, the storyteller's world is what Mircea Eliade calls "a sacralized cosmos" (Eliade, 17), in which the human condition shares a purposive role. And stories are endless, timeless; novels come to an end, as befits their secular origins as the definitive modern art, emerging coincidently with the Enlightenment; but stories—such as the ending of *Beloved*—are always continued. And finally, Benjamin states that the true storyteller, the source of "wisdom, kindness, comfort," is akin to the mother figure.

Benjamin's essay bears striking similarities to Morrison's Nobel acceptance speech. Morrison begins that address with the young people asking the definitive modernist question, one that could apply to the end of *Paradise Lost* or the end of *Paradise*: "Tell us what moves at the margin. What it is to have no home in this place. To be set adrift from the one you knew. What it is to live at the edge of towns that cannot bear your company." The wise old woman responds with story, a story that joins the alienated young and the counsel-offering old. "Look," she muses at the end, "How lovely it is, this thing we have done—together" (*Nobel*, 13). Joining together the community through story seems highly antimodernist: no indifferent artist peering above his creation, admiring his handiwork, but rather a storytelling voice intimately involved with its creation—like the creator fashioning the creation through the work of hands in clay—opening in the artwork what Morrison has called "spaces so the reader can come into it" (Tate, 164). Spaces, or, we might say, shelter, for the wandering and homeless.

Here we see the fundamental ethical quality in Morrison's writings. Not ethical in the sense of issuing edicts or graven tablets, or even in offering beatitudes that seek to lift humanity above the restrictions of law. Rather, Morrison's ethical turn consists in beholding the other, in facing the other and feeling her call in one's own being, what Emmanuel Levinas terms the "irreducible relation" of the phenomenology of the other, the "ultimate situation" of "the *direct* and *full face* welcome of the other by me." When we gaze into the face of the other, we realize that we cannot comprehend or totalize the other—she cannot be employed (and condemned) as mere object, as an instrument of our utility; she is not merely a being, but in her face we behold Being. This realization, argues Levinas, demands a radical confrontation with both ethics and ontology. It calls us to acknowledge our responsibility for our brother and sister, and to realize "the relation between the being here below and the transcendent being that results in no community of concept or totality [for which] we reserve the term religion" (Levinas, 79–80).

This "phenomenology of the other" defines *Beloved*, where Beloved looks into Sethe's face and sees her own face and the face of her mothers, sees in that face-to-face the defining call to (even the cause of) her own existence. *Beloved* is a confrontation with trauma that Morrison negotiates successfully. Its achievement consequently lays out the main ideas that will consume Morrison in her novels to follow: female friendship, the child, the ability to survive horrific trauma, and the ancient properties and remarkable endurance of the female ancestor. This ancestor figure appears in her pre-*Beloved* work, of course, particularly in the remarkable Pilate of *Song of Solomon* (the absence of such a figure is the tragedy of *Tar Baby*); but after *Beloved*, what Morrison terms "the advising, benevolent, protective, wise black ancestor"—which she argues is "the matrix of yearning" for the black character ("City Limits," 39)—shifts from a character within the book *to a presence above or behind or beyond the book*. In narratological terms, it shifts from the level of character to the level of narrator, narrative persona, or even arranger. This explains the enigmatic voice of *Jazz*, and it persists in slightly different form in *Love*. This persona constitutes the first full appearance in Morrison's work of what we may term a theology of narrative.

The opening epigraph of *Jazz* announces this radical narrative concept: "I am the name of the sound / and the sound of the name. / I am the sign of the letter / and the designation of the division" (xiii). This passage is taken from the "Thunder, Perfect Mind" section of the Nag Hammadi, the Gnostic writings discovered in 1945. This strange text offers a new narrative voice, and a theology of narrative, in Morrison's work. According to the New Testament scholars George MacRae and Douglas Parrot, this voice is "a revelation discourse by a female figure," "written throughout in the first person," containing "self-proclamation, exhortations to heed the speaker, and reproaches for failures to heed or to love," showing "the extension of the divine into the world," and asserting "the totally otherworldly transcendence of the revealer" (Robinson, xx). This is Morrison's narrative persona for *Jazz*: a divine female voice, speaking otherworldly wisdom, proffering a teaching about the need to love. This figure is located not within the narrative itself but rather above the narration, not unlike the Arranger of Joyce's *Ulysses*. This divine female voice recalls each character to her most primal longing—a longing for a mother figure and for home. And this, of course, is the longing of every character in every Morrison novel, from Pecola to Ycidra. It is even the longing of the narrator of *Jazz* itself: "I'd love to close myself in the peace left by the woman who lived there and scared everybody.... She has seen me and is not afraid of me. She hugs me. Understands me. Has given me her hand. I am touched by her. Released in secret. Now I know" (221).

The narrator touches the same female, mothering presence that each character seeks—the figure of ancient female wisdom—and receives her Gnostic knowledge. We see the same impulse in the opening epigraph to *Paradise*, also from the "Thunder, Perfect Mind" writing, suggesting that immortality will result from heeding this figure: "*And they will find me there / and they will live, / and they will not die again*" (i). The narrator of *Love* similarly gestures toward the otherworldly: if she is L, and thus the voice of a dead woman, and her name, as she says, "is the subject of First Corinthians, chapter 13" (199), hence the voice of Love itself, then we have again a divine female utterance, giving counsel and teaching from beyond this world.[2]

Conceiving of the narrative voice as a female wisdom figure opens up another aspect of Morrison's late writings: the series of so-called children's books that she and her son Slade have produced. Revisions of fables, these are didactic stories, meant to communicate a moral (as Benjamin writes, "Every real story . . . contains, openly or covertly, something useful"), though the *Who's Got Game* books seek to frustrate and confuse easy or simplistic moral endings. Morrison states, "The original stories are opened up and their moralistic endings reimagined; the victim might not lose; the timid gets a chance to become strong; the fool can gain insight; the powerful may lose their grip" (inside jacket). These books seek to move beyond or outside dead language, to tell the story in a new way—precisely what Morrison describes in her Nobel speech (another definitive post-*Beloved* writing:): "Dead language . . . is unyielding language content to admire its own paralysis.... Unreceptive to interrogation, it cannot form or tolerate new ideas, shape other thoughts, tell another story" (*Nobel*, 8). We can conceive of the storyteller in these revised fables as the wise old woman, or divine female utterance, suggested by the narrative theology of Morrison's late novels and the Nobel speech, who listens and coaxes until at last the young people create their own story. Then she trusts them, for "Look," she says, "how lovely it is, this thing we have done—together" (*Nobel*, 13). Morrison's narrative theology brings the story and the novel together, rejects exorcism for sacrifice, and replaces a willed forgetfulness with books that remember.

This narrative theology constitutes an eruption of the divine into the mundane world. Morrison's otherworldly, Gnostic voice utters itself into being in this broken world and thereby transforms our understanding of this world. In *Beloved*, when the fully dressed woman walks out of the water, this world is, in Yeats's defining modernist phrase, "transformed utterly—a terrible beauty is born." This parallels our own experience of reading *Beloved*: the haunting quality of that masterpiece is not confined to its pages—we are haunted by the book, by its voices, the uncanny effect of something from without having come into our consciousness. And what of *Paradise*? The enigmatic ending of the book, with the Convent women returned from ... where? whence? All we know with certainty is that something has returned from beyond. That novel's penultimate paragraph suggests this transformation of the world: "There is nothing to beat this solace which is what Piedade's song is about, although the words evoke memories neither one has ever had ... the unambivalent bliss of going home to be at home—the ease of coming back to love again" (318). Here "home" is not a place, or a time, but an experience of the crossing of worlds, the entrance of the sacred into our secular domain. This is Morrison's version of what Eliade calls "hierophany," or "communion with the sacred" (Eliade, 14). Such an experience, he argues, is

> a primordial experience ... a primary religious experience that precedes all reflection on the world. For it is the break effected in space that allows the world to be constituted.... When the sacred manifests itself in any hierophany, there is not only a break in the homogeneity of space; there is also revelation of an absolute reality.... *The manifestation of the sacred ontologically founds the world.* (21; italics mine)

In her late works, Morrison's narrative voice manifests the sacred and founds the world as ontological space, precisely in its *speaking*. The hierophany *is* the storyteller, the divine female wisdom figure, and thus the founding occurs in each reading, each telling of the tale. When we read Morrison's work, we participate in an uncanny and remarkably liberating experience in which our mundane world is made luminous by the eruption of this speaker into it.

This crossing of the sacred and the secular is, in some ways, a very modernist experience, like Joyce's epiphany and epicleti, Yeats's communication with otherworldly voices, or Rilke's visions of the angels. But whereas in those examples we glimpse the sacred from a distance, as through a glass darkly, in Morrison's conception the sacred crosses over to us and informs our world with the bright light of hierophany. Thus Morrison fulfills and transcends the modernist impulse of grasping for the sacred in the work of art: Morrison's art brings the sacred into this world.

Is this then a sheltering? Does this minister to the orphan's loneliness? It depends on the shelter we seek. Ultimately Heidegger was really not talking about shelter as building or structure, or about social justice or charity in which the hungry are fed with earthly bread or the wandering are brought into an earthly inn. Rather, he sought "presence, the ancient name of Being" (*Poetry*, 93), what Rilke describes as "the mysteries out of whose abundance our lives might become truly infinite" (*Selected Poetry*, 317). So too Morrison: the shelter she offers, the loneliness she assuages, is radical and transcendent, ungraspable as anything other than the experience of Being. The reader's response she seeks is what Rilke achieves near the end of *The Notebooks of Malte Laurids Brigge*, in a passage that parallels the experience of reading Morrison's late novels:

> My God, I thought with sudden vehemence, so you really *are*. There are proofs of your existence. I have forgotten them all and never even wanted any, for what a huge obligation would lie in the certainty of you. And yet that is what has just been shown to me. This, then, is what tastes good to you; this is what gives you pleasure. That we should learn to endure everything and never judge. What things are filled with gravity? What things with grace? Only you know. (211)

Notes

1. I am painting in broad brushstrokes here, and as Raymond Williams pointed out nearly four decades ago, in what remains a seminal study on these issues, the historical escalator keeps going backward until the lost, good age can be traced at least back to medievalism, if not to Eden itself. Yet Williams insists that something dramatic occurs before and following England's early Industrial Revolution, which "not only transformed both city and country" but also brought about "a very early disappearance of the traditional peasantry" (2). Morrison informs *A Mercy* with exactly this historical narrative, particularly in the migration experiences of Rebekka Vaark.

2. For a detailed reading of these issues of Gnosticism and narrative in Morrison's work, particularly *Jazz*, see Conner, 2000.

Works Cited

Als, Hilton. "Ghosts in the House." *New Yorker*, October 27, 2003, 64.

Anderson, Benedict. *Imagined Communities: Reflections on the Origin and Spread of Nationalism*, rev. ed. London: Verso, 1991.

Bakerman, Jane. "The Seams Can't Show: An Interview with Toni Morrison." In *Conversations with Toni Morrison*, ed. Danille Taylor-Guthrie, 30–42. Jackson: University Press of Mississippi, 1994.

Benjamin, Walter. "The Storyteller." In *Illuminations: Essays and Reflections*, trans. Harry Zohn, 83–109. New York: Schocken, 1968.
Bhabha, Homi. *The Location of Culture*. New York: Routledge, 1994.
———. "Postmodernism/Postcolonialism." In *Critical Terms for Art History*, ed. Robert S. Nelson and Richard Shiff, 307–22. Chicago: University of Chicago Press, 2003.
———. "The World and the Home." In *Close Reading: The Reader*, ed. Frank Lentricchia and Andrew DuBois, 366–80. Durham: Duke University Press, 2003.
Brophy-Warren, Jamin. "A Writer's Vote." *Wall Street Journal*, November 7, 2008, W5.
Conner, Marc. "Wild Women and Graceful Girls: Toni Morrison's Winter's Tale." In *Nature, Woman, and the Art of Politics*, ed. Eduardo Velasquez, 341–69. Lanham, MD: Rowman and Littlefield, 2000.
Denard, Carolyn, ed. *Toni Morrison: Conversations*. Jackson: University Press of Mississippi, 2008.
Eliade, Mircea. *The Sacred and the Profane: The Nature of Religion*. Trans. Willard R. Trask. New York: Harcourt, 1987.
Ellison, Ralph. *The Collected Essays of Ralph Ellison*. Ed. John Callahan. New York: Random House, 1995.
Franklin, John Hope. *From Slavery to Freedom: A History of African Americans*. 8th ed. With Alfred A. Moss Jr. New York: Knopf, 2005.
Habermas, Jürgen. *The Philosophical Discourse of Modernity: Twelve Lectures*. Cambridge: MIT Press, 1987.
Heidegger, Martin. *Basic Writings*. Ed. David Ferrell Krell. New York: Harper and Row, 1977.
———. *Poetry, Language, Thought*. Trans. Albert Hofstadter. New York: Harper and Row, 1971.
Levinas, Emmanuel. *Totality and Infinity*. Trans. Alphonso Lingis. Pittsburgh: Duquesne University Press, 1969.
Lukács, Georg. *The Theory of the Novel*. Trans. Anna Bostock. Cambridge: MIT Press, 1971.
McKay, Nellie. "An Interview with Toni Morrison." In *Conversations with Toni Morrison*, ed. Danille Taylor-Guthrie, 138–55. Jackson: University Press of Mississippi, 1994.
Milton, John. *Paradise Lost*. 2nd ed. Ed. Scott Elledge. New York: W. W. Norton, 1993.
Morrison, Toni. *The Bluest Eye*. New York: Vintage, 2007.
———. "City Limits, Village Values: Concepts of the Neighborhood in Black Fiction." In *Literature and the Urban Experience*, ed. Michael C. Jane and Ann Chalmers Watts, 35–43. New Brunswick: Rutgers University Press, 1981.
———. "Home." In *The House That Race Built: Black Americans, U.S. Terrain*, ed. Wahneema Lubiano, 3–12. New York: Pantheon, 1997.
———. *Home*. New York: Knopf, 2012.
———. *Jazz*. New York: Vintage, 2004.
———. *Love*. New York: Vintage, 2005.
———. *The Nobel Lecture*. New York: Norton, 1993.
———. *Paradise*. New York: Penguin, 1999.
———. "Virginia Woolf's and William Faulkner's Treatment of the Alienated." M.A. thesis, Cornell University, 1955.
Morrison, Toni, and Slade Morrison. *Who's Got Game? The Ant or the Grasshopper?* Pictures by Pascal Lemaitre. New York: Scribner, 2003.

Rilke, Rainer Maria. *The Notebooks of Malte Laurids Brigge*. Trans. Stephen Mitchell. New York: Vintage, 1990.

———. *The Selected Poetry of Rainer Maria Rilke*. Ed. and trans. Stephen Mitchell. New York: Vintage, 1989.

Robinson, James, ed. *The Nag Hammadi Library*. Rev. ed. San Francisco: Harper Collins, 1990.

Tate, Claudia. "Toni Morrison." In *Conversations with Toni Morrison*, ed. Danille Taylor-Guthrie, 156–70. Jackson: University Press of Mississippi, 1994.

Taylor-Guthrie, Danille, ed. *Conversations with Toni Morrison*. Jackson: University Press of Mississippi, 1994.

Williams, Raymond. *The Country and the City*. New York: Oxford, 1973.

RESURRECTING THE DEAD GIRL

*Modernism and the Problem of History
in* Beloved, Jazz, *and* Paradise

ANN HOSTETLER

In her afterword to *The Bluest Eye*, written twenty-four years after the book's initial publication in 1970, Toni Morrison offers a critique of her first novel about an unloved black girl: "The shattered world I built (to complement what is happening to Pecola)...does not in its present form handle effectively the silence at its center: the void that is Pecola's 'unbeing.' It should have had a shape—like the emptiness left by a boom or a cry" (215). In articulating the aesthetic desire "to shape a silence while breaking it" (216), Morrison offers a clue to reading her subsequent novels. In fact, variations on dead or discarded girls, or remnant women, haunt each of her fictions, serving as tropes for the problem of representing "unbeing"—an aporia around which historical and personal narratives are constructed. The aporia lures the reader's imagination, offering an opportunity to question, respond to, and refigure narratives that exclude or privilege certain stories at the expense of others.

This essay explores the trope of the dead girl as an accessory to articulating a silenced past in Morrison's fiction. History is articulation; the dead or discarded girl represents what remains excluded from the narrative. When the unarticulated past pressures the fictional narrative in search of language, the image of a dead girl or remnant woman intrudes, pushing the reader's imagination beyond the edge of history as narrative. By examining the dead or discarded girls in her texts, it is possible to trace the approaches Morrison's novels take toward embodying history. Although the characters and stories of the various novels are only tangentially related, the narrative obsession with rupturing historical narrative to heal its omissions deeply connects them.

In Morrison's fiction, the pressure of the past that wants to erupt into historical narrative is embodied by female figures, as in Lucille Clifton's poem "I am accused of tending to the past":

> ... this past was waiting for me
> when i came,
> a monstrous unnamed baby,
> and i with my mother's itch
> took it to breast
> and named it
> History.
> she is more human now,
> learning language every day ... (7)

Clifton's poem suggests that the past becomes history through a gestational process analogous to birth; furthermore, she figures the writer of history—the one who "names" the unarticulated past—as female. Throughout Morrison's fiction, history is also feminized: from the dead Pecola, elegized by Claudia in *The Bluest Eye*, to the ghost in *Beloved*, to the murdered Dorcas in *Jazz*. In *Paradise* the dead girl figure is replaced by remnant women whose stories are woven into the novel, told after the reader learns that the men of the town have hunted them down and killed them. In *A Mercy* the discarded girl acquires a voice. Silence presses against language until the daughter finally writes her story on the walls of the master's house.

Morrison's early novels, all meticulously set in specific time periods, experiment with variations on "shap[ing] a silence while breaking it." Her second novel, *Sula*, which explores a friendship between two girls in a post–World War I Ohio town, reverses *The Bluest Eye*'s pattern of building a narrative around a dead girl. Instead Nel and Sula form an indelible bond as they witness the accidental drowning of a boy child, Chicken Little, to which they are accessories. This death becomes the aporia around which the circles of sorrow swirl in this novel. But in Morrison's third novel, *Song of Solomon*, a story constructed around a male protagonist who follows the archetypal quest myth, the dead girl resurfaces in the character of Hagar, descendant of a line of women who live according to their own rules. In contrast to Macon Dead, real estate investor and patriarch, his sister Pilate, along with her daughter Reba and granddaughter Hagar, represent alternate versions of the past discarded by Macon's narrative for success, a narrative that excludes not only other persons but also his own emotional life. Abandoned by Milkman, Macon's son, after a brief affair, Hagar attempts to woo him back with every beauty trick in the book, then threatens to kill him. Failing to claim his attention, she finally self-destructs. Meanwhile Hagar's death propels Milkman on his own quest to find his missing history and restore his ability to feel.[1]

Such female avatars of neglect, need, and rage—strewn throughout Morrison's later work—take on special prominence in her historical trilogy of *Beloved*, *Jazz*, and *Paradise*. Each of these novels hinges on a curiously similar plotting device: the murder of a girl or woman. In *Beloved*, set in Reconstruction-era Ohio and inspired by the story of Margaret Garner, the main character Sethe has been shaped by a moment in which historical circumstances forced her into the impossible position of killing her own "best thing," slitting the throat of her "crawling already? baby" rather than allow her to be taken into slavery. The novel is also a memorial, titled after the dead, unnamed child whose tombstone, paid for by sex, bears the single word "Beloved." *Jazz*, inspired by a memorial photograph of a murdered girl taken by James Van Der Zee and set in New York during the early years of black migration, begins when Joe Trace kills his "fling"—an orphan named Dorcas—and his wife Violet disfigures the face of her husband's lover and victim. The novel explores the palpable presence of the dead girl between this estranged and dislocated pair and results in the eventual healing of their relationship as they come to nurture a similar girl, Felice, a friend of Dorcas, who serves as a kind of substitute for her. *Paradise*, which chronicles the genesis of an all-black town in Oklahoma, begins with murder: "They shoot the white girl first." "They" are a posse of self-appointed male protectors of a town (re)named in memory of a dead girl, Ruby. Their targets are a group of "remnant" women—women injured and discarded by society or unable to live by its conventional rules—characters who seem to bring to life a wide variety of the wild and unloved women hinted at in Morrison's previous novels. Meanwhile, the only deaths in Ruby appear to be the deaths of marginal women—women with traces of white, "outside" blood, or otherwise "tainted," as is the daughter of Jeff and Sweetie, Save-Marie, the product of too-close breeding within the community and a suppressed narrative of incestuous relationships between generations.

Each novel in the trilogy represents a moment of displacement in relationship to the past, echoed in the murder at the center of the text. In *Beloved* it is the disruption of mothering itself in the economy of slavery and the Middle Passage that creates the context for Sethe's murder of her own child. Sethe's own mother is unable to act as a mother in expressing her love for her daughter, save in the revelation of a brand, a sign, a slap. Sethe's passionate desire to give her own milk to her own child is disrupted by a cruel experiment imposed on her by a slave master and his male relatives. Her "crawling-already" child goes unnamed in the disrupting transition of the escape from slavery and the resulting fragmentation of her family. The (re)appearance of Beloved activates the desire of Sethe and Denver for the lost woman in their family. *Jazz* explores the fragmentation of community in migration to the city, its new technologies for narrative—such as recordings—and a disembodied narrator, possibly a record or a talking book. It reveals the disruption of traditional narratives, such as the letters, and the continuing disruption of family history but offers several versions of the same story, notably that of Joe Trace's possible mother, Wild. "Paradise" is a dystopia built on a series of displacements—from the casting out of the 8-rocks from Reconstruction-era Louisiana to the Disallowing. However, in their attempt to create a narrative that will save them from further displacement, the 8-rocks who founded Ruby create their own form of disallowing for others.

Modernism as an aesthetic is also based on the notion of a rupture with the past. It formulates itself as the eternal present, the cutting edge. It leaves behind the unsightly, the unseemly, the unruly, the stray hairs that escape the braid of modernist form. A modernist work may, like T. S. Eliot's *The Wasteland*, be made of fragments, yet the fragments express the desire for wholeness, for a totalizing formal system that breaks from the clutter of the past and redeems the present as a unified whole. The problem with the modern is that it tends to dismiss or obscure the past on which it depends. In its most unadulterated forms, modernism also refuses to historicize itself. Thus the writing of a historical novel in a modernist mode appears to be something of a contradiction in terms, since a historical narrative posits continuity between past and present.

Postmodernism historicizes modernism but sacrifices the idea of narrative as a totalizing system. Postmodern fiction, on the other hand, displays an awareness of history, as well as its own situatedness, that makes an omniscient and unifying narrative into a fiction. It acknowledges the fictionality of all totalizing narratives, so to create itself, it must forgo claims to a unifying truth. This is an artistic challenge for writers and cultures that would claim and represent historical actualities.

Modernism presupposes a notion of history as continuous narrative to posit a rupture from the past. It views itself as the ever-shifting horizon of the now, an aesthetic of progress and innovation. Form is content; content is form. In an African American context, however, the modernist aesthetic of formalism stands in opposition to the cultural necessity of healing the breach with the past imposed by the historical realities of the Middle Passage and slavery. While Eurocentric modernisms tend to "flee" historical reality for aesthetic integrity, African American modernism searches for ways to encode the past in a formally sophisticated work. At the same time, the desire to fabricate a revisionist past, or to adopt existing master narratives in the service of progress, is a powerful temptation that prevents narrators from accounting for the full range of maverick human experience. These formal challenges engage Morrison's imagination in her historical trilogy, and each of the three novels experiments with a different solution to the problem of reconciling a modernist aesthetic with a historical consciousness. This can be seen in the different ways in which Morrison uses the dead girl motif in each plot structure, the ways in which the unnarratable is shaped in relation to narration.

In *Beloved*, the title character takes the form of a ghost—a most unmodernist, or at least antirealistic, element in the novel. While modernist fictions may appear experimental, their motivation is usually toward a more realistic representation of consciousness, as in the examples of Joyce's *Ulysses* and Virginia Woolf's *Mrs Dalloway*, both stream-of-consciousness novels based on the passage of a single day as viewed through the prism of one mind—or two. Thus the overt presence of a ghost in *Beloved*, with real consequences in an otherwise realistically portrayed story, was disconcerting to many readers who expected some form of social or historical realism as they encountered the book for the first time. Yet the structure of *Beloved* is a modernist one, in which the fragments of narrative form a cohesive whole around a central dialogue between a mother and her two daughters—one living and one the ghost in which the other two fervently believe, each for her own reasons. The representation of history as the return of the repressed in the character of Beloved is also a modernist strategy born of the American love affair with Freudian psychology. In this figuration, a history of loss, betrayal, and trauma is something that must be exorcised from the psyche before healing can take place. At the center of the novel is a collaborative trio of voices all exchanging identities with one another, possessing each other in their desires for completeness. But this central narrative collapses on itself. Healing requires the creation of alternative narratives from outside the closed system, and finally the collaborative narrative of the community, and listeners who can testify to the newly emergent narrative. At the end of *Beloved*, the dead girl disappears again. She represents a story not to be passed on. Yet she resurfaces as a glimmer in *Jazz*. In fact, the repressed returns in *Jazz*.

Jazz revisits the trope of the dead girl in a new key. This time she takes the form of permanent, irrevocable death. Morrison's mode no longer requires the ghost but rather examines characters as they respond to the impact of an absence created by a violent death and come to terms with loss. This strategy seems more compatible with a modernist aesthetic in that its depiction of loss is more realistic, but the technologies of memory and the ways in which they are invoked through a seemingly mechanical narrator threaten to disrupt the modernist assumption of a unified historical narrative. Rather than offering us transparency, or at least an authoritative omniscience, the narrator—who appears to be both human and not human, both single and multiple—challenges the notion of a unified narrative. *Jazz*, like the music for which it is named, is hard to grab hold of. It has no unifying melody but a series of riffs and solos interwoven in a dialectic of call and response. The melody or theme of a jazz composition is as elusive as the figure of "Wild," a remnant woman buried at the center of the text, possibly the "disappeared" Beloved, the indeterminate object of Joe Trace's search of his mother. The narrator, like a blues song, is both personal and elusive. If, indeed, the narrator is a record(ing)—the book begins with the sound, "Sth," of a needle placed on a record—its voice reproduces overheard and borrowed narrations, posing the question: "How much of our story is made by culture, and how much by the individual?"

Whereas the fragmented narratives of *Jazz* threaten to disrupt identity, in *Paradise* the controlled and controlling narrative of Ruby's official history threatens to suppress almost everyone in the community. In *Paradise* Morrison turns to a narrative strategy that is omniscient and seemingly transparent, pushing to the novel's edge the excluded elements of supernatural and transcendent realms, which are yet essential to its structure.

The novel begins with a murder mystery: "They shoot the white girl first." *They*, the men of Ruby, shoot the motley crew of misfit women who live in the Convent because the living women tell alternate stories. Which is the most unsettling alternative, and for whom: to live with the potential disruption of narrative, or the too-tight closure of a single revisionist paradigm?

The dead girl(s) in this trilogy beg the question of how untold histories should be voiced. In *Beloved*, the impossible occurs. The missing child reappears, but in a form that is both seductive and terrifying. She must be exorcised to liberate the main character, Sethe, the mother and murderer of her child, and the community that has condemned her. Beloved, the character, represents a story that should not be passed on, but until she gains a voice, she will not disappear for good. *Jazz* begins with a funeral and a disfiguring, and Violet's attempt to de-face Dorcas, the teenage lover whom her husband Joe Trace has murdered. The death leads to soul-searching for both Joe and Violet. Violet must come to terms with her infertility and her botched attempt to kidnap a child; Joe must search for his own vanished mother—the Beloved figure in this novel. At the novel's end, Violet and Joe show their healing when they are able to create a nurturing space for another girl, Felice, who stands in for what each has lost. *Paradise* offers not just one dead girl but a host of them, rescued by Consolata, who herself was a rescued remnant girl. The novel begins with a witch hunt but ends in resurrection. How should we interpret the two parallel communities and the alternative narratives they offer?

It is hard to decide, finally, which is more unsettling: the disruption of narrative or the too-tight closure of a revisionist paradigm. In response to the too-tight narrative of Ruby that results in the hunting of the Convent women, Morrison supplies a rogue alternative, creating portraits of discarded women with such detailed empathy that the reader embraces displaced persons who do not fit into the bounds. Slipping into the novel, the reader tries on the narratives of the lost women in the worlds both of the Convent and of Ruby, sensing the holes in the text as well as the constraints of narrative. Morrison entices readers to know women in fiction whom we might refuse to know in life.

The figure of the dead girl—in particular, an unnamed, orphaned, discarded, or disregarded girl—that haunts each of these stories suggests not only the rupture with the past but a rupture within the psyche, and within narrative—the suppressed texts of gendered, feminine herstory within African American history. Thus the trope of the dead girl gestures toward a larger cultural narrative—or alternate narrative—at the margin of the text. Structurally, Morrison uses epigraphs for each novel that also direct the reader to engage historical lacunae that exist beyond the text. In *Beloved* it is the "sixty million and more" who suffered in the transatlantic slave trade. It is also the women, unable to be individuals or to be mothers, whose lives are rent and incomplete—those beloved who were not beloved. *Jazz* and *Paradise*, on the other hand, begin with epigraphs from "Thunder, Perfect Mind," from the Nag Hammadi, a fragment of noncanonical scripture. The speaker of this text is thought to be a female voice for the divine: "I am the name of the sound / and the sound of the name. / I am the sign of the letter / and the designation of the division."

The presence of a dead female—in the form of revenant, corpse, or remnant—signifies Morrison's continuing preoccupation with women's history, in particular, and the ways it has been elided in the canonical texts of African American modernism, such as Ralph Ellison's *Invisible Man* and Richard Wright's *Native Son*, or not yet fully voiced. Each novel in her historical trilogy is not only an elegy but a story of resurrections, including the resurrections of discarded narrative alternatives. Consolata, for instance, was a street child, adopted by a nun who brought her to a convent school. When her teacher dies, Connie—or Consolata—takes on the work of love and reconciliation, translating her own life the best way she can. The feminine divine figure of Piedade is merely a glimmer in a text that shows real, imperfect women at work looking for love and restoration—here, in this world, in this life, Morrison suggests, we gesture toward the divine love we have experienced or can imagine.

It is fitting, then, that Morrison brings *Paradise* to a close by invoking the mythic, rather than the historical, in the figure of Piedade (which means *pity* in Portuguese), the Black Madonna figure who was Consolata's rescuer and teacher. As Channette Romero points out, the text of the novel "does not transcend history." It refuses to side with either the materialist or the supernatural narrative but brings them into conversation:

> *Paradise* points to the necessity of a complex dialectical relation with history, a relation that requires at once an immediate, intense connection with the historical and the material and a meaningful connection with the spiritual and the mythical. Thus, the text does not privilege either method for creating beloved communities over the other. It suggests the importance of holding both of these methods open as a means of creating an earthly paradise, of keeping one eye firmly rooted to the local/material/historical and another looking beyond to the spiritual/mythical/imaginative. (425)

Thus Morrison keeps the alternate narratives in tension, the official narrative of Ruby begging for its spiritual counterpart in the story of those left out of its history.

The palimpsestic texts of Morrison's historical fictions offer layers of possible readings that richly reward successive revisionary reading of the novels. From the return of the repressed in *Beloved* to redemptive violence and the technologies of memory in *Jazz*, Morrison continually revisits the problem of history in a new key. In *Paradise* the invocation of the Black Madonna in the form of Piedade, underscored by the epigraphs from "Thunder, Perfect Mind" in *Jazz* and *Paradise*, completes the quest for a feminine divine implicit in the trilogy's earlier novels in an apocalyptic ending, a realm outside history, a perspective from which history, paradoxically, gains its meaning.

Again and again, Morrison presents a palimpsest to the reader, threaded through with precise historical references, hinting at a hidden text that will be the key to all mythologies. And yet she never lets us find it, but rather causes readers to reach for it, participating in the making of meaning through our desire to reach beyond our own narrative. As Lucille Fultz suggests, the novel *Paradise*, particularly in the embedded text of Patricia the historian, "demonstrate[s] that the borders between history and fiction are not so clearly defined—that historical and fictional narratives are interpenetrative, enabling a deeper understanding of human relations. Beyond its interplay between fiction and history, *Paradise* reveals that reading is a process involving a close relationship between the author, the text, and the reader" (98). Thus we come to know the dead girl, the representatives of those who are excluded from history, those whose narratives are unknowable, because unrecorded. Morrison's historical trilogy asks us to imagine them back to life in the process of reading disjunctive narratives and weaving them into a dialectic of meaning. And it sets the stage for *A Mercy*, in which the discarded girl, for the first time in Morrison's oeuvre, narrates her own tale.

Notes

1. Michele Gyllenhammer Pessoni has explored the dead girl in Morrison's early fiction from a different angle, in relation to the Kore/Demeter myth, in her dissertation "Rescuing the Dead Girl: Toni Morrison and Goddess Mythology" (University of Connecticut, 1995), DA9605493.

Works Cited

Clifton, Lucille. "i am accused of tending to the past." *quilting: poems, 1987–1990*. Brockport, NY: BOA Editions, 1991.
Fultz, Lucille P. *Toni Morrison: Playing with Difference*. Urbana: University of Illinois Press, 2003.
Morrison, Toni. Afterword to *The Bluest Eye*, 209–16. New York: Penguin, 1994.
———. *Beloved*. New York: Vintage, 2004.
———. *The Bluest Eye*. 1970. New York: Penguin, 1994.
———. *Jazz*. New York: Vintage, 2004.
———. *A Mercy*. New York: Vintage, 2009.
———. *Paradise*. New York: Plume, 1999.
———. *Song of Solomon*. New York: Vintage, 2004.
———. *Sula*. New York: Vintage, 2004.
Pessoni, Michele Gyllenhammer. "Rescuing the Dead Girl: Toni Morrison and Goddess Mythology." Ph.D. diss., University of Connecticut, 1995.
Romero, Channette. "Creating the Beloved Community: Religion, Race, and Nation in Toni Morrison's Paradise." *African American Review* 39 (Fall 2005): 415–30.

TO MAKE A HUMANIST BLACK

Toni Wofford's Howard Years

DANA A. WILLIAMS

"Quiet as it's kept," Toni Morrison, during her tenure as a senior editor at Random House, shepherded in the publication of over fifty books—among them books of poetry and fiction, autobiographies and memoirs, cookbooks and cultural texts. That her editorship beyond her work with *The Black Book*, which began in 1965, reached its apex in the 1970s, and ended in 1983, has gone largely uninvestigated is not especially surprising.[1] Typically, literary scholarship is guilty of focusing more on the author as producer of a text and then on the text as finished product than on the journey to publication or on the editors. But this tendency has serious limitations, since editors (and their work for and with publishers) ultimately control which texts see the light of print. In many ways, then, editors are at least one class of curators of culture.

As one such curator, Morrison helped shape the representation of African American culture in printed texts in the years immediately following the decline of the Black Arts Movement, mediated African American printed texts' vacillating shifts from the margin to center (an important feat when we consider the radical interventions that nonblack sources make in attempts to influence black meaning-making processes and cultural productions), and served both as a bridge between the radicalism of the Black Arts Movement and the mainstreaming of the Black Aesthetic and as the conduit for this bridge. In short, careful examination of Morrison's editorship facilitates the unraveling of the crucial, intently politicized elements of black intellectual and cultural history of the 1960s and 1970s and reveals her influence in shaping blackness as it was represented in contemporary printed texts.

Morrison's articulation of blackness as a distinct cultural reality with which she readily identifies makes clear that her role in shaping representations of blackness was unabashedly methodical. When we consider the texts she published in the first few years after her move from the textbook division at L. W. Singer to adult trade at Random House, the potential significance of her editorship in this regard becomes more apparent. Among the texts she either acquired (courting and recruiting authors) or adopted (serving as the final editor of record of an author acquired by another editor) during the first five years of her editorship, for example, are Huey P. Newton's *To Die for the People* (1972), Toni Cade Bambara's *Gorilla, My Love* (1972), Leslie Lacy and Edris Makward's *Contemporary African Literature* (1972), Boris L. Bittker's *The Case for Black Reparations* (1973), Leon Forrest's *There Is a Tree More Ancient than Eden* (1973), Angela Davis's *Angela Davis: An Autobiography* (1974), Middleton A. Harris, Morris Levitt, and Roger Furman's *The Black Book* (1974), Muhammad Ali's *The Greatest* (1975), Chinweizu's *The West and the Rest of Us: White Slavers, Black Predators, and The African Elite* (1975), and Quincy Troupe and Rainer Schulte's *Giant Talk: An Anthology of Third World Writings* (1975).[2] As the range of the texts suggests, Morrison's conception of blackness (or, minimally, her perception of its useful representations) was broad. How she developed this conception of blackness, then, becomes a logical query, one that I contend can be addressed in revealing ways by considering her years as a student and then as a professor at Howard University.[3]

The milieu at Howard during the years Morrison was an undergraduate student there was multifarious indeed. A cursory review of the student newspaper, the *Hilltop*, provides insight to this truth and much more. The October 10, 1950, "Outlook" column, for instance, proclaimed that "the profundity of social awareness" could be evidenced everywhere: "The average freshman and upper classman can discuss the latest show on 'U' Street, the current trend in women's fashion or the [']craziest' record in the Snack Bar, but cannot hold a decent conversation on a topic so all-embracing as world affairs"; however, the same columnist notes:

> There are numerous opportunities offered on ... campus—through visiting lectures, through our courses, through our libraries, student council and many other sources—for the construction of that type of personality necessary to our being students, and more useful people in this chaotic world of 1950. After all, humanity has placed its hopes in our generation, so let's start preparing for that all important future right now. (n.p.)

In terms of its faculty, the university was more than sufficiently equipped to prepare its students for the "all important future." Ever the traditionalists in terms of curriculum but no less interested in the ways an Africanist presence might inform or engage traditional disciplines, many members of the faculty were leading critics in their fields, even as they took nontraditional approaches to their disciplines to consider fully the implications of all things diasporic, even if the broader Howard curriculum did not fully reveal this interest. It was at Howard, for example, that William Leo Hansberry pioneered the study of African history in 1922 and where he continued to teach courses on African civilization until 1959; and it was at Howard that Sterling A. Brown pioneered the study of African American literature in the 1940s and taught the course American Prose and Poetry of Negro Life regularly while Morrison was a student there. Even the most cursory review of anthology editors or reviewers of African American literature reveals that an overwhelming majority of the seminal literary criticism in the field issued forth from Howard. And this tendency remained true at least until the mid-1950s. So just how much and in what ways did Howard contribute to the making of this humanist who would go on to be a senior editor at a major publishing company and, later, the first black woman to have her novel selected by the Book-of-the-Month Club, the first black woman to be hired as an endowed professor at an Ivy League university, and the first black woman to be awarded the Nobel Prize in Literature?

Chloe Anthony Wofford was a student at Howard from 1949 to 1953, during which time she assumed the nickname "Toni," reportedly in response to repeated mispronunciations of her name. In addition to her academic pursuits in the departments of English and classics, she was a member of the Modern Dance Club, Alpha Kappa Alpha Sorority, Incorporated, and the Howard Players, the university's official drama troupe. Since it is her work in the theater that she speaks of most fondly when she talks about her Howard years, I am limiting my comments here to her experiences with the Howard Players and its correlate, the Washington Repertory Players.

The Howard Players has its origin in the university's first drama club, which was started by students in 1907 and became an official university club in 1908, when, under the direction of Ernest Just (who was an English professor at the time), it became known as the "Howard University College Dramatic Club." In 1921 the club was reorganized as the "Howard Players" by Alain Locke and T. Montgomery Gregory, under the auspices of the Department of Dramatic Art, which Gregory chaired. When Gregory left Howard in 1924, the players were left without a department home, though Professor Brown and other members of the English department ensured quality productions by the now autonomous group, which became a charter member of the Negro Intercollegiate Dramatic Association in 1930 under Brown's direction. But it was not until 1947, two years before Morrison's arrival, that James W. Butcher Jr., Anne Cooke (Reid), and Owen Dodson established the Department of Drama, with Cooke as the chairperson. It was under the advisement of these three figures that the Howard Players emerged as one of the most renowned college theater troupes and that Toni Wofford excelled as an actress.

Her debut performance was in Alice Gerstenberg's *Overtones*.[4] The playbill for the spring 1950 production of Ernest Toller's *No More Peace* lists Toni Wofford as one of five children. In the same season, the players produced an original play titled *Boys without Pennies*, by Theodore (Ted) Smith, a junior English major. While Wofford was not cast in any role in that play, she was listed as a member of the business and publicity committee.[5] In 1952 she was cast as Elsie in William Saroyan's *The Time of Your Life* and as Cynthie, "a regular patron," in Robert Ardrey's *Jeb*. During the spring 1953 season, she received excellent reviews for her performance as Queen Elizabeth in the players' production of *Richard III*.[6] In the same season, she worked, along with Mary Nelson, who played Queen Margaret in *Richard III*, on costumes for Federico García Lorca's *The House of Bernarda Alba*, which the players presented at the university's annual Festival of Fine Arts.[7]

The 1953 summer season, which took Morrison south and garnered most of the minimal commentary on her career in the theater, was actually a function of the Washington Repertory Players, not the Howard Players.[8] Their tour stops included A&T College in Greensboro, Virginia State College, Kentucky State College, Tennessee State, Southern University, Alabama A&M, Hampton Institute, Wiley College, and Texas Southern University. The plays for the summer season were Tennessee Williams's *The Glass Menagerie*, with Morrison cast as the Daughter; Shakespeare's *The Taming of the Shrew*, where Morrison was cast as Bianca for the lone performance of the play at Virginia State College; and Ferenc Molnár's *The Guardsman*, in which Morrison was cast as Liesl. Unlike *Taming of the Shrew*, *The Guardsman* saw a number of performances, and the "who's who" of characters cited on the playbill for the Southern University production of the play revealed the following:

> Toni Wofford (Liesl) has just completed a major in English at Howard and is on her way to Cornell for further studies. She was highly praised last year for her discriminating playing of Queen Elizabeth in *Richard III*. Shakespearean authorities said she was both accurate and inspired. With considerable versatility, she has also acted more modern parts in *Jeb* and *The Time of Your Life*.

At the end of the summer 1953 season, Morrison began graduate school at Cornell. After earning her master's degree in English in 1955, she rejoined the troupe and was cast as Louka in George Bernard Shaw's *Arms and the Man*. At the end of the season, she began what was to be a two-year tenure at Texas Southern University, before returning to Howard as a faculty member in the Department of English in 1957.

Unearthing Toni Wofford as performer and her Howard years' crucial role in the formative development of an aesthetic sensibility and this development's corresponding influence on her role as editor reveals her awareness of the ways in which culture can be (re)presented with variation. As Howard and Washington Repertory Players' advisers, Butcher, Cooke, Dodson, and Lovell are exemplars of the ability of Howard faculty of that age to navigate racial representations with uncanny nuance. Each adviser was deeply committed to black culture, and each understood the significance of institutionalizing black culture and representing it with sufficient breadth.[9] At one point, Butcher directed drama activities at the University of Liberia and served as a consultant to the Liberian government, developing theater activities in the country. Cooke established the first black summer theater, which ran for forty-four consecutive seasons, and channeled her artistic energies into black colleges: Spelman, Morehouse, Hampton, and Howard. Dodson's work as a poet, novelist, and playwright speaks for itself as evidence of his commitment to black culture. And Lovell, who is perhaps best known for his seminal work on the African American spiritual (*Black Song: The Forge and the Flame; The Story of How the Afro-American Spiritual Was Hammered Out*), was active in civil rights circles long before doing so was popular. He was, for instance, the secretary of the Marian Anderson Citizens' Committee, which protested the Daughters of the American Revolution's refusal to allow Anderson to sing at Constitution Hall in 1939.[10]

How aware would an astute Toni Wofford have been of the ability of Butcher, Cooke, Dodson, and Lovell to negotiate racial spaces, and just how might some of the implications of that awareness be manifest? What might she have learned from Dodson, whose artistry was largely unparalleled at the height of his career? How might Dodson's revision of Shakespeare to make it modern and his insistence that his actors offer fresh, new interpretations of traditional texts and dialogue have influenced Morrison's willingness and ability to envision and see the value of revisions of traditional mythologies and humanities themes? How did Cooke's insistence that each actor participate in total theater—setting, budget, publicity, makeup, and costumes—endow Morrison with an unusual sense of the act of creation? In what ways did Cooke's gift of perfect diction impress on Morrison an obsession with sound in language? How did Lovell's awareness of the techniques of black music and its traditions influence her aesthetic sensibility? While we can never be certain about any of these things, when we consider that she traveled with Butcher, Cooke, and Lovell throughout the segregated Jim Crow south by car for an entire summer, it is more logical than not to argue that these experiences required her to grow increasingly aware of ways to fashioning a black cultural self.

After graduating from Cornell in 1955, she taught at Texas Southern for two years before returning to Howard as a faculty member in English, where she remained until 1964. Her students (among them Stokely Carmichael, a.k.a. Kwame Ture; Andrew Young; and Claude Brown), the junior faculty in English who made up her intellectual cohort (Clyde Taylor, Bernard Bell, and Eleanor W. Traylor, to name a few), and the activities with which she was involved (her work with Theatre Arts, the Howard Poets, and May Miller's literary salon in particular), in tandem with the sociopolitical climate, which played host to and birthed organizations like the Nonviolent Action Group (NAG) and the Student Non-Violent Coordinating Committee (SNCC), must all be considered intently to imagine their probable influence.[11] As Ture (Carmichael) wrote in *Ready for Revolution*, during that time at Howard, one could find "everything and its opposite."[12] By this he meant that there were all kinds of people at Howard and that, conversely, one could find as easily the opposite of all these kinds. At least part of what Morrison took from this experience, I would argue, is an awareness of the politics and the significance of representations of blackness, an awareness she took with her to L. W. Singer, the publishing company that moved her to New York and initiated her career as an editor.

When Morrison moved to Syracuse in 1965 to become a textbook editor at Singer, a division of Random House, she did so with a firm sense of what she might be able to do there, of how she might influence contemporary black intellectual traditions and shape modern conversations about black life and culture. When she moved from Singer in Syracuse to Random House in New York City in 1968 and then from textbooks to trade books a few years later, her objective would not change, even if the conduit for achieving it did. In both instances, her cultural and aesthetic sensibilities influenced the texts she chose to edit and, correspondingly, how they represented blackness. While I acknowledge that her way of making meaning was perpetually evolving before we see what can be considered identifiably Morrison-esque, I also imagine that significant aspects of her ways of knowing and making meaning took shape during her Howard years as a student and then as a professor.

While some of her literary ancestors may have rejected what they may have seen as the limitations of racial identity and strived instead to be an artist of Albert Murray-esqe "OmniAmerica," Toni Morrison embraces, if not demands, characterizations of her work as distinctly that of an African American. In "Memory, Creation, and Writing," for example, she writes that she is interested in knowing the truth of her "own cultural sources" (386). In the same essay, she suggests that the "interior part of the growth of a writer . . . is connected not only to some purely local and localized sets of stimuli but also to memory" and its "milieu of buried stimuli" (385). She goes on to write: "When one looks at a very good painting the experience of looking is deeper than the data accumulated in viewing it" (387). The experience of looking at Morrison's Howard years—to recover memory and its milieu of buried stimuli, and to reveal an important aspect of the interior part of her growth as curator of culture—gives us a glimpse of an excellent painting in its own right, indeed.

Notes

1. Exceptions of note include brief mentions of her work as an editor in general biographical sketches, in interviews, and in Cheryl Wall's "Recollections of Kin: *Beloved* and *The Black Book*," in her *Worrying the Line: Black Women Writers, Lineage, and Literary Tradition*; and Wall's "Toni Morrison, Editor and Teacher," in Justine Tally's *The Cambridge Companion to Toni Morrison*.

2. To be certain, Morrison published a number of texts by nonblack authors and of limited interested to black people. I am concerned foremost here with her editorship of black texts, however.

3. In this essay, I limit my commentary to Morrison's Howard years. My larger project, structured in part as a cultural biography, examines Morrison's tenure at Random House and considers her intellectual development as a critical lens through which to read the period that constitutes her editorship.

4. I must express my indebtedness to my colleague Joe Selmon, former chair of the Department of Theatre Arts at Howard, who shared with me the playbills from the Howard Players' earliest productions through the years Morrison was a member of the troupe, and provided me with access to Anne Cooke's notes and unpublished commentary about much of the players' and the department's notable history.

5. The particulars of Morrison's theater activity in 1951 have proved most elusive. Neither of the two available playbills for the plays presented that year—Albert Camus's *Cross Purpose* in the spring and J. B. Priestley's *An Inspector Calls* in the fall—cites her involvement in any capacity. It may be the case that Morrison participated in plays for which no playbill has been located. It is clear, however, that she was active on campus that year, since she is cited in the student yearbook as the dean of probates for the 1951 Alpha chapter pledges of Alpha Kappa Alpha Sorority, Incorporated.

6. Morrison also starred in this role in the June 25, 1953, television performance of *Richard and the Three Queens*.

7. Notably, the program shows considerable interest in wide-ranging diasporic African artistic productions.

8. Dated March 27, 1953, the Washington Repertory Players' articles of partnership declare James W. Butcher, Anne M. Cooke, and John Lovell Jr., all Howard faculty, equal partners. The press release announcing the launching of the troupe cites "Toni Wofford, Howard Senior, who recently won plaudits from Shakespearean authorities for her playing of Queen Elizabeth in *Richard III*," as one of its principal actors.

9. Notably, Butcher, Cooke, and Dodson were criticized when they selected DuBose Heyward's *Mamba's Daughter* and Henrik Ibsen's *The Wild Duck* as the two plays the Howard Players were to perform during their tour in Europe in 1949. The advisers' choice not to perform exclusively plays involving black life or plays written by black playwrights was a complicated one. Minimally, however, the choice reveals an attempt to avoid delimited representations of blackness.

10. Howard had sponsored Anderson's Washington recitals in 1936 and 1937, and the organizing committee had been denied requests to use Constitution Hall before they worked with the NAACP to protest publicly the refusal in 1939.

11. A number of Howard faculty, Morrison among them, formally and informally advised the group of Howard students (Walter De Legall, Alfred Fraser, Oswald Govan, Percy Johnston, Leroy Stone, and Joseph White) who dubbed themselves the "Howard poets." In an interview with Winston Napier, Govan remembers Morrison as a young faculty member who took them seriously, spent a great deal of time with them, and encouraged their efforts (58).

12. "Howard University: Everything and Its Opposite" is the title of chapter 6 of *Ready for Revolution: The Life and Struggles of Stokely Carmichael (Kwame Ture)*.

Works Cited

Carmichael, Stokely. *Ready for Revolution: The Life and Struggles of Stokely Carmichael (Kwame Ture)*. With Michael Thelwell. New York: Simon and Schuster, 2003.

——. *Stokely Speaks: From Black Power to Pan-Africanism*. New York: Random House, 1971.

Haskins, Jim. *Toni Morrison: Telling a Tale Untold*. Brookfield, CT: Twenty-first Century Books, 2002.

Hatch, James. *Sorrow Is the Only Faithful One: The Life of Owen Dodson*. Chicago: University of Illinois Press, 1995.

Keiler, Allan. *Marian Anderson: A Singer's Journey*. Chicago: University of Illinois Press, 2002.

Logan, Rayford W. *Howard University: The First One Hundred Years, 1867–1967*. New York: New York University Press, 1969.

Morrison, Toni. "Memory, Creation, and Writing." *Thought* 59 (December 1984): 385–90.

———. "Remarks Given at the Howard University Charter Day Convocation." In *Toni Morrison: What Moves at the Margin—Selected Nonfiction*, ed. Carolyn C. Denard, 164–69. Jackson: University Press of Mississippi, 2008.

Napier, Winston. "The Howard Poets." In *Washington and Washington Writing*, ed. David McAleavey, 57–67. Washington: George Washington University, 1986.

Wall, Cheryl. "Recollections of Kin: *Beloved* and *The Black Book*." In *Worrying the Line: Black Women Writers, Lineage, and Literary Tradition*, ed. Cheryl Wall, 84–115. Chapel Hill: University of North Carolina Press, 2005.

———. "Toni Morrison, Editor and Teacher." In *The Cambridge Companion to Toni Morrison*, ed. Justine Tally, 139–48. Cambridge: Cambridge University Press, 2007.

PART II

*"Regrets, excuses, righteousness,
false memory and future plans mixed
together or stood like soldiers in line"*

TRYING TO GET HOME

Place and Memory in Toni Morrison's Fiction

CHERYL A. WALL

From *The Bluest Eye* to *Home*, Toni Morrison's novels take up the subjects of place and displacement, home and homelessness, belonging and exile, memory and loss. Lorain, the Bottom, Not Doctor Street, Iles des Chevaliers, Sweet Home, the City, Ruby, Cosey's Resort, Vaark's Farm, Lotus: these places have left indelible impressions on our memories. What Robert Stepto almost thirty years ago called "this extraordinary sense of place" remains a hallmark of Morrison's fiction (213). Yet the difference in representational strategies between Lorain in the first novel and Lotus in the most recent is substantial. Lorain is a place we imagine we have been. Lotus is one that we can only imagine. The evolution suggests two questions that I explore in this essay: How is it that we know places in Morrison's fiction better than we know places where we have in fact lived? Might we in the process of mapping them miss the meanings they convey?

In "Intimate Things in Place: A Conversation with Toni Morrison," the interview that Stepto conducted shortly after *Sula* was published, Morrison acknowledged that, when writing, she at times "felt a very strong sense of place, not in terms of country or state, but in terms of the details, the feeling, the mood of the community or the town" (213). The places in Morrison's fiction are invested with history, sometimes so local and particular, as with *The Bluest Eye* and *Sula*, that readers enter worlds that seem closed to outsiders.

In other novels, the histories that animate places like the City in *Jazz* are part of our collective knowledge. Readers are always invited to bring whatever knowledge they have to the scene. Morrison's later novels evoke places that are described with verisimilitude yet inscribe spiritual cartographies, maps of places that are at once alluring and evanescent. In these places, readers are forced to confront what Morrison calls "vulnerable humanity," the selves that exist in her fiction beneath ideologies of race, selves that could exist in the world if readers summoned her domesticated "race-free paradise" into being ("Home," 9).

Place in Morrison's fiction reminds us that the so-called real and the so-called metaphoric exist in complex relationship to each other. As the geographers Michael Keith and Steve Pile assert, "The symbolic and the literal are in part constitutive of one another. That meaning is never immanent, it is instead just *marked* but also in part *constituted* by the spaces of representation in which it is articulated" (23). If the places in Morrison's earlier novels are more apt to have literal referents, they are never literal representations. The novelist selects and invents elements of landscape, speech, and ritual that produce the feeling she hopes to summon. Analogously, the places in the later novels are never merely symbolic. They, too, combine elements of landscape, speech, and ritual. The difference is a matter of degree and detail.

To illustrate the shift in Morrison's representational strategies, I have selected novels from the first and middle phase of her career, as well as her most recent novel, *Home*. But all of Morrison's fictions partake of both the illusion of realism and the artifice of metaphor. The illusion of realism enables us to know the places in the novels, while the artifice of metaphor cautions us that we do not know them as well as we think. By attending to the metaphorical, we confront the moral demands that are central to Morrison's art. These obligations, in turn, inform our reading protocol. They also, necessarily, limit the degree to which we can give ourselves over to the pleasures of the text.

Unlike William Faulkner or Zora Neale Hurston, Morrison's imagination is not tied to a particular place or region. Instead her novels map the post–Civil War migrations of blacks throughout the United States and the consequent nationalization of a culture.[1] Immediately I think of the characters in *The Bluest Eye* who find themselves in the quiet neighborhoods of Lorain, Ohio. "They come from Mobile. Aiken. From Newport News. From Marietta. From Meridian. And the sounds of those places in their mouths made you think of love. . . . You don't know what these towns are like, but you love what happens to the air when they open their lips and let the names ease out" (81).

As readers we are similarly seduced by the places Morrison's fiction invents. But we are never allowed merely to love them. They are places with particular, complex, and troubling histories. In the process of understanding them, we come closer to understanding the overarching history of Africans in the New World.

The Bluest Eye is set in the author's hometown, Lorain, Ohio. Morrison acknowledges that the information from which she drew was autobiographical: "I didn't create that town," she told an interviewer. "It's clearer to me now in my memory of it than when I lived there—and I haven't really lived there since I was seventeen years old" (Denard, 14). Morrison's Lorain is drawn from memory and imagination. When I went to a conference there in 2000, it felt very familiar—a place where I had never been before but felt in some way I knew or at least knew how it used to be: "[a] young and growing Ohio town whose side streets, even, were paved with concrete, which sat on the edge of a calm blue lake, which boasted an affinity with Oberlin, the underground railroad station, just thirteen miles away . . . facing the cold but receptive Canada" (116–17). In the beauty of the landscape and the history of political liberation on both sides of Lake Erie, Lorain embodies the American dream. It is, in short, a place so promising that on arrival Pauline Breedlove asks herself, "What could go wrong?" (117)

Rereading *The Bluest Eye*, I am surprised by how few details about the fictive Lorain the novel gives me. And yet I can sketch out a rough map of the novel's Lorain with the landmarks I have at hand: the Greek Hotel, Zick's Coal company, the steel mill, Villanucci's Café, the Washington Irving School, Yacabowski's Fresh Veg. Meat and Sundries Store, Miss Bertha's small candy, snuff, and tobacco store, Isaley's Ice Cream Parlor, the Dreamland Theatre, and, farther away, Lake Shore Park. These are sites that define the characters' world. In walking distance of each other, they are close enough for the young girl Claudia, the sometime narrator, to name and in some cases to know. Then there are the houses: The MacTeers live on Twenty-first Street (an old, cold, green house with rags stuffing the windows to keep out the cold, but where "love, rich and dark as Alaga syrup, eased up into that cracked window" [12]); Della Jones's house, where Mr. Henry Washington boards before renting a room from the MacTeers, is on Thirteenth Street. In the building on the southeast corner of Broadway and Thirty-fifth Street, the Breedloves occupy the downstairs storefront, which in sharp contrast to the home on Twenty-first is pervaded by joylessness rather than love. The three prostitutes China, Poland, and Miss Marie (a.k.a. "the Maginot Line") live on the second floor. Other residences include Bertha Reese's house, where Soaphead Church rents the back-room apartment; the house, with its doily-draped furniture, where Geraldine and her husband Louis along with their son Junior live next to the playground; and, on the outer limits of town, the lakefront houses, where the Fishers, the white family for whom Pauline works, live, and where "the orange-patched sky of the steel-mill section never reached" (105).

These places become memorable as they are invested with the histories of the people who inhabit them. In the case of the novel's main characters, these family histories hark back to the South. As Morrison asserts in an interview with Carolyn Denard, for African Americans the South is "home ... in the sense that it was the first stop when they left the ancient home.... You see my struggle with the South is to keep it from being just the old place" (20). The histories of her characters reflect the histories of people who were "very inventive, very creative," through a process by which they were forced into another culture. Black people in the 1920s and 1930s, Morrison observed, "were still operating under the aegis or umbrella of a culture that had probably been reconfigured in the new world in the South" (15). It is that culture, invested with unrecognized vestiges of West African cultures, which the characters in *The Bluest Eye* carry north. In the new environment, the rural black southern culture will be remade.

"This melting pot on the lip of America," Lorain is, in Morrison's deft depiction, a town whose economic opportunities attract immigrants from southern and eastern Europe, as well as black migrants from the South (117). The novel sketches the communities of immigrants from the outside; it tells who lives where: for example, the storefront that the Breedloves are unable to turn into a home is subsequently occupied by gypsy fortune-tellers, a Hungarian bakery, and a pizza parlor. The novel takes readers mainly inside the homes of black characters. But it facilitates the kind of "cognitive mapping" that Fredric Jameson describes.[2] As the black characters, especially Claudia, map their terrain, we are able to perceive many of the social and economic structures that govern life in the novel's Lorain, though some remain invisible. For all the characters, black or white, native or foreign born, the future depends on the steel mills whose production is both the life and the death—the orange-patched sky is evidence of industrial pollution—of the town. Set on the edge of the Black River, the mills dwarf every other building in the town. But we cannot see who owns them. The Washington Irving School and Dreamland Theatre provide the civic and popular guides to cultural assimilation. The movie house, whose toxic illusions of beauty and romantic love corrupt Pauline Breedlove, suggests how cultural meanings are produced outside the community.

"Place," writes Mindy Fullilove, "may be defined as a setting, as a set of social interactions, or as a node of the life biography. Whatever the definition, place is always a matter of politics" (18). Politics are embedded in every step of the journey the Breedloves take to reach Lorain and in the unraveling of their lives once they arrive. From rural Alabama, Pauline and her family journey north: "In shifts, lots, batches, mixed with other families, they migrated, six months and four journeys, to Kentucky, where there were mines and millwork" and indoor plumbing (111). Then, with Cholly, Pauline moves further north to Ohio, to settle just this side of the symbolic freedom that was Canada. In this new place, Pauline is completely displaced. She is alienated in an environment in which whites are not the distant oppressors that she knew in the South, but are everywhere "next door, downstairs, all over the streets— and colored folks few and far between" (117). Worse yet, the blacks are "dicty," like Geraldine, "no better than whites for meanness. They could make you feel just as no-count" (117). As a result, and in part as an act of self-protection, Pauline has no friends, no church sisters, no neighbors, save the three prostitutes who live upstairs. Pecola visits them; Pauline keeps to herself. If place is a set of social interactions, Pauline has no place in Lorain.

Geraldine, we remember, is one of those girls from "Mobile. Aiken. From Newport News. From Meridian. . . . Few people can say the names of their home towns with such sly affection. Perhaps because they don't have home towns, just places where they were born. But these girls soak up the juice of their home towns, and it never leaves them" (67). Theirs is a nostalgia that the novel holds out for our admiration, if not our envy, and then, after revealing its high price, rejects. The price the nostalgia exacts is the repression of "the funkiness of passion, the funkiness of nature, the funkiness of the wide range of human emotions" (83). These are, of course, the very emotions that must be repressed so as to accommodate oneself to the political and economic systems that govern life in the magnolia-scented towns of the South and industrial towns of the Midwest. Yet the novel offers evidence that accommodation is not the only choice. Claudia and Frieda become the first characters in Morrison's fiction to model ways of simultaneously embracing and critiquing home.

Morrison's novels offer moments of verisimilitude, moments that can be intensely pleasurable for readers, especially African American readers, who have themselves or whose parents have lived in places that resemble those the books portray, places that before Morrison had rarely been depicted in such loving detail in fiction. Nevertheless in the novels that follow *The Bluest Eye*, moments of verisimilitude more often accompany the representations of what the French historian Pierre Nora defines as sites of memory, "the ultimate embodiments of memorial consciousness that has barely survived a historical age that calls out for memory because it has abandoned it" (289). Morrison's fictions imply that for Americans generally and black Americans specifically, memory has been sacrificed on the altar of progress that is cultural assimilation. That assimilation is tied to geographical movement. For

Morrison, place and memory are inextricably bound. Tellingly, *Sula*, the preeminent representation in the African American tradition of home as already and forever lost, begins with the phrase "in that place." At a time when we are all increasingly transient, Morrison's novels give us a sense of place we largely lack in our lives. Our meeting places are more likely to be as impersonal and ahistorical as shopping malls—whose interchangeable shops and decor are intentionally designed to make us feel that we could be anyplace. In their fictive specificity, by contrast, the novels give readers a sense of rootedness. They give us access to "village values" that no real-life elders are available to impart.

Although Lenox Avenue is named in the first paragraph, the novel *Jazz* refers to its urban setting as the City. Immediately it becomes more than the historical Harlem; it becomes the symbolic city that was the Mecca of the New Negro, the City of Refuge, the Promised Land. As the narrator confides, "A city like this one makes me dream tall and feel in on things.... I'm alone, yes, but top-notch and indestructible—like the City in 1926 when all the wars are over and there will never be another one" (7). Mimicking the popular rhetoric of the Great War as the war that would end all wars, the narrator remarks that "history is over" (7). Morrison's readers know well that history is never over; it is always palpably present. The novel refers to people and events that the readers recognize as historical, including the Silent Protest Parade of 1917, the strikes at meat plants in East St. Louis, Illinois, also in 1917, and the Red Summer of 1919, when antiblack riots erupted from Chicago to Washington, D.C., to Elaine, Arkansas. Moreover, the novel conjures up iconic images of 1920s Harlem, including James Van Der Zee's photographs of the socialites dubbed the Gay Northeasterners and the dead young woman who refused to name her murderer, the image that Morrison acknowledges as a catalyst for the plot. The narrator seems more than willing to entertain whatever factual knowledge and personal recollections that readers bring to the exchange. But facts remain subordinate to the mood that the City creates. Narrator and readers together partake of "the way the City makes people think they can do what they want and get away with it," the way that it makes everyone feel new (8).

The mood is so alluring that it overtakes the novel's characters even before they arrive at their destination. Even as Violet and Joe Trace embark on their journey, they hear the City "speaking to them." In response, "they were dancing. And like a million others, chests pounding, tracks controlling their feet, they stared out the windows for the first sight of the City that danced with them, proving already how much it loved them. Like a million more they could hardly wait to get there and love it back" (32). The City's call is music, and it is irresistible. Such a lyrical rendering of the Great Migration captures the collective attraction, as well as the sense that the participants are both making a choice and being chosen. Perhaps social and economic factors determine the choice; they may well be figured in the tracks that control the migrants' feet. Rather than the causal factors that historians cite, however, the reasons the novel invokes for the migration are personal: a whim, a sense of curiosity, the fervent invitation of a friend. Once they leave their country selves behind, they fall in love, not so much with the City itself as with what it allows them to be—their "stronger, riskier" selves (33).

As the plot turns on a tale of seduction and betrayal, so does its representation of place. In a passage that ruminates on teenage sexual desire, the narrator describes how the City intensifies temptation and danger:

> The City is smart at this: smelling and good and looking raunchy; sending secret messages disguised as public signs: this way, open here, danger to let colored only single men on sale woman wanted private room stop dog on premises absolutely no money down fresh chicken free delivery fast. And good at opening locks, dimming stairways. Covering your moans with its own. (64)

The rendering of the subliminal meanings of omnipresent signs reinforces the possibilities for danger and alienation in the City. The migrants are defenseless against temptations that lie beneath the surface, temptations that involve sex and money and ignore the boundaries between public and private behavior that were observed in the places from which these country people came. Consequently they take uncalculated risks, until they recognize that they are not strong enough to survive them.

After twenty years in the City, the middle-aged Joe Trace remains unable to read the signs. As he recognizes too late, he has "changed once too often. Made myself new one time too many" (129). Persuaded that he has transcended the past of Vesper County, Virginia, and the mother who abandoned him there, he turns his jealous rage against Dorcas, the young woman who in seeming to love him has made him vulnerable to another act of abandonment. Unwilling to risk such pain, Joe kills her preemptively. The mood of the City lures him into believing his view of himself as stronger and riskier when in fact he remains tethered to a past he has never understood or confronted. The music of the City—inscribed in its everyday sounds, its garbled conversations as well as its raucous, infectious, and brilliant jazz—has drowned out the pain that has never been redressed.

Toward the end of the novel, the narrator reflects, "It was loving the City that distracted me and gave me ideas. Made me think I could speak its loud voice and make that sound human. I missed the people altogether" (220). Her words bring readers back to the artifice of metaphor on which *Jazz* depends.

Those who know the literal referents—both the historical Harlem and its music—run the risk of missing the larger meaning. The art of the novel, like the musical art for which it is named, runs the risk of masking the pain that reverberates under its surface. The narrator's reflection warns the reader away from that danger; she redirects our attention back to the vulnerable humanity of her characters.

The interplay of realism and the artifice of metaphor is recalibrated in *Paradise*. The novel's historical referents provide the illusion of realism, while its spiritual cartographies map the deepest yearning of the dispossessed. The geography of Ruby, a key setting of *Paradise*, is altogether less familiar than the geography of the City or of the Bottom; less familiar too is the story of the town's creation. Unlike the real estate bust that inadvertently opened Harlem to blacks or the "nigger joke" that is the originary myth of the Bottom, Ruby is the manifestation of black people's unalloyed will, courage, and single-mindedness. The heroic impulses that propelled the black migration to the Midwest exert a powerful hold on the descendants of Ruby's founding families:

> Over and over and with the least provocation, they pulled from their stock of stories about the old folks, their grands, and great-grands; their fathers and mothers. Dangerous confrontations, clever maneuvers. Testimonies to endurance, wit, skill and strength. Tales of luck and courage. But why were there no stories to tell of themselves? (161)

The problem is not only the inability of the descendants to view themselves as heroic, but also their unwillingness to interrogate the heroism of their ancestors. When the town's young people attempt to revise the motto inscribed on the Oven, the symbol of communal perseverance, they are thwarted. Their elders cling to the stories that have been handed down. Nathan Du Pres, the oldest man in Ruby, offers a discordant recollection, one that encapsulates the novel's fusion of the symbolic and the literal in the representation of place: "There is honey in this land sweeter than any I know of, and I have cut cane in places where the dirt itself tasted like sugar, so that's saying a heap.... But there's a sadness in me now" (204).

The images fuse the biblical (land of milk and money) with the experiential (cutting cane) and suggest that the characters have found a place of unparalleled bounty that they are willing to work hard to reap. Significantly, Nathan resorts to the metaphorical to express the wonder of his experience: "The dirt itself tasted like sugar." Yet the sadness may have been sown in the beginning, as the dream that Nathan recalls confirms. In the dream, an Indian comes up to him in a bean field and tells Nathan that the water is "foul." Nathan disagrees and points to the beautiful flowers that indicate to him that the plants are healthy. As he looks at them a second time, however, the flowers change color from white to blood red. The Indian disappears as the flowers turn white again. Nathan interprets the dream as a cautionary tale that he likens to the history the people of Ruby revere.

Apart from the Oven, the monument to the comity achieved by the ancestors, whose meaning the current generation cannot decipher, there are few visible landmarks in the fictional Ruby. What would help us retrace, for example, Deacon Morgan's walk toward Central, via St. John Street, past the corner of St. Luke, cross Mark, past the intersection of Central and St. Matthew, and on toward St. Peter to make his confession (300)? Clearly Deek's destination is not merely geographical. The street names conjure up lyrics to songs that are themselves sites of memory in African American culture: "Oh, what a beautiful city / streets are paved of gold / twelve gates to the city, *hallelu.*" The novel does not quote such songs directly. But readers who are familiar with them will hear their resonance in the novel's sermons and eulogies. Just as *The Bluest Eye* forestalls nostalgia, the pleasure that readers may take in the lyrical echoes is chastened by the recognition of the spiritual smugness they produce in the novel's characters.

The residents of Ruby believe, wrongly, that they have achieved a transcendent home, a place in paradise where, as the spiritual "Oh Glory" would have it, "there is room enough." They preserve and enact the racialized thinking that drove their ancestors from the South and then cast them out of Fairly, the all-black town that seemed to promise them safety. They invert the racial hierarchy without questioning the need for one. Instead they fetishize blackness and exclude those whose complexions indicate racial mixture; they reify maleness and establish a patriarchy as oppressive as the one that enslaved them. The result is a morally debilitated, incestuous community that secures neither freedom nor justice for its members.

Unlike the women from Mobile and Meridian or even the fugitives who have escaped from Sweet Home, Frank (Smart) Money, the protagonist of *Home,* feels no tug of nostalgia for Lotus, Georgia, the place where he grew up. Frank, a Korean War veteran, considers Lotus "the worst place in the world, worse than any battlefield" (83). Yet for most of the narrative, he is, in the words of the blues lyric, "trying to get home."[3] Discharged from Fort Lawton in Seattle, Frank reverses the trajectory of the Great Migration; his journey to the South is punctuated by episodes of violence that transpire both outwardly and inwardly.[4] Initially Lotus is as unforgiving and isolated as he remembers. In contrast to the mythical place where Odysseus's crew ate magic plants and lost the desire to find their way home, this Lotus is materially bleak (it lacks sidewalks and indoor plumbing) and emotionally barren (Frank's step-grandmother mistreats him and his sister). Frank has no desire to map this rural backwater that, with only fifty houses and two churches, one of which does double duty as a school, is "indifferent to the future" (16). After the war, he is sure that living there would be "intolerable." Ultimately, however, through an act of moral imagination, he comes to embrace it as home, a place "both fresh and ancient, safe and demanding" (132).

Frank's earliest memory is of violent dispossession; his family and neighbors are made to flee Banderas, Texas. He recalls Mr. Crawford, an elderly man who refused to leave his home; Klansmen carved the eyes out of his corpse. Frank's parents go home to Lotus, where his grandfather's new wife abuses their children while they work in the cotton fields. The novel's Lotus is a radical reimagining of Tennyson's land "in which it seemed always afternoon,"[5] and an equally radical reversal of the idealism that inspires the exodus to Oklahoma in *Paradise*. Whereas in *Jazz* the metaphorical mood and music of the City incite Joe Trace to commit murder, in *Home* the cities—Seattle, Chicago, Chattanooga, and Atlanta—are sites of violent confrontation in which the *characters* are the victims. Scenes from the narrative present are as violent as the past. A traveling couple is accosted at a station stop. Frank and the narrator disagree about whether the wife who comes to her husband's defense when he is attacked by whites will be beaten again by the husband whose humiliation she has witnessed. In Chicago, a character who befriends Frank has a son who has been shot by a "drive-by cop." Not all the violence is racialized. Outside Chattanooga, Frank happens upon a fight between two women that is orchestrated by their pimp. Frank pummels him. When Frank arrives in Atlanta, he is mugged by black men. The point is all too clear: black Americans do not need to leave the home front to be shell-shocked.

Despite its surfeit of violence, *Home* is a spare text. Scenes in Chicago and Atlanta transpire in a handful of pages. The characters with which Frank interacts are merely sketched. Lily, the woman with whom he lives in Seattle and his most important partner, is barely fleshed out. She is a striver, who, absorbed into the mythos of the American dream, is impervious to its racialized implications: "The stares she had gotten as she strolled the neighborhood didn't trouble her, since she knew how neatly dressed she was and how perfect her straightened hair" (73).

Readers get a sense of the social interactions in black communities of Chicago and Atlanta in the 1950s, but that sense depends as much on what readers bring to the text as what the text represents. To be sure, many come with an understanding of life in segregated America as a consequence of reading Morrison's nine prior novels. For example, Frank eats at a restaurant on Chicago's South Side, and the atmosphere generates such trust that he accepts a stranger's invitation to spend the night at his home. Morrison readers may remark that "village values" survive in big cities. When old men in Lotus gather on porches, they "become a chorus, inserting what they knew and felt between and over one another's observations" (139). Although readers may rue the gaps, they can fill them in. As they do, they might recognize how the absences put the moral questions that the novel raises in bold relief. What does it take to be a man? What obligations do people have to one another?

Frank returns to Lotus to save Ycidra, called Cee, an act so selfless and loving that it would seem to ensure his moral heroism. Moreover, as Frank sees how the townswomen have saved his sister, and as he observes the bonds among the townsmen, he begins to change his view of Lotus: "It was so bright, brighter than he remembered." He now hears children laughing and adults singing: "Occasionally a soprano was joined by a neighboring alto or tenor just passing by" (117). Still, Frank cannot be at home in Lotus until he has confronted his own wrongdoings. The novel performs a delicate shift here. It does not downplay the social wrongs of segregation or the questionable politics of American involvement in global wars. Frank Money is imbricated in the complex histories of his time. Yet the novel turns on his vulnerable humanity.

Frank's transgression cannot be explained by the conditions of war or society. He cannot fully explain it to himself. After sexually exploiting a Korean girl, he murders her. Belatedly, he understands that before he can claim a home, he has to make amends. After he tells the narrator, "You can keep on writing, but I think you ought to know what's true," he devises an act of atonement (134).

The impromptu ceremony that Frank improvises is a proper burial for the victim of a battle royal. As children, Frank and Cee have witnessed his body being dumped; now as adults they restore the murdered man's humanity. In so doing, Frank reclaims his own. Unable to make amends to his victim, he rights the wrong that others have done to a victim he has not known. His act is private, but not solitary. The last words of the novel belong to Ycidra/Cee: "Come on, brother. Let's go home." By performing the ritual, which conscience demands, they are able to turn the home that has been a source of pain and suffering into a place of redemption and love. Their act does not change the material conditions in Lotus; neither does it alleviate the obligation to struggle to change them. But the social realities are not the focus. Lotus is finally a place that partakes mainly of the artifice of metaphor. It is transfigured from a rural backwater, too insignificant to be mapped, to a site of memory that is stripped of verisimilitude. It centers the encounter of the self with the self that is the ultimate moral drama. Frank, like the blues singer, has waded through deep waters, climbed high mountains, and borne hard burdens, "trying to get home."

In all of Morrison's novels, place is the "ultimate embodiment ... of memorial consciousness that has barely survived a historical age that calls out for memory because it has abandoned it" (Nora, 289). The small towns, big cities, and rural backwaters that are reimagined and invented in these fictions create the semblance of a past that readers are asked to understand in its complexity. Through the scenes the novels depict and the sounds they summon, they seem to depict places that readers know better than those where we have in fact lived. The illusion of realism facilitates that response. As the novels' representations of place shift from the literal to the symbolic, they strip away the pleasures of verisimilitude and compel readers to confront directly the "vulnerable humanity" of the characters and perhaps of themselves. Whether home is an ideal that can be achieved is an abiding question. The answer, according to *Home* and to those sites of memory the novels collectively inscribe, is affirmative. The novels' spiritual cartographies show us one way to get home, if we understand home as a place in the spirit, a place that is necessarily symbolic rather than real.

Notes

1. *A Mercy* is set before the development of an African American culture, but its concern with place is illustrated by the book's frontispiece, which reproduces a map of seventeenth-century New York and its environs.

2. In one of his several writings on "cognitive mapping," Jameson describes how under monopoly capitalism, "the phenomenological experience of the individual subject ... becomes limited to a tiny corner of the social world.... The structural coordinates are no longer accessible to immediate lived experience and are often not even conceptualizable for most people" (349).

3. Recorded by Blind Willie McTell and Josh White, among other blues artists, "Trying to Get Home" includes floating lyrics such as "I'm wading through deep water," "I'm climbing high mountains," and "I'm bearing hard burdens, trying to get home."

4. In 1944 Fort Lawton was the site of a riot that started with a conflict between U.S. soldiers and Italian prisoners of war. An Italian prisoner was lynched. Forty-three soldiers, all of them black, were court-martialed. Their convictions were not overturned until 2005. One response to this history comes from Rev. Locke, a character in the novel, who comments: "An integrated army is an integrated misery" (*Home*, 18).

5. Tennyson's poem "The Lotos-Eaters" alludes to book 9 of *The Odyssey*.

Works Cited

Denard, Carolyn C. "Modernism and the American South: An Interview with Toni Morrison." *Toni Morrison Society Newsletter* 6, no. 2 (Fall 1999): 4–5, 14–22.
Fullilove, Mindy. *The House of Joshua: Meditations on Family and Place.* Lincoln: University of Nebraska Press, 1999.
Hamann, Jack. *On American Soil: How Justice Became a Casualty of World War II.* Seattle: University of Washington Press, 2007.
Jameson, Fredric. "Cognitive Mapping." In *Marxism and the Interpretation of Culture*, ed. Cary Nelson and Lawrence Grossberg, 347–57. Urbana: University of Illinois Press, 1988.
Keith, Michael, and Steven Pile, eds. *Place and the Politics of Identity.* New York: Routledge, 1993.
Morrison, Toni. *The Bluest Eye.* 1970. New York: Plume, 1994.
———. *Home.* New York: Random House, 2012.
———. "Home." In *The House That Race Built: Black Americans, U.S. Terrain*, ed. Wahneema Lubiano, 3–12. New York: Pantheon, 1997.
———. *Jazz.* 1992. New York: Plume, 1993.
———. *A Mercy.* New York: Random House, 2008.
———. *Paradise.* 1997. New York: Plume, 1999.
———. "The Site of Memory." *Inventing the Truth: The Art and Craft of Memoir*, ed. William Zinsser, 83–102. New York: Houghton Mifflin, 1987.
Nora, Pierre. "Between Memory and History: *Les Lieux de Mémoire*." In *History and Memory in African-American Culture*, ed. Geneviéve Fabre and Robert O'Meally, 284–99. New York: Oxford University Press, 1994.
Stepto, Robert. "Intimate Things in Place: A Conversation with Toni Morrison." In *Chant of Saints: A Gathering of Afro-American Literature, Art, and Scholarship*, ed. Michael Harper and Robert Stepto, 212–29. Urbana: University of Illinois Press, 1979.

THE PURSUIT OF MEMORY

CLAUDINE RAYNAUD

The conscious and memory cancel each other out.
—Freud, letter to Fliess, 1896

Memory (the deliberate act of remembering) is a form of willed creation.
—Toni Morrison, 1984

Memory—in German *Gedächtnis* and *Erinnerung*—is central to creation in Morrison's work. Indeed, remembering shapes the narratives that espouse the ceaseless returns to the not-so-distant past, the comings and the goings between now and then, and ultimately the circular motion of the production of memories. One can consequently shed light on the workings of Morrison's writing starting from a reflection on memory. What she calls "rememory" in *Beloved* helps us understand the extent to which the staging of the workings of memory is akin to phantasm ("Memory," 385–90). Derived from the Black English "to memory" or "to remember," Morrison's coinage can be read as "the narrative of a fable"—or "fabulation"—that figures the return of the repressed. The main character, the slave Sethe—with a possible wordplay on Lethe, the river of oblivion—willfully buries the memory of her infanticide. Only a hurtful process—"anything that comes back to life hurts" (35)—that requires wording can make it present to memory. *Beloved* can then be said to be about the necessity of remembering in its relation to history's trauma: the Middle Passage and slavery in America. Trying to forget may help one to survive. Yet surviving means being able to confront that traumatic memory in the very process of reconstructing the scene of its happening. This figuration, which bears the weight of the return of memory, opens the way for its transcendence. It then opens the way to "pass on" to something else, to take up the core verb that stigmatizes intransitivity: "It was not a story to pass on" (274). The "story" forbids transmission. Conversely, transmission can only happen through the paradoxical telling of that story as "no-story," as trauma.

Memory/Creation: Phantasm and Reality

If Morrison has written no autobiography, autobiographical elements nonetheless enter the composition of her novels. In her essay "The Site of Memory," she explains that the point is not to remember things precisely but to create a character or a scene that finds its origin in an impression, an association, a concentration. One could even go so far as to use the Freudian term "condensation." "Pieces" coalesce to form a "part." For the writer, the act of creation is akin to archaeological research: "On the basis of some information and a little bit of guesswork you journey to a site to see what remains were left behind and to reconstruct the world that these remains imply" (71). The metaphor is explicit: it is an archaeological site, loaded with the possibility of history, a necessarily incomplete history made of fragments, remnants. These remains retain in their very "remanence" what cannot and will not be wholly erased. Starting from these remains, the construction of the past that finds its source in the imagination can begin. In the creation of fiction, the writer mingles "recollection" with imagination, as well as with the feelings associated with the image: "What makes it fiction is the nature of the imaginative act: my reliance on the image—on the remains—in addition to recollection, to yield up a kind of truth. By 'image,' of course, I don't mean 'symbol'; I simply mean 'picture' and the feelings that accompany the picture" (71).

No wonder that the metaphor of the veil, so recurrent in black American literature—the veil of self-censorship in slave narratives, among others—should come back under Morrison's pen: "My job becomes how to rip that veil over 'proceedings too terrible to relate'" (70). In another section of the text, she uses the word "part" again: "If I'm trying to fill in the blanks that the slave narratives left—to *part the veil* that was so frequently drawn, to implement the stories that I heard," this time with the meaning of parting, lifting, pulling aside (72). The "picture" comes before the memory. It tells what the memory means. It informs it. The writer proceeds as follows: from the image, she moves to the meaning, and finally to the text. To illustrate this motion, she takes the example of the corn "that she sees" when she is working on the manuscript of *Beloved*: "I'm trying to write a particular kind of scene, and I see corn on the cob. To 'see' corn on the cob does not mean that it suddenly hovers; it only means that it keeps coming back. And in trying to figure out 'What is all this corn doing?' I discover what it *is* doing" (75).

This image keeps coming back, a sign that the compulsion toward repetition is linked to memory, but in this case not in a morbid way, since the repetition is acknowledged. The image as picture imposes itself. It is linked to childhood memories. She sees her house in Lorain, Ohio, and her parents' garden across the railroad tracks and the naps they take, which means that she and her sister are left to do what they please (75–76). Later in the summer she remembers eating corn: "I do like the corn because it's sweet, and because we all sit down to eat it, and it's finger food, and it's hot, and it's even good cold, and there are neighbors in, and there are uncles in, and it's easy, and it's nice. . . . The picture of the corn and the nimbus of emotion surrounding it became a powerful one in the manuscript I'm now completing" (76).

The personal memory of the family garden, from which the children are excluded, points to sexual difference, a distinction only faintly veiled in the little girls' inability to tell what can be eaten from what cannot. Implicitly present here, the parents' sexuality resurfaces in the vision of their joined hands and the mention of their reserved territory, barred by the railroad tracks, "this other place in the garden" (75), or the place of the Other. In the next sequence of the memory, the children play while the parents take a nap. Transgression is then possible: there is no law, which is what is spelled out, among other things, by the transfer between day (sleep) and night (work). The "disappearance" of the parents, who then cannot forbid anything, also signals lawlessness. Two taboos, the sexual, and what stands for it, the vegetable garden, are juxtaposed. Both spaces are forbidden to the children. In the narrative reconstructed by memory, the garden yields fruit, this sensual, sweet, and warm finger food. The memory also tells that it is adult food. From that space of exclusion emerges the possibility of a collective (adult and children) gathering imbued with sensuality.

Summertime, the family garden, the parents' nap, the food shared with the neighbors, the uncles, and the extended family: these elements evoke the passage in which Sethe and Paul D remember the first time when Sethe and Halle, then slaves on Garner's plantation, make love in a cornfield. From the image of food that one grabs with one's fingers, the writer frees a complex erotic scene. The ear of corn is not only food one shares but also food of partition. Slave work, field work, the separation of the ear from its sheath and its threads, call forth, in its association with food, sexual intercourse, in the same way as both elements are linked in the writer's memory. The forbidden of sexual intercourse is exposed at the same time as the forbidden of food is transgressed. (That forbidden is doubled for the slaves by a dictate for procreation, since the logic of slavery imposes sexual coupling.) Paul D and his companions have stolen corn from their master. Their *jouissance* takes place within the space of theft and of the consumption of food that does not belong to them. But the space of theft is also that of metaphor. Metaphor, the displacement from one space to another, allows the subtraction and appropriation of what necessarily belongs to the other. Eating corn is never what it appears to be: the metaphor signals theft and freedom precisely within a controlled space. The ears of corn from Morrison's memory become Sethe's memory that fuses Halle's body and the cast-off sheaths, the silk lineaments one takes off from the ears: "[Sethe] remembered that some of the corn stalks broke, folded down over Halle's back, and among the things her fingers clutched were husk and cornsilk hair" (*Beloved*, 27). Autobiographical memory is *mise en abyme*, relayed by the character who remembers. In love as they are with Sethe, the other slaves' voyeurism is elaborated textually from the gradual disclosing of the corn, the baring of the kernels of unsheathed corn: "corn shucking."

While the writer and her sister were excluded from their parents' sexuality/garden, in the fictional scene, secretive sexual intercourse becomes public knowledge. One cannot miss the space created by the broken and folded-down stalks in the field. The text constructs the scene, starting from autobiographical memory and following a logic of inversion: "The jealous admiration of the watching men melted with the feast of new corn they allowed themselves that night" (27). One moves without transition from sexual intercourse to food, whereas the garden and its produce appear before the parents' nap in the childhood memory. Corn is a metonym for sexual intercourse, and conversely, sexual intercourse is nothing but a displacement of the infant's first relationship to food, that of need. The genital stage replaces the oral stage; the oral stage stands in for the genital. As if sharing food had to be translated into the sharing of memories, the memory is also that of Paul D: "Now Paul D couldn't remember how finally they'd cooked those ears *too young to eat*. What he did remember was parting the hair to get to the tip, the edge of his fingernail just under, so as not to graze a single kernel" (27; italics mine).

The task becomes an act of sharing, of parting, which recalls the veil ripped over the unspeakable. The male character parts so as not to hurt. Excessive youth, both topos and symptom in a novel whose central theme is the murder of a little girl, is evoked by this food, which should not be consumed, while the word "hair" maintains the ambivalence between the cob and the body. Sethe cannot help associating the sharp noise of the sheath with pain: "The pulling down of the tight sheath, the ripping sound always convinced her it hurt" (27). The text then moves abruptly to Paul D's point of view: "As soon as one strip of husk was down, the rest obeyed and the ear yielded up to him its shy rows, exposed at last" (27). Thanks to characters who symbolize male and female in their relationship to sexual intercourse, the act of writing inscribes sexual difference in alternating sexual doubles: protection versus exposure, untouchability versus physical pain, shyness versus experience. The omniscient narrator passes from one to the other and thus shares with the reader the workings of sexual difference within the slaves' imaginary, "the unwritten interior life of these people" ("Site," 71). The advent of writing consists in the deployment of this repertoire of images from the core of childhood memory.

In an excess of sensuality and explicit correspondences, poetic evocation translates into a promise of freedom, chanted in the text like the lyrics of a song while the refrain calls for freedom in crescendo variations: "How loose the silk. How jailed down the juice ... How loose the silk. How quick the jailed-down flavor ran free ... How loose the silk. How fine and loose and free" (*Beloved*, 27). The narrative deliberately blurs the points of view, erases the source of utterance and recalls the presence of sexual metaphor in the slaves' work songs. The text both exposes and enacts the reappropriation of this ability to tell without telling, a skill that the slaves have always possessed. Freedom, *jouissance*, all these spaces not controlled by the master, find in the metonymic play of corn their ideal expression. The feast stands at the antipodes of the horror described by slave narratives, yet it also comes close to it, for one touches at this point on the unspeakable of *jouissance*.

This example of the workings of an image that transforms itself into text after a series of displacements illustrates the creative process at the core of writing. Contrary to analytical recollection or to an impulse that might want to reach the goal of an exhaustive description of the past, the act of creation rests content, so to speak, with details yielded up by the act of remembering. Within the act of creation, memory and its aggregate of emotions are what matters: "What is useful—definitive—is the *galaxy of emotion* that accompanied the woman as I pursued my memory of her, not the woman herself" ("Memory Creation," 386; italics mine). Creation is memory work, work that stems from memory: "The act of imagination is bound up with memory" ("Site," 76–77).

Morrison closes her essay on the site of memory with the metaphor of the Mississippi floods. In stormy weather, the river goes back to its old bed, even when dikes have tamed it. Old Man River remembers his original place and reconquers violently what man's work and willpower have taken away from him. The memory of water is both fluid and profound. Flooding shares with remembering these movements of upsurge and overflow, excesses that make them both go back to the origin, the primal site before the detour, because taming also means breaking down, redressing, straightening. A writer's memory is wild like the river's flow.

Remembering/"Rememory": The Site of the Scene of Phantasm

In Morrison's syntax, the word "rememory" changes category: from a verb it becomes a noun, whereas the noun "memory" becomes a verb.[1] Is it a reminiscence? A mnemic trace? A screen memory? Or more than that in the novel's poetic universe? Sethe explains to her daughter Denver that a memory is linked to a certain space where it dwells while the location has been transformed so as not to leave any trace of human presence, no imprint or sign that might feed memory. Sethe first mentions a time made of loss: "Some things go. Pass on" (36). The "passing" of time anticipates the sentence that, when transitive, paradoxically closes and does not close the narrative: "It was not a story to pass on" (274). But time is also made of what remains: both parting and staying, disappearing and remaining, flight and "being there." Sethe describes the workings of memory, a combination of forgetting and traces, an alternative placed under the sign of the cycle, of return: "*rememory*." Remembering gives way to "recalling," a process whose crucial role in the psychoanalytic cure Freud underlined:

> For [the physician], remembering in the old manner—reproduction in the psychical field—is the aim to which he adheres.... He is prepared for a perpetual struggle with his patient to keep in the psychical sphere all the impulses which the patient would like to direct into the motor sphere; and he celebrates it as a triumph of the treatment if he can bring it about that something that the patient wishes to discharge in action is disposed of through the work of remembering. (153)

The phantasm articulated around memory is stated in Morrison's text as a reality of places: "Places. Places are still there." Constitutive of the workings of memory and consubstantive with it, time is made of forgetting, memory lapses, and remembering, recalling. It makes room for space, or rather for place. Phantasm is anchored there, in a "being there" of place. Sethe, in fact, describes the motion from individual to collective memory. The house burns, but the place remains, or rather the picture of the place. The irreducible quality of phantasm translates into a passage from inside to outside. In this dialogue, Sethe names the fundamental phantasm of the link between place and experience. The scene of trauma is inscribed within space. Indeed, Freud spoke of "exhuming" memories. One could then say that a "territorialization" of memory takes place; a link to the soil is established in the motion from individual to collective memory. Individual memory is objectified so as to be fixed down. The scene of trauma thus moves from its presentation in the individual psyche to a presentation without a subject. The text actually passes from "*my* rememory," a remembering of the singular subject, to "place," to "the picture of the place." For the psychoanalyst Gérard Miller, "The reflection on phantasm is constructed upon the subject of the unconscious. Phantasm is actually the necessary consequence of the subject, at the same time as it constitutes the limits of the symbolic functioning of the speaking subject. There is no subject without phantasm, but phantasm is what allows the subject to think that it can escape the primacy of the signifier" (112).

According to Freud, the three phases of phantasm are (1) "a child is being beaten," (2) "I am being beaten by the father," and (3) "the father beats a child I hate." Transposed to Sethe's fiction, this "core of the individual myth of the neurotic," to take up Lacan's words (quoted in Miller, 113), or fundamental phantasm, makes the trace of the subject disappear behind the impact of the image of the place, and ultimately behind the place itself. One could read this passage from *Beloved* as an allegory of the notion of screen memory. The irreducible quality of phantasm translates into the fading of the subject behind the place of trauma. "A child is being beaten" is rewritten here as "a house has been burned out there," which becomes for Sethe "a child has been killed out there." The primacy of place is written in the passage from the singular to the plural. Collective memory is constituted on the fundamental phantasm of the link of the place to the scene of trauma—here, Sethe's rape, torture, infanticide. Thus this fable that stresses the fundamentally external character of memory tells the phantasm of a soil that maintains the link to an intersubjective collective memory.

This "mythological" narrativization of the process of memory leads to a foregrounding of the fundamentally external and indelible character of phantasm; "out there" is repeated several times. It is what phantasm comes up against. Sethe describes a visualization such that memory becomes a mental image, a "thought picture." Memory detaches itself from the subject to subsist, stay, remain permanently in the place (in place) of its experience. How can that memory be "out there," be "outside" to such a degree that it no longer belongs to the subject? Mirroring Zora Neale Hurston's inner memories ("memories within"; 3), it could be understood as outside memories or "memories without." However, how can "memory" be both the outcome of

Sethe's introspection—or her inner gaze—and be located in, "stuck" to, the very place of the experience that produced it? That place reaches a degree of utmost reality: "That place is real," Sethe tells her daughter. "The real," Lacan writes, "is always in its place" (25). Yet one could also retrace here the link to the mother's body, that "real" place of origin: the body of the mother and southern soil. Sethe's infanticide would thus be placed in relation to the mass murder of the slave trade. The subject's individual story, shaped by the murder of the child, parallels a people's history constructed on the nonbeing and the animal nature at the core of the practice of slavery. Phantasm, according to J.-D. Nasio, is "a narrative that depicts an imaginary scene with its places, its colors, its time, its light and its sounds" (168). In Sethe's narrative, memory becomes an object; it is external to the subject to the point of turning into an object. From process, memory becomes production of a series of image-objects: "thought pictures." These objects, as outside traces of the subject's memory, become obstacles into which another subject happens to bump. The object "picture" has first become bound to a subject's consciousness, to then turn into an object for another consciousness. This brutal encounter acts as a figuration of the cure in which the analytical relation contains both the analyst and the analysand: "that space in-between that encloses and absorbs the two analytical partners" (Nasio, 163).

Sethe describes a scene in which the other speaker in the dialogue is struck: he or she sees, hears, feels something that assails him or her, since it belongs to that place, the "already there" of the subjectivity that produced it. The formal matrix of phantasm contains four elements: a subject, an object, a signifier, and images. "All these elements are ordered according to a precise, generally perverse, scenario, and are generally expressed through a sentence of the patient's narrative" (Nasio, 171). Here the one who remembers becomes memory. He or she is memory. The subject becomes the process of memory. He or she gives rise to a hybrid object—a "thought picture." The *mise en abyme* of phantasm could be said to lead to the fundamental phantasm. From a psychoanalytic perspective, one is indeed dealing with phantasm, that is, with what one loses (Nasio, 172). At its deepest level, Sethe's phantasm is articulated around the loss of her child. Yet at the beginning of the novel, "she could not remember remembering" (*Beloved*, 39); that is, what she also loses is her memory. In this radical staging of the process of memory, Sethe loses what she owns, what is hers only—*her* rememory—for that object to become somebody else's, "a rememory that belongs to someone else." If one were to transpose the Freudian statement to Morrison's text, the sentence in the patient's narrative around which phantasm is articulated would be in the present tense: "You bump into rememories that belong to someone else."

In the place of "to beat" in the phantasm that Freud analyzed, one finds "to bump." The sudden chance blow may be turned around. The memory that belongs to the other hurts, strikes. These blows of the memory of the other are violent, indelible, "stuck" to the scene: "The picture is still there." The fixedness of the picture pierces through the notion of the "always already there" of rememory. Memory's repetition does not take place within an individual consciousness, but memory, which has now become a process, is watching and waiting for the other subject, ready to catch up with him or her, as if the saying "It will catch up with you one day or another" (in French, "tu ne perds rien pour attendre") were to be taken literally: "If you go there and stand in the place where it was, it will happen again; it will be there for you, waiting for you.... It's going to be *always* there waiting for you" (36; italics mine). The "always" of this waiting, halfway between pursuit and desire, its enactment in the blow, and the enigma of its happening point to the subject of *Beloved*. Like phantasm, the ghost is a hybrid being. To Freud, phantasm was like a half-breed, a being who does not specifically belong to either of the worlds from which he springs. Like a psychic formation in constant motion, phantasm is both conscious and unconscious. Freud called it the "'black-white' to show that phantasm changes register in the comings and goings between consciousness and the unconscious" (Nasio, 167).

At the end of her "mythological" narrative on memory, Sethe utters the sentence that justifies the murder of her child: "That's how I had to get all my children out. No matter what" (*Beloved*, 36). She wanted to take her children out of the grip of these phantoms/phantasms that were on the lookout for them, ready to assail them, to take them out of the site of memory, the memory of the site. If one paraphrases the Freudian phantasm of the beaten child, the murderous act may be spelled as follows: "There, a (female) child is being killed." Phantasm is acted on, but within it, the murder of the child can only be told in the following paradoxical way: "I am taking my child from the place—site of death/site of life—of her certain death, threatened as she is by the other's reminiscences, and I take her into a place where she will be free from these assaults, that is, death." Indeed, Denver sees her mother as a murderer: "There sure is something in her that makes it all right to kill her own" (205).

If remembering is taboo for Sethe in the sense that she refuses to remember, *Beloved* follows the meanderings of memory's journey to consciousness as a mechanical process where things are reordered after having been misplaced: "The click had clicked. Things were where they ought to be or poised or ready to glide in" (176). The moment of remembering is presented as a series of concentric circles—Freud uses the same metaphor of circles for memory—that Sethe describes physically around Paul D and mentally around the subject (163).

To the traditional "out there" of the scene of memory's phantasm corresponds the "over there" of the moment of the murder that is superimposed to the flight: Sethe's flight from the free states, but also her flight on to death, described here as a passage through the veil. Sethe takes her children beyond the veil, to the other side of the veil, and she performs that act literally, if one thinks of the dead child. This dead child whose name no one can remember at the end of the novel cannot be reclaimed or recalled. One comes up here against the play on transitivity and literalization that the French translates as reflexivity (*se rappeler*).

The metaphor of the mother who collects her life's most precious fragments mimics memory's effort to gather, to cull, to recollect, to give that memory a shelter. It is also akin to the creative act in its relation between pieces and parts. The "yes, yes, yes" of phantasm that inscribes the indelible character of the object-souvenir, its remanence and permanency, echoes the "nonono" of refusal (163), the rejection of violence, or its acceptance in the name of a withdrawal from a greater violence. The circle cannot be closed even if it tries to narrow down its subject. It inscribes in its center the void of the unspeakable, what writing cannot spell. Whereas the memory-object blocks, fills in, and clogs, the recall of the murder of the daughter points to a void, a hole, a place that has been emptied out, both loss and excess.

Narrative/Re-creation and the Color of Memory

The narrative re-creates reality and substitutes for it several times in the novel through the character of Beloved. The ghost, this phantom, acts as the return of the repressed. Sethe's second daughter, Denver, spins a web of words the better to hold up her fleeing sister, running away like water, who showed up one day without warning. The two sisters love to re-create in their dialogue the story of Denver's miraculous birth—"what really happened" (*Beloved*, 78)—a narrative that only the mother can tell from experience. To tell one's story is an a posteriori re-creation of experience, an act of figuration that takes time. But the metaphor of abrupt change ("quick," "sudden") and this switching between hot and cold recall the fog of that day, a necessary blurring, a liminal state between liquid and solid, "condensation." From the unspeakable of Amy's voice and breath, the narrative of birth becomes the birth of the subject in the alienation of language. It is symptomatic of the novel that Denver should ask to hear it several times and that the sisters should generate the tale through the words of the dead other. Their mother Sethe also learns that listening can be appeasing and bring satisfaction: "As she began telling about her earrings, she found herself *wanting* to, liking it. Perhaps it was Beloved's distance from the events itself, or her thirst for hearing it—in any case it was an unexpected pleasure" (58; italics mine). In the narrative of the past that Beloved demands, Sethe's pain gives way to pleasure. The loss inscribed in the memory of events changes into the production of a narrative for the other that is motivated by desire ("*want*") and an unexpected pleasure found in storytelling. The objectification of the other is a necessary step in transforming pain and suffering into pleasure.

Further on, the text describes the surprising eruption of this memory that one thought was lost but is still there. Sethe folds and refolds sheets after Paul D's visit. "The folding was too fine to stop. She had to do something with her hands because *she was remembering something she had forgotten she knew*. Something privately shameful that had *seeped into a slit in her mind* right behind the slap on her face and the circled cross" (61; italics mine).[2] Like the patient who does not want to know (that she knows)—Miss Lucy R. in Freud's *Studies on Hysteria*—Sethe's task consists in resisting the removal of the repressed once it has come back to consciousness. The removal of the repressed, as in the case of any defense mechanism, consists in acknowledging that one always already knew and in doing so through other—in the present case, traumatic—memories. They are indeed inscribed within Sethe's flesh: on the one hand, the slap her mother gives her and, on the other, the symbol of the circle and the cross (the circled cross), the master's mark. What serves for the daughter's recognition of the mother is at the same time the mark of her status as chattel.

The folds and refolds of the sheets converge to support the analysis of a multilayered memory, akin to the folds in the linen of the washerwoman or the ironing woman: the iron of slavery's shackles can be heard in the English metaphor, while the French tells of the comings and goings, the passing of the iron (*repasser*). Memory lapses can be traced back to the irreducible loss of the mother tongue Sethe no longer remembers. "What Nan told her *she had forgotten*, along with the language she told it in. The same language her ma'am spoke, and which would never come back. But the message—that was and had been there all along" (62). It is literally a language of no return, since the words are no longer there, and the African soil has been lost. The return of the trauma (rememory) is spelled in the text precisely in opposition to the impossibility of recovering this original language. Sethe's first traumatic memory is that of being raped, deprived of her mother's milk by the schoolteacher's nephews. Mother's milk, essential food and answer to need, runs into blood. But is it the blood of life (genealogy) or the blood of death (murder)? The bleeding child with the slit throat symbolically translates into self-mutilation. The infanticide is the other moment that Sethe cannot put into words, in place, around which she describes concentric circles.

Following a process that contrasts with Sethe's remembering, Halle's mother, Baby Suggs, once a courageous and powerful woman, a female preacher for unloved bodies, gradually locks herself into a gray and black universe, a colorless world. She gives up her struggle. Her mental evolution toward death is described as a progress in which she forces herself to think of colors, to go through the colors of the rainbow, one by one, in her head, to eventually reach red, a color she fails to get at—the color of murder. "Pondering color" (4) means both weighing the burden of color or "race," while thinking about what makes one go from one to the other, while maintaining this unstable balance. Dividing colors into discrete entities leads to an impossible abstraction. What is white when white is so white that it becomes blue, and blue so dark that it becomes black? That will be one of the questions asked about Sethe's eyes, which are described as wells of darkness (9). Baby Suggs dies before the moment when she could have reached red. Paul D reaches it at the bottom of a heart (a "red heart"); Amy has set off to look for "carmine" velvet in Boston (33). Stamp Paid fishes from the river a red ribbon to which still clings a bit of scalp, a macabre souvenir, a fragment of memory, a fetish that he keeps. "He kept this ribbon; the skin smell nagged him, and his weakened marrow made him dwell on Baby Suggs' wish to consider what in the world was harmless. He hoped she stuck to blue, yellow, maybe green, and never fixed on red" (181).

Sethe, who had failed to understand the meaning of the old woman's retreat, enters her bedroom and analyzes this process. In her desire "to [keep] the past at bay" (42), Sethe had reached a stage where she could no longer perceive colors. "And *she could not remember remembering* a molly apple or a yellow squash. Every dawn, she saw the dawn, but she never acknowledged or remarked its color.... It was as though one day she saw red baby blood, another day the pink gravestone chips, and that was the last of it" (38–39; italics mine).

The process of repression is described as a *mise en abyme* of remembering. Sethe does not remember that she could remember. What is lost is the ability to remember: she cannot remember the workings of memory. The visual aspects of memories fail her. Dawn is colorless. Two colors forbid the process of remembering, the red of her child's blood and the pink of the marble tombstone on which she has had the name "Beloved" engraved. Sethe passes from red to pink and stops there. To remember means to allow the memory of the narrative of the child's murder, of her child's blood that she herself has shed, to come back to her consciousness.

At the end of her essay on the site of memory—as one speaks of an archaeological site—Morrison explains that "'memories within' are the subsoil of [her] work" (71), taking up the words of her literary foremother Zora Neale Hurston. At the beginning of her autobiography *Dust Tracks on a Road*, Hurston uses the comparison with seemingly dead rocks whose apparent coldness nonetheless contains the material of the "I." "Like the dead seeming cold rocks I have memories within that came out of the material that went to make me" (3). It is within the enigma of this death-in-life that memory works on creative imagination. The geological metaphor is anything but innocent. It yokes the myth of memory as it relates to the soil ("formation" of a nation, of a people, "sites" of memory) to the metaphoric process at work in black American literature.

Notes

1. In the monologue when she addresses Beloved, Sethe remembers and asks her daughter to remember: "But you were there and even if you too young to *memory* it, I can tell it to you. The grape arbor. You *memory* that?" (202; italics mine).

2. Another narrative instance of the difficulty in remembering linked to the fragmented body is exemplified by Ella, who links the loss of her tooth and that of her child (258–59). Beloved's body is also dismembered (133).

Works Cited

Freud, Sigmund. "Further Recommendations in the Technique of Psycho-analysis: Recollection, Repetition, and Working Through." Trans. Joan Riviere. In *The Standard Edition of the Complete Psychological Works of Sigmund Freud*, vol. 12, pp. 145–57. 1950. http://www.history.ucsb.edu/faculty/marcuse/classes/201/articles/1914FreudRemembering.pdf (accessed December 29, 2013).

Hurston, Zora Neale. *Dust Tracks on a Road*. 1942. Urbana-Champaign: University of Illinois Press, 1984.

Lacan, Jacques. *Ecrits*. Paris: Seuil, 1966.

Miller, Gérard. *Lacan*. Paris: Bordas, 1987.

Morrison, Toni. *Beloved*. New York: Picador, 1987.

———. "Memory Creation and Writing." *Thought* 59, no. 235 (December 1984): 385–90.

———. "The Site of Memory." In *Toni Morrison: What Moves at the Margin*, ed. Carolyn Denard, 65–80. Jackson: University Press of Mississippi, 2008.

Nasio, J.-D. *Cinq leçons sur la théorie de Jacques Lacan*. Paris: Payot, 1994.
Raynaud, Claudine. "Figures of Excess in Morrison's *Beloved*." In *Beloved, She Is Mine*, ed. Genevieve Fabre and Claudine Raynaud, 139–50. Paris: Presses de l'Université de la Sorbonne Nouvelle, 1993.

PERSONAL AND CULTURAL MEMORY IN *A MERCY*

EVELYN JAFFE SCHREIBER

Toni Morrison has given the world a body of work that examines on the local and particular level what it means to be human. She exposes us, as readers, to the innermost recesses of our souls and our darkest hours as well as our moments of triumph. Her characters, drawn from historical events or everyday communities, search for a meaningful place in the world, succeeding or failing through personal and cultural memory. Attaining a positive sense of self occurs when personal memories can sustain subjectivity. However, traumatic memories often keep characters from achieving such fulfillment. Morrison's great gift to her readers lies in her ability to engage us in the scope and magnitude of this human struggle as individuals, as members of communities, and as citizens of the world. She touches us so as to lift us up while experiencing the tragic toll of adversity and strife.

A Mercy captures the personal and social aspects of identity, allowing us to connect with a community of strangers while separating ourselves through time and space. Her orphaned and transplanted characters reveal the vulnerabilities and fears that separate us from others at the same time that they connect us. Strangers threaten our core identity even as they allow us to reinforce our own uniqueness. Morrison examines the enduring struggle for self-ownership in an evolving society based on hierarchies. Her dispossessed characters vacilate between the New World bonding with strangers necessary for physical or spiritual survival and the prior life memories that preserve a sense of self. But what is involved in this struggle between past and future? Why does memory intrude to block attempts at adaptation? Morrison's core community in *A Mercy*—Vaark's household unit—cannot escape past cultural expectations or personal, bodily stored memory. Memory maintains subjectivity through the reactivation of past experiences in new environments and serves both to maintain equilibrium and to help one adapt.

A Mercy depicts Vaark, Rebekka, Lina, Florens, and Sorrow striving to reshape their core identities despite the reactivation of past experiences that pull them backward. To succeed, they must reenact the past so as to incorporate it into current life experiences. Characters preserve their subjectivity through memories of home, family, or a prior identity; at the same time, they restructure memories to survive in a foreign and evolving culture.

The Power of Bodily Memory

Recent neurobiological studies define memory as a reenactment of prior sensorimotor processes. As such, memory represents a complex combination of personal brain circuitry and social performance of ritual. By reactivating prior bodily activity, memory can be intrusive or can provide balm and relief. Memory also repeats, through bodily performance, the ideology of one's culture and thus defines one through the greater society. Paul Connerton explains such social memory by saying that "participants in any social order must presuppose a shared memory" (3). People who do not share a common past cannot share a "communal memory" based on "ritual *re-enactment*" (61). Through commemorative ceremonies, "a community is reminded of its identity as represented by and told in a master narrative" (70), and ritual performances become habitual. A dominant culture perpetuates its ideology through bodily performance of cultural ritual.

Conflicts between one's native culture and one's adopted society originate in a bodily memory as well as an emotional one. The blending of cultures involves the intersection of competing narratives that provide individuals with their identities. People bring their past experiences into the present through memory that takes place in the form of unconscious behavior and represents a "mental map acquired in childhood, and, as such, it is a code that is shared collectively" (Connerton, 28). Different cultures have different codes.

For transplanted and subordinate groups, the dominant culture imposes a foreign habitual performative memory. Newcomers to a culture will struggle for access because they lack the shared public historical memory of the larger group. Vamik Volkan's study of large-group behavior shows that ethnic groups have a long-term association across many generations and family involvements, often connected to religious beliefs and territorial settlement (24–25). In Morrison's New World, these attachments have not yet been established in a long-standing dominant culture but rather are based on associations with the Old World, which focus on class and hierarchies. Conflicting religious beliefs further divide the white culture and fracture a consistent ideology. Throughout the colonies, groups of Catholics, Baptists, Presbyterians, and Anabaptists vie for dominance and demand that society members conform to group expectations. These groups maintain differences to maintain a separate identity.

Current social interactions call on the retrieval of memory based on past actions, with objective memory being "constructed by analogy to previous situations with similar sensory-motor patterns" (Leuzinger-Bohleber and Pfeifer, 22). The historical truth of memory is lodged in the "neural maps" that current situations recategorize (22). This objective or sensorimotor memory combines with the subjective or emotional narrative truth of memory in the current situation. Cultural memory involves social ideology and historical conditions that shape the personal processing of memory. All our experiences, both pleasant and traumatic, mold our memories, and the reenactment of remembered experience functions like instinct; "the moment of remembrance and reenactment" fuses "the ancestral past and the experienced present" to shape the identity of the individual (Young, 93).

Personal and Cultural Memory in *A Mercy*

In the New World, essentially a country of strangers, society functions through a class system and religious practice. Ironically, the very systems of oppression that many hoped to escape in the New World set the norms for life in America. Morrison astutely describes the need to use an "other" to solidify a sense of self in *Playing in the Dark*, where she posits that the indentured or enslaved other helps to designate the "not-free," and the racial other provides "the projection of the not-me" (38). Ownership of others in early American culture is connected to class and social hierarchy rather than strictly to race, thus providing a broader boundary for separation of self and other.

A Mercy explores early conflicts based on class, indebtedness, religion, race, and ethnic origin. These various backgrounds represent a multitude of differing cultural memory, complicating an individual's efforts to assimilate or be accepted. White characters from nonaffluent families can aspire to rise in fortune and standing in the community, but only if their religious affiliations match the dominant culture in their settlement. Characters who are marked by racial differences will have more to overcome, although financial means and status as "free" can eliminate some barriers. *A Mercy* depicts the struggles of diverse individuals to establish subjectivity despite their designation as other.

The novel opens where the story ends, with Florens writing her story on the walls of Vaark's abandoned third house. The story she tells touches on the aspects of her life that she will have to accept and process. Thus she writes both for the blacksmith and for her own working through of her traumatic experiences. The reader, like Florens, will understand each poignant memory only with the full unfolding of the story.

The text moves from Florens's cryptic narration to the story of Vaark's interactions with D'Ortega, which portray the class system and hierarchies at work in the New World culture. Vaark himself has, through sheer luck, inherited money and land from an "uncle he had never met from the side of his family that had abandoned him" (11). His life experiences "of confrontation, risk and placating" have rendered him a "quick thinker," and his years as an orphan have equipped him with the keen sense of social and physical environment necessary to survive in the New World wilderness (12). His early struggle for a meager existence enables him to take advantage of the new position that money can buy him, with his race and financial circumstances opening social paths that protect him in the larger culture.

This early chapter outlines the hierarchies of the social structure. Vaark knows that he ranks below D'Ortega, and questions his summons to the plantation: "A trader asked to dine with a gentleman? On a Sunday? So there must be trouble" (14). At dinner he silently critiques D'Ortega's wasteful habits, his "turning profit into useless baubles" (19). Unable to pay his debt, D'Ortega offers Vaark his choice of slaves to either keep or sell for profit. Although angered by an option that would force him to trade flesh, Vaark hesitates to go too far in his demands for repayment.

Despite the debt, Vaark knows the consequences of "a lawsuit in a province ruled by the king's judges disinclined to favor a distant tradesman over a local Catholic gentleman" (23). Each settlement has its religious orientation and social ranking, and D'Ortega outranks Vaark by birth and prestige. Vaark hopes for the day when a man of his class, beliefs, and rank could win a case against D'Ortega, but for now he must resign himself to the situation. His early memories of his own struggles as a youth for a secure place in the social structure temper his business dealings.

Vaark will rationalize that the child he accepts in payment for the debt will bring comfort to his wife. Thinking that his own childhood experiences have taught him that "there was no good place in the world for waifs and whelps other than the generosity of strangers," Vaark knows that he can give this child a better life than she will have with D'Ortega (32). Vaark has previously taken the woebegone Sorrow as payment from a sawyer and has accepted work from Will and Scully in trade for another debt. Not totally altruistic, Vaark receives profits in these transactions.

Vaark lets D'Ortega draw him into the rum trade, intricately tied to the "remote labor force in Barbados" (35). He tells himself that his trade will be in rum, not flesh, but his desire to rise financially and be accepted as an equal to D'Ortega causes Vaark to accommodate the greater culture's values. Much as he tries to convince himself that he can preserve his higher moral ground, he succumbs to social mores. Thus, while he disdains D'Ortega's excessive spending, Vaark himself will covet useless objects that would confirm his success and wealth to the greater community. Rebekka will try to talk him out of the lavish new home, "befitting not a farmer, not even a trader, but a squire," that he insists on building to rival D'Ortega's opulence (88). D'Ortega represents the unyielding larger culture and its ideology that equates extravagant spending and display with power and salvation.

The jostling between Vaark and D'Ortega sets up the cultural structure that the women will confront. Like Vaark, Rebekka cannot ignore her community's behavioral demands. The high hopes that she and Vaark have of answering only to themselves collapse when Vaark dies, leaving Rebekka no alternative but to adopt the ways of her society. Rebekka arrives in the New World at age sixteen and relishes her "good fortune" in having Vaark as a husband, a partner with whom to build a life of mutual respect (74). Her life with Vaark is infinitely better than her life in the vicious class system at home. Rebekka knows that her options are limited, and her best option, in service, evaporates when she is fired for fighting off the master's advances. She welcomes whatever lies in the New World, since in England "her prospects were servant, prostitute, wife" (77–78).

Thus Rebekka arrives with the memory of a culture that took pleasure in public hangings and the drawing and quartering of those who transgress. No one was safe in a place where brawls, knifings, and kidnappings were common. She admires the beauty and adventure of new discoveries in America despite its hardships, discounting her mother's narrow view of "savages," as well as her opinion that Anabaptists were Satanists. Rebekka's memories make her regard religion as "a flame fueled by a wondrous hatred. Her parents treated each other and their children with glazed indifference and saved their fire for religious matters" (74). Both Rebekka and Vaark distance themselves from the community's religious fervor, relying on each other for spiritual and physical support.

Personal and Cultural Memory in *A Mercy* 85

But when Vaark dies and Rebekka becomes ill with fever, her past memories—her traumatic life in England; the crossing with the other downtrodden women and their inhumane conditions where they "shat among strangers for six weeks to get to this land"; her happy marriage to Vaark—come flooding back (72). Her personal memories of friendship and tenderness with Vaark and Lina clash with the cultural memory of rigid religious requirements as Rebekka attempts to come to terms with her human condition and faith in God. The local church, which broke off "from a larger sect in order to practice a purer form of their Separatist religion," refuses to baptize her firstborn although she has been respectful of its members, and she cannot contain her anger with God for the deaths of her children (78).

In contrast, Lina's vigil with her, her "whispering and shaking a feathered stick around the bed" (73), soothes her just as Lina's tenderness at Patrician's grave, where she "came and arranged jewelry and food on the grave, along with scented leaves, telling her that the boys and Patrician were stars now," brought Rebekka comfort (80). Weighing Lina's pagan rituals with "the I-accept-and-will-see-you-at-Judgment-Day prayers" of the Baptist church, Rebekka finds it hard to have faith in such an unforgiving God (80).

With Vaark, she could circumscribe the system; without him she must follow cultural codes. Rebekka can no longer avoid the Baptists and the village women of the meetinghouse. As she faces death, Rebekka wrestles with religious doubts: "Were the Anabaptists right? Was happiness Satan's allure, his tantalizing deceit?" (97). How can she have faith without becoming part of the church community she so distrusts? Unfortunately, she resigns herself to obey the community mores because a "widow was in practice illegal" (98). In her obedience, Rebekka changes, abandoning her humane treatment of others. She burdens her household with senseless chores, and Rebekka's seemingly capriciousness suggests, as Florens reflects, that "her churchgoing alters her" (159). She has become inflexible and irrational, repeating the behavior of her native England and the current community she and Vaark have avoided. In the end, Rebekka must succumb to the demands of her society to survive.

Rebekka's struggle for a faith to explain the greater culture, both the brutal one in England and the rigid one in the New World, runs throughout the novel. In contrast, Florens, Lina, and Sorrow cannot overcome what bars them from acceptance even if they accept the community's religion. As a result, they rely on personal memory in an attempt to accommodate the demands of a new social structure.

Perhaps Florens's strongest memory recurs in a frequent nightmare of her mother holding the little boy's hand, believing that she has chosen him over Florens when her mother sends her to live with Vaark. This seminal trauma, repeated in her dreams, represents the bodily pain of separation and grief that Florens feels in regard to the loss of her mother. At the same time that the dream defines Florens as unworthy to be chosen by her mother, it reminds her that she has missed the message in her mother's eyes.

No matter how often she dreams of their parting, Florens cannot decipher the meaning of her mother's last look. For Florens, other dreams are always better "than a minha mãe standing near with her little boy. In those dreams she is always wanting to tell me something" (101). Florens verbalizes her mother's failed attempt to warn and protect her, as well as Florens's internalization of herself as evil. Mauricio Cortina and Giovanni Liotti write that "children can construct representations of themselves as bad or evil, believing that they are causing the terror they observe of their caregivers, or construct self-representations as victims or as saviors, when parents invert roles with their children by acting with fear or helplessness" (28). Florens perceives in her mother's body language the anguish that she feels toward Florens and the lessons she has not been able to teach her, but Florens wrongly assumes that she herself is responsible for what her mother fears.

Florens lacks knowledge of her mother's past that could assist her, and in her marginalized position as a black woman, Florens lacks access to the dominant culture. Her eagerness for approval forms a survival tactic, as her acceptance depends on her being needed by others. Florens's hunger for praise is reminiscent of the slave children on her mother's journey who show off their assets for the white buyers to be chosen; unaware of their final destinations, they perform so as to be recognized as deserving and special. Lina, Florens's substitute mother, also tries to warn her about the danger that men pose for women, but Florens cannot process this message either. During her journey to fetch the blacksmith, Florens realizes that Lina has tried to teach her the things about the greater culture that Florens should know.

Florens must rely on her instincts and powers of observation to survive on her journey. For example, before eating with the Widow Ealing and her daughter, Jane, Florens dutifully says the "prayer Reverend Father taught me to say morning and night my mother repeating with me" (110). Although she starts to cross herself at the prayer's close, Florens manages to catch Jane's warning not to do so. Through these experiences, Florens processes the differences between Catholics and Presbyterians. Despite her attempts to obey the rules and to proceed on her journey, Florens cannot overcome the greater culture's equation of blackness with evil. On seeing Florens, the "little girl wails and rocks back and forth" (111), acting out the hysteria that embodies her culture's fear of foreign beliefs and practices, of the otherness that Florens's dark skin implies. For fear of contamination or damnation, the townsmen will not touch the letter from

Rebekka that has been hidden in Florens's sock. The villagers cease acting as individuals, performing instead as the larger culture demands.

To ascertain whether or not Florens is of this world or another, the villagers strip her to examine her bodily markings and physical attributes. "Naked under their examination I watch for what is in their eyes. No hate is there or scare or disgust but they are looking at me my body across distances without recognition" (113). Is she "the Black man's minion"? (113). This bodily inspection changes Florens as she feels the "wondering eyes that stare and decide if my navel is in the right place if my knees bend backward like the forelegs of a dog" (115). Stripped of her human dignity as well as her letter, Florens feels her vulnerability, concluding that she houses some type of evil: "Darkness I am born with, outside, yes, but inside as well" (115). Florens perceives from the acts by the villagers, like the rejection by her mother, that she is somehow wicked and in need of punishment.

On another level, this inspection of Florens parallels her mother's own traumatic inspection when she is put up for sale, but Florens does not have this knowledge on a conscious level. She has absorbed it through her mother's fearful and guarded body language. In the studies of Erik Hesse et al., children of frightened parents absorb their trauma:

> Parental behaviors [and] responses ... are predictive of specifiable "second-generation" effects for the child. From this point of view, the parents' frightening experience itself is of course not "real" for the second generation. What is real, however, is the developing child's interaction with a parent whose behavior at times reflects their own original traumatic experiences and/or ideation. (99)

A minha mãe's fear for her daughter's safety and her need to protect Florens by sending her away stem from her own history of abuse, but Florens does not understand that.

As Florens escapes to continue her mission, she embraces the dark self that the outer world assigns her: "I am not afraid of anything now. The sun's going leaves darkness behind and the dark is me. Is we. Is my home" (115). Thus she succumbs to her core identity, shaped by the culture's biases and her mother's fears. Florens accepts the inner "darkness" that she believes causes her mother to reject her.

Florens seeks protection in the blacksmith's love, but the foundling Malaik jeopardizes her hopes. Seeing the blacksmith holding Malaik's hand reactivates Florens's last vision of her mother holding the boy's hand, whom she believes her mother has chosen over her. Revisiting this experience leads to Florens's dream, where she looks in the water and cannot see her reflection:

"Where my face should be is nothing" (138). Malaik has erased her subjectivity, and she cannot escape the past history that defines her. In her struggle to maintain a place of safety in the blacksmith's world, Florens accidentally injures the boy.

When the blacksmith punishes Florens, he revives her feelings of inadequacy. She realizes that she is of no consequence to him, just as she does not register in the larger culture. His act of banishment reactivates a double bodily memory: the rejection of Florens by her mother and her mother's own rejection by her native and adoptive cultures as a slave. The blacksmith admonishes Florens for being a slave to her emotions: "Own yourself, woman, and leave us be" (141). Enraged by this reenactment of her mother's betrayal, Florens attacks him and thus begins to work through cultural assumptions of black as negative. Unable to rid herself of the evil within, she will live with it on her own terms.

One way to purge herself is to tell her story, and so she begins writing to the blacksmith as a way to "give me the tears I never have" (158). While she does not cry, she does have her say, whether the blacksmith can even read or will ever come that way again. As she writes on the floor and walls of Vaark's abandoned house, Florens remembers how the Reverend Father taught her to write, and with this memory she recalls the hope for advancement in society that the Reverend Father gave to both Florens and her mother. Although bereft at her inability to know her mother's message, Florens thinks that her mother would be happy that "the soles of my feet are hard as cypress" (161). Ironically, Florens has learned the lesson; the similar treatment of both women as less than human becomes stored as a bodily memory of ownership. Having once insisted on wearing the shoes of a "Portuguese lady," Florens has accepted the hardened bare feet that solidify her subjectivity (4).

Florens will begin to process what she has learned through experience as well as through the memory of lessons that Lina tried to give her. Lina warned Florens of how men abuse women by telling of her own abuse. After her man beats her, Lina wanders bleeding and staggering in the streets, but the Presbyterians reject her as drunk, leaving food for her on the porch as if she were a dog and not human. They can sell Lina to Vaark because she "had no standing in law, no surname and no one would take her word against a Europe" (52). Lina has a clear understanding of the greater culture and her vulnerabilities in its wake. Her memories of the destruction of her tribal community return to support her as she makes her way.

In the clash of the two value systems, that of the Europes and her more tolerant tribal culture, the memories of her life before the Europes' hierarchies enable Lina to preserve her integrity even as she must live among strangers.

She does not understand how the "Europes could calmly cut mothers down, blast old men in the face with muskets" (46). In contrast, Lina's home was a place "where everyone had anything and no one had everything" (60). She realizes that she must "fortify herself by piecing together scraps of what her mother had taught her before dying" (48). Thus, "relying on memory and her own resources, she cobbled together neglected rites, merged Europe medicine with native, scripture with lore, and recalled or invented the hidden meaning of things. Found, in other words, a way to be in the world" (48). To survive, Lina pays lip service to her new culture, but she bodily reenacts her native culture through dancing, medicinal rituals, and daily bathing.

In her solitude and loneliness, Lina becomes one with the natural world. Her memory also makes her a valuable asset to Vaark, as she helps him with the farming through what little knowledge she has retained. "She sorted and stored what she dared to recall and eliminated the rest" (50). In short, Lina remakes herself. At Vaark's farm, she and Rebekka become friends through necessity. "Mostly because neither knew precisely what they were doing or how. Together, by trial and error they learned" (53). Survival depends on collaboration and cooperation.

Lina also understands that survival in the greater culture also depends on having a man around. When Rebekka takes sick after Vaark dies, Lina knows that if Rebekka should die, they will be "subject to purchase, hire, assault, abduction, exile" (58). Lina assesses the reality of their situation, worrying about whether Florens will follow through with sending the blacksmith and about whether or not Sorrow will put them in jeopardy. She will need all of her cunning to secure the best outcome. When she tells Florens that we "never shape the world. . . . The world shapes us," she describes the readjustment of her personal memory to the cultural memory of the community in which she must live (71).

Sorrow, like Lina, must adapt to a strange new life as best she can. Only eleven when rescued and having never lived on land before, Sorrow has many physical adjustments to make. Her silence allows her to observe others and to remain aloof and separate. The memory of her father and their life together shipboard survives through Twin, an imagined embodiment of her past life, who protects her. With Twin's support, Sorrow abides her fate: living on land, being taken by men at their will, being rejected as incompetent and not quite all there. Through Twin, "her safety, her entertainment, her guide," Sorrow keeps her sense of who she is as separate from the culture that ostracizes her (119).

In the community's eyes, Sorrow is less than human and will always be other in this society of foreign codes. But Sorrow adjusts through the soothing songs of the sea that Twin sings to her every night. She does not share her memories with others, yet these memories sustain her. Sorrow knows enough to be discreet, accepting the cherries and walnuts the Deacon brings her but discarding the neckerchief he gives her to avoid a lecture from Lina and problems with Rebekka. Consciously employing the survival strategy of "indifference" (124), Sorrow shows her ability to understand the nuances around her.

Scully later thinks that to "dismiss Sorrow as 'the odd one' ignored her quick and knowing sense of her position" (152). When she becomes sick with fever, Sorrow reactivates memories of her father, "Laughing. Loud, raucous. No. Not laughing. Screaming" (126). His image causes her to relive the shipwreck and her loss, but she also remembers how Twin's company saves her. Twin's stories and soothing voice restore her former self and allow her to separate from the greater culture that disdains her. She takes comfort in her pregnancy, because a baby represents a connection with her father and life outside the greater culture, something hers alone that she can care for and protect. When she gives birth to her daughter, Sorrow becomes grounded with the responsibility of fulfilling her baby's needs. In a society that views her as an incompetent, troublesome problem, Sorrow will become "Complete" (134).

With Vaark's death and Rebekka's forced commitment to the meetinghouse, the women go their separate ways. "There had always been tangled strings among them. Now they were cut. Each woman embargoed herself; spun her own web of thoughts unavailable to anyone else" (133–34). Each woman must find a way to survive on her own, weaving a current relationship to the greater culture out of a personal history of prior social interactions. Vaark once united them, but now they must make their own accommodations.

Morrison ends the novel by returning us to the missed message Florens has been trying to recover in her dreams. As a minha mãe narrates the story of her life and the memories she never shared with Florens, she underscores the need to survive despite the abuses of the larger culture. Having been raped repeatedly, a minha mãe knows that there "is no protection. To be female in this place is to be an open wound that cannot heal. Even if scars form, the festering is ever below" (163). She cannot protect her daughter from the master's appetites.

A minha mãe narrates her traumatic memories, ones that chronicle the warring tribes, the burning of her village, her sale, and the chaos of their holding pens, where, in an echo of Rebekka's crossing, she says that "it is one matter to live in your own waste; it is another to live in another's" (164). At the auction block, she learns that she "was not a person from my country, nor from my families. I was negrita. Everything. Language, dress, gods, dance, habits, decoration, song—all of it cooked together in the color of my skin" (165). All hope dies with her abuse at D'Ortega's, where she feels treated like "a soulless animal, a curse" (166). The cultural codes of the New World replace her personal memories and reinforce the prevailing culture.

In her desire to spare Florens the master's abuse and the trauma she herself has experienced, a minha mãe pins her hopes on Vaark when she perceives that "there was no animal in his heart. He never looked at me the way Senhor does. He did not want" (163). Knowing that there "is no protection but there is difference," a minha mãe hopes for "a miracle" when she kneels before Vaark (166). She counts his acceptance of Florens as "a mercy. Offered by a human" (166–67). Florens will never know her mother's protective intent or the final message that would safeguard her on her own: "To be given dominion over another is a hard thing; to wrest dominion over another is a wrong thing; to give dominion of yourself to another is a wicked thing" (167). Personal memory maintains dominion over the self, despite the pressures of the greater culture.

For all the struggling characters in *A Mercy*, society betrays their prior lives, challenging their personal memory and enforcing cultural codes. A minha mãe's final message stresses the need to overcome this betrayal and to survive with one's own integrity. *A Mercy* explores the human need to control others to define the self. Morrison's work bridges the gap between self and other by delineating the personal and the cultural forces that push, pull, filter, and free us.

Works Cited

Connerton, Paul. *How Societies Remember*. Cambridge: Cambridge University Press, 1989.
Cortina, Mauricio, and Giovanni Liotti. "Building on Attachment Theory: Toward a Multi-motivational and Intersubjective Model of Human Nature." Lecture given at the annual meeting of the Rapaport-Klein Study Group, June 11, 2005.
Hesse, Erik, Mary Main, Kelley Yost Abrams, and Anne Rifkin. "Unresolved States Regarding Loss or Abuse Can Have 'Second-Generation' Effects: Disorganization, Role Inversion, and Frightening Ideation in the Offspring of Traumatized, Non-maltreating Parents." In *Healing Trauma: Attachment, Mind, Body, and Brain*, ed. Marion F. Solomon and Daniel J. Siegel, 57–106. New York: Norton, 2003.
Leuzinger-Bohleber, Marianne, and Rolf Pfeifer. "Remembering a Depressive Primary Object: Memory in the Dialogue between Psychoanalysis and Cognitive Science." *International Journal of Psychoanalysis* 83, no. 3 (2002): 3–33.
Morrison, Toni. *A Mercy*. New York: Knopf, 2008.
———. *Playing in the Dark: Whiteness and the Literary Imagination*. 1992. New York: Vintage, 1993.

Volkan, Vamik. *Blind Trust: Large Groups and Their Leaders in Times of Crisis and Terror.* Charlottesville, VA: Pitchstone, 2004.

Young, Allan. "Bodily Memory and Traumatic Memory." In *Tense Past: Cultural Essays in Trauma and Memory*, ed. Paul Antze and Michael Lambek, 89–102. New York: Routledge, 1996.

LOVE

An Elegy for the African American Community, or The Unintended Consequences of Desegregation/Integration

LUCILLE P. FULTZ

⸎

> What was the point in remembering the good old days as though the past was pure?
> —Toni Morrison, *Love*

I am being driven along Dowling Street, once a major artery of culture, commerce, and entertainment for Houston's African American community. My driver, a contemporary and a Louisiana native, has lived in Houston since the late 1950s. She has invited me to see *her* Houston. Her Houston turns out to be an erstwhile "magnificent mile" along Dowling Street,[1] once lined with churches, offices, retail shops, private clubs, parks—an area where she lived and worked until 1981. She points with verve toward boarded-up buildings, vacant lots, litter hugging curbs, and new upscale townhomes sprouting menacingly close to Dowling Street and the rest of Third Ward. She is intimately familiar with this neighborhood. When she arrived in the late 1950s, it was still a "neighborhood" where visiting African American elites came for entertainment, lodging, dining, and other services. She gestures excitedly toward the Eldorado Ballroom, where she worked as a dancer and cocktail waitress; then she adds softly, "I was a 'kept woman' by a 'high-roller' in that brick mansion," pointing at a two-story building a short distance from the Eldorado Ballroom. "That guy ditched me after I became pregnant and put me up in a dirty rooming house, where I had to share a bathroom with five other families." Her tone ambivalent—alternately full of pride and disappointment—she avers that she may have moved from the "palace to the gutter," but the "gutter is not in me. Look at how far I've come," nodding at the dilapidated rooming house, which she says appears much as it did in the 1950s. After being ditched and losing both positions at the Eldorado, she became a barber, serving some of the last popular musicians and professional athletes who came to Third Ward during the waning days of segregation. And she has indeed come far from a government housing project in Louisiana to a Dutch cottage in a low-income African American neighborhood. Her husband is white, a European with a heavy German accent that sharply contrasts with her "he do" and "she don't."

As we move along Dowling, I envision a street formerly teeming with some of the "who's who" in African America. That vision is also tinged with an inexplicable sadness for what was once the lifeblood of a distinctive part of this city. But this is a purposeful trip, not merely an indulgence of an acquaintance's nostalgia: I am searching for a "reality show"—concrete evidence of Morrison's lost communities—where "there was once a neighborhood . . . where feet in long tan shoes once pointed down from chair rungs . . . where women used to lean their heads back on sink trays and doze while Irene lathered Nu Nile into their hair . . . where the owner cooked in her hat because she couldn't remember the ingredients without it" (*Sula*, 3).

The French philosopher Paul Ricoeur refers to recognition of things from the past as the "small miracle of memory" (495)—sometimes marked by "aha" moments. For my escort, these prideful memories induce two miracles: the miracle of the neighborhood's conception and birth, and the miracle of its demise. Why do memories of the past exert such a profound hold on our psyches and imaginations? Why does the past hold such sway even in the face of our efforts to forget or embellish it? Why are certain individuals and groups castigated for their failure to recall aspects of the past or for their unwillingness to acknowledge and honor remnants of their cultural past?

I raise these issues in the context of recent and current critiques among African American writers and intellectuals about *the* African American community and the responsibilities of African American leaders to a putative unitary entity called "African America" or "black America." Perhaps in 1899 W. E. B. DuBois could write *The Philadelphia Negro* and in 1903 publish *The Souls of Black Folk* without readers raising their eyebrows. Yet a little more than one hundred years later, the debate is not whether black folk have "souls"; the issue now is *who* are "black folk"? And *where* are they? Intellectuals and public figures who identify as black or African American have begun to debate—often shrilly, sometimes threateningly—the issue of "blackness." A few pages into his most recent book, *Disintegration*, the journalist Eugene Robinson writes:

> There was a time when there were agreed-upon "black leaders," when there was a clear "black agenda," when we could talk confidently about "the state of black America"—but not anymore. Not after decades of desegregation, affirmative action, and urban decay; not after globalization decimated the working class and trickle-down economics sorted the nation into winners and losers.... These are among other forces and trends that have had the unintended consequences of tearing black America to pieces.² (4)

Toni Morrison's novel *Love* can be read as one response to Eugene Robinson, Juan Williams, and others concerned about the "disintegration" and "undermining of black America." By positing these issues under the sign of fiction, Morrison invites a studied critique of the promises, successes, and failures of desegregation and urges those on all sides of the issue to consider the unintended, perhaps unanticipated, consequences of desegregation. She also underscores the fact that these issues are more nuanced than many are willing to admit. In the foreword to the Vintage International edition of *Love*, Morrison delineates her central focus and concerns: "I became interested in the manner in which African Americans handled internecine, intraracial betrayals, and the weapons they chose in order to survive them." She cites the "civil rights revolt" and its concomitant dissent, "healthy or malign" and "frequently understood as betrayal, as lethal, as apathy." *Love* is, then, for Morrison "the story of disintegration—of a radical change in conventional relationships and class allegiances that signals both liberation and estrangement" (xi). The social historian Orlando Patterson refers to this moment of desegregation/integration as the "ordeal of integration" and the "paradox of progress," and Eugene Robinson asserts that "black America, as we knew it, is history" (4).

I want to suggest that *Love*—spanning about sixty years (1930s to 1990s)—on the one hand, raises some telling questions about a unitary vision or a united front within the African American community and, on the other hand, undermines the notion that black people were ever of one mind. While Morrison has never wavered in her conviction that African Americans share a common heritage as victims of racism, she is keen to note that their responses to white racism have varied across and within the class spectrum, and many blacks embraced or rejected desegregation/integration based on personal and self-serving interests. *Love* comprises at least two parallel narratives of betrayal, loss, and longing; one is about the loss of friendship, the other about the loss of community. This essay explores Morrison's fictional account of a community that is in some important respects like Houston's historical Third Ward and other such neighborhoods that once characterized African America. Using what Joan Silber refers to as "switch back time" (45) and her characteristic verbal artistry, Morrison offers an in-depth portrait of the inexorable but unintended outcomes of civil rights. She recalls one of the most promising and turbulent moments in American social and cultural history and provides readers with a feeling of *being there* and witnessing events as they unfolded in the sixties and seventies. Nicola King has noted that "through writing ... memory constructs itself as inevitably 'belated' ... [and] through writing ... [memory's] 'immediacy' is also re-created" (9). Morrison achieves this sense of immediacy through brevity, condensation, and a plethora of allusions.

Morrison's recollection of the "good times" in the ghetto during segregation evidences African Americans' desire, as well as their ability, to find whatever pleasures they could within the regulated, restricted spaces assigned them, in spite of the external forces—white power—that militated against them. In *Love*, African Americans are aware that not even the black doctor was exempt from this "outside evil," these "Police-heads" (5) who would intermingle with sporting black women in the "counterfeit world" of Bill Cosey's boat, then call the black doctor "boy" once the boat docked (111). And if we accept Heed's word, Cosey "forgot what every pickaninny knows. Whites don't throw pennies in your cup if you ain't dancing"—implying Cosey's dependency on money from whites to keep his resort afloat. "A little loan here, a bigger one there," coupled with bribes "to stay open and sell liquor," ensured that the business didn't actually prosper, as Heed recalls, because they "couldn't pay the bands, the police, and the liquor man" (186–87). Bill Cosey thus accedes to white power in hopes of accruing economic power to himself and some social capital for those seeking a playground of their own. As a consequence, his resort becomes a testament to black achievement and a symbol of racial pride: "All felt a tick of entitlement, of longing turned to belonging in the vicinity of the fabulous, successful resort controlled by one of their own.... A fairytale that lived on even after the hotel was dependent for its life on the people it once excluded" (42).

Cosey's Resort, like many institutions that catered to African Americans, was established to provide a comfortable environment for blacks who were barred from white establishments owing to segregation and racist attitudes. The need for such establishments is best expressed in *The Negro Motorist Green Book*: "With the introduction of this travel guide in 1936, it has been our idea to give the Negro traveler information that will keep him from running into difficulties, embarrassments and to make his trips more enjoyable"

(1). In the 1949 edition of the guide, the publisher Victor H. Green anticipated the demise of his pamphlet: "There will be a day in the near future when this guide will not have to be published. That is when we as a race will have equal opportunities and privileges in the United States" (1).

Green's statements reveal the astonishing paradox inherent in the struggle for integration: the wish to fill the vacuum created by segregation and discrimination and simultaneously the anticipation of integration, which, if accomplished, would mean the loss of what must surely have been a profitable business. The end of segregation across the country leads Cosey to the bitter realization that he is actually indebted to the racist zeitgeist for his profitable business. According to L, Bill Cosey purchased *"a broke-down 'whites only' club ... from a man honest enough to say that although he swore to God and his pappy he would never sell to niggers, he was happy as a clam to break his vow and take his family away from that bird-infested sidewalk for hurricanes"* (102).

L avers that Cosey knew that *"where there was music there was money,"* and if African American musicians *"could walk in the front door ... eat in the dining room ... eat with the guests"* (102), in a word, be treated respectfully, his business would thrive. So in spite of, or to spite, the cultural ethos, he opens a resort. L raises and answers the question of why: *"Who would have thought that in the teeth of the Depression colored people would want to play, or if they did, how could they pay for it? Mr. Cosey, that's who"* (102).

Yet Cosey himself engages in discriminatory practices against blacks. He does not associate with "local people publicly"; he "employed them." They are not "truly welcome at the hotel's tables," and "when a family collected enough money to celebrate a wedding there, they were refused. Pleasantly. Regretfully. Definitely" (41). It is to the knee-jerk, unexamined responses to the needs that black businessmen tried to meet and their untenable position in a segregated society that Morrison orients *Love* by contextualizing the disparate perspectives on integration and urges a nuanced reexamination of choices made during and after those turbulent times.

In her foreword, Morrison explains the role of one of her narrators as the moral center of the novel: "The character called 'L' is meant to exhibit and represent the imaginative and transformative nature of her name along with its constructive and destructive talents" (xi). Since the novel begins and ends with L's voice, it is useful to underscore L's theories regarding the demise of Cosey's Resort and other changes in the all-black community circumscribed by Sooker Bay, Up Beach, and the town of Silk. L seems to mirror Morrison's strategy throughout the novel. She distills experiences and emotions by speaking in brief dialogues and brief scenes. She presents a plenitude of useful information, strategically located and intricately connected to the other voices, mirroring Morrison's larger intention of presenting a wealth of information with sparse but essential details. She drops names like "Wilson Pickett," "Lil Green," and "Fatha Hines"; tosses around dates, "December 7," "Mississippi 1955," "the Holocaust," "1968," "Hurricane Agnes"; makes allusions, "First Corinthians, chapter 13"—presuming the reader's knowledge of cultural and social history. Or, she implies, if you don't know their significance, look it up. And there's always the math, someone's age, the year of her or his death, which she later restates by subtracting or adding another date or number, as if to say, you do the math. Two examples should suffice: "*Before Up Beach drowned in the hurricane called Agnes, there was a drought with no name at all*" (9); and "*Mr. Cosey told us who he was marrying the day of May's personal December 7*" (137). (When I encounter such passages, I think Morrison must have included them to provide English professors with research projects for their students.) Briefly stated, *Love* demands readers' close scrutiny and active participation.

In her initial musings about the disintegration of the community, L shares various points of view. When female guests begin to complain about the fish odor from the nearby cannery, Cosey complains that the smell "*ruined his business—that whites had tricked him*" by allowing him to purchase "*unprofitable*" beach land near the cannery. In contrast, May, Cosey's daughter-in-law, contends that it was "*freedom*" and "*civil rights*." L observes that "*folks who bragged about Cosey vacations in the forties boasted in the sixties about Hyatts, Hiltons, cruises to the Bahamas and Ocho Rios*" (8).

Both Cosey and May are partially correct about the demise of Cosey's Resort. The drive for freedom and the end of segregation would inevitably lead to an exodus of black guests who once ignored the stench of the cannery for access to Sooker Bay because their choices were few to none. As L expresses it, "*Customers will sit next to a privy if it's the only way they can hear [a fine musician]*" (8). "*Besides,*" she adds, "*who can tell one odor from another while pressed close to a partner on a crowded dance floor listening to 'Harbor Lights'?*" (9).

The poet Natasha Trethewey cites a Mr. Tims of Gulfport, Mississippi, whose business was destroyed by Hurricane Katrina. Mr. Tims describes the "two worst things" that ever happened to his business: "I did a good business—until they desegregated the white hotels. Before Katrina, the worse thing that ever happened was desegregation. I lost all my business" (87–88). Speaking with Adam Langer about *Love*, Morrison states:

> It's not about the civil rights movement not being a good idea. It was absolutely necessary particularly in terms of jobs and so on. It's just that there was a price, that's all. There were these fabulous black schools, high schools, insurance

companies, resorts, and the business class was very much involved. They had worked very hard to have their own resorts outside Detroit and New Jersey where they were all black and very upscale. Those stores are gone; those hotels are gone. (43)

Like Trethewey's Mr. Tims, who pines for the days before desegregation, Vida and Sandler Gibbons rehearse what they consider to be irreparable losses resulting from desegregation. Vida's recollections of working for Cosey, beginning in 1962, "merged with her childhood recollections of the hotel when famous people kept coming back. . . . she squeezed only sweetness from those nine years" (34). This convergence of past and present images clearly renders Vida's account suspect, but not necessarily irrelevant or invalid, as it becomes an important part of Morrison's pastiche on desegregation. For Vida, Cosey's Resort was a vital part of her segregated community because it "was more than a playground; it was a school and a haven where people debated death in the cities, murder in Mississippi, and what they planned to do about it other than grieve and stare at their children." In their segregated neighborhood, Vida and other blacks could listen to music that spoke to their pain, "convincing them they could manage it all and last" (35). Undergirding Vida's nostalgia is the implicit notion that this community of African Americans shared a common bond of discrimination and racist brutality that they could speak about and rail against without fear of recriminations. Although she has a good-paying hospital job, Vida is aware that it does not provide the cultural ties she shared in that all-black neighborhood. In that respect, Vida functions as Morrison's model for the upstanding woman who cannot totally relinquish the past, though she admits that change has brought certain advantages, like a microwave, a washer, a dryer, a smoke detector, and other appliances—a house far different from the one in Up Beach where she grew up.

After encouraging Sandler to move from Up Beach to Oceanside, Vida never looks back. But the old neighborhood has a different resonance for Sandler; he is nostalgic for moonlight, "the blanket of beaten gold it once spread over him and the ramshackle house of his childhood, exposing the trick of the world." He takes measure of his present "government-improved and -approved housing with too much man-made light" and pines for "the crackle of fire in a stingy pot-belly stove" and "the smell of clean driftwood burning" (39). Sandler's yearning for a time that clearly was fraught with hard work and struggle, contrasted with the modern conveniences of his present life, reminds us that for many African Americans, life under segregation had its treasures within its trials.

While individuals may share connections, they may differ significantly on the realities and merits of those connections. Vida dwells on Cosey's altruism; Sandler sees the limits of Cosey's commitment to helping other blacks. He cites, for example, Cosey's refusal to sell land to local blacks who had raised money for the deposit by the best means available to them, "fish fries, bake sales, rummage sales, and tithing" (45). Tellingly, Cosey had spoken to Sandler about white bankers' refusing to loan him money: "A Negro can have A-one credit, solid collateral, and not a hope in hell of a bank loan. Think about it" (44). L offers a more complex view of Cosey, observing that he "*used his heart like Santa Claus,*" quietly covering the costs of burials and college tuitions, and "*his friendship with the sheriff got many a son out of handcuffs*" (103).

If Bill Cosey represents the interests of black businessmen apprehensive about losing their establishments, it can be argued that May represents black women who are ambivalent and confused about the benefits of integration, as well as those women trying to protect their children along with their material and cultural caches:

> Once she had been merely another of the loud defenders of colored-owned businesses, the benefits of separate schools, hospitals with Negro wards and doctors, colored-owned banks, and the proud professions designed to service the race. Then she discovered that her convictions were no longer old-time racial uplift, but separatist, "nationalistic." Not sweet Booker T., but radical Malcolm X. In confusion she began to stutter, contradict herself. (80)

May's madness is real, yet her choices are understandable. May sees the potential loss of status. "A poor, hungry preacher's child," offspring of people who worked in the fishing industry (96), May achieves status when she marries Bill Cosey's son. But she is mortally afraid of whites, afraid that "any day now some Negro was going to rile waiting white folks, give them an excuse to hang somebody and close the hotel down." And "*her behavior did go strange in 1955 when that boy* [Emmett Till] *from Chicago tried to act like a man and got beat to death*" (104). So May tries to forestall the inevitable by writing urgent letters to the *Atlanta Daily World* "about 'white' honor and misguided 'freedom rides'" (96), one of many cris de coeur to her daughter and members of the movement: "Why can't you all just quiet down? Three hundred years of quiet not enough for you? We'll lose everything. All we slaved for!" (165). Out of desperation and craven fear engendered by the uncertainty of desegregation/integration, she hoards and hides whatever she can.

Given the discrete perspectives on the consequences of desegregation, we must appreciate how much was lost in the struggle for civil and economic rights. Still it remains for L to provide a more complex view that Cosey's *"life's work* [is] *a cautionary lesson in black history"* (201).

One brief conversation between Vida and Sandler reveals Morrison's project of employing Cosey as the site of disputes about segregation and the merits of integration:

> [Sandler] "You forgive that old reprobate anything."
> [Vida] "He paid us good money, Sandler, and taught us, too. Things I never would have known about if I'd kept on living over a swamp in a stilt house. You know what my mother's hands looked like. Because of Bill Cosey, none of us had to keep doing that kind of work."
> "It wasn't that bad. I miss it sometimes."
> "Miss what? Slop jars? Snakes?"
> "The trees."
> "Oh, shoot."
> "Remember the summer storms? . . . The air just before—"

When he is interrupted by Vida, Sandler continues his reverie:

> "Never seen moonlight like that anywhere else. . . . Makes you want to—. . . I'm not saying I would move back."
> [Vida] "I sure hope not." (17–18)

Bill Cosey's Resort at Sooker Bay, promising "the best good time" (33), and the neighboring Up Beach slums, home to the emergent middle class, are microcosms of African American communities across the nation clamoring for integration, achieving some goals, yet fearing the consequences of a successful outcome. L recalls that Cosey's Resort fulfilled a need by providing

> *[a] place where colored people would pay to be in [a safe] atmosphere. Those who had the money would pay it; those who didn't would find it. . . . Colored people liked it because, in those days, they trusted poverty, believed it was virtue and a sure sign of honesty. Too much money had a whiff of evil and somebody else's blood. . . . Cosey didn't care. He wanted a playground for folk who felt the way he did, who studied ways to contradict history.*[3] (102–3)

In the end, *Love* posits some potential answers to Mr. Tims's nostalgia for life before desegregation; or as Trethewey explains, Mr. Tims's "nostalgia about the days of Jim Crow" suggests that desegregation was not embraced by all African Americans. "Rather than simplifying the idea that desegregation was immediately and equally good for everyone, he focuses on the nuances of what some people lost" (88). And *Love* captures these nuances most notably through the voices of L, Vida, and Sandler.

Morrison also reveals the sordid side of the civil rights movement through an unidentified narrator who describes Christine's encounters. Christine Cosey, Bill Cosey's granddaughter, is directly and intimately involved in the youth movement, although she is somewhat older than those in her group. Setting out on a "mismanaged life" (83), Christine arrives with four suitcases at Manila's brothel, where the same night she meets private first class Ernest Holder and spends a short time in Germany as a military wife. When she returns to the United States, she meets a man called Fruit, who inducts her into the civil rights movement, where she becomes a "dedicated helpmate" and hides her "inauthentic hair in exquisite gelés" and hangs "cowrie shells from her earlobes" (163). During the nine years she lives with Fruit, he "clarified the world for her" by indoctrinating her with civil rights rhetoric and propaganda. From him she gets a new definition of Bill Cosey ("a bourgeois traitor"), May ("a handkerchief-head"), and Heed ("a field-hand wannabe") (163). As a member of the campaign, Christine is compelled to apologize for her not-black-enough physical features—anathema to a movement dedicated not just to civil rights at home but to a connection with Mother Africa. Features such as "light skin, gray eyes, and her hair threatening a lethal silk" (163) would render Christine a pariah were it not for the alterations in her phenotype.

Here Morrison directs her gaze at the contradictions and stupidities that crept into the movement: the castigation of individuals for things over which they have no control. She stresses that Christine, with her "inauthentic hair," is no less authentic than those in the movement who countenance the rape of a seventeen-year-old worker whose "violation carried no weight against the sturdier violation of male friendship" (166). However, when Christine raises the issue and urges justice for the victim, she is forced to accept the group's acquiescence to the crime so that "the good work of civil disobedience and personal obedience [can continue] interrupted only now and then by the profile, turning, offering its *uncritical* eye" (167; italics mine).

In 1968 Christine's grandfather becomes a target in the civil rights struggle when young people, prompted by the national movement, ask him to "give over some land"; he never does. The boldest gesture from the marchers is "a bucket of offal" thrown at him, to which Cosey coolly declares: "I am neither stranger nor enemy" (149). Nevertheless the die is cast, signaling that Sooker Bay and Cosey's Resort are not exempt from the larger struggle sweeping and captivating the nation. So Vida expresses gratitude that decent housing for the neighborhood trumps "pottery classes," and she is convinced that it is not a question of "whether to surrender to power or dislodge it. It was to do your duty to your family" (150).

However, changes wrought by the civil rights movement directly affect Cosey's business: "Former guests, older now, don't return to Cosey's Resort often. Their children are preoccupied with boycotts, legislation, voting rights" (171). And for that reason, Cosey's Resort and other places once cherished and relished by African Americans are *still standing. Sort of standing."* But it seems they are *"rearing backwards—away from hurricanes and a steady blow of sand"* (7). L offers an astute summation of Morrison's thesis: *"You could call [Cosey] a good bad man or a bad good man. Depends on what you hold dear— the what or the why. I tend to mix them. . . . He was an ordinary man ripped, like the rest of us, by wrath and love"* (200)—an anger at segregation and its attendant evils and a contingent love for his people, coupled with a desire to mitigate the pain of their condition while shrewdly profiting at their expense.

Heed's death scene captures one of Morrison's major themes in *Love*. If we read Heed's death as a meditation on the irrevocableness of the past and as the scene of forgiveness and reconciliation, then we must also read the disintegration of Cosey's Resort and, by extension, the splintering of the African American community as an inexorable loss. However, the scene also reminds us that memories of that once segregated but vital and vibrant community are worth keeping and sharing.

Notes

1. For a pictorial view of some of the major venues that once graced Dowling Street, see, among others, Roger Wood and James Fraher, *Down in Houston*.

2. Other African American journalists and critics have entered this discussion, which found deeper traction during Barack Obama's run for president of the United States. Consider, among others, Houston A. Baker Jr., *Betrayal*; Shelly Eversley, *The Real Negro*; Henry Louis Gates Jr., *America behind the Color Line*; Gwendolyn Ifill, *The Breakthrough*; Randall Kennedy, *Sellout*; Shelby Steele, *White Guilt*; Juan Williams, *Enough*.

3. For a detailed discussion of Florida resorts similar to Sooker Bay, see Marsha Phelps, *An American Beach for African Americans*. The 1956 edition of the *Green Book* included relevant travel information for the forty-eight contiguous states, the District of Columbia, the Territory of Alaska, Canada, Mexico, and Bermuda—revealing the scope of African American travel.

Works Cited

Baker, Houston A. *Betrayal: How Intellectuals Have Abandoned the Ideals of the Civil Rights Era*. New York: Columbia University Press, 2008.

Beeth, Howard, and Cary D. Wintz, eds. *Black Dixie: Afro-Texan History and Culture in Houston*. College Station: Texas A&M University Press, 1992.

Eversley, Shelly. *The Real Negro: The Question of Authenticity in Twentieth-Century African American Literature*. New York: Routledge, 2004.

Gates, Henry Louis, Jr., ed. *America behind the Color Line: Dialogues with African Americans*. New York: Warner Books, 2004.

Green, Victor H., ed. *The Negro Motorist Green Book*. New York: Victor H. Green, 1936, 1949, 1956.

Ifill, Gwendolyn. *The Breakthrough: Politics and Race in the Age of Obama*. New York: Doubleday, 2009.

Kennedy, Randall. *Sellout: The Politics of Racial Betrayal*. New York: Pantheon Books, 2008.

King, Nicola. *Memory, Narrative, Identity: Remembering the Self*. Edinburgh, UK: Edinburgh University Press, 2000.

Langer, Adam. "Star Power." *Book*, November–December 2003, 40–46.

Morrison, Toni. *Love*. New York: Vintage International, 2005.

———. *Paradise*. 1997. New York: Vintage, 1999.

———. "The Site of Memory." In *Inventing the Truth: The Art and Craft of Memoir*, ed. William Zinsser, 103–24. Boston: Houghton Mifflin, 1987.

———. *Sula*. 1973. New York: Vintage International, 2004.

Patterson, Orlando. *The Ordeal of Integration: Progress and Resentment in America's "Racial" Crisis*. Washington: Civitas/Counterpoint, 1997.

Phelps, Marsha Dean. *An American Beach for African Americans*. Gainesville: University Press of Florida, 1997.

Ricoeur, Paul. *Memory, History, Forgetting*. Trans. Kathleen Blarney and David Pellauer. Chicago: University of Chicago Press, 2004.

Robinson, Eugene. *Disintegration: The Splintering of Black America*. New York: Doubleday, 2010.

Silber, Joan. *The Art of Time: As Long as It Takes*. St. Paul, MN: Graywolf Press, 2009.

Steele, Shelby. *White Guilt: How Blacks and Whites Together Destroyed the Promise of the Civil Rights Era*. New York: Harper Collins, 2006.

Trethewey, Natasha. *Beyond Katrina: A Meditation on the Mississippi Gulf Coast*. Athens: University of Georgia Press, 2010.

Williams, Juan. *Enough: The Phony Leaders, Dead-End Movements, and Culture of Failure That Are Undermining Black America—and What We Can Do about It*. New York: Crown, 2006.

Wood, Roger. *Down in Houston: Bayou City Blues*. Austin: University of Texas Press, 2003.

PART III

*"Her garden was not Eden;
it was so much more than that"*

FROM EDEN TO PARADISE

A Pilgrimage through Toni Morrison's Trilogy

SHIRLEY A. STAVE

That Toni Morrison's novels treat issues of religion and spirituality is such an immense understatement that one might argue the claim to be tautological. With novels titled *Song of Solomon* and *Paradise*, characters named Pilate, Rebekka, and Grace, and multiple ministers engaging in agonistic struggle with their God(s), it is challenging to engage with a Morrison text without some recognition of her position on Christianity. However, it is in her trilogy (*Beloved*, *Jazz*, *Paradise*), I would maintain, that Morrison most deliberately undertakes an investigation of the implications of that religion in the lived experience of her characters and, by extension, the lives of all of us.

Beloved's diegesis begins on a plantation named Sweet Home, owned by a man named Garner, who claims the power "to make and call his own niggers men" (11). Sethe, years after emancipation, feels "shamed" that when she recalls the site of her enslavement, she "remembers the wonderful soughing trees" (6) instead of the carnage that transpired there. Morrison's riff on the garden of Eden—Garner as a gardener/God who "makes" men and locates them in a lush, pastoral setting—is evident but not innocent. In establishing a parallel between Eden's original inhabitants and a small group of slaves owned by Garner, Morrison enables a critique of the Judeo-Christian comprehension of God as a divine father. Garner is not a cruel man, but he is shortsighted. Baby Suggs muses that he "acted like the world was a toy he was supposed to have fun with" (52), a claim that might equally be applied to the God of the Old Testament, who, in his design of Eden, might be considered the original tempter. After all, he scapegoats Satan when the rational beings God created seek to further their understanding, as any responsible adult would do. And there we trip over the hitch in the Genesis account of creation. Although we are led to believe that Adam and Eve are adults, effectively they are infantilized by their creator, who presumably wants them to remain unthinking puppets—or, one might claim, slaves, whose basic human needs are met (and Garner's slaves do not want for quality food or decent clothing), but whose obedience is mandated and whose entire lives are circumscribed by the boundary that separates the garden/plantation from the rest of creation.

Baby Suggs observes a second flaw in Garner's plan. Although the God in Genesis initially makes one man and one woman, Garner owns five male slaves and only one female slave, an older woman who is the mother of one of the males. Baby Suggs, that older woman, ponders, "Would [Garner] pick women for them or what did he think was going to happen when those boys ran smack into their nature?" (140). Milton's claims notwithstanding, traditional Christian thought maintains that Adam and Eve did not have sexual intercourse until after the Fall, hence the cultural association of innocence with virginity. Effectively, the Judeo-Christian God might be argued to lack an awareness of the biological nature of the beings he created. In mandating rigorous prohibitions on human sexual activity, God instigates the ongoing devaluation of the body/the flesh, which, in addition to enabling a mind/body hierarchy, also might be said to be foundational in the institution of chattel slavery.

The Eden that was Sweet Home abruptly ends when Garner unexpectedly dies, to be replaced by his alter ego, the sadistic schoolteacher. Just as the Old Testament God is at times loving to, and protective of, the children of Israel and at other times petty and vindictive, so the master of Sweet Home switches character, viciously destroying his "creation." By the time schoolteacher's bloodbath ends, only Sethe and Paul D remain alive, just as after the flood only Noah and his immediate family survive God's wrathful destruction. Paul D has been sold away, and Sethe is imprisoned for the murder of the child she resolved would never live as a slave. The presumption of ownership implicit in the devastation that the God of Genesis invokes on humankind renders itself visible, exposing the master-slave relationship that underlies the Christian understanding of God's connection to his subjects.

It is through the representation of Baby Suggs, however, that the text's critique of Christianity is most evident. A self-proclaimed preacher, Baby Suggs's sermons in the Clearing in themselves manifest a theology fundamentally at odds with mainstream Christianity and its denigration of the body. Although she does not perceive her biblical exegesis as heterodox, her focus on the need to celebrate one's body and to "love it. Love it hard" (88) locates her message in a spirituality other than that typically preached in Christian churches. Lest her listeners mistake her intent, she is adamant when she intones, "This is flesh I'm talking about here" (88). The narrative claims, "She did not tell them to clean up their lives or to go and sin no more. She did not tell them they were the blessed of the earth, its inheriting meek or glorybound pure" (88). When the result of her feast of celebration for the safe arrival of her daughter-in-law and all her grandchildren, her personal miracle of the loaves and fishes, is not gratitude but resentment, such that no one warns her family of the approaching slave hunters, Baby Suggs forsakes God and life itself, taking to bed to contemplate color in what can only be read as a sign of overwhelming depression and defeat.

Baby Suggs's onetime friend, Stamp Paid, appears to have understood Baby Suggs's message more clearly than she herself did. As Bula Maddison points out, Stamp Paid renounces his original name, Joshua, after he resists his impulse for both murder and suicide when his wife, Vashti, is called to the big house to serve as his master's mistress: "With that gift, he decided that he didn't owe anybody anything. Whatever his obligations were, that act paid them off" (*Beloved*, 185). As Maddison indicates, the name Joshua aligns this heartbroken man with the compatriot of the biblical Moses. In his radical act of renaming, Maddison claims that Stamp Paid insists that "he did not owe his salvation to the Lord; he was paid up in his own coin" (21.5). Stamp Paid not only endures the disintegration of his own family but observes the nightmarish sadism of the Reconstruction years. Finding a piece of scalp to which a dark curl and a red hair ribbon are still attached, he is driven close to the kind of despair to which Baby Suggs yielded. However, Stamp Paid attributes the monstrousness to its source and does not turn his back on his community, as Baby Suggs had done. While Stamp Paid would no doubt claim he is a believer (he does, after all, talk to Jesus when he finds the ribbon), he does not expect supernatural intervention to aid him in his anguish. Instead he turns to his very human community and his connections with them to find his strength.

The power of community reveals itself most obviously in the exorcism performed by the women who choose to save Sethe for Denver's sake. While some of the women carry with them emblems of Christian faith, others bring artifacts tied to earlier belief systems or magical workings. Carol Henderson suggests that the ritual necessitates vestiges of both Western and African practices, since the women themselves embody both sets of beliefs (160). While the women do begin their rite with prayer, the text indicates that the power to purge Sethe of her ghost child comes from them, not from outside source: "They stopped praying and took a step back to the beginning. In the beginning there were no words. In the beginning was the sound, and they all knew what that sound sounded like" (259). Emily Griesinger maintains that the gathering is a "prayer meeting" and "the exorcism of Beloved is a tribute to Baby Suggs, holy, and contradicts her claim that 'sin' has won" (697). Both assertions strike me as ill founded. Sin is not an issue with which the text grapples. Sethe's decision to slit the throat of her daughter is wrought with ethical implications but is never seriously interrogated as sin.

Several critics, attuned to the text's ambiguous treatment of Christianity, have pointed toward the incipient exploration of a matriarchal religion in *Beloved*.[1] As we will see, by the time Morrison writes *Paradise*, that exploration, fueled by the author's research into Gnosticism, blossoms into a radical celebration of an alternative spirituality. In *Beloved*, however, what strikes the reader is that in a work so overloaded with Christian imagery, the figure of the Father—or the father, as the case may be—is virtually disregarded. Even Garner, a representation of the God of Genesis, is childless; no redemptive heir follows in his footsteps. The only biological father who figures significantly in the narrative is Halle, who fathers Sethe's children but runs mad at the sight of his wife being "milked" by the schoolteacher's nephews. Instead the central subject that drives the novel is motherhood in all its complex manifestations.

While it would be a stretch to insist that Sethe functions as a type of the Great Goddess, it is worth pointing out that in mythology, the Goddess often appears as a tripled figure, at once maiden, mother, and crone. In *Beloved*, this tripling recurs throughout the text. Baby Suggs is at once maiden (hence "Baby"), mother (to Halle, as well as the other children who have been sold away from her), and crone (a woman past childbearing years). Sethe begins the diegesis as maiden, becomes a mother, and, one might argue, becomes trapped in that role, unable to move on, at the mercy of the eternal child whose desires can never be appeased. Another maiden who appears in the text is Amy Denver, who has chosen to remain perpetually virgin. She claims, "I been bleeding for four years now but I ain't having nobody's baby. Won't catch me sweating milk" (83). As Sethe's midwife, she births the maiden Denver but is also aligned with the ghost child, since her first name is the anglicized spelling of the French word *aimée*, which means "beloved." Hence she remanifests in the two girls who collectively bear her name.

While Sethe is haunted by the ghost child, Beloved, she and Beloved share their inconsolable longing for mother love. Theologically speaking, Christianity, in metaphorizing God as a father, leaves one adrift insofar as a female concept of divinity is concerned. If biological, earthly mothers are inaccessible (as is certainly the case for Sethe, whose mother was lynched after an attempted escape that, had it been successful, would have left the daughter equally abandoned), then perceiving the deity as female opens up a space for solace. When Sethe most urgently needs consolation, she heads to the Clearing to commune, not with a male God but with Baby Suggs, who is able to rupture the veil between the living and the dead to comfort her daughter-in-law. Similarly, when Denver comes to comprehend that only she can keep Sethe alive, she nevertheless is terrified to take the steps that will lead to her and her mother's salvation. Again, not God but Baby Suggs comes to the girl to impart courage and sustenance:

> Denver stood on the porch in the sun and couldn't leave it. . . . And then Baby Suggs laughed, clear as anything. "You mean I never told you nothing about Carolina? About your daddy? . . . Is that why you can't walk down the steps? . . ."
> But you said there was no defense. "There ain't." Then what do I do? "Know it, and go on out the yard. Go on." (244)

Morrison's representation of Baby Suggs as a spiritual character capable of returning after death sets into motion a developing pattern that culminates in the final scene of *Paradise*.

However, between *Beloved* and *Paradise* comes *Jazz*, seemingly the least mythic, least theologically inflected novel in Morrison's oeuvre. However, the hunger for the mother that impels both Sethe and Beloved is evident in both Joe and Violet Trace. Joe's repeated unsuccessful journeys into the wild to seek some connection with Wild, the woman whom he believes to be his mother, lay the groundwork for his midlife crisis, when he is compelled to seek out Dorcas to be his child-mistress-mother. The narrative brilliantly intersperses descriptions of his trek through the woods near his youthful home in search of Wild with his excursion through several of the boroughs of New York in pursuit of Dorcas, highlighting the fusion of the two women in Joe's mind. Violet's midlife emptiness is, in part, the result of her choice to remain childless, a reaction to the suicide of her mother. After Rose Dear's death, Violet determines that "no small dark foot would rest on another while a hungry mouth said, Mama?" The child remains trapped in her orphaned status, unable to mature fully. Hence both Violet and Alice call out, "Mama," when they are forced to acknowledge that they are the seeming adults. It is intriguing to note that only Golden Grey, the young man who grew up believing himself to be white, is obsessed with finding his father; but, one might argue, his mission is more about achieving subjectivity than needing solace to confront a hostile world. Having been doted on virtually every day of his life by his white mother and her black slave (who stays on as a servant after Emancipation), Golden Grey's history is one of luxury, ease, and well-being. Upon discovering his status as a man of mixed race, Golden Grey's dilemma is fueled by the assumption of superiority he had previously presupposed. Having absorbed the racist principles of his society, he believed "there was only one kind [of black person]—True Belle's kind. Black and nothing. Like Henry LesTroy. Like the filthy woman snoring on the cot" (145). Given that he feels no commonality with the three people he references, but he cannot admit of another category of black existence, his grip on his own identity becomes tenuous. Admittedly, the text reveals that Golden Grey may to some degree be in denial about his genuine need to be acknowledged as a son to a father. However, his longing for the completion he assumes he will feel once he confronts Hunter's Hunter is mitigated by his desire to "listen to [Hunter's] crying shame" (159). When his initial encounter with his father deviates radically from the script Golden Grey had been drafting, he determines "to blow the man's head off" (173). That he does not do so has less to do with Hunter's Hunter himself than with Golden Grey's obsession with Wild.

For Joe and Violet Trace, however, the absence of a father barely registers on their psyches. Joe does not even speculate how his mother came to be pregnant, and in all his attempts to be granted a sign of recognition from her, he never indicates any desire for a father. Violet knows who her father is, but his extended absences render him virtually insignificant to her. That Morrison perhaps intends us to read this character through a theological lens is suggested in her language. The narrative voice speaks of "the joyful *resurrection* of this *phantom* father" (100; italics mine) and essentially treats him as a frivolous and cavalier ne'er-do-well: "For who could keep him down, this defiant birthday-every-day man who dispensed gifts and stories that kept them so rapt they forgot for the while a bone-clean cupboard and exhausted soil; or believed a child's leg would straighten itself out by and by" (100). Again the tension between a theology that treats the material needs of the body as genuine and one that proffers groundless hope becomes evident. In response to True Belle's admonition to her daughter, "Don't let them whip you, Rose.... He ain't give you nothing you can't bear," the narrator claims, "Maybe this one time He had. Had misjudged and misunderstood her particular backbone. This one time. This here particular spine" (99). The repeated emphasis on the specific, the personal, in the narrative language embeds a critique of a religion that, particularly in the context of a people who have been enslaved, not by a vague concept such as sin or a shadowy presence like a presumed Satan but by other humans who actually deployed that religion in defense of their depraved practices, arguably dangles otherworldly bliss in exchange for present anguish.

Several critics have explored the possibility that it is through the unnamed narrator, certainly one of the most captivating characters in the text, that Morrison encodes her critique of Christianity. Patricia Hunt maintains that "Morrison's creation of the Voice plays with the notion of the 'omniscient narrator' in fiction, which is often related to the idea of God or a 'God's-eye view'" (49). Vincent A. O'Keefe claims that "Morrison counters the conventional realist narrator of godlike power, vision, and eventual disclosure of privileged knowledge with a narrator and several characters whose 'gnosis,' or knowledge, of their reality and history is less factual, objective, and scientifically provable but more intuitive, subjective, and speculative" (331).

Although the narrator claims omniscience from the first line of the novel—"Sth, I know that woman" (3), by the end of the text, the Voice admits it has completely underestimated the characters that, presumably, it created. However, the narrator's further revelations provide a startling critique of the Judeo-Christian God. The Voice points out, "I break lives to prove I can mend them back again.... What, I wonder, what would I be without a few brilliant spots of blood to ponder?" (219). Stunned by the characters' refusal to play by the preordained rules, the narrator admits, "They knew how little I could be counted on," adding, "I was the predictable one, confused in my solitude into arrogance, thinking my space, my view was the only one that was or that mattered" (220). In her ongoing exploration of the significance of God as he is traditionally understood, Morrison unearths what one might claim is the pettiness of God, certainly as he is portrayed in the Old Testament,[2] where, in his obsession with human obedience to standards no human is capable of upholding, he whimsically makes his creations wretched and, although promising to respond to their prayers with aid, often simply ignores the pleas of the beings he claims to love. No one would understand this better than slaves and their descendants. *Jazz* is particularly rife with racial violence—entire communities burned out and people being stomped to death are portrayed virtually as asides to the main drama, since, presumably, such acts of horror are so routine they are not worthy of center stage. That a God who claims to be all-powerful and just does not intervene to impede such criminality becomes a point to ponder.

In *Paradise*, Morrison's text that most overtly interrogates Christianity, we experience the shift from God the Father to God(dess) the Consoling Mother. Simply put, throughout the novel, fathers are the problem, beginning with the Old Fathers, who, though they were former slaves who achieved freedom through Emancipation, had no qualms about perceiving their wives and children as extensions of themselves—in other words, as their slaves. So, for example, during the Disallowing that forever blights their descendants, when the townspeople who reject them do provide them with food, blankets, and money for their journey, the Old Fathers "forbade the women to eat the food" (195). Their extreme conceit renders them oblivious to the needs of their children, from the obvious realization that the young cannot endure hardships the way adults can. It is the mothers, attuned to what is most needful, who defy the fathers to retrieve the food for their young. The pattern follows throughout the book, the men (with few exceptions) smugly self-righteous and intolerant, the women generous and mindful of suffering.

Shortsighted as the Old Fathers were, their insensitivity pales in comparison to that of the New Fathers, particularly the alpha males of the herd, Steward and Deacon Morgan. While both men do cherish their wives, they also infantilize them. For example, Deacon assumes that Soane is incapable of understanding basic economics, and Steward ignores Dovey's pleasure in her small house in town and sells it out from under her, effectively making her a prisoner on his ranch. However, their treatment of everyone else, from their male peers to the young people of Ruby to, most especially, the women who inhabit the Convent, is reprehensible. And while the tiny town boasts three churches, two of the ministers are cold and judgmental, and the Reverend Misner, the one who speaks for justice and loving kindness, is shunned by even his own congregation. Thus he is away when the massacre is sanctioned by the "righteous" men of Ruby: "There were irreconcilable differences among the congregations in town, but members from all of them merged solidly on the necessity of this action" (9–10). Morrison does not pull her punches here. By specifically linking the slaughter not merely to the disgruntled men of the town but to the "congregations," she implicates Christianity, certainly as it is practiced in Ruby, in misogynistic violence. As Channette Romero maintains, "The text makes it clear that gender oppression occurs not just in Ruby's Christian churches but is historically integral to Christianity" (416).

Paradise makes vividly clear how gender oppression is an inevitable outcome of a theology that predicates itself on a mind/body hierarchy. The historical, overdetermined association of men with spirit, intellect, and reason and the foisting of all physicality and carnality onto women make the subsequent man/woman hierarchy unavoidable. Lest readers assume that only the men of Ruby have adopted a position that so obviously benefits them, Morrison indicates that the nuns who move into the Convent share in their hatred of the flesh. Although the young Consolata envisions the house as "a castle, full of . . . beauty" (225), the Mother Superior insists all the beauty must be eradicated, since it celebrates human physicality. So marble statues are either shattered or disfigured, and books are burned in an attempt to render the mansion a fit habitation for religious women. The inherent pornographic view of the body that such a theology entails becomes evident in the mislabeling of a painting that the nuns find acceptable. A representation of the martyrdom of St. Agatha, whose breasts were cut off after she refused the advances of a man, is labeled "Saint Catherine of Sienna," a saint who was never martyred and was a respected philosopher and theologian. That the nuns would scorn one of the great female leaders of their faith, who in her life fused mind with body (she spoke openly of her visions and mystical encounters with Jesus), obscuring her significance by miscataloging her as yet another victim of a theology hostile to the flesh, is telling. As Justyna Sempruch points out, Consolata, "in the environment of [a] phallocentric structure . . . has been taught to reject the ordinary female condition as impure" (100). Many of the women of Ruby share the nuns' self-hatred. Consolata is staggered by Arnette's "repugnance" toward her own body, noting a "revulsion so severe it cut mind from body and saw its flesh-producing flesh as foreign, rebellious, unnatural, diseased" (249). But cutting mind from body has been a Christian practice for centuries, and in spite of the radical theologians who argue the inherent wrongness of such a view,[3] the voices of the few have not been able to overwhelm the roar of those hostile to the flesh.

The figure who fuses the mind/body duality and opens the door to other, more wholesome spiritualities is Consolata, who, although she has lived most of her adult life in the company of nuns and has adopted, for the most part, the standards of their order, has never herself taken the veil. Prompted initially by Lone, a gifted healer who recognizes Connie's mystical abilities, Connie begins to dabble in what she perceives to be unholy magic, but which Lone insists is a way of honoring God-given gifts. After the death of her adored Mother Superior, Connie comes to understand that her true object of worship was not Jesus but the woman who saved her, quite literally, from a life of squalor, rape, and disease. The salvation that signified was that of the body, a recurring Morrisonian theme. In reflecting on her intense love for Sister Mary Magna, as well as her passion for Deke Morgan, Consolata tells the younger, lost women who have sheltered in the Convent:

> My child body, hurt and soil, leaps into the arms of a woman who teach me my body is nothing my spirit everything. I agreed her until I met another. My flesh is so hungry for itself it ate him. When he fell away the woman rescue me from my body again. Twice she saves it. When her body sickens I care for it in every way flesh works. I hold it in my arms and between my legs. Clean it, rock it, enter it to keep it breath. After she is dead I can not get past that. My bones on hers the only good thing. Not spirit. Bones. No different from the man. My bones on his the only true thing. (263)

When Consolata then resolves to help the forlorn women find a way to be in the world, like Baby Suggs before her, she does not speak of sin or otherworldly bliss. She realizes that the horrors they, and all humans, have endured have been experienced in their bodies. The psychological torment they have suffered—for example, when Seneca's mother abandons her—is realized through the flesh. Hence the girl goes hungry and brushes her teeth until they bleed, hoping against hope that being a "good girl" will make Jean return.

Once Consolata begins her "ministry," the text parallels her efforts to those of Jesus during his ministry on earth. Her words "If you have a place . . . that you should be in and somebody who loves you waiting there, then go. If not stay here and follow me," echo Jesus's exhortation "Follow me." Similarly, the night before she begins to initiate her followers, she prepares a "last supper," in that thereafter they will subsist "on bloodless food and water alone" (265); and the night before the massacre, the women experience a "baptism" as they dance in "hot sweet rain" (283). The text makes evident that the women have healed from the damage they had earlier suffered: "Seneca embraced and finally let go of a dark morning in state housing. Grace witnessed the successful cleansing of a white shirt that should never have been stained. Mavis moved in the shudder of rose of Sharon pelts tickling her skin. Pallas, delivered of a delicate son, held him close while the rain rinsed away a scary woman on an escalator and all fear of black water" (283).

How thoroughly they have integrated body and spirit becomes apparent in the novel's stunning conclusion. While critics and readers disagree about what happens to the women in the novel's final pages, I believe Morrison's text makes clear that the women do die. We are narratively present at Connie's death, and it is inconceivable that a woman shot at close range and three other women gunned down with high-powered rifles could survive such attacks. That none of the bodies are ever found riffs on the resurrection of Jesus, as does the reappearance of four of the five slain women after their deaths. Justine Tally identifies these sightings as revenants, spirits, in African beliefs, of those "who have been violently killed and [return] to visit the living" (46). I would argue, however, that Morrison reaches outside African religions *and* Christianity in the novel's final pages. When Deek and Lone's attempts to save Consolata's life fail, they "close the two pale eyes but can do nothing about the third one, wet and lidless, in between" (291). In identifying the bullet hole as Connie's third eye, Morrison suggests that Connie has achieved enlightenment, the Buddhist/Hindu concept that indicates that one is no longer trapped by maya, the world of space and time.

Therefore, in the novel's astonishing conclusion, Connie is resting her head on the lap of the Mother Goddess Piedade, who is singing to her.

Romero points out how "although not specifically geographically located, this paradise is 'down here' on earth, made up of natural water and sand but also 'sea trash.'... This paradise is recycled from the broken and the discarded, a place where the spiritual intermingles with the material" (423).

The beach scene is a far cry from the celestial Jerusalem envisioned by the writer of Revelation, and it is populated not only by believers but by both the "lost and saved" (138). Nor is this paradise the place of eternal otherworldly bliss of which Christianity speaks. Rather, it is a way station, a place of renewal, where, in the presence of the Mother, all will "rest before shouldering the endless work they were created to do" (318). Most significantly, this paradise is located "down here" (318), on earth. In its materiality, in its flaws, in its peace and beauty, Morrison's paradise is not an Eden in which an insecure Father plants snares for his unsuspecting children but a site of consolation in the arms of a loving Mother who celebrates the physicality of her children. In exploring the lived experience of her people, who must daily confront the knowledge of their all-too-recent enslavement, Morrison understandably comes to reject a theology that privileges spirit over flesh, that cannot accept the inseparable nature of the two. And once that duality is disabled, the dichotomy that would divide man from woman and establish a false hierarchy between them also dissolves. Only then will people truly be free at last.

Notes

1. Jacqueline Trace explores this idea in "Dark Goddesses: Black Feminist Theology in Morrison's *Beloved*," as do I in my article "Toni Morrison's *Beloved* and the Vindication of Lilith."

2. Such a view of the God of Genesis is consistent with the theology of Gnosticism, which essentially maintains that material creation was the work of an extremely flawed, bumbling creature who claimed to be the only existing deity. The epigraph for *Jazz* comes from the "Thunder, Perfect Mind" section of the Nag Hammadi texts, fairly recently discovered Gnostic writings.

3. Among those who resist or revise mainstream understandings of the body in favor of honoring and celebrating the body are Matthew Fox, Rosemary Radford Reuther, Sallie McFague, and Delores S. Williams.

Works Cited

Griesinger, Emily. "Why Baby Suggs, Holy, Quit Preaching the Word: Redemption and Holiness in Toni Morrison's *Beloved*." *Christianity and Literature* 50, no. 4 (Summer 2001): 689–702.

Henderson, Carol. "Refiguring the Flesh: The Word, the Body, and the Rituals of Being in *Beloved* and *Go Tell It on the Mountain*." In *James Baldwin and Toni Morrison: Comparative Critical and Theoretical Essays*, ed. Lovalerie King and Lynn Orilla Scott, 149–65. New York: Palgrave, 2006.

Hunt, Patricia. "'Free to Do Something Wild': History and the Ancestor in *Jazz*." *Literature, Interpretation, Theory* 6, nos. 1–2 (April 1995): 47–62.

Maddison, Bula. "Liberation Story or Apocalypse: Reading Biblical Allusion and Bakhtin Theory in Toni Morrison's *Beloved*." *Bible and Critical Theory* 3, no. 2 (June 2007): 21.1–21.13.

Morrison, Toni. *Beloved*. New York: Plume, 1998.

———. *Jazz*. New York: Plume, 1993.

———. *Paradise*. New York: Alfred A. Knopf, 1998.

O'Keefe, Vincent A. "From 'Other' Sides of the Realist Tracks: (A)Gnostic Narratives in Toni Morrison's *Jazz*." *Centennial Review* 41, no. 2 (Spring 1997): 331–49.

Romero, Channette. "Creating the Beloved Community: Religion, Race, and Nation in Toni Morrison's *Paradise*." *African American Review* 39, no. 3 (2005): 415–30.

Sempruch, Justyna. "The Sacred Mothers, the Evil Witches, and the Politics of Household in Toni Morrison's *Paradise*." *Journal of the Association for Research on Mothering* 7, no. 1 (Spring–Summer 2005): 98–109.

Stave, Shirley A. "Toni Morrison's *Beloved* and the Vindication of Lilith." *South Atlantic Review* 58, no. 1 (January 1993): 49–66.

Tally, Justine. *Paradise Reconsidered: Toni Morrison's (Hi)stories and Truths*. Hamburg: Lit, 1999.

Trace, Jacqueline. "Dark Goddesses: Black Feminist Theology in Morrison's *Beloved*." *Obsidian II: Black Literature in Review* 6, no. 3 (1991): 14–30.

"AND THE GREATEST OF THESE"

Toni Morrison, the Bible, Love

KATHERINE CLAY BASSARD

∽

The only way to achieve this suspension, to break the chain of crime and punishment/retribution, is to assume an utter readiness for self-erasure. And *love*, at its most elementary, is nothing but such a paradoxical gesture of breaking the chain of retribution.
—Slavoj Žižek, *Did Somebody Say Totalitarianism?*

And the greatest of these is love.
—1 Corinthians 13:13

While the subject of love takes a variety of forms in Morrison's work from her first novel, *The Bluest Eye* (1970), to her latest, *Home* (2012), I propose here to look at her meditation(s) on love in light of her readings and (re)readings of the Christian Bible, the book Northrop Frye has described as "the Great Code" of Western art and literature. In what sense is Morrison playing with the implications of the Johannine edict that "God is love" (John 4:8) as an absolute equivalence, in both its New Testament form and its inverse (love is god)? How might we survey Morrison's novels in light of the biblical insistence on agape (divine love) as a higher type of love than eros (human sexual love) or philos ("brotherly" or communal love)? Finally, how does Morrison seek to reclaim love (in any or all of these registers) as an ethical mandate to break the cycle of racism, sexism, and other oppressions?

In *Canon and Creativity*, Robert Alter examines the tension in modern writing between creativity as a modernist value and canon as a sign of scriptural authority:

> The engagement of modern writers with the Bible ... cuts sharply two ways. They frequently translate biblical motifs and themes into radically redefining new contexts.... At the same time, the Bible remains for them a value-laden, imaginatively energizing body of texts, helping make possible the novels and poems they write through the powers of expression and vision that inhere in it. (8)

Toni Morrison echoes this sentiment when she describes the Bible not as part of her reading but as "part of my life" (*Conversations*, 97) and when she notes that her frequent choice of biblical names for her characters constitutes "the gesture of getting something holy" (80).

There is a connection, I think, between Morrison's approach to the Bible in particular and her theorizing of the promises and pitfalls of reading and writing in general. At the opening of her 1993 Nobel Prize lecture, for example, she relates a folktale about a blind seer—whom she understands as "the daughter of slaves, black, American"—in an effort to comment on the nexus between language and power. That oppressive uses of language are efficacious to the point of *becoming* what they enact is central to Morrison's thinking:

> Oppressive language does more than represent violence; it is violence; does more than represent the limits of knowledge; it limits knowledge. Whether it is obscuring state language or the faux-language of mindless media; whether it is the proud but calcified language of the academy, or the commodity driven language of science; whether it is the malign language of law-without-ethics, or language designed for the estrangement of minorities, hiding its racist plunder in its literary cheek—it must be rejected, altered, exposed. (16)

Morrison's move beyond representation to embodiment also works, in her view, to reconceptualize the possibility of a nonoppressive, creative use of language. "Narrative," she writes, "is radical, creating us at the very moment it is being created." The power of (re)creation that resides in story can undo the damaging effects of oppression by meeting the language of those structures on its own terms. Moreover, the new liberationist story involves cooperation and interaction that repositions the roles of reader and writer as cocreators of the text. This concept of story as a multilayered, cooperative enterprise grounds Morrison's reading and appropriation of biblical texts.

As noted earlier, there are several words in the Hebrew Bible and New Testament translated into the English word "love." *Hesed* in Hebrew speaks primarily of the "unfailing love" of God, especially toward his covenant people, Israel (*Oxford Companion to the Bible*, 467–68). In the Greek New Testament, the English word "love" is represented by three different Greek words that divide the concept into *eros* (human sexual love), *philos* (brotherly or communal love), and *agape* (divine or transcendent love). Scholars from a variety of disciplines have long debated the usefulness of these categories as theological, ethical, and social constructs. In examining the "agape motif" in Western theology, Anders Nygren views eros and agape as initially opposed to each other: "*Agape* entered into a world that had already received the impress of *eros*" (53). Nygren laments what he sees as a deflowered agape that had "lost its purity" (53) through the ancient concept of "heavenly *eros*." Pictured as "the born rival of *agape*" (51), the heavenly eros ideal, for Nygren, sublimated agape under eros rather than allowing them to remain distinct but equivalent: "The difference between them is not one of degree," he writes, "but of kind" (51). Viewing agape from the standpoint of gender and sexual ethics, Francis Watson envisions a "reconciliation of *agape* and *eros*" (259). Ironically, Watson locates this reconciliation within the Pauline insistence on the veil or head covering to be worn by women in worship services (1 Corinthians 11). For Watson, the veil "marks the boundary that *eros* is not to transgress if *agape* is to be preserved. Forcibly separated from *agape*, *eros* is left out in the cold" (259). Like Nygren, Watson sees the two types of love as mutually exclusive categories and sublimates eros under agape. Slavoj Žižek politicizes the discussion by positing love as "self-erasure" in the Christian sense of agape as a possible break in the cycle of oppression. Similarly, Gene Outka posits that "the closer one approaches equalitarian notions of justice, the greater the material overlap with *agape*" (309).

The interplay between these differing aspects of love is evidenced in Morrison's novels in a variety of ways, most notably through her revisions of the Bible. Moreover, Morrison's use of the Bible in her fiction can be contextualized within the tradition of black women's biblicism from the nineteenth century through their extension of the Shulamite trope—"black but comely"—from the ancient love poem the *Song of Songs*.

However, unlike her nineteenth-century predecessors who steer around the poem's erotics, it is within the sexual nature of *Song of Songs* that Morrison locates black women's power and agency. This is significant for black women because of the way they have been depicted as either hypersexual or asexual, according to the dialectic that the historian Deborah Gray White has characterized as the Jezebel and Mammy archetypes. In both cases, black women were judged as unattractive or unpreferred by Eurocentric beauty standards that privileged the white female. Thus the Shulamite's claim—"I am black but comely"—has powerful implications for black women's self-image and sense of sexual empowerment. Moreover, Morrison's most innovative contribution is that in her artistic vision, eros (sexual love) and agape (divine, self-sacrificial love) are either mobilized or disallowed by the presence or absence of philos (brotherly, community love), a mediating category that none of the theorists and theologians just cited consider. Before we turn to Morrison's novels, a brief understanding of the critical reception of the Bible's *Song of Songs* will demonstrate Morrison's unique interpretation of it according to black women's historical and social position.

"Black but/and Comely": Race, Gender, and Identity in *Song of Songs*

Millennia of readings of the *Song of Songs* have tended to oscillate between two poles, that of a more literal, erotic reading and readings that spiritualize or metaphorize away the sexual urgency within its poetics. In any event, any reading of the poem must take into account that the *Song of Songs* begins with a woman's voice: "Let him kiss me with the kisses of his mouth: for thy love is better than wine" (1:2). The foregrounding of female desire is consistent throughout the erotic poem, including the female Beloved's declaration in chapter 7, "I am my beloved's and his desire is toward me" (7:10). This is a stunning reversal of the curse on Eve in Genesis 3:16, where her desire is constructed unilaterally toward her husband.

While some readers have argued that the patriarchal inscription attributing the poem to Solomon—"the Song of Songs, which is Solomon's"—eclipses the female voice within male ownership of language, others have regarded the poem as emblematic of female erotic power. For example, Francis Landy writes, "The dominance and initiative of the Beloved are the poem's most astonishing characteristics. Metaphorically aligned with a feminine aspect of divinity, associated with celestial bodies, the land, and fertility, the Beloved reverses the predominantly patriarchal theology of the Bible. Male power is enthralled to her" (317). He adds a caution: "The lovers live, however, in a patriarchal world" (317).

André LaCocque, however, argues that not only do we have a feminine voice but a female poet, noting that "it is not only possible but it is expected that a love song in the ancient Near East be written by a woman" (243). He reads the poem as potentially even more subversive in its authorship, form, and content, arguing that "the poet allegedly uses an innocent language of courtship while at the same time defying customary institutions by presenting ... a universe that is outright erotic" (236). Anchoring the poem's "subversive eroticism," for LaCocque, is not only a female protagonist who "does the talking" (241) but, in fact, the writer of the *Song*. Thus *Song of Songs* conforms to generic practices of its culture of origin. As LaCocque summarizes, "It is a woman's song from beginning to end" (243).

The Shulamite's opening declaration—"Look not at me because I am black, because the sun hath looked upon me"—raises the issue of the protagonist's outsider status: "My mother's children were angry with me; they made me the keeper of the vineyards" (1:6). Here gender, race, and class are all operative as markers of difference, and all converge under the sign "blackness." The dark skin color is attributed at least partly to being exposed to the sun due to performing outside labor.[1]

The reference to "my own vineyard" resonates with other images in the poem where the Beloved is referred to as a garden (4:12–16) and her breasts described as "clusters of the vine" (7:8). At the poem's end, the Beloved exclaims, "My vineyard, which is mine, is before me" (8:12), suggesting a progression to self-possession and the ownership of her sexuality. Thus I want to read the *Song* as a poem about desire, pleasure, and black women's ultimate possession of their bodies and selfhood through reclaiming their own sexuality, a right denied them by the institution of chattel slavery in the United States.

Just as the probability of female authorship and the certainty of female voice have been muted within the interpretive history of the *Song*, allegorical and theological readings have domesticized its message. LaCoque's words are significant: "To the *eros* of the poem was artificially opposed a disembodied *agape*" (251). The spiritualizing of the poem strips away even gender difference in an attempt to transcend the body altogether as female and male lovers become translated as "asexual personae" (251). It is in the gap between eros and agape that Morrison will situate her uniquely black and female vision, interrogating the tension between two alternatively possible translations: "black but comely" and "black and beautiful."

Reading "the sexy parts of the Bible": Morrison's *Song of Songs*

Few writers have made such lavish and complex use of the Bible as Morrison. From the names of her characters—Pilate, First Corinthians, Shaddrach, Ruth, Hagar—to the inscription at the beginning of *Beloved* from Hosea and

Romans, Morrison's novels are laden with biblical tropes, phrasing, and intonations. As the title to Shirley A. Stave's edited volume suggests, the relationship of Morrison to the Bible is one of "contested intertextualities." As one writer remarked, "those who know their Bible well will have special access" to Toni Morrison's canon (Pocock, 281).

While the *Song of Songs* may seem like a "chest which has lost its key" (Kristeva, 86), it may itself be an important key to unlocking the treasures of Morrison's artistic and intellectual vision. In "Through a Glass Darkly," Judy Pocock reads Morrison's 1977 novel *Song of Solomon* in light of its biblical predecessor, especially through Morrison's use of biblical names and typology. I would like to extend Pocock's reading to suggest that the *Songs of Songs* is possibly the biblical ur-text for much of Morrison's novelistic and discursive project, as elements of its poetics appear in several works. Not only does she exploit the subversive power of black female erotics in novels like *The Bluest Eye* (1970), *Sula* (1973), *Song of Solomon* (1977), *Tar Baby* (1981), *Beloved* (1987), and *A Mercy* (2008), but she explores and "de-metaphorizes" (LaCocque, 251) the allegorical interpretive tradition by insisting on the black female body as the site of narrative.

In "A Holy Madness: She and He," Julia Kristeva offers a useful rubric for Morrison's work in denoting the following major themes in *Song of Songs* (paraphrased here):

1. Love as the powerful antidote for death (8:6);
2. "Love as unacknowledged lament," the Lover and the Beloved as "lovers who do not merge but are in love with the other's absence";
3. The assertion of woman: "It is she who speaks and sets herself up as equal, in her legal, named, unguilty love, to the other's sovereignty. The amorous Shulamite is the first woman to be sovereign before her loved one";
4. Freedom and agency of individuals expressed through consensual intimacy and pleasure: "The enunciation of the Song of Songs is very specifically individualized, assumed by autonomous free subjects who, as such, appear for the first time in the world's amatory literature." (86–89)

The thematic "love is as strong as death" figures in *Song of Solomon* as Milkman and Guitar end in a deadly embrace, and in Morrison's *Beloved*, where Sethe's "too thick" love results in the death of her baby daughter.[2] Love as unacknowledged lament, where the lovers are "in love with each other's absence," could apply to Sula and Nel in *Sula*, as well as Son and Jadine in *Tar*

Baby, who, in the relatively isolated space of Eloe, read "the sexy parts of the Bible" to each other. The novel *Beloved* is almost entirely about absence and lamentation, as it dramatizes the pain of family separation that was a hallmark of American chattel slavery. Morrison's ninth novel, *A Mercy* (2008), is possibly her deepest meditation to date on the human need to enact gestures of agape, even within the direst of circumstances.

Two of Morrison's novels, *The Bluest Eye* and *Tar Baby*, address the issue of female desire and desirability that reenact the but/and contradiction of the Bible's *Song of Songs* 1:5. In her first novel, *The Bluest Eye*, Morrison relates the story of a little girl whose desire for blue eyes, the sign of normative white beauty standards, drives her to despair and insanity. In the afterword to the novel (1994), Morrison reflects on Pecola's predicament:

> The assertion of racial beauty was not a reaction to the self-mocking, humorous critique of cultural/racial foibles common in all groups, but against the damaging internalization of assumptions of immutable inferiority originating in an outside gaze. I focused, therefore, on how something as grotesque as the demonization of an entire race could take root inside the most delicate member of society: a child; the most vulnerable member: a female. In trying to dramatize the devastation that even casual racial contempt can cause, I chose a unique situation, not a representative one. (210)

Based on a childhood memory of a very dark-skinned girl who wanted blue eyes, Morrison writes that "implicit in her desire was racial self-loathing" (210).

Similarly, in *Tar Baby* we are introduced to Jadine, the exotic "copper Venus," who is caught between cultures as an elite fashion model. Yet it is the novel's image of the woman in yellow that represents a counterdiscourse of "transcendent beauty" (46) that proves devastating to Jadine:

> The vision itself was a woman much too tall. Under her long canary yellow dress Jadine knew there was too much hip, too much bust. The agency would laugh her out of the lobby, so why was she and everybody else in the store transfixed? The height? The skin like tar against the canary yellow dress? ... She looked up then and they saw something so powerful it had burnt away the lashes. (45)

If Pecola's desire enacts the "but" in "I am black but comely," the woman in yellow is emblematic of the alternative translation: "I am black and beautiful." Her very presence is a direct refusal of the destructive version of racialized beauty and has the power to destabilize Jadine's entire sense of her self and world. That she is described as "unphotographable" (46) suggests that she breaks the field of vision that tropes blackness as unbeautiful.

In her provocative article "Wounded Beauty," Anne Anlin Cheng writes of a fundamental *méconnaissance* "surrounding the discourse of beauty at the intersection . . . between race and gender" (191). She notes: "At the conjunction of racial and gender discrimination stands the woman of color, for whom 'beauty' presents a vexing problem both as judgment and solution. That is, between a feminist critique of feminine beauty and a racial denial of non-white beauty, where does this leave the woman of color? Can she or can she not be beautiful?" (192). For Cheng, desirability based on racialized notions of beauty at least since the Enlightenment are inherently problematic, and "efforts at racial reclamation through slogans such as 'Black Is Beautiful' seem to announce injury more than remedy" (193). Malin LaVon Walther writes of Morrison's revision of beauty in her novels as an attempt to refract the patriarchal gaze that constructs and constricts white women's sexuality. In this sense, Morrison is highlighting black women's desire for a specific type of male gaze that is objectifying and demeaning.

Morrison's choice of the name "Breedlove" in *The Bluest Eye* is important in several ways. First, Breedlove was the birth name of Madame C. J. Walker, the first African American millionaire, who made her fortune inventing hair straighteners and skin lighteners for blacks in the late nineteenth century and the early twentieth. The irony of Walker's entrepreneurship founded on beauty items that fed on African Americans' acceptance of white beauty standards is not lost on Morrison. At the center of the Breedloves' psyche in *The Bluest Eye* is a debilitating self-hatred:

> They believed they were ugly. Although their poverty was traditional and stultifying, it was not unique. But their ugliness was unique. No one could have convinced them that they were not relentlessly and aggressively ugly. . . . —Mrs. Breedlove, Sammy Breedlove, and Pecola Breedlove—wore their ugliness, put it on, so to speak, although it did not belong to them. (38)

That ugliness is constructed and not natural is clear from this passage. The Breedloves' acceptance of an outward evaluation of themselves breeds, in fact, a self-hatred that manifests in various ways, from Pecola's desire for blue eyes, to Pauline's preference for the little white daughter of her employer, to Cholly's rape of his own daughter.

There is, however, another sense in which Morrison's employs the name "Breedlove" as a signifier of the slave-breeding culture with its short-circuited desire and the desire for consensual sexual intimacy that drives both Pauline and Cholly Breedlove. Pauline's desire appears at the end of her first-person stream-of-consciousness narrative in the form of "musings, idle thoughts, full sometimes, of old dreaminess":

> *His face is next to mine. The bed springs sounds like them crickets used to back home. He puts his fingers in mine, and we stretches our arms outwise like Jesus on the cross. I hold on tight. . . . I know he wants to come first. But I can't. Not until he does. Not until I feel him loving me. Just me. Sinking into me. Not until I know that my flesh is all that be on his mind. That he couldn't stop if he had to. That he would die rather than take his thing out of me. Of me. Not until he has let go of all he has, and give it to me. To me. To me. When he does, I feel a power. I be strong, I be pretty, I be young.* (130)

The erotic equation of sexual desire with the power to be desired reenacts the erotic circuit of the *Song of Songs*. Rather than position women as objects of male desire, the woman here rewrites herself as subject of her own narrative. Yet Pauline cannot bring this narrative moment into the cultural symbolic to the novel, and it is this failure that opens the space for Cholly Breedlove's rape of his own daughter Pecola. Indeed, the novel begins with the realization of the transgression of the incest taboo, the original Fall that drives desire in the novel.

The pattern in Morrison, then, is the eruption of black women's erotic desire (black and beautiful) and the co-optation of that desire within the social structure of power (black but comely). Rebecca Degler, for example, reads Pecola as a figure of ritual sacrifice as the community "rids itself of . . . what they deem as nasty or undesirable, in an effort to rid themselves of that undesirability" ("Ritual," 232). The idea of (self-)sacrifice is important in the biblical conception of agape that Morrison will balance with concepts of philos in her reformulation of community.

(S)Mother Love: Troubled Maternity and Conflicted Community

No discussion of love in Morrison's work would be complete without a consideration of her representations of black mothers. Specifically, the prison house of slave law that mandated the child shall follow the condition of the mother comes up repeatedly in Morrison's novels in representations of what I call "lethal maternity." From Eva Peace's burning of her son Plum's drug-addicted body in *Sula*—"Is? My baby? Burning?" (48)—to Pecola's incestuously conceived and stillborn baby in *The Bluest Eye*, the barrenness of Violet Trace in *Jazz* and the barren Ruby women in *Paradise*, or the (apparently) abandoning mother in *A Mercy*, Morrison consistently gives us a troubled maternity. The lethal maternal figure, emblematic of black motherhood under slave law, references birth and death simultaneously as an iconographic reminder of a treacherous sexuality. The most chilling example of the contradictions of black maternity—the mother who simultaneously gives life and takes life away—is the character of Sethe in *Beloved*, and no writer to date has surpassed Morrison's brilliance in rendering this disturbing tableau:

> Inside, two boys bled in the sawdust and dirt at the feet of a nigger woman holding a blood-soaked child to her chest with one hand and an infant by the heels in the other. She did not look at them; she simply swung the baby toward the wall planks, missed and tried to connect a second time, when out of nowhere—in the ticking time the men spent staring at what there was to stare at—the old nigger boy, still mewing, ran through the door behind them and snatched the baby from the arch of its mother's swing.
>
> Right off it was clear, to schoolteacher especially, that there was nothing to claim. (14)

This description, around which the entire novel revolves, positions the reader in the consciousness of the slave catchers (note the word "nigger" to describe Sethe, and "old nigger boy" for Stamp Paid), as well as outside that consciousness, "staring at what there was to stare at." At the center of the horror of this representation is "a nigger woman holding a blood-soaked child to her chest"—a cruel take on nursing, especially given Sethe's history of having her milk stolen. Not only, Morrison suggests with this scene, did slave mothers struggle to nurture their children—a process interrupted by the economics of slavery—but, in fact, they birthed "dead" offspring.

While I agree with Jean Wyatt that the mother figure in *Beloved* "occupies a contradictory discourse" (475), I disagree with her premise that "the novel's discourse ... tends to resist substitution" (474). Instead substitution, in the sense not of metaphor but of allegory, is the primary drive behind the text. In the scene just referenced, the substitution—blood for milk—is completed as the dead Beloved is positioned as the substitutionary sacrifice for the living Denver in a curious evocation of the Christian Eucharist.[3]

That Sethe "reached for the baby without letting the dead one go" suggests an equivalence, as Baby Suggs "traded the living for the dead" (152). Moreover, Sethe's placing her blood-spattered nipple into Denver's mouth causes Denver to take "her mother's milk right along with the blood of her sister" (152).

"And the Greatest of These": Toni Morrison, the Bible, Love

If we see this in light of Žižek's "paradoxical gesture" of agape, we find a connection with several of Morrison's novels where characters have sacrificed (or been sacrificed) for the benefit of the larger community: Sula Peace in *Sula*, Son in *Tar Baby*, and Milkman in *Song of Solomon*, for example, can be read as enacting an agape that brings about a kind of philos or (at least) temporary community stability. In *Sula*, however, such a gesture fails to hold, as the community will ultimately meet its demise in the womblike mine. Son and Milkman both transform at the ends of their respective novels in ways that prefigure the (potential) transformation of their communities. In *Paradise*, moreover, community read as philos actually serves to block the dispensing of agape as the communities of the Convent and Ruby are on a collision course that sets one against the other. The annihilation of the female-centered Convent by the black male inhabitants of Ruby positions the women as a collective sacrifice that indeed blocks agape from fulfillment. Even when Reverend Misner gestures to the empty cross during the wedding scene, the sense of sacrifice as agape fails to register with the congregants. They certainly fail to understand its ethical implications.

In the appropriately titled *Love* (2003), Morrison stages philos experienced as agape by two female friends, Heed and Christine. That the adult others do not recognize this imperils the entire community in a collective misrecognition. In the words of the omniscient narrator "L[ove]":[4]

> It's like that when children fall for one another.... If such children find each other before they know their own sex, or which one of them is starving, which well fed; before they know color from no color, kin from stranger, then they have found a mix of surrender and mutiny they can never live without. Heed and Christine found such a one.
> Most people have never felt a passion that strong, that early. (199)

This conflation of innocence and passion that predates social categories of identity ("before they know their own sex, or which one of them is starving, which well fed; before they know color from no color") finds expression on a collective scale in *A Mercy* (2008), where Morrison depicts an almost Eden-like nascent America. The undercurrent in the novel is the difficulty of forming any meaningful sense of community, as "a love-broken girl" (58), Florens, misreads her mother's sacrificial action. Florens operates under an assumption of maternal abandonment that causes her to map agape onto eros through her infatuation with the free black male blacksmith. Driven by a desire fueled by her presumed undesirability, Florens's psyche consistently misreads what she sees as a preference for black boys (first her brother and then Malaik) with disastrous consequences. The projection of her own rejection causes her to kill her Beloved, rendering her (narratively) deaf to the mother's voice. When Florens returns blood-soaked, not only does she fail to redeem the community, but any semblance of community is foreclosed forever. In Scully's center of consciousness:

> They once thought they were a kind of family because together they had carved companionship out of isolation. But the family they imagined they had become was false. Whatever each one loved, sought or escaped, their futures were separate and anyone's guess. One thing was certain, courage alone would not be enough. Minus bloodlines, he saw nothing yet on the horizon to unite them. (156)

The hope, however, lies in the word "yet," which hovers in this passage like the mother's discourse at the novel's end: "It was not a miracle. Bestowed by God. It was a mercy. Offered by a human heart" (166–67).

Ultimately Morrison locates love within the human field of action and expression that, however flawed, continues to hope. "Now these three abide: faith, hope and love. And the greatest of these is love."

Notes

1. African American literature has a long tradition of light-skinned heroines being punished with outside labor to "darken" them, simultaneously rendering them less physically attractive and solidifying the conflation of race and class (slave) subjectivity. See Harriet E. Wilson's *Our Nig* (1859), William Wells Brown's *Clotel* (1853), and Harriet Jacobs's slave narrative *Incidents in the Life of a Slave Girl* (1861), as well as Hannah Crafts's *The Bondwoman's Narrative*.

2. Similar ideas about love and the death of children appear in Gwendolyn Brooks's poem "The Mother" and Lucille Clifton's "the lost baby poem." The representation of black motherhood and infanticide I regard as a metaphor for the law of *partus sequitur ventrem*, as the mother is deemed responsible for the slave status (and consequent "social death" à la Orlando Patterson) of her offspring.

3. I refer here, of course, to the Christian notion of drinking the blood of Christ as a sign of substituting Christ's death for the believer's life.

4. There are many different readings of who (or what) narrates the novel. I base my reading of "L" being "love" on the narrator's statement a few lines after the quoted passage: "*If your name is the subject of First Corinthians, chapter 13, it's natural to make it your business*" (199).

Works Cited

Alter, Robert. *Canon and Creativity: Modern Writing and the Authority of Scripture*. New Haven: Yale University Press, 2000.

Alter, Robert, and Frank Kermode, eds. *The Literary Guide to the Bible*. Cambridge: Harvard University Press, 1987.

Cheng, Anne. "Wounded Beauty: An Exploratory Essay on Race, Feminism, and the Aesthetic Question." *Tulsa Studies in Women's Literature* 19, no. 2 (Autumn 2000): 191–217.

Degler, Rebecca. "Ritual and 'Other' Religions in *The Bluest Eye*." In *Toni Morrison and the Bible: Contested Intertextualities*, ed. Shirley A. Stave, 232–55. New York: Peter Lang, 2006.

Frye, Northrop. *The Great Code*. New York: Harcourt Brace Jovanovich, 2002.

Kristeva, Julia. "A Holy Madness: She and He." In *Tales of Love*, trans. Leon S. Roudiez. New York: Columbia University Press, 1987.

LaCocque, André, and Paul Ricoeur. *Thinking Biblically: Exegetical and Hermeneutical Studies*. Trans. David Pellauer. Chicago: University of Chicago Press, 1998.

Landy, Francis. "The Song of Songs." In *The Literary Guide to the Bible*, ed. Robert Alter and Frank Kermode, 305–19. Cambridge: Belknap Press, 1987.

Morrison, Toni. Afterword to *The Bluest Eye*. New York: Plume, 1994.

———. *Beloved*. New York: Vintage, 2004.

———. *The Bluest Eye*. New York: Plume, 1994.

———. *A Mercy*. New York: Alfred Knopf, 2008.

———. *The Nobel Prize Lecture in Literature*. New York: Knopf, 1993.

———. *Paradise*. New York: Plume, 1999.

———. *Song of Solomon*. New York: Vintage, 2004.

———. *Tar Baby*. New York: Vintage, 2004.

Nygren, Anders. *Agape and Eros*. Trans. Philip S. Watson. New York: Harper and Row, 1969.

Outka, Gene. *Agape: An Ethical Analysis*. New Haven: Yale University Press, 1962.

Pocock, Judy. "'Through a Glass Darkly': Typology in Toni Morrison's *Song of Solomon*." *Canadian Review of American Studies* 35, no. 3 (2005): 281–98.

Stave, Shirley A., ed. *Toni Morrison and the Bible: Contested Intertextualities*. New York: Peter Lang, 2006.

Walther, Malin LaVon. "Out of Sight: Toni Morrison's Revision of Beauty." *Black American Literature Forum* 24, no. 4 (Winter 1990): 775–89.

Watson, Francis. *Agape, Eros, Gender: Towards a Pauline Sexual Ethic*. Port Chester, NY: Cambridge University Press, 2000.

Wyatt, Jean. "Giving Body to the Word: The Maternal Symbolic in Toni Morrison's *Beloved*." *PMLA* 108, no. 3 (May 1993): 474–88.

Žižek, Slavoj. *Did Somebody Say Totalitarianism?* London: Verso, 2001.

PALIMPSEST

Reading John Winthrop through the Morrison Trilogy

JUSTINE TALLY

Although Toni Morrison has herself indicated, and critics agree, that the nature of love and community is one underlying theme of her trilogy, the influence of John Winthrop's much-celebrated sermon "A Model of Christian Charity" (more commonly referred to as "The City upon a Hill"), delivered aboard the *Arbella* in 1630, has to date not been addressed as a possible inspiration for her musings on the beloved. On the face of it, Winthrop's subscription to the prevalent contemporary doctrine that God created different orders of people to his greater glory poses a contradiction in terms, for how can a society sanction slavery and indenture and yet insist that all members of the body of Christ must "strengthen, defend, preserve and comfort the other"? Winthrop affirms that the division of God's people into rich and poor, master and oppressed, is divinely ordained, yet this ordinance insists that *both* the Law of Nature *and* the Law of the Gospel emphasize not only Justice but, more importantly, Mercy.[1] Morrison takes her cues from this important urtext, but, as always, with both limitations and expansions, such that her novels comprise a thoughtful revision of Winthrop's admonitions and exhortations to his Puritan community.

Although the enigmatic epigraph for *Beloved* is taken from Romans 9:25, and those for *Jazz* and *Paradise* are taken from "Thunder, Perfect Mind" in the Nag Hammadi, the subject of the end of Romans 9 is actually the Law of

Righteousness, an underlying theme of both Winthrop's sermon and the third novel of the trilogy, *Paradise*:

> 31 But Israel, which followed after the law of righteousness, hath not attained to the law of righteousness.
> 32 Wherefore? Because they sought it not by faith, but as it were by the works of the law. For they stumbled at that stumblingstone.

For Winthrop, whether governed by the Law of Nature or the Law of the Gospel, the Law of Mercy lies incumbent on each member of the community, also instructed in Romans 1:31: "Without understanding, covenant-breakers, without natural affection, implacable, unmerciful." And what makes the act of mercy possible is its foundation in love:

> Love is the bond of perfection. First it is a bond or ligament. Secondly, it makes the work perfect. There is no body but consists of parts and that which knits these parts together, gives the body its perfection, because it makes each part so contiguous to others as thereby they do mutually participate with each other, both in strength and infirmity, in pleasure and pain. (Winthrop)

It is the absence of love, smothered by pride and envy, that is so notable in *Beloved*, the first novel of the trilogy, first in the betrayal of Baby Suggs and Sethe by their community, and second by the ostracism of their family after "The Misery." And it is the absence of mercy that propels the community of Ruby to tragedy in *Paradise*. Though Winthrop uses the metaphor of the body of Christ and the membership in a Christian community that will embrace and sustain its members through love,[2] Morrison uses this same trope in her emphasis on "re-member-ing," not only the tragedies of the past but most importantly reuniting a sundered community. Whereas in *Paradise*, what the founding father Zechariah (Coffee) most dreaded was the "scattering," or the dismembering of his band, this dismemberment is visibly enacted in *Beloved* through the physical dismemberment of the eponymous character, who literally flies apart at one point, or worries about her teeth falling out as the beginning of her bodily disintegration, fearing that her head will be next. Sethe, of course, having faced all odds and having given birth on the journey to reunite her family, has in fact begun its dismemberment by slicing her baby's throat, attempting to sever her head from her body.

Sethe's explanation is that she loved her child so much, she wanted to put her out of harm's way so that schoolteacher could never sully her the way she herself had been sullied by the nephews. In his discussion of "how this love comes to be wrought," Winthrop begins with his views on maternal love. As God loved his only son, so he "loves his elect because they are like Himself, He beholds them in His beloved son. So a mother loves her child, because she thoroughly conceives a resemblance of herself in it." Yet Sethe's problem is that she loves her daughter so "self-less-ly" that her love of self is annihilated; in Foucauldian terms, her obsessive "thick love" impedes any development of an "ethics of the self" so necessary for a full, healthy development of the psyche.[3] Beloved's continual references to "the face that is mine," and the triad of voices (Beloved, Sethe, and Denver) that insist "you are mine," (sub)merge their distinct personalities into an unholy trinity. Sethe's maternal love literally invites her "daughter" to devour her.

In *Jazz*, Violet belatedly yearns for the daughter she might have had, and resorts to trying to steal a baby, and then sleeping with a doll in her arms. Her yearning begins to uncover the cracks in her sense of self. And in *Paradise*, Soane, in an attempt to discourage Consolata from continuing her affair with Deacon, walks all the way to the Convent to ask the woman to help her abort the new life she is carrying: "This was a mother here, saying a brute unmotherly thing that rushed at Consolata like a forked tongue" (239). Soane loses the pregnancy anyway and is haunted by her sin for having used her unborn child as a weapon against her husband's infidelity. It is one thing to recognize (aspects of) the self in one's offspring; it is quite another to deposit all sense of self in a maternal role to the exclusion of one's very being, or to use a child for ulterior purposes. Alarmed by Sethe's fading away after the banishment of Beloved, Paul D attempts to return a sense of self to her: "You your best thing, Sethe. You are"; and there is a glimmer of hope in her tentative "Me?" (273).

Winthrop's emphasis on mercy is intrinsic to his arguments on love, because "the way to draw men to the works of mercy, is not by force of Argument from the goodness of necessity of the work . . . but by *framing* these affections of love in the heart" (Winthrop; italics mine). The degree to which white racists in *Jazz* have abandoned the precepts of their Puritan forefathers is alarming (Joe and Violet's land is repossessed, and then they are burned out, propelling their migration to the City).[4] In the opening section of this novel, Morrison uses the word "frame" four times in eight pages, far too many to be coincidental in the writing of an author so concerned with her use of language:

> Do what you please in the City, it is there to back and frame you no matter what you do. (8–9)

> The mantel over the fireplace used to have shells and pretty-colored stones, but all of that is gone now and only the picture of Dorcas Manfred sits there in a silver frame waking them up all night long. (13)
>
> And while she sprinkles the collar of a white shirt her mind is at the bottom of the bed where the leg, broken clean away from the frame, is too split to nail back. (16)
>
> And both of them stand in the door frame a moment while the borrower repeats for the lender a funny conversation.[5] (16)

And later in the novel:

> Lower and lower, until the music was so lowdown you had to shut your windows and just suffer the summer sweat when the men in shirtsleeves propped themselves in window frames, or clustered on rooftops, in alleyways, on stoops and in the apartments of relatives playing the lowdown stuff that signaled Imminent Demise. (56)

Winthrop specifically includes Dorcas among the names of five biblical characters who framed their good works through mercy toward those less fortunate. Dorcas, Joe's teenage lover, becomes not only the "gazelle" Joe tracks in the City but also the well-off yet generous woman of the first century AD, who as a seamstress made cloaks for older widows who could not sew for themselves, and clothed the children of younger poor widows who could not provide for them. The biblical Dorcas was much beloved by her community at Joppa "for the charitable use of the needle" ("Dorcas") and was exceedingly mourned when she died, so much so that they entreated Peter to bring her back to life (Acts 9:36–41). In *Jazz* Dorcas is also resuscitated in that her picture in the silver frame becomes lifelike for Joe and Violet and haunts their minds and memories. And, of course, it is Dorcas's aunt, Alice Manfred, who as a seamstress demonstrates compassion toward Violet and both stitches Violet's torn coat and figuratively stitches her fractured self back together through their frequent visits and talks.

While reviewers and critics have pointed out that *Jazz* takes up notions of romantic love, the novel contrasts the (ultimately) old-timey love Joe feels for Violet with the obsessive and passionate nature of his love for the teenage Dorcas. Once again it is the obsession with a love that resides outside the self (in Joe's case, the fusion of his frustrated search for mother love from "brain-blasted" Wild with the intimacy he shares with his young lover) that leads to tragedy. Yet passion between lovers is more intricately taken up in *Paradise*: "He [Deacon] was twenty-nine. She [Consolata] was thirty-nine. She lost her mind. Completely" (228). Interestingly, Winthrop does not at all eschew dealing with sexual love, reinforcing John Beardsley's opinion that in this particular sermon, "Winthrop's genius was logical reasoning combined with a sympathetic nature. To remove this work's central arguments about love and relationships is to completely lose the sense of the whole" (Beardsley). And to remove the inclusion of sexual love would have seriously limited his comprehensive overview. Drawing on the appearance of Eve in Adam's life, Winthrop aptly describes the devotion a person feels for the beloved:

> Now when the soul, which is of a sociable nature, *finds anything like to itself*, it is like Adam when Eve was brought to him. She must be one with himself. This is flesh of my flesh (saith he) and bone of my bone. So the soul conceives a great delight in it; therefore she desires nearness and familiarity with it. She hath a great propensity to do it good and receives such content in it, as fearing the miscarriage of her beloved, she bestows it in the inmost closet of her heart. She will not endure that it shall want any good which she can give it. If by occasion she be withdrawn from the company of it, she is still looking towards the place where she left her beloved. If she heard it groan, she is with it presently. If she find it sad and disconsolate, she sighs and moans with it. She hath no such joy as to see her beloved merry and thriving. If she see it wronged, she cannot hear it without passion. She sets no bounds to her affections, nor hath any thought of reward. She finds recompense enough in the exercise of her love towards it.[6] (Winthrop; italics mine)

Saved from the streets of Brazil as a nine-year-old, educated and protected by Catholic nuns and following in their chaste ways, Consolata is struck by her recognition of a "sameness" of which she was totally unaware, or had suppressed. On a trip into Ruby with Mary Magna, she happens upon the horse race in which the young KD will ultimately be declared winner:

> As Consolata watched that reckless joy, she heard a faint but insistent Sha sha sha. Sha sha sha. Then a memory of just such skin and just such men, dancing with women in the streets ... Consolata knew she knew them....
> It was while Consolata waited on the steps that she saw him for the first time. Sha sha sha. Sha sha sha.... Consolata saw his profile, and the wing of a feathered thing, undead, fluttered in her stomach. (226)

While Winthrop initially couches his conception of the reciprocity of love by alluding to the "body of the church"—"First in regard that among the members of the same body, love and affection are reciprocal in a most equal and sweet kind of commerce" (Winthrop)—his second point alludes more clearly to the pleasures of the "exercise of love" in the "natural body," and he employs a metaphor that is clearly dominant in *Paradise*:

> The mouth is at all the pains to receive and mince the food which serves for the nourishment of all the other parts of the body; yet it hath no cause to complain; for first the other parts send back, by several passages, a due proportion of the same nourishment, in a better form for the strengthening and comforting the mouth. Secondly, the labor of the mouth is accompanied with such pleasure and content as far exceeds the pains it takes. (Winthrop)

After the abuse she suffered as a young child in Brazil, Consolata, under the tutelage of Mary Magna, never knows "any male or want[ed] to, which must have been why being love-struck after thirty celibate years took on an edible quality" (*Paradise*, 228). So intense is this newly awakened bodily passion that the capacity for describing her lovemaking with Deacon deserts her, becoming "un-memorable, -controllable or -translatable" (229). Losing all notion of time and circumstance, Consolata abandons logic and reason; the landscape for their adventure is described in terms of Genesis: "Out here where wind was not a help or threat to sunflowers, nor the moon a language of time, of weather, of sowing or harvesting, but a feature of the original world designed for the two of them" (229). Deek tells Connie that her "eyes are like mint leaves," and she replies, "And yours are like the beginning of the world" (228). When she mentions that she is older than he is, Deacon replies, "Nobody's older than me" (231). Not only is Deacon described as Adamic, but Consolata's abandonment to pleasure and the erotics of the body again echoes Winthrop: "Nothing yields more pleasure and content to the soul than when it finds that which it may love fervently; for to love and live beloved is the soul's paradise both here and in heaven" (Winthrop).

But the "agonized trunks" of the fig trees (231), the site of their passionate rendezvous (apparently under the two trees for which Gigi is searching), never give fruit, and as autumn grows cooler, Consolata endeavors to entice Deek into the cellar of the Convent to continue their *affaire de coeur*:

> He laughs a low, satisfied laugh and she bites his lip, which, in retrospect, was her big mistake. (237)

> ... He'd sucked air sharply. Said, "Don't ever do that again." But his eyes, first startled, then revolted, had said the rest of what she should have known right away. Clove, cinnamon, soft old linen—who would chance pears and a wall of prisoner wine with a woman bent on eating him like a meal? (239)

Too late she realizes her error: "Dear Lord, I didn't want to eat him. I just wanted to go home" (240); "Sha sha sha, she wanted to say, meaning, he and I are the same" (241). Deacon never appears, and devastated, Consolata returns to Mary Magna, who replaces her "Sha sha sha" with the "Sh sh sh" of erotics denied: "Never speak of him again" (241).

> While the light changed and the meals did too, the next few days were one long siege of sorrow, during which Consolata picked through the scraps of her gobble-gobble love. Romance stretched to the breaking point broke, exposing a simple mindless transfer. From Christ, to whom one gave total surrender and then swallowed the idea of His flesh, to a living man. Shame. Shame without blame. Consolata virtually crawled back to the little chapel. (240)

Later, after futile attempts to keep Mary Magna (the only mother figure she has ever known) alive, Consolata retreats to the cellar, feeling like a little "curl of paper—nothing written on it—lying in the corner of an empty closet" (*Paradise*, 248), literally disconsolate (dis-Consolate), waiting, hoping to die. Consolata has deposited her sense of self outside herself, first in Christ, then in a man, and then back to Christ again through Mary Magna.

In contrast to the voraciousness of Consolata and Deacon's passion, Steward has totally lost his capacity for taste, a result of his craving the hot peppers grown out at the Convent. He "loves" Dovey as his wife (and in her fulfillment of her role, according to *his* understanding of gendered difference) and cannot imagine sleeping without the smell of her hair next to him, but his capacity for the erotic has abandoned him. Dovey measures the changes in him not through his achievements but through his losses, the loss of taste only the "outward and visible sign of an inward and spiritual [dis]grace." Notwithstanding the New Fathers' concern with the "biblical" overtones of the Old Fathers' migration first from Louisiana and then their own from Haven to Ruby, the generation represented by Deacon and Steward Morgan has abandoned the early precepts to which they have been historically called: "We know that there were many that corrupted the service of the Lord" (Winthrop). Dovey does not understand why Steward cannot allow Menus, who is unable to pay his loan to the Morgan bank, to keep his house; Misner is incredulous that Deacon chooses to arrive at the bank on time rather than succor Jeff's wife, Sweetie, exhausted and beside herself with worry over her sick children, stumbling her way out to the Convent (124). Yet it is worth noting that the original surname of the Morgans was something like "Moyne," an anagram of "money," which has conditioned all their choices.

Winthrop admonishes his flock that under both the Law of Nature and the Law of the Gospel, "Duty of mercy is exercised in the kinds: giving, lending and forgiving (of a debt)," quoting not only Matthew 6:19 and John 3:17 but also Judges:

> "If thou pour out thy soul to the hungry, then shall thy light spring out in darkness, and the Lord shall guide thee continually, and satisfy thy soul in draught, and make fat thy bones, thou shalt be like a watered garden, and they shalt be of thee that shall build the old waste places," etc. On the contrary most heavy curses are laid upon such as are straightened towards the Lord and his people (Judg. 5:23). (Winthrop)

The curse laid upon the Morgan twins is, of course, no living progeny, for which they must rely on K.D. and Arlene for the continuity of the 8-rock people. Yet Arnette, "insulted" by K.D., who is protected by his uncles, has already pummeled the life out of the first baby she was expecting so that she can go on to college and avoid the shame of having a child out of wedlock. At first appealing to the women at the Convent to abort the unwanted pregnancy, on the night of her wedding, she returns, demanding that they give her the baby she tried so desperately to eliminate.

Much as the Fathers of Ruby would like to scapegoat the Convent women for things going awry in their perfect town, it is the wayward, "slack" females who, in fact, most closely adhere to Winthrop's concept of mercy, a mercy that arises from love, which "is the fulfilling of the law, not that it is enough to love our brother and so no further" (Winthrop). It is this concept of love that is so on view at the Convent, as Winthrop's words make evident: "John 3:17, 'He who hath this world's goods and seeth his brother to need and shuts up his compassion from him, how dwelleth the love of God in him?' Which comes punctually to this conclusion: If thy brother be in want and thou canst help him, thou needst not make doubt of what thou shouldst do; if thou lovest God thou must help him" (Winthrop).

And yet Consolata's "conversion" while sitting in the garden is not to the Christian God of Mary Magna, like Saul on the road to Damascus; rather, it is effectuated through a vision of a male version of herself (252). Morrison moves here beyond the world conceived by John Winthrop and into an exploration of the nature of self-love and love of others using feminist theory. In Consolata's first words to her little band of disciples after her rebirth from utter desolation, fittingly uttered over a sumptuous Last Supper during whose preparations the references to "juices," "breast," "Thick. Pale. Slippery," "rose cavities," "tender," "liquids," sighs of "Oh, Yes," and "sweet warm fluid" (252–53,

255, 257, 260) all call to the sexuality of the female body, Consolata's admonition never to separate the body from the spirit again carries distinct echoes of "A Model of Christian Charity":

> Love cometh of God and every one that loveth is born of God, so that this love is the fruit of the new birth, and none can have it but the new creature. Now when this quality is thus formed in the souls of men, it works like the Spirit upon the dry bones. Ezek. 37:7—"Bone came to bone." It gathers together the scattered bones, or perfect old man Adam, and knits them into one body again in Christ, whereby a man is become again a living soul. (Winthrop)

Having reclaimed her self, Consolata begins her sermon to her charges with "I call myself Consolata Sosa"[7] and tells them that if they want to stay with her, she will "teach you what you are hungry for" (*Paradise*, 262). What Consolata explains to her charges is crucial:

> My child body, hurt and soil, leaps into the arms of a woman who teach me my body is nothing my spirit everything. I agreed her until I met another. My flesh is so hungry for itself it ate him. When he fell away the woman rescue me from my body again. Twice she saves it. When her body sickens I care for it in every way flesh works. I hold it in my arms and between my legs. Clean it, rock it, enter it to keep it breath. After she is dead I can not get past that. My bones on hers the only good thing. Not spirit. Bones. No different from the man. My bones on his the only true thing. So I wondering where is the spirit lost in this? It is true, like bones. It is good, like bones. One sweet, one bitter. Where is it lost? Hear me, listen. Never break them in two. Never put one over the other. Eve is Mary's mother. Mary is the daughter of Eve. (263)

Consolata's fractured self is knit together not through the body of Christ but through the acceptance of her wholeness, her integrity, not only by integrating her body and her spirit but also by reclaiming the masculine aspects of her self. Calling to the Gospel according to St. John's "In the beginning was the word," Morrison depicts Consolata's taking the young women into the cellar (symbolic of the womb or the *chora* or the *semiotique*[8]): "In the beginning the most important thing was the template" (*Paradise*, 263). And through the "writing of the body," drawing their silhouettes on the floor of the cellar, projecting their individual traumas, and fusing their voices in mutual help and mercy, the women begin their own process of healing and becoming whole. The baptism effectuated by dancing in the warm rain effectively cleanses them of their past, though their sins were committed not by them but against them.

As the townspeople rewrite the story of the massacre to suit their needs and their self-approval, only Deacon repudiates what he recognizes in his twin as an abandonment of the covenant that the Old Fathers had entered into with their God. As he walks barefoot as a sign of humility along the straight streets of Ruby, named for the Evangelists, Deacon's contrition calls again to Winthrop's warning:

> The Lord will surely break out in wrath against us, and be revenged of such a people, and make us know the price of the breach of such a covenant.
>   Now the only way to avoid this shipwreck, and to provide for our posterity, is to follow the counsel of Micah, to do justly, to love mercy, to walk humbly with our God. For this end, we must be knit together, in this work, as one man. We must entertain each other in brotherly affection. We must be willing to abridge ourselves of our superfluities, for the supply of others' necessities. We must uphold a familiar commerce together in all meekness, gentleness, patience and liberality. We must delight in each other; make others' conditions our own; rejoice together, mourn together, labor and suffer together, always having before our eyes our commission and community in the work, as members of the same body. (Winthrop)

Now it is Deacon who is disconsolate. Humbly walking a path he hopes will reconnect him with Soane, Deacon searches for the integrity he had abandoned in his adherence to the "works of the law" rather than the Law of Mercy. Reading the trilogy in light of Winthrop's sermon also facilitates an interpretation of the end of the epigraph Morrison chose for *Paradise*: "And they will find me there, and they will live, and they will not die gain." Or in the stirring final words of John Winthrop: "Therefore let us choose life, that we and our seed may live, by obeying His voice and cleaving to Him, for He is our life and our prosperity." The final coda of *Paradise* re-members the sundered body of the mother and daughter of *Beloved* and reiterates the reconciliation of Joe and Violet in *Jazz*, "the ease of coming back to love again," and the other passengers on this boat of life: "lost and saved, atremble, for they have been disconsolate for some time" (*Paradise*, 318). Mercy is, in Consolata's last humanly word, "Divine."

Notes

1. Winthrop's thoughts clearly continue to spark the author's contemplation, as both her eighth and ninth novel attest: *Love* (2003) and *A Mercy* (2008). For the purposes of this essay, however, I focus on the novels of the trilogy, most particularly on *Paradise*.

2. "First of all, true Christians are of one body in Christ (1 Cor. 12). Ye are the body of Christ and *members of their part*. All the parts of this body being thus united are made so contiguous in a special relation as they must *needs partake of each other's strength and infirmity; joy and sorrow, weal and woe. If one member suffers, all suffer with it*, if one be in honor, all rejoice with it" (Winthrop; italics mine).

3. For a full discussion of the narrativization of Foucauldian theory in *Beloved*, see Tally, "Literary Archeology," chap. 1 in *Toni Morrison's Beloved*, 1–28.

4. Winthrop's citations from the scriptures condemn precisely those actions: "On the contrary most heavy curses are laid upon such as are straightened towards the Lord and his people (Judg. 5:23), 'Curse ye Meroshe . . . because they came not to help the Lord. He who shutteth his ears from hearing the cry of the poor, he shall cry and shall not be heard.' (Matt. 25) 'Go ye cursed into everlasting fire,' etc. 'I was hungry and ye fed me not.' (2 Cor. 9:6) 'He that soweth sparingly shall reap sparingly.'"

5. In *The Story of Jazz: Toni Morrison's Dialogic Imagination*, I argued that this specific use of framing is at once a call to the hard-boiled detective novel (a "ghost text" for the imitation of a popular genre) and an illustration of Bakhtin's theory of alterity. As Pam Morris writes, "It was the author's condition of outsidedness which allowed him to visualize the hero as a unified image *framed* against the surrounding world. The existence of heteroglossia constituted of multiple social discourses allows speakers to achieve a similar position of outsidedness to a language. It is possible to recognize the ideological contours of one social discourse by outlining it against other discourses. In this way any monologic truth claims made by one social language will be relativized by the existence of other views of the world" (Morris, 16; italics mine).

6. Winthrop also takes up the love that springs of devotion between other notable characters in the Bible, mentioning Ruth and Noemi (a story basic to understanding *A Mercy*), and Jonathan and David, whose love he describes in some detail. Modern-day Bible critics disagree about whether this relationship was indeed platonic or whether, as some gay-rights advocates insist, this example of such dedicated love between men also included a sexual aspect; but this interpretation is not a noticeable thrust in Winthrop's sermon, as is to be expected.

7. The syntax here is important: not "Call me Consolata" (as in Melville's Ishmael) but the claiming of the self and the foregrounding of the first-person personal pronoun as a sign of wholeness.

8. For a discussion of an interpretation of this scene using French feminist critique, see Tally, "The Nature of Erotica in Morrison's *Paradise*."

Works Cited

Beardsley, John. Introduction to "A Model of Christian Charity," by John Winthrop. http://religiousfreedom.lib.virginia.edu/sacred/charity.html (accessed September 12, 2010).

"Dorcas." http://www.essortment.com/bible-woman-dorcas-43988.html (accessed September 7, 2010).

Morris, Pam. *The Bakhtin Reader: Selected Writings of Bakhtin, Medvedev, Voloshinov*. 1994. New York: Edward Arnold, 1997.

Morrison, Toni. *Beloved*. New York: Alfred A. Knopf, 1987.

———. *Jazz*. London: Chatto and Windus, 1992.

———. *Paradise*. New York: Alfred A. Knopf, 1998.

Tally, Justine. "The Nature of Erotica in Morrison's *Paradise* and the Em-body-ment of Feminist Thought." In *Complexions of Race: The African Atlantic*, ed. Fritz Gysin and Cynthia S. Hamilton, 83–95. Münster: Lit, 2005.

———. *The Story of* Jazz: *Toni Morrison's Dialogic Imagination*. Hamburg: Lit, 2001.

———. *Toni Morrison's* Beloved: *Origins*. New York: Routledge, 2009.

Winthrop, John. "A Model of Christian Charity." http://religiousfreedom.lib.virginia.edu/sacred/charity.html (accessed September 12, 2010).

MAGICALLY FLYING WITH TONI MORRISON

Mexico, Gabriel García Márquez, Song of Solomon, *and* Sula

DAVÍD CARRASCO

"Finally," she says. "I trust you now. I trust you with the bird that is not in your hands because you have truly caught it. Look. How lovely it is, this thing we have done—together."
—Toni Morrison, Nobel Prize lecture, 1993

I want to reflect on two religious dimensions in Morrison's language of catching, of doing, and of togetherness in a hybrid essay mixing fragments from journals with interpretations of magical flight and sacred place in *Song of Solomon* and *Sula*. I kept the journals during two trips to Mexico with the author and her son Ford, during both of which she met with Gabriel García Márquez. Toni Morrison and García Márquez first met in 1996 at the home of the Mexican novelist Carlos Fuentes, and we returned to Mexico again in 2005 for a second meeting with him. The sacred appears in Morrison's writings in various ways: (1) traditional Christian ritual and symbols, (2) African-influenced themes and characters, and (3) what Morrison calls "Strange Stuff." The themes of magical flight and sacred place link the literary strategies of both Morrison and García Márquez and also refer to the emotional thrill we all felt traveling to Mexico for these meetings. As we shall see, one of the primary elements in magical flight as portrayed in many religious traditions

Mexico, Gabriel García Márquez, *Song of Solomon*, and *Sula*   145

Morrison in Frida Kahlo's garden at her "Blue House" in Coyoacán, Mexico, 1996. Photo by Fabrizio Leon Diez.

is the search for a spiritual ally, often in the form of a bird, who enables the seeker in the face of some profound challenge to change place.

Flying to Mexico City, 2005

As we are flying to Mexico City on our second journey, we reminisce about Morrison's first meeting with García Márquez at Carlos Fuentes's home in 1996, about our visit to the great pyramids at Teotihuacan (the Abode of the Gods), and about the guided tour by Eduardo Matos Moctezuma of the Museum of the Templo Mayor in downtown Mexico City. She speaks of her experience as a judge at the Cannes International Film Festival, and I tell her about my work on the film about undocumented Mexican farmworkers, *Alambrista: The Director's Cut* (2003). She speaks enthusiastically about her upcoming project at the Louvre, "The Foreigner's Home." She tells me that she listened to Nina Simone while writing the last pages of her eighth novel, *Love*, and gives an emphatic recommendation of Tommy Lee Jones's "out of this world" movie *The Three Burials of Melquíades Estrada* (2005).

Morrison's comments on film remind me of her deep interest in art as we viewed Diego Rivera's murals at the Secretaría de Educación Pública in

Mexico City nine years before. I have never seen anyone look so intensely at paintings and landscapes. She would grow extremely quiet and seemed to physically connect with the images and colors of Rivera's murals and the plants in Frida Kahlo's garden at her "Blue House" in the Coyoacán district of Mexico City—so much so that those of us around her felt an impulse to step back a few paces and give her unimpeded access to what she was gazing at.

Day 1, November 23, 2005: Toni Morrison and García Márquez Meet Again

"Señor Davíd Carrasco," the voice on the room phone of the hotel near the Colegio de México said, "el señor García Márquez llegó y está esperándolos a usted y a Toni Morrison en el lobby." As I walk to the elevator, I wonder whether I am awake or dreaming. At the lunch, a top-notch translator helps to keep the compliments and stories flowing between them. García Márquez insists we all have the fish dish they make for him at this restaurant; after some repartee about the right lunch choice, we all go with the fish. There is wordplay about whether it will be Morrison's white wine or García Márquez's champagne—champagne wins, but only after he says, "Toni invents things I say, and it comes out better than when I say it."

A bit later in the lunch, Morrison is angling to get him to come to Paris the following November to be part of her project called "The Foreigner's Home," and insisting on the meaning of the apostrophe in the title. He, in turn, angles to get her to come to Mexico on March 6 for his birthday party, and so they continue their repartee to see what they can work out. Morrison talks about how her project on the foreigner's home has led her to realize that "an illness is a foreigner in a strange home—in a different body," and how she's thinking of writing about how this kind of foreigner—an illness—takes over the family and the people once it hits. She is to give a talk on "The Foreigner's Home" tomorrow night to open the Guadalajara Festival de Libros, and the talk is much on her mind.

Watching Toni Morrison and Gabriel García Márquez converse makes me wonder whether the two of them are seeking spiritual allies in each other. Although they do not share a common language—she speaks in English and he in Spanish—they do catch each other's meanings and enter into each other's worlds. Toward the end of the meal there is a moment of exchange between them. Morrison picks up her napkin and writes a private message to García Márquez. He takes his napkin and writes a private message to her.

Carlos Fuentes, Gabriel García Márquez, and Morrison at Fuentes's home in 1996. Photo by Fabrizio Leon Diez.

They then exchange them as gifts, and he notes with a broad smile, "I'm going to frame this."

Now, nine years later, his words at the restaurant, "I'm going to frame this," point me to a way I can enter into *Song of Solomon* by focusing on the framing scenes of flight and magical flight that open and close the novel.

Magical Flight and Spiritual Helpers in *Song of Solomon*

From the opening epigraph to the final paragraph, Morrison develops the theme of the flying African. It teaches us, among other lessons, the importance and power of magical flight as a strategy to deal with profound racial suffering. The novel's epigraph reads, "The fathers may soar and the children may know their names," linking the experience of celestial flight to the acquisition of crucial knowledge about lineage and identity. In the novel's final sentences, it is the children who fly as Milkman and Guitar, once dear friends and now mortal enemies, jump into each other's arms and soar into the air: "Without wiping away the tears, taking a deep breath, or even bending his knees, he leaped. As fleet and bright as a lodestar he wheeled toward Guitar and it did not matter which of them would give up his ghost in the killing arms of his brother. For now he knew what Shalimar knew: if you surrendered to the air, you could *ride* it" (337).

Morrison has partially hidden in her narrative thread of magical flight one of the key meanings of shamanic transport and elevation, namely, the vital importance of finding a spiritual ally who enables the seeker to transcend the terror of one's historical condition. She hints at the importance of gaining a spirit-helper in the epigraph where the children learn the names of their fathers, and thereby their own names, because of a magical flight. In the final scenes, Milkman has found, through his ordeal of returning to Solomon's Leap, his own spiritual allies. At several points in the novel, Morrison signals the presence of the spiritual ally through the strategic positioning of bird imagery and birds flying. It is Morrison's focus on this ordeal and this acquisition of a spiritual ally in relation to the symbolism of birds and the flight *to a new place* that I see as one religious dimension of this novel.

Mercy Hospital (which the colored people call "No Mercy Hospital" because it is for whites only) becomes the site of racial trauma at the opening of the novel. The theme of the flying African enters this tense scene almost immediately when Pilate, who is wrapped in an old quilt and standing in the small crowd watching Robert Smith up on the hospital's cupola, with his two blue wings wrapped around him, begins to sing in her powerful contralto just before Smith "leaped on into the air" (9):

> O Sugarman done fly away
> Sugarman done gone
> Sugarman cut across the sky
> Sugarman gone home. (6)

Morrison notes the religious character of the scene when she writes that the hospital personnel first thought the gathered crowd represented "a political action group" but then thought they represented "some form of worship." This flight and song serve as the first side of the religious frame of *Song of Solomon*. In the final chapters, the frame is closed as Morrison transforms the meaning of flight/suicide into "magical flight," a basic motif in the shamanic imagination of spiritual renewal found in the history of religions.

While on his journey of ordeals and discoveries, Milkman, spending the night with Sweet, has a "warm dreamy sleep all about flying, about sailing high over the earth ... floating, cruising ... over the dark sea, but it didn't frighten him because he knew he could not fall. He was alone in the sky but somebody was applauding him, watching him and applauding" (298). This "somebody" is invisible to him. In the days leading up to this dream, Milkman makes a crescendo of discoveries about his flying African ancestor and exclaims to Sweet with overflowing delight the story of Solomon's escape from slavery.

> Oh, Man! He didn't need no airplane. He just took off; got fed up. *All the way up!* No more cotton! No more bales! No more orders! No more shit! He flew, baby.... Flew on home. Can you dig it? Jesus God, that must have been something to see. And you know what else? He tried to take his baby boy with him. My grandfather. Wow! Wooee! Guitar, my great-granddaddy could flyyyyy and the whole damn town is named after him. Tell him, Sweet. Tell him my great-granddaddy could fly.... He sailed on off like a black eagle. (328)

In the 2004 edition of *Song of Solomon*, Morrison notes that the three flights of the novel—Robert Smith's, Solomon's, and Milkman's—are "ambiguous, disturbing." She emphasizes that the verb she uses in the first sentence of the book, referring to Robert Smith's leap, works to ignite the story not merely of a suicide but rather of "a radical gesture demanding change, an alternative way, a cessation of things as they are" (xiii). The first verb of the novel is "promised," and it has a religious inflection that grows into a religious theme in both Solomon's leap to freedom from slavery and Milkman's jump at the novel's end. Morrison states that Solomon's leap to freedom is "the most magical, the most theatrical, and, for Milkman, the most satisfying," and it drives the novel's movement forward from a point in a mythical past (xiv). It is this combination of ambiguity, magic, and satisfaction that points me to the underlying religiosity of the story.

Anthropologists and historians of religion have gathered abundant evidence from religions around the world about the ecstatic states, magical flights, and helping spirits associated with shamanic vocations. Shamans, who sometimes face physical and spiritual dangers, practice ecstatic techniques that enable them to go into trances, leave their bodies, enter a labyrinth, and ascend to the sky or the underworld, where they meet monsters, allies, and seek helping spirits. One historian of religions in particular, Mircea Eliade, has noted in *Myths, Dreams, and Mysteries* that "the 'flight' expresses in spatial terms the ability of certain individuals to leave their bodies at will, and to travel 'in the spirit' through the three cosmic regions.... The soul abandons the body and flies away into regions inaccessible to the living. By his ecstasy the shaman renders himself equal to the gods, to the dead and to the spirits; the ability to 'die' and come to life again—that is voluntarily to leave and to re-enter the body—denotes that he has surpassed the human condition" (101–2).

The radical action of a human being flying through the air reflects the desire to abolish history, or the terror of one's history, and undergo the feeling and experience of freedom. The symbolism of magical flight among shamans often includes the following elements, relevant to Morrison's framing of *Song of Solomon*: (1) the experience of a dream, in which (2) the protagonist flies into the celestial sphere (or enters the underworld through a cave), where (3) he suffers ordeals and, most importantly, (4) finds a spiritual ally, sometimes in the form of a bird or another animal from which he learns a new language, and (5) returns to earth and the community with new knowledge and sometimes the power to heal. When we turn back to the text in light of these religious motifs, our eyes are drawn to the language of Milkman's dream and exclamatory statement to Sweet. He dreams of a celestial ascent, of "sailing high over the earth," and says his ancestor "went all the way up." He delights that his great-grandfather Solomon flew above the historical weight of "cotton bales" and "orders" and "shit." What stands out especially are the two key phrases "he sailed off like a black eagle" and (from his earlier dream) "[Milkman] was alone in the sky but somebody was applauding him, watching him and applauding. He couldn't see who it was" (298).

These two images, the unseen celestial watcher and the black eagle, point to the religious pattern of the acquisition of a spiritual ally or helper during a magical flight experience. These allies often lead the seeker out of the terror of their history and into a new place or dimension. His dream experience reveals to him—and gives him new emotional power—that he has a spiritual ally in the form of the celestial being who is applauding him, watching over him. At some level, he must have identified this watcher with his great-grandfather Solomon. And as in shamanic motifs from many parts of the world, the black eagle symbolizes his new spiritual ally, who mediates between the celestial and earthly levels and signifies the potential of spiritual rebirth after physical death. It is after this dream and its awareness that he unleashes the speech to Sweet signifying that he has learned a new and sacred story.

The importance of the bird as spiritual ally appears at the novel's climax when Milkman's aunt, Pilate, the woman with no navel, is murdered by Guitar and dies in Milkman's arms. Milkman and Pilate have returned to Solomon's Leap to carry out a burial—the interment at long last of the bones of Macon Dead the First, Pilate's father and Milkman's grandfather. The ascent to Solomon's Leap resonates with ancient and even biblical ascents of mountains: "It was the higher of two outcroppings of rock. Both flat-headed, both looking over a deep valley. Pilate carried the sack and Milkman a small shovel. It was a long way to the top but neither stopped for breath. At the very top, on the plateau, the trees that could stand the wind at that height were few" (335). Far away from society, where the winds blow trees down, the two travelers carry out a long-overdue burial. Refusing the suggestion to put a "cross or a rock" on the grave, Pilate rips off the ancestral "earring"—a snuffbox—she has been wearing for years on her ear and buries it with the bones. Then out of the darkness and the wind, Guitar fires a shot and wounds her mortally.

As she lies dying in Milkman's arms, he sings loudly to her a new version of the song she had sung at the start of the novel just before he was born, only now he replaces "Sugarman done fly away" with "Sugargirl don't leave me here." His singing awakens two birds that "shuddered off into the air. Milkman laid her head down on the rock. Two of the birds circled round them." And then in a gesture that brings sky down to earth and takes a human up to the sky and reveals to Milkman the spiritual secret of life over death, one bird descends to near where Pilate lies dead. "One bird dived into the new grave and scooped something shiny in its beak before it flew away" (336). The "something shiny" is the earring containing her name, and we are taken back to the novel's opening epigraph, which links the flight of an ancestor and the knowledge of one's name; only now it is the female who soars and whose life is fully recognized by Milkman. The meaning of this bird's feat comes to Milkman immediately as he recognizes Pilate's spirit and destiny in the action of the bird. "Now he knew why he loved her so. Without ever leaving the ground, she could fly" (336). By using this framework of flight becoming magical flight in a novel about a family named Dead, Morrison illustrates the religious motif of acquiring spiritual allies to overcome the realities of racial suffering and death.

In addition to signaling a profound religious dimension to the framework of the novel, Morrison also sets up an ironic parallel between Mircea Eliade's writings on the spiritual meaning of magical flight and the author's language about the family called the Deads. If we read the following sentence and merely change one letter—a capital *D* for the little *d* in the word "dead"— we grasp a summary of the novel's religious framework. Writing of the special quality of knowledge about death and rebirth that a shaman in training gains, Eliade writes, "Little by little, the world of the dead [or Dead] becomes knowable, and death itself is evaluated primarily as a rite of passage to a spiritual mode of being" (Eliade, 108).

Day 2, November 24, 2005: Toni Morrison Lectures beneath the Murals of José Clemente Orozco

At breakfast Morrison expresses concern that her talk tonight at the University of Guadalajara on the novel *The Radiance of the King* may not "work well" for a Mexican audience. She likes the novel, and it relates to her upcoming

Paris project "The Foreigner's Home." She tells me over her scrambled eggs, "It's about a white man who goes to Africa and his ONLY credential is that he's white. He's got no money, no entourage, and no porters—just his white skin. White people usually go to Africa with lots of 'stuff.'"

Morrison's talk works very well with the Mexicans after she is introduced by Carlos Monsiváis to a standing-room-only crowd. What a surprise it is to see her lecturing onstage in front of a furious mural titled *El pueblo y sus líderes falsos* (The People and Their False Leaders) by the Jeremiah of Mexican muralists, José Clemente Orozco. Looking up from the audience at Morrison with this mural looming behind and above her gives one the impression that Orozco is laying down a challenge of truth telling for any speaker or event on this stage. Morrison proves up to the challenge, and in the minds of many Mexicans, for this one night, Morrison and Orozco become magical allies—partners of deep import—and the Mexicans are enthralled by the drama of it all.

In a convulsive scene, wrapping around the three walls of the stage, we see an uprising of oppressed people whose naked, writhing, cadaverous bodies seem about to erupt from the wall and join Morrison on the stage. Their ferocious outrage, poignantly expressed by their screaming faces and emaciated arms upraised with clenched fists, signals that the world, some kind of world, is coming to an end. One emaciated human body at the bottom of the mural lies on the ground, leaning against the stage with his head partially covered by a wrapping—either a bandage covering wounds or perhaps a wrapping for the dead. His eyes are covered, and one wonders if this is a Mexican Lazarus—perhaps awakening from the dead at this moment of uprising. The protesters are leaning toward a group of bosses and scholars while a conflagration of hot red and white flames roars between the two groups and in the background. A hefty labor boss with one of his boots shoved into the naked abdomen of the lead rebel holds a saw in one upraised hand while gripping an open book in the other. One of the scholars is pointing into a book that is stained with blood. Is it a law book? A bearded scholar with weak eyes shaded by dark glasses points a finger into another book while brandishing a knife in the direction of the moving mass of the living dead. Watching this action from the side wall stand three armed men in uniforms—one, the *comandante* with his bayonet raised; the other two, bulky guards with one hand on their holstered pistols and the other grasping steel clubs. Is the message that the military might back up the "scholar bosses" and the labor bosses? Or is Orozco warning the viewers that following false prophets and teachers can lead to yet another kind of subservience, another catastrophe for Mexico?

When Morrison gets up to speak, her voice, her body, and the theme of her talk join quickly with the Mexican audience and the mural. The hall is filled with a sense of electricity and hope. She addresses the theme of the foreigner's home and the struggle of belonging, living in the margins and in exile. She acknowledges the incredible movement of peoples and ideas all over the globe—she compares it to the colonized going to the homes of the colonizer.

Borders for Toni Morrison are the places where the concepts of home are threatened. Borders stoke the worry of the metropolis because the foreigners are challenging the sense of belonging that the folks in the United States are *already* losing with all their talk of globalization. Globalization, she says, is a new form of Manifest Destiny and has the energy of that idea, for it has been given a level of majesty. The language of globalization promotes an abhorrence of diversity, minority languages, and cultures. She notes that foreigners coming across the borders are viewed as (1) threatening, (2) depraved, (3) incomprehensible, (4) inaccessible, and (5) with common hostility, because they are said to bring it. She turns to Camara Laye's novel *The Radiance of the King* to illustrate her case. In the book, a white man whose only currency in Africa is his white skin brings a menacing jungle *along in his head*. Once there he goes through a peregrination of being slowly, slowly opened to a different realization. He faces the pressures we face today of "denying the foreignness in ourselves as we resist, to the death, the commonness between us" (author's journal).

I sense the deep emotional impact these words by Toni Morrison have on the Mexican audience sitting in front of her and Orozco's ominous vision. She tells us how the white man in the novel comes to realize the void in himself only after "protecting himself from disclosure to himself." She leads us to the climax of the novel, when the white man, who has come to Africa in search of an African king, arrives in the king's presence and can only crawl forward to meet him. To his amazement, the king is a young boy all dressed in wonder and gold. The white man, then, allows himself to surrender to the king's gaze. Morrison's last words to the Mexicans listening and watching her beneath those curving murals above us are the final words of the novel, spoken by the African to the white man, "Did you not know that I was waiting for you?"

Thunderous, standing ovation.

Morrison and the Mythic "Bottom" in *Sula*

Toni Morrison's performance beneath José Clemente Orozco's apocalyptic mural recalls for me the social catastrophe in her novel *Sula*. This novel is also framed by the opening and closing structure of a myth, only this time about sacred places in the black community. The original place is, of course, the

Bottom, the neighborhood where Sula and other black people lived, loved, and died in their shacks, visited the Time and a Half Pool Hall and went to Irene's Palace of Cosmetology, struggled with the legacy of slavery and cried out "long and loud—but it had no bottom and it had no top, just circles and circles of sorrow" (174). The catastrophe is the final National Suicide Day in which Shadrack, whose name resonates with Orozco's white-hot flames above Morrison on the stage that day, leads many of the people from the Bottom down to the desired and hated coal tunnel, "in their need to kill it all," all of whom are swallowed up in water and the collapsing earth. For a historian of religions sensitive to the cosmologies of sacred places and millennial dreams and nightmares among people of color, the scene in Mexico and these episodes in *Sula* have profound religious dimensions of cosmic order and change.

What historians of religions who look at novels know is that religious meanings are often disguised in characters, scenes, places, and episodes because, as with myths narrated in words, music, and dance, some scenes in literary fiction reveal the drama and structure of the universe as well as its undoing. When we remember that creation stories are symbolic narratives that people tell about how their world began, was ordered, and what their destiny will be, we can see the mythic quality of Morrison's passages in *Sula*. In these two short episodes, Morrison gives us, in camouflaged form, religious symbols of (1) black origins in the bottoms of slave ships and the bottoms of social well-being in America, and (2) memories and fears of black destinies in individual and collective graves. She is doing what Charles Long means by *religion*, which he defines as *orientation*: "orientation in the ultimate sense, that is how *one comes to terms* with the ultimate significance of one's place in the world" (Long, 7; italics mine). This emphasis on orientation points to both stories *of* beginnings and stories *at the* beginning of ceremonies and novels (orientation in time), as well as the places that serve as the *center* of a community's world (orientation in space).

Morrison orients the black universe in the first three and one-half pages by describing the Bottom as a geographical, social, and psychic spatial order that leaves its imprint on the actions and characters throughout the novel. She is thereby *orienting* the narrative in these pages to show us how the black people of the Bottom *come to terms* and *make the terms* to find significance, even ultimate significance, in their lives. And just as anthropologists have shown how folklore, music, lifestyle, dance, clothes, and forms of speech can be clues to religious dimensions of African American life, so Morrison shows us that dance ("a bit of cakewalk ... a bit of black bottom"), music ("mouth organ ... the man breathing music in and out of his harmonica"), and church (going to Greater Saint Matthew to "let the tenor's voice dress him in silk") are how black folks are coming to terms with living in the Bottom (4). But most of all, the terms for surviving in space and time appear in a creation story that takes the form of a "nigger joke" about the origin of the Bottom. "A joke. A nigger joke. That was the way *it got started*" (italics mine). The "it" that got started was a place, "the part of town where the Negroes lived, the part they called the Bottom in spite of the fact that it was up in the hills" (4). This kind of clever reversal where the top becomes the bottom and the bottom the top parallels the paradoxes of many creation stories; for instance, in the Judeo-Christian tradition, the paradise of the garden of Eden is where evil and pain and banishment *from a sacred place* make their first appearance; for the Aztecs, each new universe had the name of the force that would destroy it.

That this opening section of *Sula* can be compared to a creation story is evident in Morrison's repetition of the phrase "was all about." Creation stories set the order of the universe in motion and contain the kernel of what the new cosmos *is all about*. Morrison ends the preface by telling us that the black people would not have agreed with the white hunters who sometimes went up there and thought that maybe the Bottom was, after all, "the bottom of heaven," as the joke had claimed. The blacks didn't have the time to think about that, for their lives were filled with "wondering ... what Shadrack *was all about*, what that little girl Sula who grew into a woman in their town *was all about* and what they themselves *were all about*, tucked up there in the Bottom" (6; italics mine).

Sula is about so many things and at the same time circles *all about* those things; the characters and turning points in the story are the atmosphere and asymmetry of the Bottom as described and evoked in mythic tones in the opening pages. The mythological sacred space of the novel is also framed by the creation story of its beginnings and the circles of sorrow that close the work.

One circle of sorrow is closed on the final National Suicide Day, when many in the community, fed up with their years of pain and false promises, flood out into the streets, marching and dancing behind their pied piper, Shadrack, toward the other "bottom," the unfinished underground tunnel that leads to nowhere. At this crucial moment in the journey, Morrison again employs the word "promise," but in a different way than she did in *Song of Solomon*. Standing at the mouth of the tunnel excavation "in a fever pitch of excitement and joy ... it dazzled them. ... Their hooded eyes swept over the place where their hope had lain since 1927. There was the promise: leaf-dead. The teeth unrepaired, the coal credit cut off, the chest pains unattended ... the slurred remarks and the staggering childish malevolence of their employers"

(161; italics mine). Now in a release of rage and not promise, they begin to smash and "kill" the tunnel but soon get jammed too deeply inside when it collapses, and they "all died there" in the earthquake that had been waiting for them all this time, underground. A place of destruction.

As Mircea Eliade observes, "In the same way as a writer of fiction, the historian of religions is confronted with different structures of sacred and mythical space, different qualities of time, and more specifically by a considerable number of strange, unfamiliar and enigmatic worlds of meaning. Each literary piece creates its own proper universe, and the creation of such imaginary universes through literary means can be compared with mythical processes" ("Literary Imagination," 22). Just as Orozco's mural embraces the convulsion and turmoil of Mexican history, so Morrison frames the history of black people in the United States within mythological spaces of both belonging and becoming. The circles may be of sorrow, but they rise in the possibility of religious flight.

Works Cited

Eliade, Mircea. "Literary Imagination and Religious Structure." In *Waiting for the Dawn: Mircea Eliade in Perspective*, ed. Davíd Carrasco and Jane Marie Law, 17–24. Boulder: Westview Press, 1985.

———. *Myths, Dreams, and Mysteries: The Encounter between Contemporary Faiths and Archaic Realities*. Trans. Philip Mairet. New York: Harper, 1960.

Long, Charles H. *Significations: Signs, Symbols, and Images in the Study of Religion*. Philadelphia: Fortress, 1986.

Morrison, Toni. *The Nobel Lecture in Literature*. New York: Alfred A. Knopf, 1993.

———. *Song of Solomon*. New York: Vintage, 2004.

———. *Sula*. New York: Penguin Books, 1982.

PART IV

*"Now it seemed both fresh
and ancient, safe and demanding"*

PROPERTY AND AMERICAN IDENTITY IN TONI MORRISON'S *BELOVED*

LOVALERIE KING

> Even as thoughts and the ideas of things are arranged and associated in the mind, so are the modifications of body or the images of things precisely in the same way arranged and associated in the body.
> —Spinoza

Beloved (1987) is part of a collective intertext that provides African America's perspective on racialized discourse and practice in American history, particularly as it relates to race and the rights and privileges associated with citizenship. This essay is part of a larger project that explores the relationship between property ownership and American identity. Property includes "not only external objects and people's relationships to them, but also all of those rights, liberties, powers, and immunities that are important for human well-being, including freedom of expression, freedom of conscience, freedom from bodily harm, and free and equal opportunities to use personal faculties" (C. Harris, 279–80). The point is not that items or commodities are essential to self-identity; rather, the *right to claim ownership* of tangible and intangible property is an essential aspect of American identity and the full expression of liberty under the Constitution, as America's founders imagined it. Indeed, Thomas Jefferson included the Lockean phrase "pursuit of property" rather than "pursuit of happiness" in an early draft of the Declaration of Independence. The question of whether human beings could be considered property was answered in the affirmative by the framers of the Constitution. Morrison imagines a community of enslaved and formerly enslaved individuals whose experiences made them acutely aware of the difference between free people who owned property and enslaved people who were themselves property.

The conflict between property rights and human rights is intrinsic to the American experience and its history of racialized slavery. In colonial America, racial difference was used to reduce indentured blacks to the status of slaves; enslaved blacks were gradually reduced to the status of owned (subhuman) property with no rights and privileges protected by law.[1] The definition of "slave" included the condition of being black and unpropertied. Over time, "white" came to be associated with "free," and "black" with "slave":

> By the 1660s, the especially degraded status of Blacks as chattel slaves was recognized by law. Between 1680 and 1682, the first slave codes appeared, enshrining the extreme deprivations of liberty already existing in social practice. Many laws parceled out differential treatment based on racial categories; Blacks were not permitted to travel without permits, to own property, to assemble publicly, or to own weapons—nor were they to be educated.... The ideological and rhetorical move from "slave" and "free" to "black" and "white" as polar constructs marked an important step in the social construction of race. (C. Harris, 278)

The linking of property entitlement and other rights to whiteness made whiteness inherently valuable property in itself (277–79). Because enslaved blacks, defined legally as property, were forbidden to own property above certain basic items, the means to acquire property was necessarily defined as *outside the law*.

Legal scholars and historians have shown that under slavery, law and custom worked in tandem to advance the notion of white supremacy, to cultivate the relationship between whiteness and property, and to secure for property-owning white Americans all the rights, privileges, and protections of citizenship that were simultaneously denied to enslaved blacks.[2] Even as the legal system affirmed the connection between whiteness and property, it gradually curtailed the rights of both enslaved and free blacks to own property. Various states forbade blacks and other nonwhites to own certain kinds of livestock. Blacks accused of theft were subject to different and more severe punishments than white Americans accused of the same act. Blacks who were discovered owning property had to prove that they were legally entitled to said property. Resources generated by slave labor became the legal property of slaveholders who, with few exceptions, were white and male.

Laws set in place to facilitate the regime of American chattel slavery "propertized" human life. Under the law, an enslaved person could assert no claim to property of any sort, particularly her own body, a fact that the North Carolina Supreme Court makes explicit in *State v. Mann* (1829). The Mann case involved the shooting of Lydia, an enslaved woman who was fleeing after having been punished for some minor offense. When John Mann ordered her to stop and she continued to run, he shot her. The court noted that there was no available legal remedy for the enslaved person because it could not "allow the right of the master to be brought into discussion in the courts of justice. The slave, to remain a slave, must be made sensible that there is no appeal from his [or her] master; that his power is in no instance usurped; but is conferred by the laws of man at least, if not by the law of God" (Morris, 190). Further, the court noted that endowing the slaveholder with such unlimited dominion was "essential to the value of slaves as property, and to the security of the master, and the public tranquility" (quoted in Higginbotham, 9). The result, however, was not merely an erosion and denial of personal freedom; it was also a reaffirmation of white supremacy and the legal expropriation of certain natural rights.

In *Beloved*, Toni Morrison illustrates the profound implications of such a legal climate. Basing her central protagonist on the real-life Margaret Garner, who was tried for grand larceny, found guilty, and eventually died in slavery after a long illness,[3] Morrison revisits Garner's story and changes the outcome. Her protagonist is charged with murder rather than larceny; she subsequently serves a period of incarceration and then lives as a free person. *Beloved*, like the slave narrative tradition it invokes, explores the effects of slavery's many deprivations (legal or otherwise), and none so prominently as its interference with the capacity for healthy expressions of love and the development of love relationships. Such conditions breed desire, and Morrison's spiteful title character is the essence of insatiable desire, distilled from the extreme deprivations and abuses that emanate from slavery.

Legally circumscribed and prevented from acquiring property through legal means, black Americans recognized the inherent inequality of the situation and devised strategies for coping with and resisting such conditions. The historical record reveals that enslaved blacks felt entitled to what their labor produced and defined their acts as "taking" when the property in question was appropriated from white Americans.[4] As one woman put it: "Law, mam, don't say I's wicked; ole Aunt Ann says it allers right for us poor colored people to 'popriate whatever of the wite folk's blessings de Lord puts in our way" (quoted in Stampp, 127). Enslaved persons who were accused of stealing recognized that the law supporting that charge was meant to protect not their interests but those of the slaveholder. They defined their acts as "taking" when such acts involved the *legal* property of whites, with whom they associated the greater theft of kidnapping and the plunder of home, family, labor, identity, and history. In other words, the existence of early codes dealing with theft suggests not that blacks (and other nonwhites) were naturally inclined to steal but that theft (as that term is defined under the law of the dominant class) naturally thrives in an environment such as that created in America at the time.[5] The historian Eugene Genovese writes that slaveholders believed all blacks stole by nature, and they defined "'a thieving Negro' simply as one who stole much more than the average" (599). Indeed, Genovese noted that white Americans, more often than not, attributed theft and stealing to blackness rather than to the condition of servitude. The historian Kenneth Stampp concurs in part, noting:

> If slaveholders are to be believed petty theft was an almost universal "vice"; slaves would take anything that was not under lock and key. Field-hands killed hogs and robbed the corn crib. House servants helped themselves to wines, whiskey, jewelry, trinkets, and whatever else was lying about. Fugitives sometimes gained from their master unwilling help in financing the journey to freedom, the advertisements often indicating that they absconded with money, clothing, and a horse or mule. Thefts were not necessarily confined to the master's goods: any white man might be considered fair game. (125–27)

Well aware of the stereotype of the black thief in American culture, I set out to determine why so many African American authors explored the topic, which one finds in texts including Douglass's autobiographies of 1845 and 1855, Charles Chesnutt's novels, Paul Lawrence Dunbar's novels and poetry, Ellison's *Invisible Man*, most of James Baldwin's novels, as well as works by Octavia Butler, Kristin Hunter, Richard Wright, Charles Johnson, Alice Walker, Dorothy West, Ann Petry, and numerous others (including WPA narratives) that are featured in my larger project. Nevertheless the following dialogue from *Beloved* sparked my initial interest:

> "You stole that shoat, didn't you?"
> "No, sir," said Sixo, but he had the decency to keep his eyes on the meat.
> "You telling me you didn't steal it, and I'm looking right at you?"
> "No, sir. I didn't steal it."
> Schoolteacher smiled. "Did you kill it?"
> "Yes, sir. I killed it."
> "Did you butcher it?"

"Yes, sir."
"Did you cook it?"
"Yes, sir."
"Well, then. Did you eat it?"
"Yes, sir. I sure did."
"And you telling me that's not stealing?"
"No, sir. It ain't."
"What is it then?"
"Improving your property, sir."
"What?"
"Sixo plant rye to give the high piece a better chance. Sixo take and feed the soil, give you more crop. Sixo take and feed Sixo give you more work." (190)

Sixo is *enslaved* but not *a slave* and thus poses a direct threat to the institution and schoolteacher's regime. Indeed, if one begins with the legal definition of "slave," the various references to Sixo define him gradually in terms of how he does not fit that definition. Morrison constructs him via small backward glimpses leading up to Sethe's and Paul D's recollections of Sixo's confrontations with schoolteacher—the one involving the pilfered shoat, and the one in which Sixo is killed. The narrator first refers to "Sixo, the *wild* man," a few pages into the novel (11).[6] Next Paul D recalls that at Sweet Home he often sat with Sixo under a favorite tree that he called "Brother." Sixo was "gentle then and still speaking English." He had indigo skin and a flame-red tongue, and he "experimented with night-cooked potatoes," which he never got right because his timing was always off (21). Paul D recalls that Sixo walked seventeen hours each way to visit Patsy, who was, Sixo said, a friend of his mind: "She gather me, man. The pieces I am, she gather them and give them back to me in all the right order. It's good, you know, when you got a woman who is a friend of your mind" (272–73). Sixo's excursions violate a Sweet Home rule (before and after schoolteacher's presence there), and he is so fatigued after his trips that his fellow workers must cover for him the following day. During one of Sixo's excursions, he discovered a "deserted stone structure that Redmen used way back when they thought the land was theirs." Sixo asked the structure for permission to enter and to bring Patsy there. Feeling comfortable among trees, he danced alone among them at night to "keep his bloodlines open" (24–25). Sixo provided backup support for Sethe when her Sweet Home duties—which increased after schoolteacher came—mandated that she neglect her children. Sixo especially hated schoolteacher's questions; he was not amused when Sethe, Paul D, and the others laughed at schoolteacher's questions, thinking him a fool for measuring their heads. Paul D suspects that

Sixo did not need Garner to pronounce him a man, and he remembers that Sixo learned about the "train" (the Underground Railroad) because he was the only one of them who crept away at night. Thus the small community of blacks at Sweet Home depended on Sixo, along with Halle, to plan their escape, a necessary response to schoolteacher's harsh regime. The law would define their acts as grand theft of property. Toward the end of the novel, after he has survived physical slavery, Paul D looks at himself through Sixo's eyes and feels ashamed.

Thus Sixo stands apart from the other enslaved inhabitants of Sweet Home in that he refuses to speak the language of his oppressors and deliberately ignores certain rules that deny his humanity, including a refusal to submit to the limitations placed on his options for heterosexual expression. Sixo also adheres to certain behaviors, traditions, and customs that comport with his understanding of what is natural, organic, and appropriately human; he helps to plan the exodus from Sweet Home, resists capture when he understands that he will be killed for doing so, and laughs in the face of physical death. Upon witnessing Sixo's laughter and song in the face of death, the more "suitable" Paul D—as he sat locked in a three-spoke collar—thought that "he should have sung along" with Sixo, "loud, something loud and rolling to go with Sixo's tune, but the words put him off—he didn't understand the words" (226). The scenario in which Sixo faces death with laughter prefigures Sethe's signal act in the novel.

Morrison has explained that "in shaping the experience [slavery] to make it palatable to those who were in a position to alleviate it, they [ex-slave narrators] were silent about many things, and they forgot many other things" ("Site of Memory," 90–91). She adds, "On the basis of some information and a little bit of guesswork you journey to a *site* to see what remains were left behind and to reconstruct the world that these remains imply. What makes it fiction is the nature of the imaginative act; my reliance on the image—on the remains—in addition to recollection, to yield up a kind of truth" (92; italics mine). Using memory as the subsoil for her archaeological work, Morrison reveals a treasure trove of local knowledges that assist in various projects of resisting the self-denying effects of slavery and racism in *Beloved*. Significantly, we learn of the confrontation between schoolteacher and Sixo through Sethe's memory when she wants to justify pilfering after she is physically free from slavery. Sethe's attempt to remove her children from the grips of slavery and Sixo's taking of the shoat are related in that the enslaved individual acts in each case to resist the institution's constraining influences on her or his will toward subjectivity and freedom.

When schoolteacher encounters Sixo with forbidden loot, he naturally categorizes Sixo's act as petty theft, a property crime for which the law prescribed punishment of thirty-nine lashes. Sixo resists the easy reduction of his act of self-preservation and self-assertion to one of petty theft by explaining that he is actually improving the slaveholder's property, not reducing it. Rather than provide the response schoolteacher expects, Sixo serves up his own assessment of the situation and demonstrates a capacity for reasoning, as well as an awareness of arbitrary meaning, by reversing the objective of schoolteacher's formulaic discourse. Sixo points out that slavery is a closed economic system and that it is economically astute to maintain a healthy labor force. By providing nutrition for his body, Sixo positively enhances Sweet Home's chances for prosperity.

Sixo's reasoning parallels that of Frederick Douglass in *My Bondage and My Freedom* (1855), where Douglass asserts that taking meat that belonged to his owner did not deprive his owner of anything:

> Considering that my labor and person were the property of Master Thomas, and that I was by him deprived of the necessaries of life—necessaries obtained by my own labor—it was easy to deduce the right to supply myself with what was my own. It was simply appropriating what was my own to the use of my master, since the health and strength derived from such food were exerted in his service.... It was not always convenient to steal from master, and the same reason why I might, innocently, steal from him, did not seem to justify me in stealing from others. In the case of my master, it was only a question of *removal*—the taking his meat out of one tub, and putting it into another; the ownership of the meat was not affected by the transaction. (118–19)

Indeed, Douglass goes on to state, "The morality of a *free* society can have no application to *slave* society," or as the slave-owning founding father Thomas Jefferson would write of blacks:

> That disposition to theft with which they have been branded, must be ascribed to their situation, and not to any depravity of the moral sense. The man, in whose favour no laws of property exist, probably feels himself less bound to respect those made in favour of others. When arguing for ourselves, we lay it down as a fundamental, that laws, to be just, must give a reciprocation of right: that, without this, they are mere arbitrary rules of conduct, founded in force, and not in conscience: and it is a problem which I give to the master to solve, whether the religious precepts against the violation of property were not framed

for him as well as his slave? And whether the slave may not as justifiably take a little from one, who has taken all from him, as he may slay one who would slay him? That a change in the relations in which a man is placed should change his ideas of moral right and wrong, is neither new, nor peculiar to the colour of the Blacks. Homer tells us it was so 2,600 years ago. (11)

Douglass concludes, "Slaveholders have made it almost impossible for the slave to commit any crime, known either to the laws of God or to the laws of man. If he steals, he takes his own; if he kills his master, he imitates only the heroes of the revolution" (119). Douglass's assertions are clearly represented in the often-analyzed dialectic between Sixo and schoolteacher, in which Morrison deftly links the material implications of slave pilfering with the ethical questions surrounding it. At that time and place, schoolteacher beat Sixo anyway, exercising his right under the law. Nevertheless, Sethe recalls Sixo's reasoning, his resistance to schoolteacher's attempt to define him, and his assertion of subjectivity.

In constructing the confrontation between Sixo and schoolteacher, Morrison illuminates the contingent factors surrounding the event and reveals competing ethical codes at work in the dynamic interaction between slave and master—the stakes and stakeholders being so obviously different for each party. When Sethe recalls the exchange about the stolen shoat, she remembers that schoolteacher acted "like he was just going through the motions"; however, the exchange is structured like a religious catechism, the objective of which is to elicit specific prefigured responses, ultimately arriving at some overall, predetermined "truth" to be used in manipulating individual or group behavior. Ultimately the dialectic results in two versions of truth about the same event, revealing that the label "thief" is neither fixed nor absolute; rather, it is produced in discourse and contingent on the contexts that inform that discourse. Sethe's recollection of the event reveals the contingent circumstances that lead to Sixo's truth, an *unofficial* truth in the dominant sphere that emanates from the local knowledge acquired through experience, which in turn becomes local knowledge that Sethe can call into service later.

Sethe recalls that even before schoolteacher took over at Garner's "false" paradise, deprivation of certain basic rights and privileges had intensified desire and longing among the members of the enslaved black community. Deprived of young women with whom to form intimate connections and sexual relationships, the enslaved men at Sweet Home lived on fantasy and had sex with cows. When Sethe arrived, she became the focus of their sexual fantasies. Deprived of seven of her eight children, Baby Suggs experienced a perpetual longing for their presence and for knowledge about them during and after her time at Sweet Home. Baby Suggs had lived for a long time with the desire that replaced her snatched, stolen, and chased-away children: "What she called the nastiness of life was the shock she had received upon learning that nobody stopped playing checkers just because the pieces included her children. Halle she was able to keep the longest. Twenty years. A lifetime." Indeed, "Anybody Baby Suggs knew, let alone loved, who hadn't run off or been hanged, got rented out, loaned out, bought up, brought back, stored up, mortgaged, won, stolen or seized" (23).

After Sethe chose Halle to be her husband, she expressed the desire to mark her marriage as a special event, as a day that would mark the two of them as something more than chattel. She resolved to make a wedding dress "on the sly," pilfering bits of fabric and later realizing that Mrs. Garner knew of the thefts (59). Sethe's "stealing" and "pilfering" express a will toward subjectivity, which is also represented by her attempt to make some part of Mrs. Garner's kitchen her own, as if "a handful of myrtle stuck in the handle of a pressing iron propped against the door in a whitewoman's kitchen could make it hers" (23). Sethe recalls also that before schoolteacher took over at Sweet Home, Sixo, the Pauls, and Halle used rifles to hunt game, but schoolteacher took the guns away from the Sweet Home men, and deprived of game to round out their diet of bread, beans, hominy, vegetables, and a little extra at slaughter time, they began to pilfer in earnest, and it became not only their right but their obligation (190–91).

The act of deprivation that produced the strongest response from Sethe involved schoolteacher's nephews' forceful taking of her milk. Sethe's outrage at this particular violation streams through the text and culminates in the appearance of rampant desire in the form of Beloved, the outraged presence of the child whose killing can be tied directly to the existence of the harsh new Fugitive Slave Law that took effect in 1850.[7]

Although Denver never actually lived as a slave, her longing is part of the legacy of slavery, for the institution is directly or indirectly responsible for the absence of her father, sister, brothers, and grandmother. Denver longs for the father who will never show up; even his absence had not been hers alone: "Once the absence had belonged to Grandma Baby—a son deeply mourned because he was the one who had bought her out of there. Then it was her mother's absent husband. Now it was this hazelnut stranger's [Paul D's] absent friend. Only those who knew him ('knew him well') could claim his absence for themselves" (13). After Beloved arrived, Denver's desire poured out in a stream of claims: "my sister," "her blood," "my mother's milk," "my secret company," "my company," "my daddy," " my brothers," "her own," "my mother," "my sister," "my sister's ghost." She repeats the words "BELOVED is my sister" and ends her *claiming* section with "She's mine, Beloved. She's mine" (205, 209).

Paul D's and Sethe's thoughts reveal that (not unlike the "flying" Pilate in Morrison's *Song of Solomon*) Sixo had managed throughout his tenure at Sweet Home to resist both the definitions and the limitations of a constraining master narrative. The scenario in which Sixo faces death with laughter prefigures Sethe's choices: enslavement or transcendence through death. Sethe's rememory of the confrontation between Sixo and schoolteacher links that event to Sethe's attempt to kill herself and her children. Schoolteacher's appearance at 124 Bluestone Road propels Sethe into action. Her resolve to take control of her children's lives away from schoolteacher through death can be compared to her assertion that under the extreme conditions schoolteacher imposed, stealing became not only a right but an obligation.

She tells Paul D later that during her one month of freedom, though Halle was "missing," she had allowed herself to love her children "proper":

> It was a kind of selfishness I never knew nothing about before. It felt good. Good and right. I was big, Paul D, and deep and wide and when I stretched out my arms all my children could get in between. I was *that* wide. Look like I loved em more after I got here. Or maybe I couldn't love em proper in Kentucky *because they wasn't mine to love*. But when I got here, when I jumped down off that wagon—there wasn't nobody in the world I couldn't love if I wanted to. (162; italics mine)

Freedom had also allowed Sethe to go further, to claim (or reappropriate) a *self*: "Bit by bit, at 124 and in the Clearing, along with the others, she had claimed herself. Freeing yourself was one thing; claiming ownership of that freed self was another" (95).

In representing Sethe's most profound act of resistance, Morrison makes subtle use of the myth of the flying Africans: newly enslaved Africans who, upon arriving at Ibo Landing in South Carolina and sensing the nature of things, turn and fly (or walk) back to Africa. Blacks who jumped over the sides of slave ships are said to have taken flight. Flight signals spiritual rebirth in freedom, so the question of whether those who take flight to escape oppression survive in a physical sense is less important than the fact that they are no longer oppressed.[8] In rendering Stamp Paid's and Sethe's thoughts about Sethe's actions, Morrison writes: "So Stamp Paid did not tell him how she flew, snatching up her children like a hawk on the wing; how her face beaked, how her hands worked like claws" (157). Sethe recalls, "She just flew. Collected every bit of life she had made, all the parts of her that were precious and fine and beautiful, and carried, pushed, dragged them through the veil, out, away, over there where no one could hurt them. Over there. Outside this place, where they would be safe" (163).

Sethe's attempt to end their lives as slaves is deliberate (156, 63).[9] Considering Sethe's investment in her role as mother, she might easily be compared to Paul D's "witless" duck collector. Her act was an extreme manifestation of her desire to claim her children as her own and to exercise control over their lives. In Morrison's hands, the killing of the child becomes the more important consideration, rather than the fact that schoolteacher claimed the child as his property. Sethe was tried, found guilty, served time, and was set free.[10] Schoolteacher filed a claim for reimbursement of his property and left town.

Sethe's rememory of the Sixo/schoolteacher incident at a moment when she is about to pilfer from her employer strongly links her to Sixo and his acts of resistance. The killing of someone like Sixo is all but inevitable in that context, but his presence in the collective memories of slavery's survivors ensures that his spirit of resistance will endure and will, perhaps, be incarnate in his offspring, Seven-O, and as long as there are numbers in the number line.[11] Sethe's ultimate act of resistance, however, is characterized by the community's outrage, the whole situation becoming a major dilemma for Baby Suggs, who can neither condone nor condemn Sethe's actions. The weight of the dilemma eventually *deprives* her of the will to live. From that point on, Baby Suggs (like Paul D) keeps her own desire to a minimum.

The two acts, Sethe's taking of her child's life and Sixo's theft of the shoat, are connected to self-assertion and the will toward freedom; their acts challenge the slaveholder's legal authority over their physical selves while also refusing his definition of them as subhuman and property. Thus Morrison's work acknowledges the larger philosophical and psychological considerations of being that the acquisition of material property cannot resolve; however, she refuses to dismiss the importance of attention to corporeal matters and the significance of the relationship between property ownership and American identity.

Notes

1. Such status changes applied to other groups in America.
2. For a discussion of how citizenship rights for free blacks declined over time during the colonial era, see Malone, *Between Freedom and Bondage*.

3. See Weisenburger.

4. See Aptheker; Franklin; Higginbotham; and Stampp.

5. See Higginbotham and Morris. Genovese observes that throughout history, wherever slavery existed, enslaved persons have argued that, being property, they cannot steal from their owner (603). For me, this is the same as saying that wherever slavery has existed, the problem of theft has existed.

6. "Wild" is an often-used characterization in Morrison's fiction. It is usually associated with a character who resists being subsumed under the normalizing tendencies of various societal institutions.

7. The text of the 1850 act is available at a number of Web sites, including http://www.yale.edu/lawweb/avalon/fugitive.htm.

8. See, e.g., Julius Lester's "People Who Could Fly," in *Black Folktales* (New York: Richard W. Baron, 1969). For an excellent representation of the myth in film, see Haile Gerima's *Sankofa* (1993). The most obvious use of the myth of the flying Africans in Morrison's work is as a structuring device in the novel *Song of Solomon* (1977).

9. In his book-length work on Margaret Garner and the trial surrounding her escape attempt, Steven Weisenburger notes that a fictional treatment of Garner's life by the lawyer John Jolliffe also represents the act of infanticide as deliberate. Interestingly, the child in Jolliffe's novel, *Chattanooga* (1858), comes back as a ghost to haunt a white reverend who assisted in the pursuit and capture of Margaret. Hattia M'Keehan had previously used the fictionalized ghost story centered on Margaret Garner's experience in her novel *Liberty or Death!; or, Heaven's Infraction of the Fugitive Slave Law* (1856), reprinted in 1862 as *Liberty or Death!; or, The Mother's Sacrifice* under the author's married name, Mrs. J. P. Hardwick. As Weisenburger notes, both Jolliffe and M'Keehan/Hardwick found it necessary to "lessen" the presence of Margaret Garner's husband, Robert, who was present throughout her ordeal (271–75).

10. See, e.g., Higginbotham and Morris. According to Stampp, "Every state provided stiff penalties for the theft of a slave" (198); under the law, Sethe had stolen not only herself but also her three children and the child she was carrying. Margaret Garner was tried for the theft of the slaveholder's property. Joseph Cox, the county prosecutor, felt that the jury would never deliver a guilty verdict on a charge of first-degree murder. Her attorney, John Jolliffe, felt that even if she were convicted and temporarily imprisoned on a murder charge (as Sethe is in *Beloved*), it would be a preferable outcome to her being sent to the deep South. Garner died of typhoid fever after a substantial period of suffering. See Weisenburger, 117.

11. See Trudier Harris, 178–79, for a discussion of the folkloric dimensions of the Sixo character.

Works Cited

Aptheker, Herbert. *American Negro Slave Revolts*. New York: Columbia University Press, 1943.

De Spinoza, Benedict. "On the Power of Understanding, or of Human Freedom." Proposition 1, pt. v in *Ethics*. 1677. http://www.mtsu.edu/~rbombard/RB/Spinoza/ethica5.html.

Douglass, Frederick. *My Bondage and My Freedom*. 1855. Urbana and Chicago: University of Illinois Press, 1987.

Franklin, John Hope. *From Slavery to Freedom*. New York: Knopf, 1956.

Genovese, Eugene. *Roll Jordan Roll: The World the Slaves Made*. New York: Random House, 1976.

Harris, Cheryl. "Whiteness as Property." In *Critical Race Theory: The Key Writings That Formed the Movement*, ed. Kimberlé Crenshaw, Neil Gotanda, Gary Peller, and Kendall Thomas, 276–91. New York: New Press, 1995.

Harris, Trudier. *Fiction and Folklore: The Novels of Toni Morrison*. Knoxville: University of Tennessee Press, 1991.

Higginbotham, A. Leon. *In the Matter of Color: Race and the American Legal Process; The Colonial Period*. New York: Oxford University Press, 1978.

Jefferson, Thomas. "The Administration of Justice and the Description of the Laws." Query XIV in *Notes on the State of Virginia*. 1785. New York: Harper and Row, 1964.

Malone, Christopher. *Between Freedom and Bondage: Race, Party, and Voting Rights in the Antebellum North*. New York: Routledge, 2007.

Morrison, Toni. *Beloved*. New York: Knopf, 1987.

———. "The Site of Memory." In *Inventing the Truth: The Art and Craft of Memoir*, ed. William Zinnser, 85–102. Boston: Houghton Mifflin, 1995.

Stampp, Kenneth. *The Peculiar Institution: Slavery in the Ante-bellum South*. New York: Knopf, 1956

Weisenburger, Steven. *Modern Medea: A Family Story of Slavery and Child-Murder from the Old South*. New York: Hill and Wang, 1998.

AESCHYLUS, EURIPIDES, AND TONI MORRISON

Miasma, *Revenge, and Atonement*

TESSA ROYNON

In its determined confrontations with the past, Toni Morrison's oeuvre repeatedly portrays an America characterized by both black and white recourse to vengeance. At the same time, it represents the process of revenge as a flawed means to moral purification. My specific purpose here is to demonstrate and analyze the ways in which Aeschylus's *Oresteia* and Euripides' *Bacchae* inform Morrison's exploration of the themes of vengeance and atonement. The close readings from *Song of Solomon*, the trilogy (*Beloved*, *Jazz*, and *Paradise*) and *Love* that follow also consider Richard Schechner's controversial *Dionysus in 69* (1970) and Wole Soyinka's *The Bacchae of Euripides* (1973). The need for a new relationship between Nietzsche's Apolline and Dionysiac forces (a predicament that recalls the *Bacchae*) and the need for practicable alternatives to violent revenge (a predicament that recalls the *Oresteia*) drive nearly every plot. Morrison's often-ambivalent and revisionary engagement with Aeschylus and Euripides, and in particular with the ancient Greek concept of *miasma*, or "pollution," gives rise to a devastating critique of American justice as it is pursued in the courts and in domestic and foreign policy.

Throughout her work, Morrison explores the conception of crime as a pollutant that also structures the Aeschylean representation of Clytemnestra's killing of her husband and Orestes' reciprocal killing of his mother. The

Oresteia is useful to Morrison's project in part because in the Greek trilogy (as in her work) personal and political kinds of violence are always and already inextricably intertwined. While Sethe's murder of Beloved must be the ultimate act in which personal and political motivations are inseparable, Morrison also implies that the community's oppressed condition in *Sula* explains their alienation of the eponymous character, or that the disappointing realities of life for blacks in 1920s Harlem are a factor in Joe's affair with and subsequent murder of Dorcas in *Jazz*. This commonality between the Greek plays and the African American novels is counterbalanced by Morrison's widespread critique of the American legal system as black people experience it, to which skepticism about Athena's acquittal of Orestes, and about Aeschylus's celebration of the establishment of the Areopagus, is integral. The novels show that the American implementation of justice has more in common with the irate recourse to force epitomized by Pentheus in the *Bacchae* than with the ideal of rational law that the *Eumenides* endorses and to which the United States aspires in its rhetoric.

In the *Agamemnon*, the murderous Clytemnestra claims that "the savage ancient spirit of revenge" has acted through her, and Aegisthus declares over Agamemnon's body that it is a "brilliant day" for "vengeance" (*Ag*. trans. Fagles lines 1530, 1605–6). That the pair kill the "black, impure, unholy" Agamemnon in the bath emphasizes the purifying element of the act, but that "the bath swirls red" indicates the new pollution that they have incurred (*Ag*. trans. Fagles lines 218, 1131). In the *Libation Bearers*, while the Chorus optimistically equates justice and vengeance, Orestes is immediately aware that his "victory" in killing his mother is "soiled" (*L.B.* trans. Lattimore line 1017). And in the *Eumenides* Athena intervenes in the infinite cycle in which "each charge meets counter-charge" (*Ag*. trans. Fagles line 1588). She establishes in her law court the "first trial of bloodshed" (*Ag*. trans. Fagles line 695), reassigns the Furies to a new role as guardian spirits of Athens, and redefines the concept of justice. In his celebration of the democratic advances of fifth-century BCE Athens, Aeschylus is to some extent prophetic, in that, as the classical scholar Robert Parker writes in his study *Miasma* (1983), the cultural preoccupation with "murder-pollution" did indeed recede as the new legal system took hold (126–28). By the fourth century BCE, Parker writes, "murder-pollution had outlived its utility," and "the function of 'purification' . . . had been taken over by legal process" (128, 322).

It is not hard to understand the appeal of the *Oresteia* to Enlightenment-bred America, a nation in which the Greek facade of the Supreme Court connotes the ideal of the "equal justice under law" that is engraved on its architrave. Both Fagles's and Lattimore's translations of the Pythia's opening speech in the final play bring dominant American ideology to mind. Fagles describes the Athenians who led Apollo to Parnassus as "the highway-builders, sons of the god of fire who tamed / the savage country, civilized the wilds" (*Eum.* lines 13–14), while Lattimore calls them "the builders of roads," who "changed / the wilderness to a land that was no wilderness" (*Eum.* lines 13–14). The commentaries by these American classical scholars likewise reveal their sense of an analogy between the Athens portrayed in the *Eumenides* and their homeland. Lattimore observes that the myth's resolution "merges into the history of civilization at Athens, which represents in fact the world's progress" (Introduction, 2), while Fagles and Stanford write of "an Athens radiant with civic faith and justice" (14), and of the trilogy as "our rite of passage from savagery to civilization" ("Reading," 16, 20). Fagles and Stanford even conflate lines of the *Agamemnon* with Julia W. Howe's "Battle Hymn of the Republic" (*Ag.* trans. Fagles lines 971–72; see their footnote on 35). It is presumably these scholars' "civic faith" in their own nation's political and judicial systems that enables their unambivalent celebration of the *Eumenides*.

In his *Violence and the Sacred* (1972), René Girard's analysis of the effects of the legal process accords strikingly with Parker's analysis of the demise of "murder-pollution" in Athens. "Our judicial system rationalizes revenge," Girard writes. "The system treats the disease without fear of contagion and provides a highly effective technique for the cure and . . . the prevention of violence" (22). If an effective legal system eliminates the pollution of crime and the imperative for private revenge, then the inverse is also true: a persisting conception of crime as a pollutant that provokes direct vengeance suggests that a legal system is ineffective. Thus the recurrent representation in Morrison's novels of crime as a miasmatic force that propels individuals to seek violent revenge can be read as an exposure of African American alienation from American justice.

In *Song of Solomon*, Guitar speaks the language of Aeschylus's Clytemnestra in his articulation of white violence as a contamination that (in the absence of a meaningful legal process) can only be purged by revenge. But Morrison also deploys the terms of *miasma* and a skeptical allusiveness to the *Oresteia* to protest the injustices to which white America has subjected blacks in the trilogy, though the central crimes and pursuits of revenge in these novels are intraracial rather than interracial. Given the recurrence of murder in Morrison's plots, the fact that representation of judicial proceedings is virtually nonexistent in her novels is striking. Absenting the law courts is one means by which she discredits them. At the same time, she shows that despite the enlightened aspirations it professes in the guise of "law" or in the name of "democracy," the dominant culture wreaks a vengeance that is as irrational as Pentheus's attempt to deploy force against Dionysus and as primitive as the *Agamemnon*'s "ancient spirit of revenge" (*Ag.* trans. Fagles line 1530). The hypocrisy of the moralistic and the disordered violence on which the maintenance of "law and order" depends are recurring themes in the Morrison's work, and her allusions to Aeschylus and Euripides in *Paradise* in particular expose the corrupt and corrupting practices of a nation that claims to act in a purifying capacity both at home and abroad. But all these novels—*Song of Solomon*, the trilogy, and *Love*—ultimately articulate alternative means to atonement, ones that eschew both the legal system from which African Americans have historically been alienated and the infinite violence of revenge.

"He who has wrought shall pay," declares the Chorus of the *Agamemnon*, "that is law" (trans. Lattimore line 1563). In *Love*, the character L gives a different perspective: "The problem for those left alive is what to do about revenge—how to escape the sweetness of its rot" (139). In the aftermath of Emmett Till's murder, Guitar rages that "there ain't no law for no colored man except the one that sends him to the chair" (*Song of Solomon*, 82). He is impassioned and articulate about black people's legal disenfranchisement: "The only thing left to do" about white-perpetrated violence is to "balance it" (154), and "if there were anything like or near justice when a cracker kills a Negro, there wouldn't have to be no Seven Days" (160). Morrison here initiates the analysis of the relationship between justice and retribution in the civil rights movement that she continues in *Paradise* and *Love*.

The critic Leslie Harris indicates the affinity between Guitar's vengeful outlook and the "unenlightened" Greek worldview when she describes the Seven Days as a "Fury-like society" (72). But scholarship has not discussed the extent to which the character's idiom recalls the archaic conception of murder as a pollution necessitating revenge that the *Oresteia* expounds. The activist men of the Blood Bank deploy "blood"—the visible pollutant in murder—to express their rationale and purpose (81, 158). Here Morrison has transposed to interracial American conflict the intrafamilial violence of the House of Atreus, of which the Chorus in the *Libation Bearers* observes, "Through too much glut of blood drunk by our fostering ground / the vengeful gore is caked and hard," and asks, "What can wash off the blood once spilled on the ground?" (*L.B.* trans. Lattimore lines 66–67, 47).

At the same time, Guitar's conviction that his guerrilla group's reciprocal attacks on whites are justified by the need to "keep things on an even keel" and to maintain "numbers. Balance. Ratio" recalls the insistent choric imagery of the *Agamemnon* (*Song of Solomon*, 154, 156). In that play, the old men of Argos claim that "justice turns the balance scales" and "no pain can tip the scales" (*Ag.* trans. Fagles lines 250, 567). Both Morrison and Aeschylus undermine this "primitive" view that vengeance straightforwardly equates to justice. Paradoxically, Guitar also speaks the language of the Enlightenment in his ambition to "help keep the numbers the same," matching his sentence structures to the society's principle of "balance" (153–55). Guitar points out that the dominant culture deploys scientific rationalism to legitimate the irrationality of racist violence (157), yet he shares his enemy's "depravity," justifying the Seven Days' actions on the grounds that white people have a biologically determined "disease" (157). Through Guitar's outlook, Morrison demonstrates the actual primitivism of Enlightened racial politics and also the futility of imitative revenge.

Song of Solomon does configure one atonement, however, that does not involve reciprocal violence. The author makes conventional use of the imagery of *miasma* in describing the Butler Place as Milkman finds it: "The house looked as if it had been eaten by a galloping disease, the sores of which were dark and fluid" (19). The simile unambiguously conveys the corruption of the Butler family and is the logical correlative to the familiar injustices meted out to the black population that the Reverend Cooper describes (231–32). Cooper tells Milkman, however, that as far as vengeance against the Butlers is concerned, "any evening up left to do, Circe took care of" (233). Circe's mode of revenge turns out to be passive but entirely effective. She boasts to Milkman that she will "never clean [the house] again. Never. Nothing. Not a speck of dust, not a grain of dirt, will I move" (247). In Circe's neglect of the Butler Place, Morrison may be recalling the Choric description of filthy halls in the *Agamemnon* (see *Ag.* trans. Fagles lines 761–65). The housekeeper strategically literalizes the defilement that the Butlers' crimes have incurred, without incurring further pollution on herself.

"What to do about revenge" is, of course, a dilemma that unifies *Beloved*, *Jazz*, and *Paradise*, and by the end of the trilogy, it is to some extent resolved. Allusion to the Aeschylean Furies is a principal means by which Morrison establishes a dialectic between her own trilogy and the *Oresteia*. Several critics have noted the author's obvious engagement with the Greek trilogy in *Beloved*'s description of 124 Bluestone Road as "palsied by the baby's fury" (5). But there is much more to be said about the connection between the avenging Beloved, Alice Manfred's "trembling fury" at Dorcas's murder in *Jazz* (76), and Billie Delia's fantasy that the dead Convent women will "return" as Furies in *Paradise* (308). What is important is not the fact of Morrison's allusiveness to Aeschylus but rather the ambivalent nature of that allusion and the radicalism that the ambivalence enables.

A second means by which Morrison both unifies her trilogy and maintains a dialogue with the *Oresteia* is the emphasis she places on the staining blood of the novels' murdered characters. As a manifestation of the contamination of both victims and perpetrators, this recalls the Furies' obsession with blood in the *Eumenides*, for example, in their description of Clytemnestra's death (see *Eum.* trans. Lattimore lines 261–66). But while Morrison shares Aeschylus's condemnation of vengeance and cyclical violence, she eschews recourse in the *Eumenides* to the legal process as a resolution of the impasse. Her deployment of the paradigm of murder pollution is itself a refutation of the American judicial system, and each of the three novels seeks an alternative to violent revenge that is also an alternative to a court case. As each novel comprises both murder and its resolution or purification, each can be seen as a revised *Oresteia* in itself—*Beloved* is even in three parts—as well as combining to form an allusive trilogy.

Given Morrison's interest in the facts of Margaret Garner's trial, which was for "stolen property" rather than for murder (Moyers, 272), the absence of detail about Sethe's trial in *Beloved* is striking. In the opera *Margaret Garner* (2005), Morrison as librettist devotes an entire scene of the second act to Garner's trial. But in *Beloved*, although Sethe rehearses a few memories about her time in jail, she never mentions appearing in court (182–84). She does not care whether she is guilty or not guilty in the eyes of the law, but is concerned (in Vernant's words on purifying the impurity of murder in ancient Greece) "to appease the rancor of the deceased" (125). She realizes that "rutting" with the stone engraver to pay for Beloved's gravestone has not appeased her dead daughter's "rage" (5).

The blood that "pump[s] down" Sethe's dress and is ingested by Denver at the time of the murder, however, is not the only evidence of the miasmatic nature of the crime (149–50). Denver, whose "tears" that she "dripped into the stovefire" (*Beloved*, 17, 54, 67) recall the "hearth soaked in sorrow" that the Chorus of *Libation Bearers* laments (trans. Lattimore line 49), is at pains to hide the fact that her returned sister is a polluted and polluting presence. Robert Parker writes that the Greek Erinyes (or Furies) are "animate agents of pollution who embody the anger of one slain by a kinsman" (107). Beloved embodies her own anger: when the community gathers to exorcize her, they notice "the stench, the heat, the moisture" to which her haunting gives rise (258).

The closing vision of *Beloved* largely rejects the revenge paradigm, and both Sethe and the ghost are purified through ritual that is implicitly Christian. The novel's rejection of vengeance is symbolized by a positive redeployment of the "net" and "web" imagery that punctuates the *Agamemnon*. While in the Greek tragedy these recurring net/web motifs symbolize the inescapable and perpetual nature of reciprocal violence, in the novel they are powerful means to healing. Denver creates a "net" of stories with which to "hold

Beloved" (76), while Amy dresses Sethe's back with "spiderwebs" (80). Yet in the novel's unsettling epilogue, a faint ambivalence about the desire for revenge persists. We are told that Beloved's "footprints come and go, come and go." Our feet "will fit" if we step into them, but "take them out and they disappear again as though nobody ever walked there" (275). Here Morrison creates a conflicted, tentative reconfiguration of the famous "recognition" between Orestes and Electra in the *Libation Bearers*, to which the fact that Electra's foot fits into Orestes' print is pivotal (see *L.B.* trans. Lattimore lines 205–10). In that play, the reunited siblings go on to plot the deaths of Clytemnestra and Aegisthus. The Christian vision of *Beloved*'s ending rejects such vengefulness, but the novel's epilogue nonetheless acknowledges the pain of the wronged who can never be avenged.

In the *Agamemnon*, Calchas describes the polluting presence of the dead but unappeased Iphigenia: "For the terror returns like sickness to lurk in the house / the secret anger remembers the child that shall be avenged" (*Ag.* trans. Lattimore lines 154–55). This *miasma* resonates clearly in *Jazz*, where, in the Trace home three months after the death of Dorcas, "the girl's memory is a sickness in the house" (28). In her representations of the sheer contaminating bloodiness of that character's dying, Morrison once again configures crime as a pollutant to highlight and protest the absence of a meaningful criminal justice system.

While the memory of Dorcas haunts Joe, Alice Manfred is possessed by a "trembling fury" toward him (76). Alice and her relatives have suffered much at the hands of white people as well as black (57); these details and the account of Violet's dispossession continue the focus on the contribution of white violence to black violence that *Song of Solomon* and *Beloved* initiate. As in the earlier novels, personal and political crime and vengeance are inextricable from each other, and the polluting crimes of whites against blacks highlight the moral ambiguities inherent in black-on-black revenge. Yet this novel as well as the earlier two also contain powerful processes of atonement that eschew violent vengeance. One example is the Fifth Avenue march protesting the 1917 riots: Morrison configures this as a kind of cathartic purification ritual, in that afterward Alice Manfred realizes that "the hurt hurt her but the fear was gone at last" (54). A second example is the main plot's unexpectedly peaceful resolution, in which Joe and Violet find a kind of absolution through their confessions to Felice.

Morrison's refutation of vengeance and her insistence on alternative means to atonement are most fully expressed in *Paradise*. Through the Rubean Fathers' attack on the Convent women, the author exposes the justification of violence on the grounds of exacting revenge or upholding moral righteousness.

As she does so, she implies an affinity between the town's ruling class and Euripides' voyeuristic, irrationally rational Pentheus; her engagement with the *Bacchae* illuminates the hypocritical irrationality of the state's handling of home-based racial conflict and of the war in Vietnam during the 1960s and 1970s. By first associating the Convent women with, and finally disassociating them from, both the Euripidean Bacchantes and Aeschylean Furies, Morrison shows that moral purity has nothing to do with violent revenge.

Of ancient Greece, Parker writes that "because pollution and guilt can be closely associated, the imagery of pollution may be used to express moral revulsion" (312). This is exactly the discourse the men of Ruby use against the Convent women, who complain of their soon-to-be victims "drawing folks out there like flies to shit" and that "the mess is seeping back into *our* homes" (276). In language that recalls the Pentheus of Soyinka's *Bacchae of Euripides*, who laments "the filth, the rot and creeping / Poison in the body of the state" (27), the men claim that the Convent is "diseased" and that it "rots" the town (8, 5). Morrison's representation of the men's scapegoating and vengefulness engages the similar tendencies of the nation itself during both the 1990s, when the novel was written, and the 1960s and 1970s, when it is predominantly set.

In the introduction to C. K. Williams's translation of the *Bacchae*, Martha Nussbaum notes that in Schechner's "famous and controversial" *Dionysus in 69*, "the play became linked with both the 'sexual revolution' and the opposition to the Vietnam War" (xxv). Morrison, who moved to New York City in the momentous year that Schechner's interpretation opened there—1968—may well have been conversant with the production and with its identification between Bacchic ecstasy and what Schechner calls "the carnival spirit of black insurrectionists," as well as with the sexual liberation and antiwar movements ("Politics," 217). In "Unspeakable Things Unspoken," Morrison describes 1969, the year in which she began *Sula*, "as a year of extraordinary political activity" (24). It is interesting to consider her juxtaposition of the citizens of Ruby with the Convent women in light of the contrast Schechner draws between the men of Thebes and Dionysus in his essay "In Warm Blood: The Bacchae." In two columns, he sets these against each other (see "Warm Blood," 95). The commonalities between Schechner's men of Thebes and Morrison's men of Ruby are striking.

Both the Vietnam War and the violent response to black agitation in the 1960s form an insistent backdrop to the main plot of *Paradise*. The state's use of excessive force against a perceived threat in Asia and against the rioters in Watts, Detroit, and Newark resonate in the Rubean Fathers' massacre of the Convent women. Pentheus, who is condemned by Dodds for his "willingness to believe the worst on hearsay evidence" and his "brutality towards the helpless" (xliii), and is described by Nussbaum as "rigid and militaristic" (xxv), resonates in all three conflicts; different versions of the *Bacchae* have given varying emphases to Pentheus's embodiment of what Schechner calls the "repressive machinery civilization constructs to keep itself intact" ("Politics," 217). Morrison in turn shows the irrational rationality of the men who "take aim ... for Ruby" (18), and of those responsible for the "body bags" from Vietnam, the "tear gas" in the cities, and the assassinations of King and Robert Kennedy that so traumatize Gigi (68, 64).

The etymology of "Ruby" from the Latin *rubeo* ("I redden" or "I blush") exactly illuminates the relationship between the citizens' moralistic shame and their descent into hot-blooded Dionysiac bloodshed. Lone DuPres realizes she has misunderstood the significance of Apollo's new handgun; in that short phrase, Morrison encapsulates the violent disorder of the dominant culture (273). When the men invade the Convent, their worst suspicions about the women are confirmed by the discovery of Christian iconography "trimmed in grapevines" (4). But the author constructs only a selective affinity between the Convent dwellers and followers of Dionysus. The "dancing in hot sweet rain" that follows their shared confrontation with their trauma has affinities with ecstatic Bacchic ritual (283): it is a process that is truly cathartic. Furthermore, the women's liberating effect on the young people of Ruby during K.D. and Arnette's wedding recalls the fact that in the *Bacchae* it is the Asian Bacchantes who draw out the Theban women. But while the newly converted Rubean youth are bloodthirsty in a way that recalls the intoxicated Agave, Morrison does not imbue the Convent women with either the desire for or the reveling in revenge that is so repellent, as Nussbaum points out, in the Asian Bacchic chorus (xii).

In the attitudes of Ruby's rebellious young people, Morrison echoes Schechner's interest in the potential destructiveness of anarchic counterculture. "Total, public, communal, sensual freedom is civilization's death throe," Schechner writes in "In Warm Blood" (107). In *Paradise*, Gigi's realization about her demonstrating days that "the point" of "the fray" was "lost to entertainment and adventure" effects a similar cautionary evaluation of the 1960s protest culture (257), and Morrison develops this theme through Christine's negative experience of civil rights activism in *Love*. Schechner goes further in "The Politics of Ecstasy," where he argues that "an unrepressive society" can "come perilously close to ecstatic fascism" (228); at the end of *Dionysus in 69*, the god himself has become obsessed with power in a manner that recalls Pentheus, ordering his "fellow Americans" to "grab a thyrsus" and "Napalm the decay." Similarly, the young people of Ruby who interpret "Be the Furrow" as a command to act, in the battle for civil rights, as God's "instrument, His justice...His retribution" (87) are as blindly thirsty for revenge as are both the Fathers against whom they rebel and the Euripidean Asian Bacchantes. Yet the massacred Convent women, unlike the assaulted Dionysus and his followers, have no interest in revenge on their attackers, and in this divergence Morrison revises both Euripides and Aeschylus.

Toward the novel's end, Billie Delia imagines the murdered women returning, Fury-like, to avenge themselves on the people of Ruby (see *Paradise*, 308; Jessee, 10). But the final pages of *Paradise* discredit such urges for reciprocal violence. Billie's fantasy is dispelled by the description of each resurrected woman absolutely at peace, getting on with her future, refusing even to dignify revenge by contemplating it. In the final play of Aeschylus's trilogy, the Furies become the "Kindly Ones," the guardian spirits of Athens. But the Convent women never give Ruby another thought. And like every other Morrison novel, the work departs from the *Eumenides* in that the legal system is once again dismissed as an irrelevance: the men of Ruby are relieved that the absence of bodies results in the continued absence of "white law" from their town (298). The emphasis on forgiveness and redemption (though Deacon's conversion, for example) at the end of *Paradise* posits these doctrines as an alternative to either vengeance or the legal process. It also anticipates the concerns of *Love*.

Morrison's dialectic with the *Eumenides* continues in *Love* in the conflict between Romen and Theo. In the characters' experience of shame provoked by the gang rape of Pretty-Fay, the basketball court functions both literally and metaphorically. Romen's school friends humiliate him during the game following his rescue of the girl: "They just tripped him and walked off the court" (48). Later, in his shame, Romen hears the "trumpet" (marking an on-court foul) "sputtering in his head" (49). This can be read as an ironic revision of the "stabbing voice of the Etruscan trumpet" that accompanies Athena's opening of the court in the *Eumenides* (*Eum*. trans. Lattimore lines 567–69). And L observes the guilty Theo in his father's café, "*dribbling air balls in his dream court behind the register*" (67). "Not a bad way to work off shame," she remarks (67). Instead of atoning for their guilt through the judicial process that Athena establishes, it is through basketball that Romen is confronted with his ignominy and though which Theo tries to purify himself of shame. The author expresses her habitual cynicism about the American legal system by substituting one "court" for another.

The notion of revenge as a contaminating rather than a purifying process also finds expression in *Love* through a series of briefly illuminated identifications between the central women characters and key female figures in Greek mythology. But only L, obviously a version of Venus, is an effective Athena, as well: when Heed and Christine fight at Cosey's funeral, "L restored order, just as she always had" (34). *Love* creates new syntheses between love and wisdom and between the irrational and the rational. This new equation epitomizes the redemptive potential inherent in the transformed Christianity and transformed classicism that Morrison's novels visualize as an alternative to vengeance through either violence or the legal process. As *A Mercy* makes explicit, the oeuvre challenges Puritanism, with its vengeful God and its repressiveness that becomes perverse. It also rejects the opposition of the Apolline and the Dionysiac and thereby rejects the identification of enlightened America with Apollo. The novels embrace the impure as the pure—an impulse exemplified by the fact that (through its name sounding as "Celestial Pallas") Heed and Christine's treasured "Celestial Palace" reconciles the prostitute Celestial with the classical Pallas Athena of order and of wisdom (*Love*, 188).

Morrison's commitment to synthesis over binary opposition explains why her project at once depends on and reconfigures the *Oresteia* and the *Bacchae*. In *Tar Baby*, when Jade tries to persuade Son to go to law school, she gives him some weighty advice. "There is nothing any of us can do about the past," she says, "but make our own lives better.... That is the only revenge" (274). Does Morrison concur with this view? Perhaps she does. And yet Son, as we know, refuses to apply to law school; he runs off to find the galloping horsemen instead. Lickety-split. Lickety-split. Lickety-lickety-lickety-split. What would the Greeks have had to say about that?

Works Cited

Aeschylus. *Agamemnon*. Trans. Richmond Lattimore. Ed. David Grene and Richmond Lattimore. 2nd ed. Chicago: University of Chicago Press, 1991.

———. *The Eumenides*. Trans. Richmond Lattimore. Ed. David Grene and Richmond Lattimore. 2nd ed. Chicago: University of Chicago Press, 1991.

———. *The Libation Bearers*. Trans. Richmond Lattimore. Ed. David Grene and Richmond Lattimore. Chicago: University of Chicago Press, 1960.

———. *The Oresteia: Agamemnon, The Libation Bearers, The Eumenides*. Trans. Robert Fagles. 1975. New York: Penguin, 1979.

Dodds, E. R. Introduction to *The Bacchae*, by Euripides. Trans. E. R. Dodds. 2nd ed. 1944. Oxford: Clarendon Press, 1960.

Euripides. *The Bacchae*. Trans. William Arrowsmith, David Grene, and Richmond Lattimore. 2nd ed. Chicago: University of Chicago Press, 1991.

———. *The Bacchae*. Trans. C. K. Williams. New York: Farrar, Straus and Giroux, 1990.

———. *Medea*. In *Medea and Other Plays*, trans. and ed. James Morwood, 1–38. Oxford: Oxford University Press, 1998.

Fagles, Robert, and W. B. Stanford. "A Reading of *The Oresteia*: The Serpent and the Eagle." In *The Oresteia*, by Aeschylus, trans. Robert Fagles, 13–97. 1975. New York: Penguin, 1979.

Girard, René. *Violence and the Sacred*. Trans. Patrick Gregory. 1972. Baltimore: Johns Hopkins University Press, 1977.

Grene, David, and Richmond Lattimore, eds. *Greek Tragedies*. Vol. 1. 2nd ed. Chicago: University of Chicago Press, 1991.

———. *Greek Tragedies*. Vol. 2. Chicago: University of Chicago Press, 1960.

———. *Greek Tragedies*. Vol. 3. 2nd ed. Chicago: University of Chicago Press, 1991.

Harris, Leslie. "Myth as Structure in Toni Morrison's *Song of Solomon*." *MELUS Journal* 7, no. 3 (1980): 69–76.

Jessee, Sharon. "'The Gods Are Laughing at Us': Toni Morrison's Trilogy and Classical Greek Lyric Tragedy." Paper presented at Third Biennial Conference of the Toni Morrison Society, Washington, June 28, 2003.

Jones, Bessie W. "Greek Tragic Motifs in *Song of Solomon*." In *The World of Toni Morrison: Explorations in Literary Criticism*, ed. Bessie W. Jones and Audrey L. Vinson, 103–14. Dubuque, IA: Kendall Hunt, 1985.

Lattimore, Richmond. Introduction to *Agamemnon*, by Aeschylus, trans. Richard Lattimore. In *Greek Tragedies*, vol. 1, 2nd ed., ed. David Grene and Richmond Lattimore. Chicago: University of Chicago Press, 1991.

Morrison, Toni. *Beloved*. 1987. London: Picador, 1988.

———. *The Bluest Eye*. 1970. London: Picador, 1990.

———. *Jazz*. 1992. London: Picador, 1993.

———. *Love*. London: Chatto and Windus, 2003.

———. *A Mercy*. Vintage, 2008.

———. *Paradise*. 1997. London: Chatto and Windus, 1998.

———. *Song of Solomon*. 1977. London: Picador, 1989.

———. *Sula*. 1974. London: Picador, 1991.

———. *Tar Baby*. 1981. London: Picador, 1991.

———. "Unspeakable Things Unspoken: The Afro-American Presence in American Literature." *Michigan Quarterly Review* 28 (1989): 1–34.

Moyers, Bill. "A Conversation with Toni Morrison." In *Conversations with Toni Morrison*, ed. Danille Taylor-Guthrie, 262–74. Jackson: University Press of Mississippi, 1994.

Nussbaum, Martha. Introduction to *The Bacchae*, by Euripides, trans. C. K. Williams, i–xliv. New York: Noonday Press, 1990.

Parker, Robert. *Miasma: Pollution and Purification in Early Greece*. Oxford: Clarendon Press, 1983.

Rankine, Patrice. *Ulysses in Black: Ralph Ellison, Classicism, and African American Literature*. Madison: University of Wisconsin Press, 2006.

Roynon, Tessa. "A New 'Romen' Empire: Toni Morrison's *Love* and the Classics." *Journal of American Studies* 41, no. 1 (2007): 31–47.

———. "Toni Morrison and Classical Tradition." *Literature Compass* 4–6 (2007): 1514–37.

———. *Toni Morrison and the Classical Tradition: Transforming American Culture*. Oxford: Oxford University Press, 2013.

Schechner, Richard, ed. *Dionysus in 69*. New York: Farrar, Straus and Giroux, 1970.
——. "In Warm Blood: The Bacchae." In Schechner, *Public Domain*, 93–108.
——. "The Politics of Ecstasy." In Schechner, *Public Domain*, 209–28.
——. *Public Domain: Essays on the Theater*. New York: Bobbs-Merrill, 1969.
Soyinka, Wole. *The Bacchae of Euripides: A Communion Rite*. London: Eyre Methuen, 1973.
Taylor-Guthrie, Danille. *Conversations with Toni Morrison*. Jackson: University Press of Mississippi, 1994.
Vernant, Jean-Pierre. *Myth and Society in Ancient Greece*. 1974. Trans. Janet Lloyd. Brighton, Sussex: Harvester Press, 1980.

TONI MORRISON'S PERFORMANCE OF THE WORD IN *SONG OF SOLOMON*

The Folkloric, the Fantastic, and "Some Old Folk's Lie"

ALMA JEAN BILLINGSLEA BROWN

The characteristic "response trait" of black performance, the convention of running assents by audience or listener to what is being said by speaker or performer, is observable in a number of creative expressions by African Americans and viewed as a notable feature of African and African diaspora cultures. Identified by Melville Herskovits as a "reworking" of African polite behavior (52), this affective participatory relationship between speaker and listener, audience and performer, reader and writer, is a defining feature in Toni Morrison's fiction. In *Song of Solomon*, Morrison's third novel, this feature is actualized as textual performatives of "make-believe," which sustain the boundary between reality and the fictive world, and performative utterances as "make-*belief*," which intentionally blur that boundary to create the effect and affect of performativity.[1]

Replicating essential features of African oral art forms, performative utterances in *Song of Solomon* generate multiple meanings and interpretations, but are especially linked to the novel's thematic explorations of identity and the rootedness of community and culture. With a protagonist who discovers individual, cultural, and collective identity by tracing his origins to flying ancestors, *Song of Solomon*, like the Gullah folktale on which it is based, speaks pointedly to the phenomenon of rootedness and continuity through flying. At the same time, through stories and the storytelling event, the novel encodes the contending utterances of the folkloric and the fantastic. As the utterance for the "tribal" or communal sensibility of social cohesion and cultural continuity, the folkloric in *Song of Solomon* is what makes things cohere. As the utterance for individual creativity and imagination, the arbitrary constructs of mind, the fantastic creates the one great ambiguity that drives things apart. Dialogically implicated in each other, the folkloric and the fantastic exist for each other. Each challenges, penetrates, and carries the accent of the other to sustain and mediate the oppositional belief systems which, in Bakhtin's sense, mark the "style of the whole" (263).

To assist in defining the theme of rootedness, the narrative focalizes a quest to find gold, a quest that takes the protagonist geographically and ontologically from the urban Midwest to the rural South. Unraveling and connecting the stories told to him by his father and his aunt, Milkman Dead learns that there is gold in his family's past. He also learns that his own uncanny obsession with flight has a legitimate source: his great-grandfather could fly. Equally important, Milkman discovers not only that the "gold" is identity, personal, communal, and cultural, but that identity itself emerges from recognizing and accepting the creative tension between "two modes of life," the individual and the communal, each of which threatens to exclude and annihilate the other.[2]

In the first chapter, when Robert Smith attempts and fails to fly from the roof of Mercy Hospital, the narrative situates two conflicting belief systems. Even with artificial blue silk wings, Robert Smith's abortive leap into the air validates the belief that humans cannot fly. Moments before his leap, however, Pilate Dead renders through song the legend of the slave Solomon, who, in remembering how to "surrender to the air," escapes slavery and flies back to Africa. Solomon's great-grandson is born the morning after Robert Smith's death. The narrative then charts the attempts of the "flying African's" descendant, Milkman Dead, to unravel the legend, retrieve history, and gain rootedness.

The mechanism for all three is the storytelling event. Reifying African oral traditions in the form of the novel, Morrison appropriates African oral art forms and configures the novel as a series of oral narrative performances or storytelling events. Throughout the novel, stories, songs, and legends are recollected and performed, told and retold, to inscribe the folkloric. From the account of how his grandfather acquires his name from a drunken Union soldier to the story of why his aunt suspends a sack of bones from her ceiling, stories provide the vital "cord and pulse of information" (Bakhtin, 293) that enable Milkman to achieve rootedness.

At the same time, stories like those associated with Pilate's birth and Ryna's Gulch situate the textual antinomy between the natural and the supernatural, the real and the surreal, to inscribe the fantastic.[3] As heteroglossic sites for contending discourses, "stories, gossip, legends and speculations" (323), one of which becomes "some old folk's lie" at the end of the novel (322), constitute one vehicle by which Morrison "performs the word" in this text and the primary vehicle by which the folkloric and the fantastic penetrate, contravene, and carry the accent of each other.

The first arena for these competing utterances and a singular example of how performativity enacts multiple meanings and interpretations in this novel is the song Pilate sings in the opening chapter.

> O Sugarman done fly away
> Sugarman done gone
> Sugarman cut across the sky
> Sugarman gone home. (6)

The song of Solomon's or Sugarman's "going home" to Africa by "flying away" from a wife and twenty-one children articulates the utterance of rootedness. It does so, however, by the "flying ambiguity" of the fantastic. As a dominant, unifying motif, this "song of Solomon" functions in much the same way as the "core cliché" functions in African oral narrative art forms. A song or chant that can be repeated any number of times to form an expansible image, the core cliché is the visualized action or set of actions that mediate between the audience and reality (Scheub, 353). In this novel, the song of Solomon in its several iterations functions as core cliché.

In addition to the core cliché, Morrison structures another patterned image to serve as "plot cliché": the story of the murdered father, Solomon's youngest son, Jake; his orphaned children, Pilate and Macon Dead; and their individual strategies for survival in a hostile world. After seeing their father "blown five feet into the air" (40), the twelve-year-old Pilate and sixteen-year-old Macon are hidden first by the midwife and family friend Circe. Fearing that their father's murderers would kill them too, Circe sends the children away where they wander into the woods, take refuge in a cave, murder a man, and discover gold.

As with Solomon's song, the action of this story occurs before the narrative begins, and unfolds by means of repetition, alteration, and expansion. While Solomon's song serves to reveal the novel's thematic definitions, the story of the murdered father, the orphaned children, the cave, and the gold functions to construct plot. This central sequence of events, the primary plot cliché, originates when Pilate meets her nephew Milkman for the first time since his birth. Explaining that had it not been for her brother Macon, his father, she would have "died in the womb" and "died again in the woods" (40), Pilate begins with the details of their father's murder and the terror it generated. "We were some scared children" (41), she tells Milkman. In the midst of remembering their fear, Pilate actualizes her role as performer and interposes an unexpected transformation in the story to elicit a certain affective response from her nephew.

Pilate tells another story—that of a former employer in Virginia who believes he is about to fall off a cliff and asks her to hold on to him. The man's wife, insisting on the impossibility of anyone falling off a cliff while standing in the middle of the kitchen, demands that Pilate release him. And Pilate does just that. She lets him go. When she does, the man takes three full minutes to fall "stone dead" to the floor (42). In terms of the novel's dialogized background, this story is told not only to prepare Milkman for future encounters with the fantastic but to affirm that there is no correct side for the categorical dichotomies of real and unreal. As Pilate explains before telling the second story, her brother Macon had insisted the things that frightened them in the woods were not "real." She believed differently. To manipulate and control audience response and to actualize "make-belief," Pilate then poses a question to Milkman: "What difference do it make if the thing you scared of is real or not?" (40).

On two separate occasions, Macon performs two different versions of the same story for Milkman, each version reflecting his own recollection, sensibility, and purpose. In the first version, with every detail clear in his mind, Macon re-creates for his twelve-year-old son the image of his own father's farm, Lincoln's Heaven, the land for which his father had been killed, the "land that was to have been his" (52). While this version of the story functions to express Macon's materialistic and individualistic belief system, it is also the device Morrison uses to express the value and function of orature. In telling this story, Macon reconnects with the tradition of communal performance and storytelling. The narrator explains:

> He had not said any of this for years.... When he first married he used to talk about Lincoln's Heaven to Ruth. Sitting on the porch swing in the dark ... when he was just starting out in the business of buying houses, he would lounge around the barbershop and swap stories with men.... That was the way he knew what history he remembered. (52)

With the oral transmission of not only stories but history through stories, the narrative situates the folkloric in this first version Macon tells his son. In

Macon's second version, told to Milkman ten years later, the narrative elaborates the superreal specifics of the cave, the murder, and the gold to inscribe the fantastic. To enact yet another instance of performance as "make-belief," that is, belief in the reality of the dead reappearing to communicate with and guide the living, the text again frames the character's speech with the words of the narrator.

The narrator's account appropriately begins with the supernatural, with the children waking on their third day in the woods to find a man who "looked just like their father" sitting on a tree stump and beckoning them eventually into a cave. With "ominous signs of a presence" (168) following and searching for the children, this version stages the fantastic not only in the dead father's multiple reappearances, the last one as the "very old and very white man" whom Macon kills,[4] but also in the father's finally whispering two words, "Sing. Sing" (170).

A double-voiced utterance, these two words first inscribe the fantastic, for they are articulated by a man who has been murdered twice but reappears after each murder. To contravene and recuperate the ambiguity created by the fantastic, the utterance inscribes the folkloric. Pilate, believing her father's presence is real, takes his words literally and becomes, as the novel progresses, a woman who sings by candlelight at home, who sings "in the streets," and who by her singing functions as griot-historian (Omolade, 285). As in oral traditions, it is through singing and telling stories that the griot weaves the network of history and tradition in which individual, family, and community are rooted.

The murdered father's utterance serves not only to inscribe the dialogics of the fantastic and the folkloric but also to advance narrative action. In Macon's second telling of the story, he prods Milkman to find the cave and retrieve the gold—a mission that takes him first from Michigan to Pennsylvania, where he meets Circe. Circe, who is alternately deliverer, healer, and ancestor, tells Milkman that his grandfather's name was Jake and that his grandmother's name was Sing. Milkman's meeting with Circe begins with the fantastic. Appropriating the magico-realist technique of the sensuous paradox,[5] this episode begins with an abrupt shift in the character's sensory perception. The shift prepares Milkman for the movement to the oneiric, spiritual world of the fantastic. When he finally reaches Circe's door, Milkman is repulsed by an odor so foul it makes him vomit. But within seconds, the odor changes to the "sweet spice perfume" of gingerroot, a clean and seductive smell that makes him turn back to meet the woman who everyone thinks is dead. Having calculated that Circe must have been "at least a hundred years old when she died" (233), Milkman is psychically seduced by this woman who is so old she is colorless but has the "mellifluent voice of a twenty-year-old girl" (240).

Milkman embraces her and finds that the "dry bony hands" rubbing his back and the gummy "floppy mouth" babbling into his vest "made him dizzy" (239). Then to expand, clarify, and enact new meanings, the two exchange stories. Circe re-creates the image of Milkman's "mixed, mostly Indian" grandmother Sing and his newly freed grandfather Jake in 1869. Milkman in turn recounts the material success of their son in 1963 and tells Circe how his family was named. As ancestor Circe informs, teaches, and advises Milkman. She gives him directions to Hunters Cave (where he does not find the gold), and she provides another vital "cord and pulse of information." She tells Milkman that his grandparents, Jake and Sing, were from a place in Virginia called Charlemagne or "something like that" (244).

To discover what happened to the gold, Milkman journeys to a rural community in Virginia named Shalimar, a place where the local grocer and over forty other families have named themselves "Solomon." After joining a hunt and surviving an attempt on his life, Milkman eventually learns that his grandmother had lived in Shalimar and had a relative still living—a niece named Susan Byrd. Because Susan Byrd thinks Milkman is "too dark" to be a part of her family, a family with members light enough "to pass" (290), she intentionally misleads him on his first visit. But after he hears children playing a game in which he recognizes fragments of the blues song about Sugarman that Pilate had sung and the name of his grandfather, Jake, Milkman visits his cousin for a second time.

On Milkman's second visit, Susan Byrd alters and amplifies her first story. The most important alteration is that Sing, Susan Byrd's aunt and Milkman's grandmother, had not gone to Boston to attend a Quaker school as she had insisted earlier, but had married instead a man named Jake who was leading a wagon load of former slaves north. The major expansion is that Jake had been the youngest of twenty-one sons sired by Solomon, who was himself "one of those flying African children" (321). When Susan explains that, according to "some old folk's lie" (322), Solomon, whose real name was Shalimar, one day just "flew off" from the cotton fields, Milkman queries her more specifically. "When you say, 'flew off,' you mean run away don't you?" But Susan replies, "No, I mean flew. Oh, it's just foolishness, you know, but according to the story, he wasn't running away. He was flying. He flew. You know, like a bird" (323–24).

To give coherence to the ambiguity of Susan's story, Milkman attempts to ground it in conventional reality. Humans cannot fly. He assumes, as in so many African American folktales and folk songs, there must be an encoded message, one alluding to escape from bondage. Then too, because Susan had prefaced her story with the explanation of its being "some old folk's lie" (322), she encourages the notion of its being "just foolishness." Her final explanation, however, not only reinserts the tension and ambiguity of the fantastic but also blurs the boundary between her performance as "make-believe" or as "make-belief." "Like a bird," she reiterates, Solomon actually "flew."

As "some old folk's lie," this final re-creation of the legend of the flying African, like the first, is a vital link in Milkman's quest for rootedness and a battleground for competing utterances. On the one hand, the story, as Susan tells it, is "foolishness," a "lie." But on the other, the "foolishness" and the "lie" have been passed down from "old folks." Consequently while the utterance of the fantastic (the "foolishness" and the "lie") penetrates the interior of the folkloric, the utterance of the folkloric (the story passed down from "old folks") carries the accent of the fantastic. In this double-voiced utterance, perhaps the most complex and enmeshed performative feature in the whole of the novel, the fantastic justifies its ambiguity in the lore of the community. At the same time, the folkloric locates a code of coherence for the fantastic in culture.

In folklore genres, specifically those for oral narrative art, certain features of performance and historical content are used to distinguish conceptual and formal categories. Among the oral art forms of the West African Mende, for example, Marion Kilson has recognized two categories: the *njia wova* (old talk) and *dome* (tale).[6] Dan Ben-Amos has recognized similar categories, the *alo* (folktale) and the *itan* (history) among the Yoruba in Nigeria (231). Like the Yoruba *alo* and *itan*, the Mende *njia wova* and *dome* differ with respect to content and performance. While the *njia wova* recounts "truth," the *dome* creates "fiction." The *dome* incorporates song or chant, but the *njia wova* does not.

These formal categories bear relation to the dialogized background, to performance and performativity in *Song of Solomon*. Just as the categories of "folktale" and "fiction" permit the performer to exercise her wit and imagination, the other categories restrict her to "history" and "truth." Because, however, in virtually every category for oral narrative performance, the image still mediates between audience and reality as well as among different realities, the performance of oral narrative itself constitutes a heteroglossic site. As Donald Consentino discerns, "That [the performer] can argue either side of a categorical dichotomy by constructing thematically polar narratives from an identical image suggests that there is no *correct side*" (Consentino, 304; italics mine).

For the competing utterances of the folkloric and the fantastic, for the conflicting claims of the individual and the communal, for the incongruent conventions of orature and literature, Toni Morrison's "performance of the word" in *Song of Solomon* likewise suggests that there is no correct side.

Notes

1. As used here, "performativity" refers to the reiteration of a textual element to such a degree that it carries out, enacts, or "performs" a host of meanings and interpretations in a text. But both performativity and the performative have been theorized extensively and used in widely varying contexts. In the context of speech-act theory, a performative is an utterance "in which to say something is to do something." Judith Butler, using Lacanian psychoanalysis, phenomenology, and structural anthropology, builds on speech-act theory to explore performativity in relation to identity. In everyday life, people perform the conventions and ideologies of the social world, including race and gender, and thereby enact the reality constructed in and through that world. Richard Schechner, distinguishing between performance as "make-believe" and performance as "make-belief," likewise contends that performances in everyday life shape and influence identity. With scholars like J. Hillis Miller, John R. Searle, Jacques Derrida, and Michel Foucault having theorized the term, the concept of performativity now infuses not only everyday life but the media and the Internet. My intent in this essay is to demonstrate how the overall performative quality of *Song of Solomon* is linked in notable and distinct ways to speech-act performance and oral narrative art forms in African and African diasporic cultures and, to some degree, to the theorizing of folklore as performance. I would also add here that Morrison's extensive background and creative work in the performing arts may also have shaped and influenced the multilayered performances in *Song of Solomon*.

2. This perspective derives from my reading of the novel in the context of Morrison's comments in the essay "Rootedness: The Ancestor as Foundation." In that essay, Morrison writes, "There is a conflict between public and private life, and it's a conflict that I think ought to remain a conflict. Not a problem, just a conflict. Because there are two modes of life that exist to exclude and annihilate each other" (339).

3. The definition of the fantastic as the sustained tension between the real and the superreal derives from Amaryll Chanady's examination of magical realism and the fantastic. Like Chanady, I see the unresolved antinomy between natural and supernatural occurrences, or the "fantastic," informing magico-realist fiction. But I have also discerned that this kind of fiction resolves or recuperates the antinomy by situating the expressive forms of culture, the myths, songs, legends, and tales that constitute folklore, as a code of coherence. It is also useful to note that at one point, Morrison eschewed the use of most of the contemporaneous terms used to describe this element in her fiction, indicating a preference for the term "enchantment."

4. The perspective that Macon's murder of the man in the cave is a "bizarre parricide" is Komla Messan Nubukpo's, but the details in the novel, particularly the fact that only a set of bones is recovered from the cave, makes such a view possible.

5. For the concept of sensuous paradox to describe this technique in magico-realist fiction, I am indebted to Professor Rainer Schulte at the University of Texas, Dallas. For their valuable assistance in reading and responding to the ideas presented in this paper, I am grateful to Chinosole, professor emerita from San Francisco State University, Paul K. Bryant Jackson from Miami University of Ohio, and my mentor, David Thomas.

6. Donald Consentino refers to and explains these categories in his review and analysis of Marion Kilson's *Royal Antelope and Spider: West African Mende Tales.*

Works Cited

Bakhtin, M. M. *The Dialogic Imagination.* Trans. Michael Holquist. Austin: University of Texas Press, 1988.
Ben-Amos, Dan. "Analytical Categories and Ethnic Genres." In *Folklore Genres*, ed. Dan Ben-Amos, 213–42. Austin: University of Texas Press, 1976.
Chanady, Amaryll. *Magical Realism and the Fantastic: Resolved versus Unresolved Antimony.* New York: Garland, 1985.
Consentino, Donald. Review of *Royal Antelope and Spider*, by Marion Kilson. *Research in African Literatures* 10 (1979): 296–307.
Herskovits, Melville. *The Myth of the Negro Past.* Boston: Beacon Press, 1958.
Morrison, Toni. "Rootedness: The Ancestor as Foundation." In *Black Women Writers (1950–1980): A Critical Evaluation*, ed. Mari Evans, 339–45. New York: Anchor, 1984.
———. *Song of Solomon.* New York: Knopf, 1977.
Nubukpo, Komla Messan. "Through Their Sisters' Eyes: The Representation of Black Men in the Novels of Toni Morrison, Alice Walker and Toni Cade Bambara." Ph.D. diss., Boston University, 1987.
Omolade, Barbara. "The Silence of the Song: Toward a Black Woman's History through a Language of Her Own." In *Wild Women in the Whirlwind: Afra-American Culture and the Contemporary Literary Renaissance*, ed. Joanne M. Braxton and Andree McLaughlin, 282–95. New Brunswick: Rutgers University Press, 1990.
Schechner, Richard. *Performance Studies: An Introduction.* New York: Routledge, 2002.
Scheub, Harold. "Oral Narrative Process and the Use of Models." *New Literary History* 2 (1975): 353–77.

"A KIND OF RESTORATION"

Psychogeographies of Healing in Toni Morrison's Home

VALORIE THOMAS

Once I redemption neither sought nor knew.
—Phillis Wheatley

While dissenting with itself over the possibility of reliable narration and interpretation, *Home* is stabilized by two principles that span Morrison's relationship to fiction: valuing black diasporic literacies and identifying black vernacular culture as a space of knowledge and healing. Using African diasporic spiritual archetypes along with black vernacular communal sensibilities, Morrison constructs an alternate imaginative landscape, or "psychogeography" (Debord, 1). In *Home* the author's mapping of this restorative psychogeography serves as a template for healing in the midst of trauma. The landscape of black vernacular culture in *Home* is structured by the liminal space of the crossroads archetype and related concepts in Yoruba-Bantu-Kongo spiritual systems that evoke a studied relationship to existential and social precarity that I term African diasporic vertigo.

African diasporic vertigo puts a black vernacular spin on what Judith Butler calls "precarity."[1] Vertigo is both sign of colonial dislocation and disorientation and (ancient) methodology for healing and, in modern terms, decolonizing. It invokes a continuum of vernacular experience and knowledge available to mediate contemporary experiences of diasporic rupture and recovery. Vertigo contemplates diasporic (dis)locations while asserting the power of finding equilibrium in the spiritual freefall of the crossroads. African diasporic vertigo foregrounds indigenous epistemologies, diasporic literacies, and African-derived spiritual systems with particular emphasis on their extensive consideration of the crossroads and the trickster as spatiotemporal and affective pedagogies.

In this analysis of *Home*, I am interested in how the novel constructs black psychic landscapes accented by vertigo. I argue that such narratives prioritize the black subject's ability to embody psychic balance and cultural equilibrium over the quest for purification and redemption. In *Home*, stereotypically racialized identity broken by trauma produces cultural and social vertigo, a state of suspension and displacement. Black vernacular culture, African-derived spirituality, and rituals remedy their disorientation by restructuring relationships to place, nature, and communities joined by folk knowledge. The crossroads is a key concept represented in the Yowa cosmogram, pictured as a cross inside a circle or diamond, and is governed by the divine trickster, Eshu-Legbara, master of "Signifyin(g)" rhetorical play (Gates, xxi), hybridity, transgressing borders, transformation, and limiting "excesses of evil" (Neimark, 76). Eshu, the "very embodiment of the crossroads" (Thompson, 19), emerges, throughout the diaspora, wearing disguises and shifting identities. Eshu is a jokester who overturns hierarchies and topples authorities, stirring conflict and catastrophe to spur spiritual and ethical growth. The crossroads graphic encodes information about volatility, the instability of forms, the potency of emptiness, and the necessary vertigo of being unmoored to transform. Morrison's allusions to vertigo through the crossroads and the trickster, through liminality, and through sacred space provide a structured view of social, emotional, and spiritual precarities through which Frank and Cee assemble agency. Morrison insists that "life becomes comprehensible when we know what rules we are playing by" (Jones and Vinson, 182), and she employs Bantu-Kongo-Yoruba rules to define modes of self-recovery that embrace precarity.

By locating Frank in the liminal psychic space of an ethical crossroads, Morrison engages Judith Butler's theorizing on the limits of self-knowledge and the inseparability of subjectivity and social mechanisms beyond the subject's control in *Giving an Account of Oneself* (2005). Frank dismisses the narrator's ability to grasp his state, connecting the moral, emotional, visceral, and material in the lines "*You don't know what heat is until you cross the border from Texas to Louisiana in the summer. You can't come up with words that catch it. Trees give up. Turtles cook in their shells. Describe that if you know how*" (41).

The turtle cannot see or escape its shell and under extreme conditions will succumb to it. The chaos of Frank's panic and rage in the throes of war punctuates his killing of Korean civilians. In recalling the Korean child, he admits, "*I didn't think. I didn't have to. Better she should die. How could I let her live after she took me down to a place I didn't know was in me? How could I like myself, even be myself if I surrendered to that place?*" (134).

Frank's liminality is early defined in the dislocated space of a mental hospital as he imagines faking the liminal state of a "semi-coma" (7). Frank escapes in the transitional moment just "before sunrise" (10). The hospital was a brush with death because "they sell a lot of bodies out of there" (12). He runs barefoot on "curb snow" (11), hazarding the possibility of being arrested for "vagrancy, meaning standing outside or walking without clear purpose anywhere" (9).

Cee's space is also liminal; when Frank leaves her, she is cut loose, "adrift in the space where her brother had been, ... [with] no defense" (48). Frank's habit of covering her eyes is protective but resembles closing a corpse's eyes, suggesting that her dependence perpetuates social death. Frank thinks of "her eyes ... suspended.... She was a shadow for most of my life, a presence marking its own absence, or maybe mine" (103), a reflection of his alienation. "She be dead" can mean, in black vernacular, both she will die and she is dead; Cee suffers from a deathlike absence of self-esteem and agency. Blocking Cee's vision parallels Frank's lost self-image, his focus on spaces that "stirred no feelings, encouraged no memory" (8), Mr. Crawford whose "eyes had been carved out" (10), and the tree, "beheaded, undead" (144). Frank and Cee linger in liminality in a manner of hysterical blindness on the borders of actual and social death. While Frank initially thinks, "*Nobody in Lotus knew anything or wanted to learn anything*" (83), and Cee sees "a no-count, not-even-a-town place" (47), the women of the community come to constitute a "healing zone." Morrison frames Cee's sickness as an "invading" entity (121), taking her through a healing ritual in three stages: "First the bleeding ... Next the infection ... then the repair" (121). The healers "love mean" (121), rejecting sentimentality like Mrs. MacTeer in *The Bluest Eye*. After Cee is physically safe, they arm her by sharing wisdom and survival skills and telling her to "locate her" (126), in effect providing Cee with a "sacred space."

In Morrison's view of ancestral influences in African diaspora cultures, the "civilization of black people, which was underneath the white civilization, was there with its own everything," providing a compass, but has been dismantled in ways that leave individuals "out there, strung out. There is nowhere for them to go" (Ruas, 105). Frank finds a space in which to "sort out what was troubling him and what to do about it" (132) by exercising a selfless devotion toward Cee that transforms his perception of Lotus. Frank's agency in changing his personal psychogeography reflects Morrison's assertion that "home is an idea rather than a place ... where you feel safe. Where you're among people who are kind to you—they're not after you; they don't have to like you—but they'll not hurt you. And if you're in trouble they'll help you" (Leve). This is the context in which, "hostile as he was" (22), Reverend Maynard helps Frank, and the women help Lenore although "they knew that the woman they were helping despised them all" (92). Relational practices shape the space in which Frank registers "the pleasure of being among those who do not want to degrade or destroy you" (118). Danille Taylor-Guthrie notes that Morrison writes "to take the 'tribe' via art ... to a healing zone" (Taylor-Guthrie, x). Indeed, Morrison asserts that she writes to and about communities "under siege" (Jones and Vinson, 183). For Morrison, "novels are important because they are socially responsible.... A novel written a certain way can do precisely what spirituals used to do ... what blues or jazz or gossip or stories or myth or folklore did" (183). Calling attention to "modes of agency that are possible" in precarity (Butler, "Conversation"), Morrison locates such modes in a black vernacular ethos.

Markers of sacred space in *Home* are further elaborated through Bantu-Kongo-Yoruba motifs of verticality and vectoring. In Bantu-Kongo thought, the V figure represents life energy. "To grow, to mature is to ... enter into this powerful zone of the V ... to stand vertically" (Fu-Kiau, 28). The V "is the center of balance for the human being, his health and that of his community.... The human (muntu) is fundamentally a vertical being" (Fu-Kiau, 149). This verticality is associated with horses, trees, Frank's "very tall" (22) stature, and the "perpendicular" (144) burial of the remains of the lynched man. Frank's conflicts correspond with the Bantu-Kongo concept of descent into life-or-death struggle with negativity, an initiation through which one becomes "a true knower of what is marked on one's own mind and body" (Fu-Kiau, 33). Frank undergoes the psychic crisis and realignment with the V associated with initiation of healers (Fu-Kiau, 30). When Cee trembles, Frank instinctively places "one hand on top of her head, the other at her nape. His fingers, like balm" (51), and through him she "recognized poisonous berries, shouted when in snake territory, learned the medicinal uses of spider webs" (52). In West African tradition, the spider Anansi, archetypal weaver of stories, emerges here as an instrument of Cee's healing through her learning to sew.

Additional vectors abound: the Y in Ycidra, the tree, "spreading its arms, one to the right, one to the left" (144), the cutting of the "girl" (66) melon that foreshadows Cee's dissection. In the battle royal–style knife fight, Jerome and his father first "slashed each other a bit—just enough to draw a line of blood" (138) before they are sadistically forced to fight to the death. Frank factors that story with the year that it happened and the memory of seeing the body dumped, three facts that lead to the sudden understanding that the body being dumped was Jerome's father. In Seattle, Frank is "wide open" (69) for Lily. In contrast, "as soon as Lily shut the door behind him . . . his anxiety became unmanageable" (15). Closing the vector sends Frank into emotional suspension and disarray. He is soothed by open vectors. After the man in the zoot suit visits him on the train, Frank watches the scenery and tries "to redecorate it, mind-painting giant slashes of purple and X's of gold . . . trying and failing to recolor the western landscape" (27). The name "Cee" teeters rhetorically between homophone, homograph, and hieroglyph; played through black vernacular signifyin(g) and vertigo as a hard *C*, it becomes "key." This might technically be the "wrong" pronunciation according to the rules of Standard English, but it has the right effect. In the Greek alphabet the letter *X* is chi, sign of chiasmus: Cee is the key, and the key is Cee. Chi is pronounced "kai" in Greek, but as Qi in Buddhism, it represents life force, known as Ashe' in West African spiritual systems. Frank retreats to the liminal space of "no scenery, no trains, just endless, endless tracks" (8), the stopover of "a Chevron station, its black flames shooting out from the V" (23), the angularity of "bebop" (108), a trumpet's "screech . . . from down a short flight of steps ending at a half-open door" (108), and "the little wishbone V" of feminine softness that, through Lily, "took up residence . . . and made itself at home" in him (68). Though they part, Lily begins Frank's healing by planting that seedling V. As Frank's relationship to the V implies, these spatiotemporal configurations remediate the meaning of humanity in the novel.

In Frank's eyes, Lotus changes from "the worst place in the world" (83) to a space of "blessed peace" (118). The narrator observes of the healer's yard, "Honeybees gathered to salute *Illicium* and drink the juice. Her garden was not Eden; it was so much more than that" (130), specifying this member of the Schisandra plant family as part of the healing landscape. Bees are sacred to San Ysidro, in English Saint Isidore (meaning "gift of Isis"), gatherer of fragments who produced the first encyclopedia; Ysidro is a palimpsest to Ycidra/Cee's naming, a namesake reputed for his tendency to disappear into the texts he authored. *Illicium* often refers to star anise, *Illicium verum*, which is edible. *Illicium parviflorum*, yellow anise, grows abundantly in Georgia, also has a star-shaped seedpod, and is highly toxic. While either can suffice as a ritual symbol, choosing the right *Illicium* for the intended purpose is critical. Morrison inscribes this riddle to underscore the women's skill at managing "evil" (124) in situations where "the point was to know the difference" (124). For Morrison, their knowledge, including "the skills of the illiterate: perfect memory, photographic minds, keen senses of smell and hearing" (128), is critical information that forms the basis of African diaspora cultural literacy.

In alternative medicine, star anise is an adaptogen used to manage trauma. In the African diaspora, star anise is used in Bantu-Kongo and Vodun-derived systems as an offering to Eshu, often to request protection and goodwill when entering the crossroads. Star anise is also known as "five-flavor fruit" because it balances the five sensations: sour, sweet, bitter, spicy, and salty. In a novel so painfully concerned with bodily suffering, it is notable that star anise alludes to the five-pointed star, or pentagram, which in European folk magic signifies the human body and sacred space. In occult science, star anise is a protective herb associated with spiritual wisdom, dreams, and money, all of which concern Eshu. Morrison's privileging of African and African-derived spiritual systems is interwoven with cross-cultural knowledges, diasporic memories, palimpsests, and transgressive histories.

Though Frank's journey as a warrior resembles Odysseus's, it is Cee, also a survivor of the atrocities of institutionalized "medicine," who is effectively admitted to Elysium (a homophone of *Illicium*), a garden in the Greek realm of the dead where resurrected heroes experience paradise. The Elysium of Greek myth has its own sun and stars, which for Cee translate to *Illicium*, star anise, and her healing beneath the sun's burning rays. Cee's recovery is guided by women she is unaccustomed to, "their talk ... songs ... instructions ... they shared everything ... had a use for everything ... took responsibility for their lives and for whatever, whoever else needed them ... gathering strength for the coming day" (123). Cee comes to respect their vernacular knowledge, recognizing that their world is a battleground in which "an aggressive gardener ... destroyed enemies" (130). In effect, the women heal her blindness as well as her womb and, in ceremonial terms, deliver "unto him [Frank] a Cee who would never again need his hand over her eyes" (128). Thus diasporic vertigo is a method not of redemption but of reinvention or, as Morrison terms it, "repair" (121). This strategy acknowledges the historical trauma of enslavement, colonization, and genocide and invokes the ancestral spiritual principles associated with the trickster and with the crossroads as sacred transformative space.

From the perspective of Bantu-Kongo-Yoruba spirituality, Frank is a trickster stuck in vertigo, a sacred fool surviving by being "lucky" (12), managing perilous conditions such as hiding from the men who stage Jerome's killing of his father, and subverting hierarchical authority such as that typically invested in narrators, authors, and doctors. In some situations, Frank is actually phenomenally skilled as a trickster. We enter the novel as he works on "breathing. How to do it so no one would know he was awake. Fake a deep rhythmic snore, drop the bottom lip. Most important, the eyelids should not move and there must be a regular heartbeat and limp hands.... The trick of imitating a semi-coma" (7). The irony with Frank is that while he can control his autonomic nervous system, he lacks autonomy.

Because the trickster and crossroads are one and the same in Bantu-Kongo-Yoruba thought, The trickster and crossroads motifs in *Home* often coincide and overlap. Frank sees the "little man" (33) in the zoot suit three times in the course of the novel. This playful figure refers to both the discursive possibilities of Eshu and Ellison's "Little Man at Chehaw Station." The number three, which is sacred to Eshu and a sign of the trickster, arises more than thirty times in the novel. Three has philosophical, structural, and numerological importance in many cultures, including Christianity, Hinduism, Greco-Roman antiquity, Buddhism, and Western secular culture. Threes in *Home*, however, produce a chantlike pattern, as well as a webbing of vectors; this rhythmic pattern imbued with Eshu's presence conveys a possession of the text that parallels how "the rhythm was in charge" of the drummer (109). References to three include Frank escaping on his third day at the mental hospital (9), the "three syllables" (40) of Ycidra and three letters of Cee, the little man disappearing "after three steps" (33), and Frank and Cee's "three years with Lenore" (46).[2] The symbolism of the lotus in Buddhism and Hinduism evokes the three syllables contained in the primordial sound, Aum, and the unfolding of the soul symbolized by the roots, stem, and blossom.

Defined by liminality—"empty space" (81), not "there or anywhere" (53)—Frank is a man with "no goals at all" (76), whose affect is "clear indifference" (79). Yet Lily also wonders about his capacity to "change so quickly" (77); this is part of the trickster's influence on his character and a quality that will be Frank's saving grace. As Frank's subjectivity heals, the dissociations and emptiness shift in meaning, so that he becomes "serene" (111), a man who transcends his performance of the Fool, evolving from sleight-of-hand trickery to a persona "not to be fooled with" (111). Though he survives the encounter with Dr. Beau by chance, the gun's "empty chamber" (111) also represents the solace of a state in which the last name "Money" begins to resonate with good fortune. Money, in Bantu-Kongo-Yoruba spirituality, is the province of Oshun, the orisha (deity) of abundance and love (Neimark, 141).

In effect, Frank attains a higher vibration in his embodiment of the Trickster. He has an epiphany in which he sees that "not having to beat up the enemy to get what he wanted was somehow superior—sort of, well, smart" (114). This is a pivotal shift. He begins to see a black community contextualized by vernacular social patterns and a thriving natural environment that resists the "white heaven ... torturing its landscape" (117). Frank's early experiences of colorlessness correspond to the West African world of the dead, but later in the novel he becomes immersed in nature, saturated with "crimson, purple, pink, and China blue ... deep, deep green" (117), and an alternate temporality of "timeless time" (120) symbolized by the watch with "no stem, no hands—the way time functioned in Lotus, pure and subject to anybody's interpretation" (120). Mindful of how "color, silence, and music enveloped him" (118), Frank's feelings of "safety and goodwill" (118) free him to reinterpret himself. Frank becomes a study in the equanimity of nonattachment, stillness, surrender, and nonviolence.

Frank's signifying on the narrator's limitations also constitutes an Eshu move that destabilizes authority and control of knowledge. Reading through African diasporic vertigo, as a critical practice that highlights the aesthetic deployment of vernacular African-derived spiritual systems, suggests a view of Frank as an Eshu in training. Frank embodies the trickster's ability to subvert hierarchical authority, "breaking the aesthetic contract," as Clyde Taylor characterizes it in *The Mask of Art*. His signifying on the author/narrator's limitations constitutes an Eshu move that reveals and deliberately exploits tensions along fissures of authority and the control of knowledge. Reserving the right, as a vernacular African American practice, to be contrary and self-defined under any and all circumstances suggests there will always be more stories than a single author, narrator, or narrative can contain, gesturing backward to riff on Ellison's "infinite possibilities" and *Invisible Man*'s shifting subjectivity as a prototypical diasporic trickster figure.

Though Frank fears that he is unknowable, he trusts the narrator's cultural ethos. He upbraids the narrator but keeps communicating and eventually confides his own moral depravity, saying, "*I have to say something to you right now.... I hid it from you because I hid it from me.... You can keep on writing, but I think you ought to know what's true*" (133–34). Insofar as Morrison inscribes the trickster as a rhetorical presence in *Home*, she surrenders narrative authority while using authorship as a means of meditating on text as a healing technology and privileging the principle of limitless story.

Morrison's punning allusion to the 1952 play *The Morrison Case* (72) by the blacklisted Hollywood writer Albert Maltz exemplifies her use of the trickster principle as narrative device. Maltz is an important influence for Morrison, but there is another, more recent "Morrison case" beneath this reference, one that the author is privy to that the characters do not have access to within the narrative present of the novel. This is the additional dimension of ironic allusion that extends to the 2000 Supreme Court case *United States v. Morrison et al.*, which found that certain aspects of the 1994 Violence Against Women Act were unconstitutional under the Commerce Act and the Fourteenth Amendment. Morrison is here signifying on, and closing the distance between, similarities in Cee's gender landscape and the one we continue to inhabit. Morrison's highlighting of Maltz's work sends a series of resonances into play, revealing additional intertexts and critical amplifications.

Maltz's 1956 novel *A Long Day in a Short Life* is deeply connected to Morrison's preoccupations in *Home* with its contemplation of the dissonance between noble language and evil actions, the impact of learned hatred, and the moral condition of the human heart. The novel opens with two epigraphs: "In the center of all, and object of all, stands the Human Being, towards whose heroic and spiritual evolution poems and everything directly or indirectly tend," by Walt Whitman; and "You got a right, I got a right. We all got a right to the tree of life," from a "Negro spiritual." The tree of life reference resonates with Morrison's figuration of the bay tree where Frank and Cee bury Jerome's father. Morrison brings Maltz into her literary lineage alongside Ellison, whose *Invisible Man* was also published in 1952; this inclusion strategically expands an intertextual discourse on American identity, race, gender, class, and the politics of capitalism. It is relevant to Frank's ability to find good in himself that in *A Long Day* Maltz writes of his incarcerated protagonist: "There ain't nobody who's ever been born bad. . . . God don't start nobody off with hate in his heart" (72). Yet the scars that Frank bears from both racial hatred and the atrocities of war leave him in a liminal state from which he can only be released by grief, for himself, for his sister, and for the child he murdered.

While Butler asserts that "war designates certain populations 'ungrievable'" (Butler, "Conversation"), African diasporic ethos demands that the "ungrievable" must in fact be reclaimed and acknowledged and that grief must be incorporated to restore psychic balance. Morrison's pedagogy of restoration in *Home* rejects the amnesia of redemption in favor of remembrance, self-acceptance, and acts of compassion.

The dead man later identified as Jerome's father, the Koreans, and the deaths of Mike, Red, and Stuff evoke the "grotesque" (98), the prehistory and the "irresponsibility" confronting Frank. He changes his narrative by becoming accountable to Cee, confessing his awful secret, and giving the forgotten dead a proper burial. Of these three actions, fighting for Cee's life entails surrendering to the healers' knowledge; confession renders the dead grievable; and the burial at the bay tree connects Frank, through ritual, to those who earlier buried the lynched body of Mr. Crawford "beneath his beloved magnolia" (10).

Cee eventually stations herself in a present that is "as sad as it ought to be" (131), balanced by the process of becoming restored and self-located; a process without an end point. It is a vernacular psychogeography formed through equanimity, communal relationships, and sacred knowledge. Within the scaffolding of African diasporic vertigo, the trickster archetype, the crossroads motif, the Yowa, and Morrison's cross-cultural narrative aesthetics, *Home* becomes a sacred space of restoration, its pages leaves of healing.

Notes

1. In Judith Butler's formulation, precarity means exposure to "illness, unemployment, or violence, and that one has insufficient resources available to solve or address those problems" ("Conversation").

2. Other examples include "thief, fool, hussy" (50), "Frank, Mike, and Stuff" (52), "a bit over three dollars a day . . . enough left for a fifteen-cent movie" (55), "three melons from a peck basket" (66), "the third one" (66), "a few afternoon strolls" (73), "six months of pressing" (74), "Those three years" (88), "three pennies' change. At three-thirty in the afternoon . . . in the half hour until the train pulled out of the station" (97), "three hundred yards" (100), "the final three" (106), "a trio" (108), three repetitions of "take me to the water" (117), "First . . . Next . . . Then" (121), "Okay. . . . Okay. . . . Okay" (129–30).

Works Cited

Butler, Judith. "Conversation with Judith Butler." Conservatorium, University of Stellenbosch (July 21, 2011) posted July 26, 2011, Stellenbosch Literary Project. http://slipnet.co.za/view/event/judith-butler.

———. *Giving an Account of Oneself.* Bronx: Fordham University Press, 2005.

Debord, Guy-Ernest. "Introduction to a Critique of Urban Geography." http://library.nothingness.org/articles/SI/en/display/2 (accessed March 2, 2013).

Ellison, Ralph. *Invisible Man.* New York: Random House, 1952.

———. "The Little Man at Chehaw Station." In *Going to the Territory.* New York: Vintage, 1995.

Fu-Kiau, Kimbwandende Kia Bunseki. *African Cosmology of the Bantu-Kongo: Tying the Spiritual Knot: Principles of Life and Living.* New York: Athelia Henrietta Press, 1980.

Gates, Henry Louis, Jr. *The Signifying Monkey: A Theory of African-American Literary Criticism.* New York: Oxford University Press, 1988.

Jones, Bessie, and Audrey Vinson. "An Interview with Toni Morrison." In *Conversations with Toni Morrison*, ed. Danille Taylor-Guthrie, 171–87. Jackson: University Press of Mississippi, 1994.

Leve, Ariel. "Toni Morrison on love, loss and modernity." *Telegraph*, July 17, 2012. http://www.telegraph.co.uk/culture/books/authorinterviews/9395051/Toni-Morrison-on-love-loss-and-modernity.html.

Maltz, Albert. *A Long Day in a Short Life.* International Publishers, 1957.

———. "The Morrison Case." 1952.

Morrison, Toni. *The Bluest Eye.* New York: Alfred Knopf, 1970.

———. *Home*. New York: Vintage International, 2012.

Neimark, Phillip J. *The Way of the Orisa: Empowering Your Life through the Ancient African Religion of Ifa*. New York: Harper Collins, 1993.

Ruas, Charles. "Toni Morrison." In *Conversations with Toni Morrison*, ed. Danille Taylor-Guthrie, 93–118. Jackson: University Press of Mississippi, 1994.

Taylor-Guthrie, Danille, ed. *Conversations with Toni Morrison*. Jackson: University Press of Mississippi, 1994.

Thompson, Robert Farris. *Flash of the Spirit: African and Afro-American Art and Philosophy*. New York: Vintage, 1984.

United States v. Morrison et al., 529 U.S. 598 (2000).

PART V

*"You can keep on writing but
I think you ought to know what's true"*

AESTHETIC ACTIVITY

CLAUDIA BRODSKY

In considering the relation of meaning to memory in the work of Toni Morrison, it is well worth recalling, from the outset, that few celebrated writers of this century have been as dedicated as Morrison to the proposition that the reader of her work *lives*. This simple yet powerful conviction is often aligned with the political dimension of Morrison's prose, and indeed, *political* is as good a word as any for fiction that assumes the reading public also lives public lives, and that forming a reading public forms those lives, as nothing else can. Such a conviction, as obvious as it is rare, benefits us all, whether we care to be its beneficiary or not. In direct relation to the kind of aesthetic activity whose practice and analysis Morrison's writing compels are two of the rewarding differences in mind I have found—and believe we all find in our own ways—in Morrison's work.

There is a statement at the close of a now canonical essay written by the critic Walter Benjamin, which, despite its nearly aphoristic status in contemporary culture and criticism, and despite years of reading and teaching this essay, has never appeared persuasive in its logic to me. The essay, first published in 1936, is "The Work of Art in the Age of Mechanical Reproducibility" (Das Kunstwerk im Zeitalter seiner technischen Reproduzierbarkeit); its final paragraphs describe the technological wars waged by fascism as "the consummation of *l'art pour l'art*," an aesthetic pleasure in destruction stated in the dictum *Fiat ars—pereat mundus* (make art and perish the world). "This is how it stands," the essay concludes, "with the aestheticization of politics, which fascism carries out. Communism answers fascism with the politicization of art" (270).

The symmetry of this statement is immediately satisfying, but upon a moment's inspection it becomes clear that the chiasmus, or crossing of terms, on which it is built threatens to make no real difference at all. A politicized aesthetics is just as germane to fascism as an aestheticized politics; despite different conceptual origins, the results of the two operations verge on the same: politics rendered aesthetic and aesthetics rendered political are names of things supposedly transformed into something they previously were not.

Toni Morrison's writing departs from the very different assumption that aesthetic experience—the experience, identification, and fabrication of beauty—*is* political, an assumption in fact akin to the oldest political theory we know, which openly viewed poets as disruptive of the smooth running of the state and just as openly banned them therefrom. In keeping with Plato's warning that these ventriloquizing poets can turn up anywhere, can prove everywhere persuasive, Morrison's prose turns out poetry where you least expected it, where you never even paused to look before. And indeed, what could be more political than seeing beauty—new, irrefutable beauty—where nothing had been seen at all: than rendering what had been viewed, paradoxically, as invisible, the most compelling thing your mind's eye can imagine, and which imaginings it cannot then erase.

I say "new beauty" in odd, historical conjunction with the ancient view of the inherently political force of poetic imitation, and this is where a second difference, made by Morrison's writing, to our understanding of others' writing comes to mind, the epic and explicitly subjective narrative of the greatest French novelist of the twentieth century, Marcel Proust. Readers of Proust's *A la recherche du temps perdu* know well the recurrent caveat, regarding our temporal experience and knowledge of such experience, that punctuates every personal realization recounted in that great work: "ce n'était que plus tard" (it wasn't until later), "ce n'était que bien d'années plus tard" (it wasn't until many, many years later). Such routine temporal injunctions introduce the narrator's own revisions of the exquisitely detailed representations and recoveries of his past he has just narrated at length—a past that Marcel, the narrator, now states he had never understood at all, almost always got exactly wrong. It is not some new fact but a new perception of the factual that marks the passage of time—the occurrence of a distinct, perceptible difference within time— just as it alters and expands the narrative horizon in Proust's writing. Morrison is not a Proustian writer, whatever that may mean—she is, of course, Morrisonian instead. But she may be, conceptually speaking, the Marcel of *our* past, the mostly unimagined past whose status *as* unimagined has always affected and continues to affect our private and public lives. It wasn't—to borrow from Proust—until many, many years later (1987, for example) that national cataclysms of a hundred and of hundreds of years before came to be understood, known as never before, by millions nationally and internationally, millions who—to expand on Proust's first-person narrator—never, whether deludedly or lucidly, *personally* experienced them (before the publication of *Beloved*) at all.

In reading Proust, in other words, each reader may well say along with Marcel, I, too, never knew even my own private life (including the political views I held in that life) before. In reading Morrison, we may see that we have never known our *public* life any better, the life of previously unnoticed, unknown beauty, as of unfelt because unimagined horror, that Morrison has made us see, "only later," for the first time. Even more evidently than in Proust, personal history is national history in Morrison, which is to say, our ability or failure to perceive the lived reality of past events, their always personal history, is demonstrated to shape not only the plotlines of "the past," such as we receive it narrated, but our own experience of the past in the present, as real and effective temporal difference, as well as all our ensuing attempts at its personal and historical representation. And so, for the same ancient reasons that it would be wrong to view her writing as either political *or* aestheticist, as if the two could ever be extricated to stand alone, it would be wrong to view Morrison's writing, when, with Proust's, it finds itself "in search of lost time," as solely historical, as if the past, our past, seen and unseen, were not ongoing, indeed, going on right now. As the distortions of the past extend, as if across empty time, into the appearance of present norms and our current events (including the latter's so-called reporting), so Morrison's writing, disrupting time lines that efface all possible difference between past and present, is the writing, the representation in the present, of a past still unknown and a future yet unknowable.

In this, too, Morrison's writing recalls the distinctly historical theory of the enhanced political effectivity of art advanced by Benjamin. An analysis of the effect of technical means of reproduction on the public and private reception of artworks, Benjamin's essay signals by its very title that, with the advent of "the age of mechanical reproducibility," all art is already the future of art, an inherently temporal act of representation made—by its reproduction—strangely ageless. That is, Benjamin does not pose the more commonplace question—already familiar in 1936—of whether reproduced art is still art. Defining what does and does not constitute art in itself did not concern Benjamin; indeed, any experience-independent definition of art would appear to him misconceived from the outset. Benjamin raises instead the more interesting interpretive question, itself directly related to Morrison's work, of how art permitted to turn up anywhere at any time by technical means, art thus unhinged from its original historical purpose and context, would affect the historical subjects who perceive it.

The technical arts of reproduction, Benjamin argued, fundamentally change the way artworks are undergone; his well-known analogy in the "Reproducibility" essay for the encounter with decontextualized art is the experience of a "shock," the parrying by consciousness of the force of unexpected, inassimilable events. Just as art is not art in itself but in what it does, so shock—Benjamin, following Freud, suggests—is not a blank muteness in itself but the external sign of all the more indelible and intricate psychic work. Visible—palpable or legible—aesthetic work that sets the psyche invisibly to work is the defining experiential basis for a specifically modern lyric, according to Benjamin. And the poet of this lyric of new beauty, whose verbal representations rendered those refused the status of the beautiful no less aesthetically than politically unforgettable in effect, who attempted to embrace and contain, as if *in propria persona* ("J'ai plus de souvenirs que si j'avais mil ans"[1] [I have more memories than if I were a thousand years old]), all historical experience no less than an entire, inassimilable city and its people, is the writer who, in his impassioned, erotic, while ironic attempt to make the historical live in the present, effectively wrote the modern: Baudelaire. The uncontainable "crowd" (*la foule*) of Baudelaire's attraction, and the shifting present-tense action of the city he represents, resemble freely circulating copies of art, Benjamin suggests, for the same reason that the object, or singular and original work of art, of which they are the "double" (*dédoublement*), may be viewed instead as similar to an individual person—similar in the sense that when you look at such an artwork, as opposed to a crowd of infinitely circulating reproductions, you bestow on it a human quality, the peculiar, specular ability to look back at you. This is Benjamin's remarkable definition of the so-called aura of the original in the essay "Some Motifs in Baudelaire," the 1939 companion piece to the essay on reproduction: "The person we look at, or who feels he is being looked at, looks at us in turn. To experience the aura of an object we look at means to invest it with the ability to look at us in return" (338).

The objects Benjamin writes about, here and elsewhere, are concrete; in the reproduction essay, it is figurative art objects whose reproduction by photograph, and their ensuing loss of a specular, auratic quality, he principally has in mind. For the same reason, the opposition between auratic and reproduced art that these seminal essays construct must exclude from consideration the figurative, concrete, yet never entirely "original" art of the word. Even when spoken in conversation between two persons, words, by their very nature, are reproductions, repetitions that first attained meaningful, objective identity *with repetition*: objects that were never "original" to begin with. When, in addition, they are written and made available to reading—available, that is, as it is the very nature of writing alone to enact, always, to anyone anywhere, at any time, and in any place—words originate (so to speak) in the same graphic state of decontextualization that photography first dramatically imposed on the world of the plastic arts, the world of "originals" versus "reproductions," which, for the written word, does not and cannot obtain. No verbal art is or can be an exception to this rule of reproducibility *as* the rule, or essential norm: a structural necessity inhering in the very definition and possibility of language (as repeatable and reproducible form) that Gutenberg's Bible and the subsequent invention of Protestantism only made historically clear.

Yet Morrison's *verbal art* dislodges the skewed opposition between original and originary copy, artwork and word, by altering our experience of the inescapable if infinitely forgettable, iterable quality of the word itself, the premise of reproduction and infinite reproducibility that makes all words literally prosaic, essentially different from every other medium we class as aesthetic. Just as, I think, for Morrison, the aesthetic is by nature political, the prosaic word is, or rather is *made*, aesthetic in appearing anew in her narrative prose. By this I do not only mean that Morrison writes beautifully—although, as it happens, she does—nor do I mean to understate that feat. We all know it is hard enough to render beauty, and its experience, beautiful in words—such is the insuperable difference between the sentient and the verbal worlds. Yet Morrison's writing takes the additional, extraordinary step of rendering refuse beautiful—"refuse" very much in the Baudelairian sense of the rejected, *les refusés*—and it does so, moreover, without resorting to false aestheticization, the prettifying that ultimately underlies most conventional, and unthinkingly political, notions of what counts as beautiful in any society. Prettification that renders the conventionally unbeautiful conventionally beautiful is the form of aestheticization we describe as sentimentalism. However one judges Morrison's prose, it has never been deemed sentimental; indeed, that absence, not of sentiment but of the sentimental—Morrison's painstaking avoidance of prettification—may be just what makes her writing, for some readers, so hard to read. To maintain, at all costs, an actual sympathy for the real without expressing that sympathy through sentimentalism may be the most daring and enduring stylistic trait to mark her novels overall, to make them both difficult *and* available in the long, indeed, the *very* long, run, when current pleasure and displeasure with them are as anecdotal as even that historic act of recognition whose very sound seemed to echo what it celebrated, a Nobel Prize so nobly won.

As exceptional as that stylistic trait—the rendering of sympathy without sentimentalism—is and will, I think, remain, this is still not what I have in mind in considering the aesthetic activity of Morrison's prose. And here Benjamin's definition of the aura of the artwork is worth recalling again. Morrison's narratives neither politicize the aesthetic nor aestheticize the political, which is to say simply, they do not effect propaganda. But they do attempt to effect a version of the experience that Benjamin accords to certain objects and to original, plastic works of art: they attempt to do what already decontextualized words cannot naturally do, to cause the reader to join *them* in a specular relationship. That is to say, it is not the reader who, like the viewer of an aesthetic object, invests that object with the ability to return the human gaze. Rather, it is that least "original" or aesthetic or immediately sensory of objects—the printed and reprinted, hardback or paperback, pristine or underscored and dog-eared, lush vellum, virtual, or yellowing, and, in every case, infinitely reproducible text: it is the text here that invests the reader with the ability to return *its* gaze. Yet, rather than a kind of reverse anthropomorphism, what Morrison enacts in the aesthetic activity of her writing is a specifically textual representation instead, one that states—of necessity, *in* writing—the *inability* of writing to say what such writing would say: "If I were able I'd say it. Say make me, remake me. You are free to do it and I am free to let you because look, look. Look where your hands are. Now." Unable to say it, because a book; able to say it—saying it—because a book: the unparalleled sensuousness of a book speaking its "envy" of human lovers who "have no need to say" what it says it cannot and *does* say. And yet somehow that sensuousness is and is not the point, just as human lovers, no matter how enviable in their "public love," can never, forever, say, "now," can never ever say, "look where *your* hands are," not to each other but to a public without number.

That unforgettable enactment of a gaze *conferred* in love at the ending of *Jazz* may seem so seductive as to circumvent the necessity for any reflection. Yet the question of what or whom we gaze upon in the act of reading remains unanswered, the "secret" each reader so enjoined must ponder. The equally celebrated opening of the same novel seems poised to alienate rather than invite the reader's participation. Also written in the first person, it addresses, however, no one:

> Sth, I know that woman. She used to live with a flock of birds on Lenox Avenue. Know her husband, too. He fell for an eighteen-year-old girl with one of those deepdown, spooky loves that made him so sad and happy he shot her just to keep the feeling going. When the woman, her name is Violet, went to the funeral to see the girl and to cut her dead face they threw her to the floor and out of the church. She ran, then, through all that snow, and when she got back to her

apartment she took the birds from their cages and set them out the windows to freeze or fly, including the parrot that said, "I love you." (*Jazz*, 3)

There you have it ("you" who have not been named): the whole story, even "I love you," spoken to anyone at anytime by its most prosaic, mechanically reproductive speaker. In the beginning is the end of *Jazz*, and its middle, and, as unsensuous, unseductive, as this apostrophe-less opening is and is surely meant to be, it performs what only Lone in *Paradise* is said to know: "what neither memory nor history can say or record: the 'trick' of life and its 'reason'" (272). This gazing, knowing "I" performs what neither memory nor history can say or record, because in stating the story it knows it shows that story is neither life nor its reason; its "trick" is to make you ask what it, in its outspoken omniscience, denies, to engage it as it conceals itself from view. And the trick works, even if in parrotlike fashion: "Who is the narrator at the beginning of *Jazz*?"; or for that matter, "who is the narrator at the end of *Jazz*?"—the question, who is speaking here, asked over and over in private and in public,[2] itself indicates that the text has made us meet or at least attempt to meet that narrator, what or whomever we want or imagine that narrator to be.[3]

If openly at the close of *Jazz*, and in a closed manner at the opening of *Jazz*, then blindingly does the text of *The Bluest Eye* invest us with the specular—the aesthetic and political—ability to look. For there it is, the text we all read when learning to read and so never really *read* at all—the text lacking all substance or context but the thin text of unfathomable subtext, the invisible, the exemplarily transparent text—there they are, Dick and Jane. Mother and Father are there, the green and white house is there, the dog, the cat: all there as they have never, however, been anywhere before. The command to "see" them is there, too; it is part of the very text of them ("See Jane.... See the cat.... See Father.... See the dog run" [1]), and, for the first time, see them we do—literally, in different typefaces, in upper case or lowercase, with or without the spacing needed to set their letters, the characters of these otherwise characterless characters, apart. Framing each section of the narrative in a run-on segment we can only read with effort, reproduced in and as themselves, are the words we learned to read by, and learned not to read by, the words that made reading an exercise in the exercise of reading, its own self-reflexive, palindrome-like reward, as meaningless, homogeneous, and impossible to imagine as it was to imagine otherwise, with any other words: the "original" first-person evocation of "Dick and Jane." There *they* "are": not the nonsubjects of a nonnarrative they name, but the words that force us now to read *them* as such, that compel us to see them for what they *are*: words, only words, weapons, only weapons, representing nothing else than their exemplary status.

And in reading "Dick and Jane" as the reproductions they are, emblematic words made displaceable by their own emptiness, we, for the first time, need, read, and see more. To see "Dick and Jane" shorn of the illusion of their existence is to experience the revelation of the nightmare aesthetic that seeing—and not being—Dick and Jane represents, the private *and* public politics the green-and-white house domesticates and the command to "come and play" codifies, with all the apparent universality of the alphabet: a primer, a propaedeutic for the failure to read, for self-defeat, for reality ruled by unreality. See me, *that* reality, *The Bluest Eye*, commands. If, now, you will learn to read, come and see the Breedloves, gaze upon them whose gaze is not returned, where even "the loved one is shorn, neutralized, frozen in the glare of the lover's inward eye"; see a place, a context whose objects hold one in a kind of anti-aura, an investment that *becomes* specular for the reader exactly in its own admission that it is of the least specular kind—where the soil, the narrator Claudia states, is believed "bad for certain kinds of flowers," and

> we acquiesce and say the victim has no right to live. We are wrong, of course, but it doesn't matter. It's too late. At least on the edge of my town, among the garbage and the sunflowers of my town, it's much, much, much too late. (*The Bluest Eye*, 20)

> In ocean hush a woman black as firewood is singing. Next to her is a younger woman whose head rests on the singing woman's lap. Ruined fingers troll the tea brown hair. All the colors of seashells—wheat, roses, pearl—fuse in the younger woman's face. Her emerald eyes adore the black face framed in cerulean blue. Around them on the beach, sea trash gleams. Discarded bottle caps sparkle near a broken sandal.
>   A small dead radio plays the quiet surf. There is nothing to beat this solace which is what Piedade's song is about, although the words evoke memories neither one has ever had ... (*Paradise*, 318)

Set up against the closing words of *The Bluest Eye*, these lines from the close of *Paradise* show the works as each other's bookends. In more than the formal and developmental sense—of an early and singular narration of the mental refuge of single-mindedness, and a later, multiply reflective and refractive narrative voice—they are, face to face, each other's double and inversion. On the one side, no possible aesthetic, no gaze returned, the real and contagious madness of lived victimhood, and political death—"among the garbage and the sunflowers of my town, it's much, much, much too late"; on the other, the history of the propagation of an aesthetic reproduction that, anti-aesthetically, renders all gazes nearly as superfluous as they had long been between the founding, proprietorial Morgan twins, the real madness of the success of such an ideal of reproduction without difference, and, likewise, political death. And just as in Morrison's first novel what is novel is a distinctly human voice that has never been heard, a voice that identifies beauty nearly inhumanly with an unattainable superlative, "the bluest eye," in the later novel, narratives within narratives are shot through at every turn with all form of sensuous beauty: flowers grow thick upon flowers, their very names an inventory of naturally, almost too perfectly fertile soil, beauty, turned to for its own sake, gone wild:

> The moon's light glittered white fences gone slant in an effort to hold back chrysanthemums, foxglove, sunflowers, cosmos, daylilies, while mint and silver king pressed through the space at the bottom of the slats. The night sky, like a handsome lid, held the perfume down, saving it, intensifying it, refusing it the slightest breeze on which to escape.... The dirt yards, carefully swept and sprinkled in Haven, became lawns in Ruby until, finally, front yards were given over completely to flowers for no good reason except there was time in which to do it. ... The women kept on with their vegetable gardens in back, but little by little its produce became like flowers—driven by desire, not necessity. (*Paradise*, 89–90)

If both *The Bluest Eye* and *Paradise* unexpectedly mirror each other by representing *an* aesthetic, the real political consequences of imposing a definition of beauty on the world, their own aesthetic interaction demonstrates that beauty is not but does, and the mind that undergoes it as an *activity* may resemble "white fences gone slant" with flowers, an imagination that has grown thin. But look, the text *made* aesthetic, *made* political, seems to say, these words you read "evoke memories you have never had," cancel the aesthetic you believed you had. Along with murder committed in the name of paradise—an aesthetic one believes one owns and a genealogy of beauty one believes one knows—*Paradise* shows you how to gaze upon "white fences gone slant" with flowers, when the paradise one has imagined for oneself has grown as thin and brittle as the infertile soil of its imagining, and one's "driv[ing]" "desire" is not for the unpredictable beauty, the individual efflorescence of "flowers," but for the power, promised by "fences," to exclude these and all other unexpected encounters with the aesthetic, to make reproduction of sameness its own reason and reward.

The active achievement of Morrison's singular art, in works accomplished *so as* to be permanently unfinished, to be re-*produced differently*, as a newly present experience, by every individual reader, is to prove, in writing, our prior, prosaic imaginings thin, and our sight, before reading the writing, its own barrier to seeing, a fence barely capable of withholding new beauty from view. Pressing us to read "through the . . . slats," she makes visible our own "slant" of vision by revealing its impotence, like that of any fence, forever "to hold" the "flowers" "back," to remain upright against the weight of words in flower "now," which is to say, at any moment they are read. With Baudelaire, Morrison shares the modern view that the challenge and *reality of art* are to exclude nothing and no one from representation: that, just as every glimpse of beauty suggests something even better, greater than itself, evil can breed irrepressible flowers, too. The originality of her art is to represent, in infinitely active, inherently reproducible words, the present flowers, pressing even now among the historically "discarded," of beauty's enduring good. "Look," the aesthetic activity that is *Paradise* would seem to say to its reader, "look at the slant of your mind attempting without success to hold the flowers back."

Notes

1. Baudelaire, *Spleen II*, line 1.
2. The two related questions formed a plurality of all those submitted to Morrison at her 1999 reading at New York's Ninety-second Street Y, seconded only by "who was the white girl?" (in *Paradise*).
3. A brilliant critic and early admirer of Morrison once announced to me that she had in fact figured out who the narrator of *Jazz* was. Thinking more, I am sure, of Flaubert's faithful Félicité than of Walter Benjamin's politicized art, even while effectively minimizing the difference between them, Barbara Guetti laughingly, half-seriously, declared, "The parrot!"

Works Cited

Benjamin, Walter. *Selected Writings*. Vol. 4. 1940. Cambridge: Harvard University Press, 2003.
———. "The Work of Art in the Age of Mechanical Reproducibility" (1934/35; rev. 1939), first version published in French translation by the Institute for Social Research (1936); revised version published in Benjamin, *Gesammelte Schriften* (Frankfurt, 1955); English translation of first version published in *Illuminations*, trans. Harry Zohn, introduction by Hannah Arendt (New York, 1968); English translation of revised version by Edmund

Jephcott, published in *Selected Writings*, vol. 4, ed. Howard Eiland and Michael W. Jennings (Cambridge: Harvard University Press, 1996–2003).

Baudelaire, Charles. "Spleen II." In *Baudelaire: Oeuvres complètes*, ed. Marcel A. Ruff. Paris: Editions du Seuil, 1968. Translations mine.

Morrison, Toni. *The Bluest Eye*. New York: Vintage, 1999.

———. *Jazz*. New York: Alfred A. Knopf, 1992.

———. *Paradise*. New York: Alfred A. Knopf, 1998.

Proust, Marcel. *A la recherche du temps perdu*. 3 vols. Paris: Gallimard, 1954. Translations mine.

"'There is the Power,' he thought, 'Right There'"

Dramatizing Entropy in Tar Baby *and* Paradise

HERMAN BEAVERS

I begin with the assertion that Toni Morrison's fiction often portrays the lives of characters and communities that can be understood in terms of fluctuation, turbulence, and entropy.[1]

These terms come to us from the realm of systems or chaos theory, and they can serve us well as instruments of critical inquiry. Such an assertion finds validity, first, through the identification of recurring tropes, but subsequently the argument must move beyond mere identification in favor of elucidating how chaotics inform Morrison's overall critique of human endeavor, particularly in terms of how it has moved from modernity to postmodernity. As Philip Page points out, "Readers are familiar with Morrison's tendency to delve beyond the what into the more problematic *how* and *why*; with her nonlinear, polyvocal, multistranded narratives; and with such challenging techniques as jump-cutting radically from one scene and/or perspective to another and dropping unexplained tidbits that leave readers suspended, waiting for more information" (637).

This approach is indicative of Morrison's ongoing and multifaceted critique of repressive systems, and it is evident even in her earliest novels. In this essay, I argue that central to Morrison's investigation into "the more problematic *how* and *why*" is her investment in fictions that complicate what we think we know. Which is to say that Morrison is often at her most intriguing when she creates instability within systems of meaning (race, gender, class, etc.) where we are most comfortable resting on well-established assumptions. Morrison is highly dubious of the kinds of thinking that emerges from moribund systems of thought, and thus she seeks to unsettle how we understand the family, the village, and the traditions to be found in each. In light of this, I have identified four postulates at work in Morrison's fiction, each of which reflects terms drawn from systems (or chaos) theory:[2]

1. Systems in a state of fluctuation are often characterized by local (micro) disruptions that lead to global (macro) instability.
2. Negative feedback loops characterize stable systems; positive feedback loops characterize systems undergoing rapid change.
3. Systems facing entropy enact strategic measures that establish clear boundaries between inside and outside.
4. Turbulence can represent an opportunity for either self-renewal or self-delusion.

Morrison's fiction dramatizes the turbulence that results when sensibilities or entities that might be said to represent strategic forms of power and those that represent tactical exercises of power are in a state of violent opposition. As Malin Walther Pereira argues in a persuasive essay on *Tar Baby* (1981), Morrison's early fiction "struggles with the effects of colonization on African American individuals and the community, while her later fiction moves into an exploration of decolonized African American culture and history" (72).

However, it would be a mistake to assume that Morrison sees the processes that led to decolonization as either complete or absolute in their effects. What this could mean, especially when we observe the many instances where blacks put forward divergent perspectives, have incompatible agendas, and assume dogmatic postures in Morrison's fiction, is that decolonization is a necessary step to something yet unrealized in Morrison's characters or the society they inhabit. While we might hazard a set of speculations regarding what form this missing perspective or impending epiphany might assume, it seems much more efficacious to conclude that her most consistent answer to the question lies in her unwillingness to adopt a conventional approach to novelistic closure. The open-ended nature of her novels suggests that Morrison is less motivated to find out what the next stage in African American liberation might be than she is to explicate the obstacles to reaching it. Which is to say that to read her fiction as a set of ruminations on the nature of systems and disorder is, paraphrasing William Paulsen, to locate it among texts that seek to oppose structures of symbolic authority by troubling the very sanctity of symbolism (110).

This conflict lies at the heart of Morrison's *Paradise* (1997), where the inhabitants of Ruby have created the illusion of equilibrium, but at a tremendous cost. As James Clifford intimates, knowledge and how it is acquired (and how the acquisition is judged) can lead to divergent perspectives that can only be resolved by violent means.[3] Those whose knowledge grows out of their familiarity with people and their surroundings often distrust and come into conflict with those for whom knowledge is only legitimized when it is acquired en route to someplace else.

Two of Morrison's novels, *Tar Baby* and *Paradise*, demonstrate her affinity for interrogating the complexity of racial politics as they unfold *inside* the black community. In this, we see Morrison dramatizing what the legal scholar Kimberlé Crenshaw terms intersectionality,[4] where race and gender intersect to constitute both the site at which black female subjectivities begin to cohere and the site of dualistic forms of oppression. But such a move does not, in my view, constitute sufficient grounds for reading the novels as complementary texts. What makes elucidating them worthwhile is the manner in which, when read together, they demonstrate the shift in Morrison's approach to rendering the complexity of racial identity politics. Most significant, perhaps, is the manner in which both novels realize the third and fourth postulates with their representation of systems in danger of collapse that create effects that redound across temporal and spatial contexts and their use of turbulence as an opportunity for self-renewal or self-delusion.

Further, in *Tar Baby* and *Paradise* we find a fifth postulate: the propensity for closed systems to create the illusion that outsiders have insider status. The manner by which individuals seek to engage this conundrum pivots on whether their approach is recursive or iterative. As Gordon Slethaug observes, recursion "refers to the replication of acts, occasions, and patterns within a given object, subject, or system," and iteration involves "the ongoing incorporation of various changes wrought by successive repetitions" (98). This dichotomy leads us to reflect on how the communities represented in Morrison's fictions arrive at decisions regarding self-sustenance and the ways those decisions establish boundaries that become so rigidified that strategic symbolism becomes the order of the day. At issue here, I would conjecture, is that despite the ways that Morrison is read as an author who values cultural memory and its role as a regenerative modality in the black community, she is perhaps more aptly understood as an author who resists simple binaries, who seeks to render all assumptions fluid. Indeed, *Beloved*, with its insistence that "this is not a story to pass on," argues for an iterative relationship to the past, which means that cultural memory functions as the source of corrective behaviors, as opposed to a recursive posture characterized by replicating patterns of erroneous thinking.

Of course, it is clear that, of the two novels, *Tar Baby* has been considered by critics to be a lesser work, whose conclusions and characters have left readers less than satisfied. But as Pereira argues, we are better served by viewing the novel as a transitional text between the aforementioned paradigm shift and her first three novels that locate the ancestral past as a necessary aspect of black survival (72). Though I see the merits of this argument, I would further insist that Morrison's portrayal of intraracial dynamics in *Tar Baby* was enacted in a time before critics had internalized the need to abandon racial essentialism, on the one hand, and on the other, as the feminist insistence on the necessity for women to embrace acts of self-making was being distilled through the divergent experiences of women of color and white women. As we read the novel through the lens of the early 1980s, then, Morrison's portrayal of the relationship between Son and Jadine gets read as an encounter best understood as a reflection of the ways black nationalism constitutes an interpretive logic governing romantic relationships. The novel's proximity to Ntozake Shange's *for colored girls who have considered suicide/when the rainbow is enuf* (prod. 1975; pub. 1977) and Michele Wallace's *Black Macho and the Myth of the Superwoman* (1979), being mindful of the nationalist backlash directed against both, led readers to conclude—given the novel's conclusion—that Morrison was writing in support of the idea that black women's "confusion" had deleterious effects on the lives of black men.[5]

But it is here that reading *Tar Baby* and *Paradise* together becomes both productive and interventionary. By teasing out each novel's enactment of principles found in systems theory, what I argue is that, despite the sixteen-year gap between the two novels, *Tar Baby* anticipates *Paradise*'s rumination on the foreclosures to which notions of racial purity will inevitably lead in the town of Ruby. As Linda Krumholz insists, *Tar Baby* represents Morrison's effort to "show readers that we are all implicated in the construction of blackness" (263). Hence Philip Page's apt declaration that *Paradise* "requires the readers' participation by forcing them into complex acts of interpretation" (638) points to how Morrison is seeking to find a way out of the conundrum of making racialized identities an end in themselves.

Reading *Tar Baby* alongside *Paradise* begins with an acknowledgment of their contrasts: the former is set on an island in the Caribbean, at a house owned by Valerian Street, the latter in Ruby, an all-black town, founded by the progeny of ex-slaves. The oppositions in *Tar Baby* have to do with the collision that results when Son's "village values" come into contact with Jadine's cosmopolitanism. In *Paradise*, the men of Ruby conclude that they need to eradicate the threat represented by the women in the Convent because they threaten to contaminate the town, whose "purity" is the sign of 8-rock superiority. A first point of contact lies, however, in the fact that both novels provide us with enactments of paradise, of utopian spaces free of the dictates that might be imposed by the instability of capital or the social negation of white supremacy.

To be clear, my decision to place *Tar Baby* into conversation with *Paradise* issues from my sense that both novels exemplify Morrison's propensity to portray systems in decline (entropy) in search of new sources of energy (physical, material, or ideological). An even greater similitude between the novels is the manner in which entropy determines how the action unfolds in both texts.[6] For our purposes, Morrison's fiction can be said to represent moments when systems are in danger of falling into a state of irreversible dissipation.[7]

Since a system is defined as any organized, orderly set of processes, it seems counterintuitive to suggest that Morrison's fiction seeks to portray instances when order is breaking down as the most fertile sources of human possibility.[8] However, systems in need of new sources of sustenance are often forced to recognize the necessity of relaxing the boundaries characterizing closed systems.

Though both *Tar Baby* and *Paradise* end in ways that suggest Morrison's tendency to eschew neat methods of closure, I submit that she sees the moments when meaning undergoes destabilization as the most favorable conditions for human freedom and innovation to thrive. One of the best examples in *Paradise* of this kind instability is the Oven. Built by the men who founded the all-black town of Haven, the predecessor to Ruby, the Oven is dismantled and then lovingly reassembled upon the arrival of the fifteen families that start over in Ruby after Haven's failure. In this sense, the Oven is a relic of the past, but one that holds significance for the elders of Ruby, who continue to believe that the inscription on the door of the Oven states, "Beware the furrow of his brow." Though the women have long abandoned it as a means of preparing food, the Oven nonetheless represents the legacy of the Morgans, Deek and Steward.

But the Oven, in all its historic resonance, has fallen into disuse, become an instrument of idolatry rather than social utility. Morrison's use of the Oven as a point of conflict in the early pages of the novel points to its importance as an instance where the prospect of entropy occasions an increase in possibility. Although it is no longer a source of the heat necessary to prepare meals, it is nonetheless a source of ideological heat. When the young men in the town state a desire to change the inscription on the Oven to "Be the Furrow of His Brow," the elders object with disdain and revisit the process of the Oven's construction and its dismantling and reconstruction. After hearing the debate, Deek Morgan rises and declares:

> They made good strong brick for that oven when their own shelter was sticks and sod.... Nothing was handled more gently than the bricks those men—men, hear me? not slaves, ex or otherwise—the bricks those men made. Tell them, Sargeant, how delicate was the separation, how careful we were, how we wrapped them, each and every one. Tell them, Fleet. You, Seawright, you, Harper, you tell him if I'm lying. Me and my brother lifted that iron. The two of us. And if some letters fell off, it wasn't due to us because we packed it in straw like a mewing lamb. (85–86)

As Philip Page brilliantly points out, what Morrison depicts here is significant; not only "are there multiple meanings of the text—multiple signifieds—but here are multiple texts, multiple signifiers" (639). Here she suggests that the dialogue the Oven generates is a new form of heat, a way to reinvigorate Ruby's waning power, at the very least a discussion that should signal that the young are ready to take their place among the town fathers.[9] But the dispute over meaning, whether the Oven begins with "Be," "We," or "Beware," also signals a fluctuation of meaning. In Morrison's universe, this is a good thing, for she is at her most distrustful of strategic forms of power when meanings are stable, unimpeachable. However, what is also at work is the collision between tactical and strategic symbolisms.[10] For the young men, the word "Be" suggests a reframing of the Oven's purpose, a shift from conservatism to radicalism, from passive vessel to political agent. For the elders, the word "Beware" is their most visible link to the past, not only to the vengeance their predecessors sought to bring about in the face of the Disavowal, but also the license that signifies their authority. Following Page's argument that the Oven requires "law, order, and the preservation of the status quo," I submit that the elder's vision is recursive. In imagining Ruby as a liberatory space, the elders use the Old Testament and the narrative of the Israelites as God's chosen people as sources of meaning. Thus when Steward Morgan declares, "If you, any one of you ignore, change, take away, or add to the words in the mouth of that Oven, I will blow your head off just like you was a hood-eye snake" (87), he shifts from the compensatory rhetorics that accompany narratives involving the achievement of a liberated consciousness to the strategic rhetoric we associate with a repressive state. His threat forecloses the possibility that dialogue creates, and points to the Oven as a false idol wrought from a reified past.

Ruby comprises the penultimate negative feedback loop: its future all but nullified by the dominance of the 8-rock families, its present characterized by a combination of self-congratulation and isolationism, and the past romanticized till it resembles Greek mythology. Any fluctuation in the town's routine is met with a determined effort to eradicate it, such that "the one or two people who acted up, humiliated their families or threatened the town's view of itself were taken good care of" (8). It is the reason the Convent represents such an obvious threat. Peopled by women, many of whom are defined by their status as either outcasts, castoffs, or malcontents, the Convent is actually the space that undermines Ruby's ability to remain a closed system.

An equally compelling moment occurs in *Tar Baby*, when Jadine accompanies Son back to his hometown of Eloe, Florida. Though Jadine and Son have returned to New York, which for her is a place of familiarity and possibility, where she has rediscovered that "if ever there was a black woman's town, New York was it" (222), she becomes instantly aware that Eloe is the antithesis of New York. Son's insistence that they visit Eloe bespeaks both his lasting ties to his rural upbringing, with its divergent notion of space and progress, and his distrust of urban modernity. And just as Son feels out of place in New York, so Jadine is unsure of how to engage Eloe's inhabitants. The men, like Son's friend, Soldier, look at her with dismay, unsure of how she and Son have settled the matter of control in the relationship. The older women, like Son's Aunt Rosa, are embarrassed by what they see as Jadine's immodesty, while the younger women look at her with "outright admiration" and wonder "where did she know Son from and how much did her boots cost" (250).

During a night when Son sneaks into Jadine's room to make love, she "struggles to outdo [Son's deceased wife] Cheyenne and surpass her legendary gifts" (257). Because they are "paying attention only to each other," they forget that Son has left the door leading outside open, allowing the "night women" to come into the room to watch Jadine in action. Cheyenne, Son's dead wife, is the first to arrive. Then she is joined by "Rosa and Therese and Son's dead mother and Sally Sarah Sadie Brown and Ondine and Soldier's wife Ellen and Francine from the mental institution and [Jadine's] dead mother and even the woman in yellow" (258). Though they are apparitions only visible to Jadine, they are "all there spoiling her lovemaking, taking away her sex like succubi," as if her presence is a spectacle for all to see. When she asks what the women want with her, without a word, the women each look as if "they had just been waiting for that question and they each pulled out a breast and showed it to her.... They stood around in the room, jostling each other gently, gently—there wasn't much room—revealing one breast and then two and Jadine was shocked." After Jadine responds, "I have breasts too," the night women are not convinced: "They just held their own higher and pushed their own farther out and looked at her. All of them revealing both their breasts except the woman in yellow. She did something more shocking—she stretched out a long arm and showed Jadine her three big eggs" (258–59).

The night women denote the manner in which Jadine is haunted by a recursive loop, in which the exposed breasts signify the "funk" Morrison describes in *The Bluest Eye*. They represent, moreover, what would seem on its face to be a propensity for self-display but is actually the declaration that female sexuality gains purchase only within the context of maternity, a model of womanhood that transcends race, in which womanhood is a function of how fully a woman can embody tradition because she can, in the words of Gayl Jones's Ursa Corregidora, "make generations." What makes this a distinctive moment in the novel, moreover, is that it points to Morrison's depiction of a system falling into decline. But because a reading sympathetic to nationalist identity politics often interprets the omniscient narrator as being sympathetic to Son, Jadine's emotional response to the night women is easily read as the measure of her dislocation from the black community, her confusion about who she is, her misalignment with conventional notions of black womanhood.

To the contrary, I submit the moment is indicative of the emotional turbulence that accompanies Jadine's novelty. If the reader interprets *Tar Baby* as a brand of melodrama now familiar to readers of black romance novels, then it is not a leap to conclude that the night women's presence signals her alienation and the necessity of being in line with tradition. But it is my sense that Morrison conceptualizes Jadine as a way to destabilize the forces circumscribing notions of womanhood. As such, it is Jadine's unsettledness, her location *in the process* of self-making, that makes her distinctive.

In light of this, let us return to a point earlier in the novel, during Jadine's exchange with Soldier, who considers Son and Jadine and wonders, "Who's controllin it?" During that exchange, Soldier interrogates Jadine about her background while she seeks information about Cheyenne and her relationship to Son. Soldier relates that Son "wouldn't know a good woman from a snake" (255). But when Jadine challenges that assessment with a put-down of her own, Soldier's rejoinder, "You a hot one, ain't you?" signals that his understanding of relationships rests on the assumption that women who give off the figurative heat of self-assertion must be subordinated. Thus his question of who controls the relationship intimates that he sees what happens between a man and a woman as a matter of heat transfer, where the man's dominance is the means by which the "heat" possessed by independent women like Jadine can be subdued. Soldier's declaration that "Son don't like control. Makes him, you know wildlike" (255) likewise signals his incredulity in the face of Jadine's insistence that "nobody controls anybody." Though her defensiveness is disingenuous, Jadine's sentiment, when viewed through her cosmopolitanism, is apparent. But because Soldier can only conceptualize men's relations with women in terms of heat, Jadine's assertion is problematic because it rests on a thermodynamic dilemma: when two objects with the same relative temperature are in proximity, how can "work" be done? If sexuality can be thought of as a form of heat exchange, Soldier's question points to his sense that someone must be in control, to maintain the negative feedback loop all relationships seek to sustain. Knowing that Son has driven his car into the house he shared with Cheyenne, causing the fire that kills both her and her lover, Soldier's declaration that control makes Son "wildlike" means that a woman who fails to make Son the center of her world, to love him exclusively, sends him into a state akin to boiling. Which is also to say that Son's response to efforts to control him takes the form of a positive feedback loop.

In my two examples, Morrison points first to the dangers of recursive approaches to history. Second, we see the ways that recursive loops can assume spectral forms that "haunt" or trouble the conditions in which iteration might occur. *Tar Baby* is a novel that, on its face, contains characters who enact the fifth postulate: systems in danger of decline can sustain themselves by creating conditions in which "outsiders" can assume "insider" status. However, I would argue that to reach such a conclusion, the reader has to cast Jadine into what has often been her traditional role as Son's foil. I would insist, by way of dissent, that Jadine is an iterative figure; she seeks to establish a new pattern, one that might run afoul of previous models of black womanhood, but one that is nonetheless rich in possibility. One could read Jadine's exchange with Ondine, near the end of the novel, as a sign of her rebelliousness. However, I submit we need to be more critical of Ondine's declaration "Jadine, a girl has got to be a daughter first. She have to learn that. And if she never learns how to be a daughter, she can't never learn how to be a woman. I mean a real woman: a woman good enough for a child; good enough for a man—good enough even for the respect of other women" (281). While this is an observation that might have had merit for women of Ondine's generation, it has diminishing value for women like Jadine because it is recursive. It casts women's relations in the traditional terms of mother, daughter, and wife and implies that positive relationships with other women hang in the balance. However, Jadine's experiences in New York and Paris, the fact that she has an education and can think critically (albeit in ways that are Eurocentric to a fault), mean that she constitutes a new iteration of black femininity. As if to confirm this, the omniscient narrator declares, "If ever there was a black woman's town, New York was it" (222), and provides a list of the ways that black women entering the professional ranks create a level of turbulence that announces that they are a force to be reckoned with. The jobs the narrator lists would be recognizable to readers in the twenty-first century as service-economy jobs, and the women described as single heads-of-households, first demonized in the Moynihan report and later by then-presidential candidate Ronald Reagan as kin to the notorious "welfare queen." But this does not diminish Jadine's importance as an iterative break from convention. Indeed, if we are to value Morrison's insistence, "No more dreams of safety. No more. Perhaps that was the thing—the thing Ondine was saying. A grown woman did not need safety or its dreams. She *was* the safety she longed for" (290), we must struggle against the prevailing tendency to marginalize Jadine's iteration of black womanhood.

When we bring *Paradise* to bear on this discussion, then, we can conclude that Morrison returned to tropes that functioned just below what readers in 1981 understood as the "surface" of the text and amplified them. Her portrayal of the violent attack on the women of the Convent demonstrates the ways that systems in decline are always already in a state of exigency, ready to survive "by any means necessary." The generational dispute over the Oven leaves the efficacy of violence uncritiqued. We find a complementary moment in *Tar Baby* when Jadine happens upon Son and Valerian "laughing to beat the band." What signals Morrison's critique of masculine privilege is not only the joke that Son tells Valerian about "the three colored whores who went to heaven" but also Son's preceding pronouncement, "I know all about plants. They like women, you have to jack them up every once in a while. Make em act nice, like they're supposed to" (148). What I'm insisting on here is that Son's notion of women, like the men who murder the women in the Convent, is predicated on "heat." Unlike the men of Ruby who are "packing heat," Son's version is, at root, violent and coercive. Son's attractiveness, his resistance to the dictates of white supremacy, notwithstanding, he nonetheless leads us to conclude that masculine privilege is recursive and strategic. Though we might find all sorts of reasons to be critical of Jadine or the women who inhabit the Convent, while we might view the conclusions of both novels as unsatisfying, noncommittal, we must contend with Morrison's desire to destabilize what we think we know about how to manifest forms of community. In *Tar Baby* and *Paradise*, she gives us fictions that help us to understand that the performance of blackness in the postmodern moment is at its most vibrant when we are uncertain about its methods and anxious about its designs.

Notes

1. In his essay "A Philosophical Evaluation of the Chaos Theory 'Revolution,'" Stephen H. Kellert provides a highly useful definition of chaos theory: "While qualititative questions can be asked about almost any dynamical system, chaos theory focuses on certain forms of behavior—behavior which is *unstable* and *aperiodic*. Instability means that the system never settles into a pattern of behavior that resists small disturbances. A system marked by instability, on the other hand, will shrug off a small jostle and continue about its business like a marble which, when jarred, will come again to rest at the bottom of a bowl.... Aperiodic behavior occurs when the state of the system never exactly repeats itself. Unstable aperiodic behavior is thus highly complex: it never repeats and it continues to manifest the effects of any small perturbation" (34; italics in original).

2. In making such a declaration, I follow Peter Francis Mackey's formulations in *Chaos Theory and James Joyce's Everyman*, where he proposes that the life of Leopold Bloom in Joyce's *Ulysses* presents the reader with four ideas that affect both Bloom's life and that of the reader. Thus some of the postulates are lifted from Mackey, and others are the product of trying to think across the breadth of Morrison's fiction (cf. Mackey, 1).

3. As Clifford notes: "The currency of culture and identity, as performative acts, can be traced to their articulation of homelands, safe spaces, where the traffic across borders can be controlled. Such acts of control, maintaining coherent insides and outsides, are always tactical. Cultural action, the making and remaking of identities, takes place in contact zones, along the policed and transgressive intercultural frontiers of nations, peoples, locales. Stasis and purity are asserted—creatively and violently—against historical forces of movement and contamination" (7).

4. Stephanie Wildman and Adrienne D. Davis credit Crenshaw and other scholars for their invention of a phrase meant to describe black women's dual oppressions in the spheres of race and gender, what Wildman and Davis refer to as "intersections of subordination" ("Language and Silence," 578).

5. Such a profound misreading of the text was only possible in a critical atmosphere in which black male critics had left gender politics in the black community completely uncritiqued, most particularly black men's deep and abiding investment in patriarchy and male domination. Thus we must consider the ways that, as Clifford might have it, "the currency of culture and identity" was not yet understood as a performative act, and efforts at "maintaining coherent insides and outsides," those "policed and intercultural frontiers of nations, peoples, locales," were understood as a necessary means of racial identification even as they resulted in black women's marginal status (7).

6. As N. Katherine Hayles points out in her book *Chaos Bound*, the concept of entropy, as it was coined by Rudolf Clausius in 1850, is best understood through the field of thermodynamics (38). Strictly defined, the term refers to "a measure of the heat lost for useful purposes." The concept became explicit in 1852 when William Thomson (Lord Kelvin), a British thermodynamicist building on the second law of thermodynamics, which states that "in a closed system entropy always tends to increase" (38), concluded that "within a finite period of time ... the earth must again be unfit for the inhabitation of man as at present constituted" (quoted in Hayles, 39).

7. If entropy can be described as the moment when heat ceases to be added to a closed system, leading to a chaotic state, where random possibility assumes singular importance, then we must also think about the ways that a closed system's main priority is to stabilize sources of input and thus remain "ordered."

8. Though entropy is a product of scientific discourse, Hayles insists that we recognize that entropy is a product of the Victorian age. "The convergence of social formation," she notes, "with the complex connections among repressive morality, capital formation, and industrialization in Victorian society" (39), highlights the anxiety that accompanies system failure. Thus the "universal tendency toward dissipation" links entropic heat loss semantically to deplorable personal habits (39). Kelvin's conclusion regarding the impending uninhabitability of the earth must be understood as both a scientific and a moral claim, a chiasmus reflected in the claims of imperialism, suggesting that entropy, when we view it in a political context, "represents an inescapable limit on the human will to control" (40).

9. As the novel's first moments demonstrate, it is this generational collaboration that lies at the heart of the attack on the Convent. The young men's rhetoric, harkening back to the nationalism of the sixties, becomes instrumental in the violent response to difference. Which is to say that I do not dismiss the notion that the dispute over the Oven—which is an implement we usually associate with domestic space—is finally a dispute over control, to be sure, but perhaps more directly, how and when the use of force is sanctioned.

10. In *The Practice of Everyday Life*, Michel de Certeau distinguishes between strategic and tactical imperatives. A strategy "assumes a place that can be circumscribed as *proper* (propre) and thus serve as the basis for generating relations with an exterior distinct from it." A tactic is "a calculated action determined by the absence of a proper locus. . . . The space of a tactic is a space of the other. Thus it must play on and with a terrain imposed on it and organized by the law of a foreign power" (36–37).

Works Cited

Clifford, James. *Routes: Travel and Translation in the Late Twentieth Century.* Cambridge: Harvard University Press, 1997.

Davidson, Rob. "Racial Stock and 8-Rocks: Communal Historiography in Toni Morrison's *Paradise*." *Twentieth-Century Literature* 47, no. 3 (Fall 2001): 355–73.

De Certeau, Michel. *The Practice of Everyday Life.* 1984. Berkeley: University of California Press, 1988.

Hayles, N. Catherine. *Chaos Bound: Orderly Disorder in Contemporary Literature and Science.* Ithaca, NY: Cornell University Press, 1990.

Jones, Gayl. *Corregidora.* Boston: Beacon Press, 1975.

Kellert, Stephen. "A Philosophical Evaluation of the Chaos Theory 'Revolution.'" In *PSA: Proceedings of the Biennial Meeting of the Philosophy of Science Association*, vol. 2, *Symposia and Invited Papers*, 33–49. Chicago: University of Chicago Press, 1993.

Krumholz, Linda. "Blackness and Art in Toni Morrison's *Tar Baby*." *Contemporary Literature* 49, no. 2 (Summer 2008): 263–92.

Mackey, Peter Francis. *Chaos Theory and James Joyce's Everyman*. Gainesville: University Press of Florida, 1999.

Morrison, Toni. *Beloved*. New York: Signet, 1987.

———. *The Bluest Eye*. 1970. New York: Plume, 1993.

———. *Paradise*. New York: Plume, 1997.

———. *Tar Baby*. 1981. New York: Plume, 1982.

Page, Philip. "Furrowing All the Brows: Interpretation and the Transcendent in Toni Morrison's *Paradise*." *African American Review* 35, no. 4 (Winter 2001): 637–49.

Paulsen, William. *Literary Culture in a World Transformed: A Future for the Humanities*. Ithaca: Cornell University Press, 2001.

Pereira, Malin Walther. "Periodizing Toni Morrison's Work from *The Bluest Eye* to *Jazz*: The Importance of *Tar Baby*." *MELUS* 22, no. 34 (Autumn 1997): 71–82.

Slethaug, Gordon. *Beautiful Chaos: Chaos Theory and Metachaotics in Recent American Fiction*. Albany: SUNY Press, 2000.

Wildman, Stephanie, and Adrienne D. Davis. "Language and Silence: Making Systems of Privilege Visible." In *Critical Race Theory: The Cutting Edge*, ed. Richard Delgado, 573–79. Philadelphia: Temple University Press.

TELLING STORIES

Evolving Narrative Identity in Toni Morrison's Home

JAN FURMAN

∽

Structure is meaning, according to Toni Morrison. Plot is information about *what* happened, she says. The structure, what lies underneath plot activity, manifests the writer's intention and shapes readers' experience of the text. Morrison "work[s] very hard" at this "sort of deep structure" (Silverblatt, 218). *Jazz*'s (1992) narrative hipness—improvisational story, syncopated first-person voice, 1920s vernacular—captures the energy, possibility, and adolescent self-regard of transplanted blacks in New York City's jazz scene, for example. *Love*'s (2003) crystalline accretion of polyphonic narrative voices reveals characters' delusions of isolation. "They may feel separate," Morrison points out, "but everything they do and think is connected to the behavior, or what they think was the reason for the behavior of somebody else" (Silverblatt, 219). In *Home* (2012), Frank Money's dual-voiced narrative signals the psychological effects of war and racial violence on masculine self-identity in 1950s America. Speaking retrospectively, in first person, Frank continually queries and contradicts the third-person center-of-consciousness account of his experiences. Because a first-person retrospective view of one's life is not different from a third-person center-of-consciousness perspective of the same life, his is, in effect, a voice divided. "In both," Shlomith Rimmon-Kenan points out, "the focalization is a character within the represented world. The only difference between the two is the identity of the narrator" (73). That the voices are not in accord suggests Frank's unresolved psychic conflict. His autobiographical vignettes painfully unearth secrets that forestall his emergence from adolescence into manhood, while a third-person rendering of his consciousness looks forward to the immediate and distant future. One view is to the past, the other to the future, but the novel moves toward integrating this bifurcated vision and reconciling its competing narratives.

Complex, fragmented, and a major source of cues to the novel's themes and motifs, Frank's "I" occupies very little text space and is a fraction of the novel's multilayered narrative in which Frank, a twenty-six-year-old Korean War veteran, recounts major episodes of his life to Morrison, in her role as *Home*'s author. As Morrison phrases it, "I let the character sit on my shoulder and talk to me" (Rose). That approach, she notes, was "my great discovery! I didn't want to take on the 'I' persona, so he and I are in this relationship" (Shea). Such an arrangement begs the question of how, in critical language, one might characterize Morrison's role in the text. Morrison clearly authors *Home*, a fully envisioned work of fiction, including its narrative strategy that involves Frank telling Morrison the story that she is creating. A fictional writer inside the story to whom Frank might speak would be familiar literary ground. It would be light work, indeed, to distinguish between Frank and a fictional writer within Morrison's plot frame. *Home*, however, requires a more demanding critical discussion. And given Morrison's emphasis, both inside and outside the text, on her writerly relationship to Frank, it seems appropriate, if a little awkward in an age of literary studies that insists on the distinction between author and narrator, to speak of *Frank's* first-person narrative in the one instance and *Morrison's* third-person focalization in the other.

Italicized passages suggest Frank's spoken monologue and distinguish his first-person retrospective voice from Morrison's focalization. As Frank looks backward, in Morrison's words, to "learn about what he does . . . learn about himself, and learn . . . with the aid of community" (Shea), Morrison's focalization keeps the novel's temporal pace, what Susan Stanford Friedman refers to as a text's horizontal dimension, which "involves the linear movement of characters through . . . space and time" (14). It begins with Frank's escape from a Seattle mental ward in 1952 and ends days later in the small community of Lotus, Georgia, where he returns with his sister, Cee. Through Frank's focalized point of view, Morrison also constructs Friedman's "vertical narrative axis," which generally constitutes a text's "literary, social, and historical intertexts" (14). Thus Frank's journey by bus and train across the northwest to Atlanta with a stop in Chicago captures, especially, the precariousness and danger of blacks' encounters with white society in the 1950s and the black community's organized and ad hoc responses. A public and underground network of accommodation and rescue includes extravagant generosity from churches, train porters, and strangers, which made travel reasonably safe and survival possible. The fifties were a decade of "violent racism," Morrison notes in her commentary on *Home*. "I wished to rip the scab off that period," she says. "There's all this 'Leave It to Beaver' nostalgia. That it was all comfortable and happy and everyone had a job [but].... There was McCarthy. There was this horrible war we didn't call a war, where 58,000 people died" (quoted in Minzesheimer). And there was "A lot of medical apartheid, the license of preying on black women, the syphilis trials on black men" (quoted in Shea).

While plot renders these elements of meaning, Frank's meta-narrative raises and answers *Home*'s animating question about what it means to be a man, perhaps especially a black man, at midcentury (Bollen). That, according to Morrison, is Frank's dilemma, and the alternating conviction and doubt about the quality of his manhood shape Frank's narrative identity. Frank's telling is not continuous or consistent. Each of his eight chapters is a different memory or reflection, and each is Frank's attempt to reconcile his self-defining master narrative with contradicting experience. The narrative resolves the dissonance between what Frank believes and what he experiences by the novel's end. But Frank's is not a quest. Morrison does employ elements of questing, beginning with Frank's call to adventure in Korea, the long road home, tests and allies along the way, death and rebirth in midjourney and at the conclusion. However, because *Home*'s deep structure is its narrative dissonance, Frank is quick to warn Morrison away from romantic myth. "*Don't paint me as some enthusiastic hero*," he tells her. "*I had to go* [rescue Cee] *but I dreaded it*" (84). In Morrison's thinking, "It's a learning process—his going back and forth" (quoted in Ashbrook). *Home*, then, is the story of Frank's maturation, rendered as a process of narrative integration. Tension between the two voices relaxes in Frank's deepening willingness to see all the parts of himself over the course of the novel's lean plot.

These first-person and third-person focalized points of view, which may also be understood as the "I" and "Me," facilitate Frank's storytelling about the past and allow him to achieve purpose and wholeness in the present. This narrative model of human development is the interdisciplinary work of the psychologist Dan McAdams and others who position narrative identity within a broadly integrated (rather than fragmented) framework for conceptualizing human selfhood (McAdams, 102). As McAdams explains it, integrated narrative identity is essential to a generative life, and in Morrison's words, "Wordwork is sublime ... because it is generative" (*Nobel Lecture*, 22). McAdams presents the narrative self in terms of the I and Me paradigm articulated by the psychologist William James, who saw personal identity as an integrated self, composed of the "empirical person," or Me, and the "judging Thought," or I (371). Here I am positioning Morrison's center-of-consciousness as the empirical, observing voice and Frank's as the judging I. McAdams offers this comprehensive outline:

> Over the life course, the I develops increasingly sophisticated and nuanced understandings of the Me as it develops from an actor to an agent to an author. Reflecting our evolutionary heritage as social animals, human infants begin life as ... social *actors*. Around one's second birthday, an initial actor-self begins to form, as the I begins reflexively to take note of the basic traits and proclivities that make it (the Me) up. With its collection of fixed traits and essential features, the actor-Me is similar to what Chandler (2001) describes as an *essentialist* rendering of selfhood. With the development of theory of mind (Wellman, 1993) in the fourth and fifth years of life and with the establishment of goals and motives in later childhood, human beings begin to see themselves from the standpoint of ... motivated *agents*, as well, whose goals, plans, desires, programs, and long-term aims take up residency in the newly expanded Me. In adolescence and young adulthood, the I becomes ... an *author* too, seeking to fashion the Me into a self-defining story, consistent with what Chandler (2001) describes as a *narrative* rendering of selfhood. That story, or narrative identity, explains what the social actor does, what the motivated agent wants, and what it all means in the context of one's narrative understanding of the self. By providing a story regarding how the Me came to be over time, as well as what the Me may become in the future, the self-as-author extends the Me back into one's personal history and forward into the imagined distant future. Narrative identity, then, is that feature of human selfhood that begins to emerge when the adolescent or young-adult I assumes the guise of a storyteller. (103)

Frank's developing narrative identity reliably hits McAdams's markers and invites useful cognitive comparisons. At age four—the earliest period he chooses to recall—Frank knew the workings of his world, in which he experienced himself as part of a vulnerable family and community. Forced to leave Texas by vigilantes, his community and life broke open. At four these events were hypersensory: the discomfort of a flapping shoe, searing heat that defies description, piercing hunger, the sweetness of a newborn sister whose name was like music. Frank relates these details as a kind of coming out, a personal story of opening to new worlds—the birth; his namesake, Uncle Frank; crossing the geographical border from Texas to Louisiana; awakening to sensate effects of racial hatred.

At age ten, as mapped on McAdams's continuum, Frank acquired agency. His defining beliefs about manliness grew from a seminal childhood encounter with horses and bad men. In a brief first-person account, Frank recalls standing awestruck in waist-high grass, witnessing the brute force of two determined stallions, "*their raised hooves crashing and striking, their manes tossing back from wild white eyes*" (3). Ten-year-old Frank and six-year-old Cee had ignored posted warnings and crawled under a fence to stand within fifty feet of the action. When the fury subsided and Frank and Cee attempted to retrace their steps to the fence, they stopped just short of a group of men burying a body. Hiding and terrified, the two children were unable to see the men's faces but could make out the foot of their victim, "*that black foot with its creamy pink and mud-streaked sole being whacked into the grave*" (4). Fourteen years later, Frank's strongest memory of the afternoon is the way the horses reared up to a standing position. He insists that in the time since, he has not remembered the grave or the body. "*I really forgot about the burial*," he declares to Morrison. "*I only remembered the horses. They were so beautiful. So brutal. And they stood like men*" (5).

Frank is wrong, of course. Both scenes have haunted his thoughts and shaped his sensibilities and ambitions. Form and movement on the imposing scale of horses, the danger explicit in that movement, and what Frank perceived as the dignity of their brave instincts called forth his own authority. He experienced a distinct inkling of manhood. The subsequent violence, however, competed with that emerging authority. The brutality and courage of the horses took on different meaning as he crouched in the grass. When the men drove the protruding foot into its hole, Ycidra trembled, and Frank, rising to the occasion, protected her. In that moment the awesome beauty and force of nature were perverted; anger and fierce fidelity supplanted what had been noble and manly. Frank remembers that Ycidra

> *was the first person I ever took responsibility for. Down deep inside her lived my secret picture of myself—a strong good me tied to the memory of those horses and the burial of a stranger. Guarding her, finding a way through tall grass and out of that place, not being afraid of anything—snakes or wild old men. . . . In my little boy heart I felt heroic and I knew that if they found us or touched her I would kill.* (104)

The scene's meaning derives, in part, from the stalwart intimacy of sibling relationships. Absent rivalry, impatience, jealousy, and competition, Frank's attention to Cee is heroic. In privileging their bond, Morrison was "trying to think of when a man would love a woman without the baggage. Who is the female that he would love selflessly? Not a mother, not a lover, not a wife—only a sister" (quoted in Shea).

Afterward, as a growing boy, Frank lived his heroic vision, protecting Cee and being generous to others. Cee tells how he took a baseball bat to a flasher standing near her and kept the step-grandmother from her worst mistreatments of the little girl she called "gutter child." In fearful times, Cee could count on Frank to "touch the top of her head with four fingers, or stoke her nape with his thumb. Don't cry, said the fingers; the welts will disappear. Don't cry; Mama is tired; she didn't mean it. Don't cry, don't cry girl. I'm right here" (53). Even the young girl Jackie, whom he had not seen in years, remembers Frank as "the one long ago [who] had made a collar for her puppy" (116). Frank skips these events in his first-person narrative. It is as if the horses and burial were all. "*I wonder,*" he asks regretfully, "*if succeeding at that* [protecting Cee from wild old men] *was the buried seed of all the rest*" (104). Did he later fail in war and love because notions of manhood at age ten set up false ambitions of bravery, honor, and duty? As a teenager, the army had been a welcome relief; he "*couldn't wait to get out and . . . far away*" (84). He wanted more than what he believed was his parents' hopeless life. Frank understood that "*having been run out of one town, any other that offered safety and the peace of sleeping through the night and not waking up with a rifle in your face was more than enough*" for them. "*But it was much less than enough for me,*" he insists (84).

Korea, however, harnessed his bravado and dreams: "*I dragged Mike to shelter and fought off the birds but he died anyway. . . . I staunched the blood finally oozing from the place Stuff's arm should have been. I found it some twenty feet away and gave it to him in case they could sew it back on. He died anyway*" (103). And his starkest failing was the Korean girl. In chapter 9, the middle of the seventeen chapters, he paints a scene in which a small girl, perhaps seven, rummages through soldiers' garbage for anything edible. His first sight of her hand had reminded him of "*trying to steal peaches off the ground under Miss Robinson's tree*" with Cee (94). In one instance, the girl was scavenging; in the next she was making a sexual gesture; in the final moment of her life, the relief guard, according to Frank, "*blows her away*" (95). But five chapters later, in the next to last of Frank's stories, he reveals that he shot the little girl. He was the one she touched. He was the one she "*aroused*" (133). Rhetorically, he asks, "*How could I let her live after she took me down to a place I didn't know was in me? How could I like myself, even* be *myself if I surrendered to that place where I unzip my fly and let her taste me right then and there? What type of man is that?*" (134).

Manhood was beautiful horses who "*stood like men*" (3) and, by extension, the heroic effort of protecting a sister. The irony is that he killed "*a child. A wee little girl*" about the age his sister had been fourteen years earlier to protect the heroic image of himself as a little girl's protective older brother. It is the same logic he uses to interpret the aftermath of racial violence against a young black couple on the Chicago train. Morrison, focalizing the scene through Frank, writes:

> The abused couple whispered to each other, she softly, pleadingly, he with urgency. He will beat her when they get home, thought Frank. And who wouldn't? It's one thing to be publicly humiliated. A man could move on from that. What was intolerable was the witness of a woman, a wife, who not only saw it, but had dared to try to rescue—rescue!—him. He couldn't protect himself and he couldn't protect her either, as the rock in her face proved. She would have to pay for that broken nose. Over and over again. (26)

Later Frank corrects this account. Addressing Morrison, he notes: "*Earlier you wrote about how sure I was that the beat-up man on the train to Chicago would turn around when they got home and whip the wife who tried to help him. Not true. I didn't think any such thing. What I thought was that he was proud of her but didn't want to show how proud he was to the other men on the train*" (69). He is not so predictable or myopic, he insists. Previously Frank had appreciated the feminine as a lovely weakness, "*the small breakable thing inside each one. . . . Like a bird's breastbone, shaped and chosen to wish on*" (68). He notes how easily he could have broken that bone "*if I wanted to*" (68). He adds, "*But [I] never did. Want to, I mean*" (68). Such knowledge gave him an advantage.

But, Frank intimates, the old heroic masculinity no longer pertains. First Korea and then Lily intervened—war broke him, and Lily ultimately dismissed him. She had wanted a partner whose aspirations matched her own, not a savior or hero. Frank could be neither. Each felt his leaving as an unburdening and deliverance. Frank does not dispute Morrison's focalization of Lily as a displacement for the "rage and shame" of Korea. The displacement "had convinced him the emotional wreckage no longer existed. In fact, it was biding its time" (108). Indeed, in denying a misogynistic instinct in response to the couple on the train, Frank, in effect, confirms what is left of the old manly bravado. Better to silence a husband's pride, in his thinking, than to risk that other men might distrust his manhood.

The trip south unravels these (self-)deceptions and gives Frank historical perspective. He had come of age in Lotus, Georgia, as a restless adolescent, brave and stifled. After discharge, he had refused to return to Lotus in defeat and resents the current inevitability of going back, not only refuting that he is the "enthusiastic hero" but insisting, defensively and perhaps disingenuously, that Lotus was not and is not a place to live. "*Nobody in Lotus knew anything or wanted to learn anything*," he claims. As if Morrison might doubt his story, Frank warns, "*You never lived there so you don't know what it was like*" (83–84). Likely, Frank also sees Lotus as he believes others see it, such as the taxi driver dropping him at Ethel Fordham's and getting, in Morrison's characterization, "as fast and as far away as he could from Lotus and its dangerous bed-bug-crazy country folk" (115). Frank's anger conceals what would otherwise be enervating feelings of inadequacy and guilt. He survived; Mike and Stuff did not. How can he face their parents? What would he say to them? Can he save Cee? He had been wrong to leave his sister to manage a difficult life on her own. The decision had largely been the result of teenage angst: "*marbles, fishing, baseball, and shooting rabbits* [were not] *reason enough to get out of bed in the morning*" (84). But the consequences of leaving have been disastrous, and condemnation of the community disguises disappointment in himself. Were Lotus the witless society Frank asserts, he might have considered taking Cee out of the state or, realizing that her condition made that impossible, might have sought help other than from Ethel Fordham. Frank clearly trusts her skill enough to obey her instructions to "get out" and allow women's work to proceed.

As the third-person focalization unfolds, Frank finds refuge for Cee and himself in Lotus, now seen as a verdant haven where "every front yard and backyard sported flowers protecting vegetables from disease and predators—marigolds, nasturtiums, dahlias. Crimson, purple, pink and China blue" (117). In direct contradiction of the earlier first-person denunciations, a newly envisioned Lotus offers a "feeling of safety and goodwill"; he takes "pleasure [in] being among those who do not want to degrade or destroy you" (118). Before, in first person, an angry Frank had substituted complacency for the community's steadfastness, and ignorance for an ancient reliance on nature. He had marked every Lotus resident with meanness and indifference. But two months in this place, tended by exceptional women, strengthened Cee and reinvented Frank. "His sister was gutted, infertile, but not beaten. She could know the truth, accept it, and keep on quilting" (132). His own acceptance of the hard truth was not far behind: "He had covered his guilt and shame with big time mourning for his dead buddies. Day and night he held on to that suffering because it let him off the hook, kept the Korean child hidden. Now the hook was deep inside his chest and nothing would dislodge it. The best he could hope for was time to work it loose" (135).

Toward the end of *Home*, Frank's narrative voice is no longer at war with itself—not intratextually, among first-person passages, or intertextually, between first- and third-person accounts. This latter interplay is especially significant. By refuting, goading, and deceiving Morrison as she executes the focalized portion of his narrative, Frank struggles to justify old versions of himself as the watchful brother and good friend. In the opening chapter, he warns, "*Since you're set on telling my story, whatever you write down, know this*" (5). In his next encounter with Morrison, he issues the challenge, "*Write about that, why don't you? ... Describe that if you know how*" (40–41), suggesting, perhaps, that only he is equipped to recount a four-year-old's experience of hunger and privation. Later he accuses the author of misrepresenting his thoughts, and charges, "*I don't think you know much about love. Or me*" (69). Setting the record straight after lying about his crime, Frank is unapologetic: "*You can keep on writing, but I think you ought to know what's true,*" he tells Morrison (134). These attempts at discursive authority do not work. Morrison's focalized response to Frank's assertions is to effect a gradual narrative shift—about Lotus, the meaning of home, and of manhood: Lotus is not the worst place; it is vibrant, communal, and resilient. Home is where one feels safe, and manhood is not heroism but self-possession. While his first-person narrative tells its restrictive stories of a past life, his third-person narrative embraces a healing truth in the present. This response pattern continues until there is integration of the narrative selves, first and third, I and Me. Once Frank admits his crime in chapter 14, the next time he speaks is chapter 17, the novel's conclusion, and at this point he seems to have achieved emotional clarity. After chapter 14, he issues no more challenges to Morrison's knowledge or authority. The two are in sync.

Chapters 15 and 16, then, pivot the narrative dynamic. There the burial, Korea, Lotus, and Frank's understanding of their lessons for him align. Frank's meta-narrative I, as McAdams would see it, joins with "the Me into a self-defining story, . . . [the] *narrative* rendering of selfhood" (103). In chapter 15, Frank acknowledges he can never be redeemed for taking a child's life. The reburial in chapter 16 moves him and the text toward resolution. Encouraged by the prospect of a home and future, he rights a wrong from his and the community's past and eases tension in his disjunctive experiences of beauty, violence, and heroism. His gradual change of perspective allows for the resolution of his conflicting feelings of obligation for the beauty of horses, the violence implicit in a black man's quivering foot, and the heroic stance of brotherly vigilance. Excavating the bones, placing them in the quilted shroud, and removing them to the base of the sweet bay, thereby honoring the dead father's sacrifice, discharge his obligations to the past and synchronize three previously competing impulses into a harmonious trilogy. Thus reburial restores Frank's intuition for what is beautiful in the world, replaces the men's savagery, and acknowledges his sister's independence. This time Cee does not look away. She is not "the terrified child who could not bear to look directly at the slaughter that went on in the world, however ungodly. This time she did not cringe or close her eyes" (143). Linda Krumholtz calls this sort of reversal in Morrison's novels "repetition with a difference." Morrison employs this narrative trope, Krumholtz says, "to create multiple versions of stories, to revise dominant history, and to represent processes of healing, transformation, and insight" for character and reader (21). Though in childhood Frank's emerging manhood has been tainted by society's inhumanity, this time he has complete understanding and can finally say of Jerome's father, "Here Stands A Man" (145). To save his son, a father had refused to fight for his own life. Past and present are at last reconciled: "Wishful thinking, perhaps, but he could have sworn the sweet bay was pleased to agree. Its olive green leaves went wild in the glow of a fat cherry-red sun" (145). A final image of the sweet bay tree, "*strong / So beautiful / Hurt right down the middle / But alive and well*" (147), is his lyrical tribute to Cee. And to himself.

In the novel's final scene, past and present give way to a future as suggested by the last appearance of the man in the zoot suit. His is the energy of tomorrow and the new sort of manhood. When a little man appeared, somber and distant, days earlier at the beginning of the journey, Frank had dismissed both man and suit. "If they [zoot suits] were the signal of manhood, he would have preferred a loincloth and some white paint artfully smeared on forehead and checks. Holding a spear, of course" (34). This cavalier attitude barely hides the irony that it is Frank's romantic narrative of manhood that is, in fact, regressive. The man's changed demeanor, "swinging a watch chain. And grinning" (144), is confident and prophetic. He signifies, in Morrison's words, that "there was something [about the forties and fifties] that became the seeds of the Civil Rights struggle" that was to come in the sixties and seventies (Brown). For the author, the novel ends on a hopeful note (Brown).

Home explores Morrison's continuing interest in an author's relationship to her story and characters—the vaguely defined distinction between an author's omniscience and psychoanalysis of her characters. Morrison has said:

> I take control of them [characters]. They are very carefully imagined. I feel as though I know all there is to know about them, even things I don't write—like how they part their hair. They are like ghosts. They have nothing on their minds but themselves and aren't interested in anything but themselves. So you can't let them write your book for you. (Schappell, 106)

Song of Solomon's (1977) Pilate is the example Morrison uses of a character who threatened to expand a role that she chose to contain. Morrison notes, however, that "if I come to a place where I am unsure, I have the characters to go to for reassurance. By that time they are friendly enough to tell me if the rendition of their lives is authentic or not" (Schappell, 106). It is this hard-to-grasp area between authorial certainty and dynamic doubt that Morrison explores in *Jazz*, where narrative instability suggests the ungovernable nature of creative insight. As *Jazz*'s narrator explains, the characters

> knew how little I could be counted on; how poorly, how shabbily my know-it-all self covered helplessness. That when I invented stories about them—and doing it seemed to me so fine—I was completely in their hands, managed without mercy.... Busy, they were ... being original, complicated, changeable—human, I guess you'd say, while I was the predictable one, confused in my solitude into arrogance, thinking my space, my view was the only one that was or that mattered. (220)

In *Home*, Morrison says she was "a little bit more aggressive about that"— about showing the essential collaboration between storyteller and characters (Ashbrook).

Nicholas Royle, building on the work of Sigmund Freud, Jacques Derrida, and others, calls this relationship between author and character telepathy. Royle objects to the term *omniscient*. "Omniscience," he argues, "serves to promote and protect a thinking of the 'world' of narrative fiction as holistic, unified, and closed.... It thus helps to ward off the transformative possibilities of reading, to limit and close down in advance what is incalculable and unprogrammable in the experience of the text" (Royle, 97).

Morrison agrees that "the [narrative] voice of assumed knowledge, the voice that says 'I know everything,'" causes trouble. "So," she says, "I had to get rid of the conventions, which I distrust" (Carabi, 42). She is describing, in this instance, her approach to voice in *Jazz* but could just as plausibly be speaking about *Home*, in which she continues to explore novelistic form by way of narrative innovation. In *Home* Morrison moves beyond conventional assumptions of omniscient knowledge to expand the creative possibilities of rendering character as narrative identity.

Works Cited

Ashbrook, Tom. "Toni Morrison." *On Point*. May 11, 2012. Radio. http://onpoint.wbur .org/2012/05/11/toni-morrison.

Bollen, Christopher. "Toni Morrison." *Interview Magazine*. http://christopherbollen.com/ portfolio/toni_morrison.pdf (accessed June 15, 2012).

Brown, Jeffery. *The News Hour*. PBS. May 29, 2012. Television. http://www.pbs.org/newshour/bb/entertainment/jan-june12/tonimorrison_05-29.html.

Carabi, Angels. "Toni Morrison: The Nobel laureate concludes her trilogy of interviews with Angels Carabi by musing on the historical and musical background of her most recent novel, *Jazz*." *Belles Lettres* 10, no. 2 (Spring 1995): 40–43.

Friedman, Susan Stanford. "Spatialization: A Strategy for Reading Narrative." *Narrative* 1, no. 1 (1993): 12–23.

James, William. *The Principles of Psychology*. Vol. 1. New York: Henry Holt, 1890.

Krumholtz, Linda J. "Reading and Insight in Toni Morrison's *Paradise*." *African American Review* 36, no. 1 (Spring 2002): 21–34.

McAdams, Dan P. "Narrative Identity." In *Handbook of Identity: Theory and Research*, vol. 1, ed. Seth J. Schwartz, 99–116. New York: Koen Luyckx and Vivian L. Vignoles, 2011.

Minzesheimer, Bob. "New Novel *Home* Brings Toni Morrison Back to Ohio." *USA Today*, May 7, 2012. http://usatoday30.usatoday.com/life/books/news/story/2012-05-07/toni-morrison-home-books/54814002/1.

Morrison, Toni. *Home*. New York: Alfred A. Knopf, 2012.

———. *Jazz*. New York: Alfred A. Knopf, 1992.

———. *The Nobel Lecture in Literature*. New York: Alfred A. Knopf, 1994.

Rimmon-Kenan, Shlomith. *Narrative Fiction: Contemporary Poetics*. Florence, NY: Routledge, 1983.

Rose, Charlie. *CBS This Morning*. May 28, 2012. Television. http://www.cbsnews.com/video/watch/?id=7409962n.

Royle, Nicholas. "The 'Telepathy Effect': Notes toward a Reconsideration of Narrative Fiction." In *Acts of Narrative*, ed. Carol Jacobs and Henry Sussman, 93–109. Stanford: Stanford University Press, 2003.

Schappell, Elissa, with additional material from Claudia Brodsky Lacour. *Paris Review* 128 (Fall 1993): 82–125.

Shea, Lisa. "Toni Morrison on 'Home.'" *Elle*. http://www.elle.com/pop-culture/reviews/toni-morrison-on-home-655249 (accessed June 15, 2012.).

Silverblatt, Michael. "Michael Silverblatt Talks with Toni Morrison about *Love*." In *Toni Morrison: Conversations*, ed. Carolyn C. Denard, 216–23. Jackson: University Press of Mississippi, 2008.

"NEWNESS TREMBLES ME"?

Representations of White Masculinity in Toni Morrison's A Mercy

MAR GALLEGO-DURÁN

∽

Toni Morrison's ninth novel, *A Mercy* (2008), provides an account of the nature of slavery in late-seventeenth-century America by exploring the myriad ways in which indentured servitude was still raceless but already delineating the contours of the so-called New World. Tackling issues such as class and religious allegiances, Morrison depicts a primitive society in which material wealth and possession are deeply and inextricably intertwined with notions of power and the establishment of rigid hierarchies. *A Mercy* conjures up a description rich in interpretive potential, in which readers are eagerly invited to witness the coming into being of a profoundly racist and sexist value system. Indeed, not only racial but also gender divisions figure prominently in Morrison's rewriting of this pivotal moment in the history of what later came to be known as the United States. More concretely, Morrison offers a compelling critique of the harmful effects of the subservience to a European-imported ideology of patriarchal supremacy by dealing specifically with the politics of representing normative masculinity.

At the very outset, *A Mercy* plunges into an extremely suggestive "confession" (2), which is nonetheless an unprecedented effort on Morrison's part to reclaim a historical period, in this case the 1680s and 1690s. Moreover, she also readily acknowledges a definable purpose: "I really wanted to get to a place before slavery was equated with race.... Whether they were black or white was less important than what they owned and what their power was" (quoted in

Kachka, 1). Readers are awed and seduced by the powerful call of Morrison's magnificent reconstruction of those foundational encounters among Europeans, Native Americans, and Africans that would pave the way for the "birth of the nation." Such encounters are proved to be misleading from the beginning, as they are guided by the urgency to tame "chaos," understood as the lack of barriers or clear-cut divisions. What is really at stake in this notion of chaos has to do with the stark regulation of an appropriate social and legal order that would eventually be drawn along racial and class lines: first, the new laws would function to separate and protect "all whites from all others forever," and then they would also enforce a convenient separation between gentry and laborers "in the interests of the gentry's profits" (*A Mercy*, 8). Thus Morrison addresses the complex process of planting and legalizing the connection between forced servitude and race that is at the core of the formation of the New World.[1]

As John Updike has brilliantly phrased it, Morrison manages to expose "a new world turning old," which is "poisoned from the start."[2] My contention is that the institutionalization of this socially sanctioned "chaos" as race and class based is also gender biased, that is, intimately related to the configuration of a code of gender behavior that must be honored by all. This ruling code affects both men and women alike and, in turn, delimits gender relations. And here another contradiction emerges in this "brave new world": gender stereotypes and roles are shown to be inherited from a conventional conception of patriarchal supremacy that chokes any newness that could flourish in this new setting. In spite of the many tempting promises that this pervasive sense of newness could entice, in the end gender relations fall prey to an extremely conservative worldview that Morrison is intent on contesting. To explore the constrictions and limitations of the inherited patriarchal hold, I focus exclusively on the way in which white male characters in the novel are unable to overcome accepted representations of hegemonic masculinity along with its racial and class discriminatory practices.[3] Yet Morrison praises their timid attempts to undermine the status quo by dwelling on issues of sexuality and class conflict.

The adherence to a Western patriarchal outlook undeniably prevails in the novel, conveniently represented by Jacob Vaark, a Dutch trader with a burgeoning inherited estate. One of the most telling instances of that normative definition can be exemplified in a conversation between Jacob and his wife Rebekka, in which Jacob's forceful assertion—"What a man leaves behind is what a man is"—is immediately followed by Rebekka's apparently dispassionate response: "Jacob, a man is only his reputation" (87). This brief exchange evokes recurring traits of traditional patriarchy: the intricate link between manhood, material possessions, and reputation.

This definition of masculinity is tied up with the basis for the patriarchal order in American thought, which has been the subject of great controversy over time. Philip Weinstein traces it back to John Locke and his defense of hard labor over class or ancestry, which led to an endorsement of the defining traits of masculinity coming from European ideology, namely, "autonomy, agency, and power, control over one's self, family and environment" (Read, 529). Joseph Armengol also elaborates on this version of masculinity: "Being manly entailed ruling one's life, liberty, and property" (64), thus corroborating once more the importance of these key concepts for attaining "true" masculinity. In *Manhood in America* (1996), Michael Kimmel delineates three models of masculinity: the "Genteel Patriarch" and the "Heroic Artisan" from the late eighteenth to the nineteenth century, and then the "Self-Made Man" from the beginning of the nineteenth century, probably the best-known one to date. While the Genteel Patriarch and the Heroic Artisan value virtues such as honesty, morality, kindness, and compassion, the Self-Made Man would incarnate economic success in the public sphere.

Although not strictly corresponding to the historical period under revision, Jacob Vaark clearly denotes an early version, a veritable precursor, of the Genteel Patriarch who cherishes landownership above all. Indeed, Morrison chronicles the incipient formation of the planters' class in early America by means of Jacob's social upward mobility and his unremitting obsession with property. Moreover, Jacob's stubborn insistence on building a great mansion—"something befitting not a farmer, not even a trader, but a squire" (86)—speaks to his need to ground his masculinity on material wealth and social recognition. But he can also be categorized as a pioneering self-made man who struggles against all odds to achieve his goals. Up to a point, he can personify a typically American rags-to-riches story: "a ratty orphan become landowner" (10). But soon in the novel readers get insightful glimpses into his true objective: that of shedding unwanted invisibility. As Rebekka fittingly thinks: "Invisibility was intolerable to men" (89). Briefly put, she highlights the importance of social status for men like Jacob, signaling the extent to which class divisions were already at work in this new/old world.

This desperate need on Jacob's part to be socially successful is ultimately conditioned by his fateful visit to D'Ortega, who functions, at least initially, as Jacob's alter ego. A despotic and insidious Portuguese slave owner, D'Ortega possesses a plantation in Maryland, forcing Jacob to travel there to settle an outstanding debt. As an unexpected partial payment for it, Jacob eventually accepts the eight-year-old slave Florens at the behest of her mother, who begs him to take the child away and leave her behind instead. This act of mercy resonates with unforeseen consequences for Florens, but also for

Jacob.[4] At first he is utterly revolted by his firsthand experience of a horrid slave plantation, especially by the moral corruption and the countless signs of physical and psychological mistreatment of the slaves he spots or otherwise senses. But what he deeply resents is D'Ortega's condescending attitude toward him, enacted in the tedious and intolerable dinner that he is invited to: "Intentional, he decided; a stage performance to humiliate him into a groveling acceptance of D'Ortega's wishes" (15). His deep-seated resentment at the intentional humiliation to which he is subjected leads him to plan a "grand" house that can elevate him to a superior social position. At the bottom of his determination, the distress aroused by the humiliation inflicted by D'Ortega sets the stage for Jacob's (over)reaction and his unwavering determination from then onward. Thus the building of the house stands for his ambitious plan to attain unquestionable social relevance, even grandeur, which would prevent his ever yielding again to men like D'Ortega.

Apart from material possession, another element in Jacob's encounter with D'Ortega becomes a sine qua non for the normative definition of masculinity that Jacob subscribes to: control over the "other," be it nature or other beings (women, children, slaves or indentured servants, etc.).[5] Indeed, Jacob's positioning lends insight into the crushing need for control in this "untamed world" (16). Again the chaotic nature of the New World is used (and abused both literally and figuratively) by European men as a justification for their wrongdoings. This view of the New World would legitimize a hegemonic concept of masculinity in which mastery over others is construed as a desirable and unavoidable destiny.[6] Legitimization acquires a more ominous significance when religious motives are invoked to further bless European men's undertakings, signifying a whole history of pillaging and massacre for the "divine purpose" of Christian civilization. In Jacob's conversation with D'Ortega, they conveniently recall the "unbreakable connection to God's work and the difficulties they endure on His behalf" (16). Hence Jacob's pharaonic task of erecting his mansion is almost seen as a "mission" he has been called to fulfill that exalts his direct dealings with God. Not only that, but he also accommodates a paternalistic view of himself when he shares D'Ortega's opinion that "caring for ill or recalcitrant labor was enough . . . for canonization" (16). These comments are especially poignant given the source of D'Ortega's wealth in slavery, and even more so when Jacob's later fortune comes from the same exploitation and inhumanity. Incidentally, too, considerable irony resides in the fact that Jacob has never had any problems with his laborers, neither when his conversation with D'Ortega takes place nor thereafter.

Moreover, to illustrate the incongruence involved in the aggressive model of European masculinity that was unfolding in the colonies, Morrison seems to prefigure in Jacob's version of masculinity the roots of the contemporary and often-debated "crisis of American masculinity." As Cristina Alsina and her coauthors affirm, the "crisis of no identity" that American men suffer from involves "personal insecurity, lack of self-esteem and lack of referents," which results in an "incapacity for affective relationships" and "for transmitting a positive model for the next generations" (14). At first, Jacob is presented almost as a raw model for "tough" masculinity, completely sure of himself, even envisioning himself as God's intermediary. I would argue, however, that Jacob's facade easily crumbles as the novel progresses because he does not comply with the prescriptions of self-made masculinity.[7] On the one hand, his incapacity for affection is repeatedly hinted at by his wife, for instance, when she explains their lack of communication and emotional involvement beginning with their first meeting. Later he provides her with lively accounts of his journeys that are eventually discontinued: "It was some time before she noticed how the tales were fewer and the gifts increasing, gifts that were becoming less practical, even whimsical" (86). These impractical presents are indicative of the kind of relationship they will share over the years, which reaches its climax when he finally discloses his plans for the new house:

> "We don't need another house. . . . Certainly not one of such size."
> "Need is not the reason, wife." (86)

This tense dialogue between the two effectively mirrors the wide gulf that cannot be bridged: while Rebekka centers on their needs and their appropriate status, Jacob takes into account only his preferences and dreams, thereby revealing his selfish and self-serving interests.

What is particularly striking about this conversation is that it precedes their clash about warring definitions of masculinity mentioned earlier, which also foreshadows their emotional alienation resulting from the early death of their progeny. Revisiting that scene, Jacob's problematic version of masculinity also accounts for his "bitterness" (17) over the lack of surviving children, and therefore heirs for his estate. He places the blame for his frustrated sense of fatherhood on his wife, who also assumes her own guilt on her deathbed (93).[8] In addition, Jacob's frustration coalesces into feelings of envy for D'Ortega's six children, once more connecting his resentment over what he perceives to be an uneven and bluntly unfair distribution of patriarchal status. Thus his stifled potential in not being able to become a model for the next generation renders him emotionally vulnerable, enraged, but resolute in his determination to build that house at all costs. By the end of the novel, it is evident that his construction of masculinity rests on the building of a useless and inappropriate house that would also stand for his lack of adaptation and even his (figurative) sterility.[9] Hence his futile attempt to secure his estate is ultimately mocked and thwarted when the house becomes his tomb in an ironic twist of fate.

It is also interesting to note that the house could have been the medium that would allow Jacob to become a planter, even to resemble D'Ortega. His (un)timely death is thus seen as the punishment he deserves for his wishful thinking, but also for the way in which he has amassed his large fortune. Toying with the idea of a "more satisfying enterprise," Jacob decides to venture into the prospect of profitable sugar plantations, thinking that "there was a profound difference between the intimacy of slave bodies at Jublio and a remote labor force in Barbados" (33). Despite his apparent dislike for both an intimate contact with slaves and Jublio (D'Ortega's ostentatious plantation), Jacob's reliance on sugar plantations as the means for his fortune indicates his wish to replicate the decadence of the plantation model. Here Morrison deliberately objects to white men's expectations in early America of becoming a sort of new aristocracy. Jacob's desire for a plantation is opportunely truncated by his death, even endowed with a certain poetic justice. Morrison ferociously attacks the endorsement of racial slave trade by enabling a significant correction of a mistaken history, a history that should not be repeated. Ironically, the only legacy that Jacob leaves is the light of Florens's candle as she writes on the walls and floor of the now-abandoned house, which to the eyes of Willard and Scully becomes Jacob's specter.

That the house seems haunted by his "presence" reminds readers of haunted houses in gothic narratives.[10] One of the first descriptions of the house prefigures this possibility: "His dreams were of a grand house of many rooms rising on a hill above the fog" (33). The gothic dwelling signifies different things at once. First, the house is considered a metaphor for the patriarchal family, another basic principle in gothic narrative. The house is also identified with the psyche. According to Hantke, "Gothic horror has always dealt with the return of the repressed" (2). Although Hantke alludes to the traumatic legacy of Nazism and the Holocaust, it is equally applicable to institutionalized slavery, one of the most recurrent themes in American gothic fiction.[11] In more than one way, the empty house becomes a figure for these nuances because there is a direct identification between the house and Jacob's construction of his fragmented and uncertain subjectivity.[12] By the same token, Jacob ends up "impersonating" the gothic villain, roaming the house at night, as he is pictured by his helpers Willard and Scully:

> They did not see him—his definitive shape or face—but they did see his ghostly blaze. His glow began near midnight, floated for a while on the second story, disappeared, then moved ever so slowly from window to window. (142)

This benign "visitation" may suggest his deceitful nature, as is the case with many gothic villains, although there are also significant discrepancies.[13] Undoubtedly he incarnates the Law of the Father, the patriarchal authority, but the dynamics of domination and subversion at work in the novel do not follow the conventional gothic structure.[14] In short, he fails as a gothic villain because he remains humane.

While alive, Jacob is deeply admired and cherished by most of the characters in the novel for his humanity. In Florens's mother's description, "His way ... is another way.... There was no animal in his heart. He never looked at me the way Senhor does" (161).[15] Indeed, the comparison with D'Ortega is effectively grounded on what Florens's mother perceives as sexual greed and possession. The lack of any sexual threat and violence in Jacob's mien (insinuated by the telling term "animal") is thus an encouraging sign for the mother. As in other previous works,[16] Morrison rewrites the Eurocentric script of Africans as "subhuman" by transferring it to the white owner who would project wanton libido onto his enslaved women.[17] Moreover, the stark contrast between D'Ortega and Jacob is further emphasized by Jacob's unstereotypical gaze: "because I saw the tall man see you as a human child" (164). The reiterative use of the term "human" in the closing paragraphs of the novel applies to both Florens and Jacob while excluding D'Ortega.

Two other male figures provide extremely interesting and sympathetic representations of white masculinity in the novel: the two indentured servants Willard and Scully. Prompting alternative configurations of masculinity, these characters help to foreground Morrison's investment in a more nurturing politics of manhood. I would further contend that Morrison's intentional meditation on "alternative masculinities" embodied by these two men has a twofold objective: to dispel widespread assumptions about the desirability of dominant heteronormativity, and to bring into the forefront class struggle in the seemingly "classless" society of seventeenth-century America.

At first, Willard and Scully seem to feel perfectly at ease re-creating "family" on Jacob's farm: "a good-hearted couple (parents), and three female servants (sisters, say) and them helpful sons" (142). They are so closely bonded to their master and their surrogate family that they remain loyal to Jacob's widow until Scully senses its disintegration, which he blames on the women, never on the kind master. The alleged reason for their sense of family is easily dismissed, as it fails to foster lasting links among them once Jacob is dead. Thus the patriarchal unit is again viewed as the only possibility for a harmonious coexistence, further reinforced by Lina's view: "As long as Sir was alive it was easy to veil the truth: that they were not a family" (57). Moreover, this assertion is also substantiated by the great changes that Willard and Scully notice in all the women after Jacob's passing, but especially the tremendous transformation Florens undergoes that makes it difficult to recognize her as "a living person" (145). As Waegner observes, many women in Morrison's fiction seek "a unit which could at least provide a psychological hold if not a legal one" (99). I would extend Waegner's view by proposing that the patriarchal system in the novel seems to be working as a psychological hold for both women and men, intimating the need for patriarchal primacy.

This last comment obfuscates Willard's and Scurry's *otherness*: they are white gay men in forced servitude. Their particular marginality sets them apart from Jacob and the planter class from the outset. Scully's and Willard's lives basically revolve around hard work but good company, always meaning male company. Male "camaraderie" (147) is emphasized in Willard's Virginia days, compared to the solitude before Scully's arrival: "Willard had suffered hard and lonesome days" (146). Before his arrival at Jacob's farm, Scully's homosexuality is also presented in an explicit way: "Scully had no carnal interest in women. Long ago the world of men and only men had stamped him" (150). His sexual initiation by an Anglican curate is also detailed in the story, as well as the punishment he was subjected to for his "lasciviousness" when they were caught (151). It goes without saying that this scene evokes moral and ethical problems. The correlation, however, between Scully and a slave is plain enough, as the disruption caused by a homosexual relationship is entirely blamed on the victim, not on the victimizer. Furthermore, that Scully does not voice any sense of revenge or remorse may also prove the normalization of those kinds of practices in seventeenth-century America.[18] But with Willard he finds a lasting relationship. They seem to be true companions, even soul mates: "For Scully and Mr. Bond it was enough to imagine a future" (154).

Within the framework of gothic fiction, I would also argue that Willard and Scully function as vehicles to set off a yet more profound reflection on the nature of the legacy of colonialism, and concretely on the "unspeakable" (Booher, 125). Their decisive defense of the patriarchal family mentioned previously is tainted from its inception, because they should allegorically try to end the tyranny of the Law of the Father and celebrate the disruption of the family as a socially repressive system. Moreover, their relationship alone should invalidate the heterosexual politics that rule the patriarchal notion of family. It signals the transgression of sexual borders as well as the ambiguous sexual male self that is present in many gothic novels.[19] This view throws new light on Scully's dealings with the curate, which can be read as rape. But what is truly unspeakable is their homoerotic relationship, which raises anxieties about traditional heterosexuality. Their homosexual desire and coupling would be labeled in conventional gothic fiction as "abnormal sexuality." By "speaking the unspeakable," in this case, homosexual desire, Morrison skillfully reveals the patriarchal family as a site for repression and discrimination. Morrison's critique of the Western ideology of patriarchal supremacy by (re)placing the sexual other at the center of the contemporary discursive controversy challenges sanctioned sexual practices.

Willard and Scully, then, are indentured servants oppressed by an unjust and elitist system also targeted in gothic fiction. Nonetheless their complicity with the system is also a corrective to the ideologies of the culture that system engenders. For instance, Willard's troubled relationship with the free blacksmith is resolved by the smith's deferentially calling him "Mr. Bond": "Although he was still rankled by the status of a free African versus himself, there was nothing he could do about it. No law existed to defend indentured labor against them" (149). This passage hints at the shift from class to racial politics during the fluctuating social system of the period. Moreover, Morrison quickly forecloses any romantic assumptions about their relationship by stating what really determines that they remain on the farm after Jacob's death in Rebekka's employment—wages. In this return to material acquisition as substitute for family and love, materialism is once more strategically fused with whiteness. While Willard and Scully may trespass certain sexual boundaries, they still subscribe to a materialistic vision of society, understandable enough because of their overwhelming desire to terminate their terms of forced servitude.

Morrison's meditation on the faulty colonial inheritance in seventeenth-century America prompts an interrogation of the internal workings of not only racial but also class and gender politics of the time. *A Mercy* effectively explicates the difficulties inherent in overcoming the social prescriptions of the period by foregrounding the moment when race began to displace class as its structuring principle. But her deliberate deconstruction of a race-based ideology is obviously complicated by the interaction of other key issues such as class struggle and heteronormativity. Morrison unravels the impositions of patriarchal supremacy in her depiction of the white male characters that populate her novel, who fail either as patriarchal figures or as subversive masculine models. These characters ineluctably test the limits of hegemonic masculinity in ways similar to gothic fiction by transgressing social and sexual boundaries. Though ostensibly a novel of a "pre-racialized" society, *A Mercy* confronts an increasingly sexist, racist, and class-conscious value system designed for white men's lives and well-being. Thus the novel also becomes a cautionary tale for later configurations of America.

Notes

1. Several critics have expressed similar views concerning Morrison's mapping of what Ellen Emry Heltzel calls "pre-racial" America. The critical reception of the novel confirms Morrison's successful re-creation of the intentional forging of race-based slavery at its very infancy (Jennings, 645; Waegner, 101).

2. This critiques the classical notion of America as the virginal, uninhabited Promised Land or "unfallen America" (Massa, 1). Radically departing from saccharine tales about the New World, Morrison proposes a particularly subversive account of America "doomed to fall" from the start.

3. Here I endorse claims made by a growing body of masculinity studies that strive to promote the analysis of gender as conditioning both women and men (Kimmel and Messner, x–xi).

4. The title refers to Jacob's acceptance of Florens as the crucial act of mercy that fortunately saves her from predictably brutal treatment and misuse at the hands of the lusty D'Ortega and his wife. Florens, however, misinterprets the act as utter abandonment instigated by her mother's alleged preference for her brother.

5. Athena Mutua insists on this when she claims that "normative masculinity is predicated on the domination of others" (17). In *Playing in the Dark*, Morrison makes a similar observation by demonstrating the way in which the notion of the white male depended on the subjugation of African Americans (6).

6. Although it is far beyond the scope of this essay to discuss the legacy of European aggression in its encounters with the New World, Morrison illuminates the irreducible complexity of such (dis)encounters by moving beyond stereotypical representations of white pioneers such as Jacob and convincingly discussing their complicity with what Kang terms the "*status* of whiteness" (844; italics in original).

7. Armengol touches on some of the reasons that may explain the chronic crisis of American masculinity, since he argues that self-made manhood is by definition "unattainable" and leads to unforeseen consequences such as "anxiety, restlessness, fears, loneliness, frustration and failure" (65). If the pattern of manhood to which American men aspire is unattainable, then the crisis should be, and actually is, a permanent feature, a fixture, in American society.

8. Typically it is the woman who needs to answer for not fulfilling her obligation as a self-sacrificing and devout mother.

9. Although not in a literal sense, Jacob's lack of surviving children points tangentially to his inability to live up to the expectations of the figure of the patriarch. On the other hand, his figurative sterility derives precisely from a sense of patriarchal sterility that can only produce death and violence at both a familial and a social level.

10. The haunted house is one of the most pervasive supernatural elements in gothic works. The gothic strain in Morrison has been successfully addressed in publications such as David Dudley's *Gothic Writers* (2002) or, more recently, Marisa Parham's *Haunting and Displacement in African American Literature and Culture* (2010).

11. As Alan Smith mentions, the "trauma of guilt, race and slavery" has been ever present in American gothic fiction (8).

12. However, the house is also Florens's preferred setting, where she manages to carve her story on its walls, which is an act of self-empowerment. Her appropriation can also be read as a demand for wholeness on her part, an attempt to erase the script of "gothic terror" from the house.

13. As David Punter observes, "The villain was always the most complex and interesting character in Gothic fiction" (25), frequently associated with the figure of an authoritarian and abusive father with Faustian drives. This description would not correspond to Jacob's case entirely.

14. In gothic fiction, the evil villain exerts his authority and free will over the helpless innocent maiden. Florens could arguably be characterized as an innocent maiden, but her transformation at the end of the novel and subsequent appropriation of the house completely subvert the formula. Additionally, Jacob is not a heartless tyrant but is only tormented by a definitive lack of closure, and Florens could also be defined as a destructive Dark Lady.

15. Obviously her words are prompted by a highly wrought relationship with D'Ortega, which ultimately motivates her choice to offer Florens instead of her brother to go away with Jacob.

16. An often-quoted text that bears witness to Morrison's insistence on the crippling and devastating effects of accusations of the animality of slaves can be found in *Beloved*. Indeed, *A Mercy* diligently delves into the origins of race-based ideologies of slavery that Morrison develops in-depth in her groundbreaking re-creation of the excesses of the slave system.

17. Obviously, on Florens's mother, who is sexually assaulted by D'Ortega, but she also notices his intentions to sexually abuse her daughter: "But you wanted the shoes of a loose woman . . . and you caught Senhor's eye" (164).

18. Even more shocking when religious considerations are also analyzed, as the Anglican curate is not accountable for his misdeeds.

19. The overall presence of sexual issues is not overtly addressed as a specific motif in gothic fiction, a direct outcome of the dysfunctional patriarchal family. As Andrew Smith and Diana Wallace assert, the gothic is a "form which has traditionally given space to the representation of transgressive sexualities" (6).

Works Cited

Alsina, Cristina, Rodrigo Andrés, and Ángels Carabí, eds. *Hombres soñados por escritoras de hoy*. Universidad de Málaga: Servicio de Publicaciones, 2009.

Armengol Carrera, Josep M. "Rereading American Masculinities: Re-visions of the American Myth of Self-Made Manhood in Richard Ford's Fiction." *Revista de Estudios Norteamericanos* 11 (2006): 63–80.

Booher, Michelle. "'It's Not in the House': *Beloved* as Gothic Novel." *Readerly/Writerly Texts* 9, nos. 1–2 (2001): 117–31.
Dudley, David. "Toni Morrison." In *Gothic Writers: A Critical and Bibliographical Guide*, 295–302. Westport: Greenwood Press, 2002.
Hantke, Steffan. "German Film: Stefan Ruzowitzky's *Anatomie*." 2001. http://www.kinoeye.org/01/01/hantke01.html (accessed July 25, 2010).
Hetzel, Ellen Emry. "Toni Morrison's Powerful New Novel *A Mercy* Tracks, Examines Forces of Slavery." *Seattle Times*, November 6, 2008. http://seattletimes.nwsource.com/html/books/2008355833_br09morrison.html (accessed August 15, 2010).
Jennings, La Vinia Delois. "*A Mercy*: Toni Morrison Plots the Formation of Racial Slavery in Seventeenth-Century America." *Callaloo* 32, no. 2 (Spring 2009): 645–49.
Kachka, Boris. "Toni Morrison's History Lesson." *New York Magazine*, August 24, 2008. http://nymag.com/guides/fallpreview/2008/books/49499 (accessed August 12, 2010).
Kang, Nancy. "To Love and Be Loved: Considering Black Masculinity and the Misandric Impulse in Toni Morrison's *Beloved*." *Callaloo* 26, no. 3 (Summer 2003): 836–54.
Kimmel, Michael. *Manhood in America: A Cultural History*. New York: Free Press, 1996.
Kimmel, Michael, and Michael Messner. *Men's Lives*. Boston: Allyn and Bacon, 1998.
Massa, Ann. *American Declarations of Love*. London: Macmillan, 1990.
Morrison, Toni. *A Mercy*. London: Chatto and Windus, 2008.
———. *Playing in the Dark*. London: Picador, 1993.
Mutua, Athena, ed. *Progressive Black Masculinities*. New York: Routledge, 2006.
Parham, Marisa. *Haunting and Displacement in African American Literature and Culture*. New York: Routledge, 2010.
Punter, David. *The Literature of Terror*. Malaysia: Longman, 1996.
Read, Andrew. "'As If Word Magic Had Anything to Do with the Courage It Took to Be a Man': Black Masculinity in Toni Morrison's *Paradise*." *African American Review* 39, no. 4 (2005): 527–40.
Smith, Alan Lloyd. *American Gothic Fiction*. London: Continuum, 2004.
Smith, Andrew, and Diana Wallace. "The Female Gothic: Then and Now." *Gothic Studies* 6, no. 1 (2004): 1–7.
Updike, John. "Dreamy Wilderness: Unmastered Women in Colonial Virginia." *New Yorker*, November 3, 2008.
Waegner, Cathy Covell. "Ruthless Epic Footsteps: Shoes, Migrants, and the Settlement of the Americas in Toni Morrison's *A Mercy*." In *Post-national Enquiries*, ed. Jopi Newman, 91–112. Newcastle: Cambridge Scholars, 2009.
Williams, Anne. *Art of Darkness*. Chicago: University of Chicago Press, 1995.

THE SOUND OF CHANGE

*A Musical Transit through the
Wounded Modernity of* Desdemona

LENORE KITTS

The persistence of the past into the present through song is a consistent theme of Toni Morrison's work. The two temporalities refer to and enrich each other, as when a jazz player or singer of spirituals reanimates an old standard even while reworking it. This creative principle guides Morrison's *Desdemona*, which she created with the African singer-songwriter Rokia Traoré and the American opera and theater director Peter Sellars.[1] In a provocative experiment, they reimagine Shakespeare's tragic representation of the legacies of gender, race, and class domination in *Othello* (1603) as these issues reverberate in our global present.

Many crises of modern life find a voice in *Desdemona*, whether the physical and spiritual battering of women, the exploitation of child soldiers, dislocations caused by slavery, poverty, and hunger, or racism's legacy of interpersonal distrust and cultural alienation. These themes unfold in a charged dialogue between Desdemona and Barbary, who also represent the West and Africa, respectively. Morrison thus modernizes the ambiguities about Africa in Shakespeare's play with the aid of Traoré's socially charged music. Together they work to update the legacy of colonialism from a woman's perspective.

Barbary (Rokia Traoré) confronts Desdemona (Tina Benko) in *Desdemona* at Vienna's Theater Akzent, May 3, 2011. © Ruth Walz. Reprinted with permission.

Genesis of the Work

The *Desdemona* project grew out of Sellars's dialogue with Morrison about *Othello*—to which he responded by mounting a new production in Vienna for the Vienna Festival in 2009, and she by developing a new script in conversation with Traoré. The project aims to rescue from obscurity Barbary, the character whose "Willow Song" (adapted by Shakespeare from a popular English tune) rises to Desdemona's memory as a premonition of her imminent death:

> My mother had a maid call'd Barbary;
> She was in love, and he she lov'd prov'd mad
> And did forsake her. She had a song of "Willow,"
> An old thing 'twas, but it express'd her fortune,
> And she died singing it. That song to-night
> Will not go from my mind; I have much to do,
> But to go hang my head all at one side,
> And sing it like poor Barbary. (*Othello* 4.3.26–33)[2]

Up to now, attentive readers have only known Barbary as Desdemona's mother's "maid." Invented by Shakespeare (but not listed in his dramatis personae), she is missing from his Italian source, Giraldi Cinthio's novella *Un capitano moro* (A Moorish Captain) (1565), which may hearken back to a historical incident of murder in Venice in 1508. Scholars have long recognized, however, that Barbary's name recalls Iago's description of Othello as a "Barbary horse" (1.1.110–11)—one of several equivocal references to Africa in the English play.

In an interview, Sellars explained to me why this term mattered to Shakespeare: "Two high diplomats from the Barbary Coast came to London in 1600 to meet with Queen Elizabeth. And it was the first time Londoners saw Africans of high degree, and that was widely commented on in the British press at the time. So for Shakespeare to use the term 'Barbary' in 1603 was extremely vivid."[3] The queen met the envoys to discuss a military alliance against Catholic Spain, sparking controversy among her subjects, who alternately regarded the North Africans as welcome allies or else religious infidels they should shun (Vaughan, 14). In those same years, their sovereign had banished low-placed "Blackamoors" from her realm,[4] while the public decried the enslavement of English sailors by "Barbary" pirates. These political anxieties complicated the English fascination with various dark-skinned peoples known from popular travel literature,[5] such as Leo Africanus's *A Geographical Historie of Africa, written by . . . a More . . . brought vp in Barbarie* (1600), which may have informed Shakespeare's play.[6]

It was Sellars's colleague Avery Willis who suggested to Toni Morrison that, by calling the maid "Barbary," Shakespeare allows us to imagine Barbary herself as African, and her songs to Desdemona as a medium transmitting another history. It is Desdemona's prior familiarity with this African heritage, Morrison suggests, that allows her to recognize the "glint" in Othello's eye and empathize with his history

> Of moving accidents by flood and field,
> Of hair-breadth scapes i' th' imminent deadly breach,
> Of being taken by the insolent foe
> And sold to slavery, of my redemption thence. (*Othello* 1.3.35–38)

The idea that Barbary was not just her mother's maid but also Desdemona's own nurse was the creative seed for the *Desdemona* project.

Resisting Morrison's reading, critics point out that the nurse is sometimes called "Barbara," or its variant "Barbarie," in older editions of the play (Littlejohn). In response Morrison recalls how the cultural footprint of Africa and its diasporic peoples has been overlooked in the West. Filling in such gaps has been one of her artistic aims throughout her many works. Here she addresses the problem by engaging with classical Greek and Roman sources, particularly Herodotus, whose tales of Amazons and other fabulous creatures are reimagined by Othello. I will return to the legendary "killers of men" (whom Herodotus called Oiorpata, 4.110) at the end of the essay. By invoking the Greek "Father of History," Morrison reminds us that the authority of Greek antiquity was embedded into Western culture to the detriment of African (and Asian) interactions. In one derogatory passage, Herodotus compared the speech of North Africans to "bats squeaking," which has nothing in common with human language (4.183). Morrison rejects his cultural bias, but not his famed receptivity to oral tradition, his interpretative agency, or his narrative skill.[7] Similarly, her characters work hard to identify, interpret, and relate the hidden impulses that led each of them to their demise in the Shakespearean tragedy, which, as one critic describes, is characterized by "obsessive speculation" about offstage actions and distant geographies (Neill, 397). As Morrison told a New York audience, her chief aim in *Desdemona* is to "reveal interior lives and characters' motives unexamined in *Othello*."[8] She challenges us to reevaluate the actions of Shakespeare's characters, particularly his women. It is from their perspective that we study Othello, while Iago's presence is almost entirely erased.

Another aim is to bring Africa back into focus by reshaping our dialogue with it. The African continent has been mined for many things by outsiders over the centuries, but rarely for its history.[9] Sellars told me that it was important that Africa no longer be "ventriloquized" by Shakespeare, or even by Morrison, for that matter. He proposed the collaboration with Traoré, a native of Mali, because the project "required a voice of an African woman to speak as an African woman and to sing as an African woman. Rokia was the logical choice because Rokia is a completely extraordinary figure." In *Desdemona*, finally, the voice of "Barbary"—Africa—is . . . African.

A Charged Feminine Space

It is fitting that as a singer, Barbary should come to life via the translucent music of Traoré, who sings her own songs in Bambara and French together with music she revises from the ancient griot tradition in which she is schooled. The only exception is one set of lyrics that Morrison penned for her in response to Shakespeare's "Willow Song," which Traoré also recalls for us in her softly accented diction. The songwriter accompanies herself on acoustic guitar with a small band of traditional string players (on the *n'goni* and *kora*) and three backup singers whose apparent ease masks the careful choreography of their rhythmic dance. Overwhelmed by the beauty of the ensemble, Morrison said that writing for it was like "asking a cello what it is saying."[10]

This African collaboration was new for Morrison. Although she spoke eloquently about her prior collaboration on the opera *Margaret Garner* when I interviewed her in 2005, I think her working relationship with Traoré is unique. A protégée of the renowned guitarist Ali Farka Touré (who famously connected American blues and Malian traditions), Traoré has distinguished herself within Mali's vibrant musical culture by developing an unusually intimate style that promotes thoughtful consideration of her intricate lyrics. The root sounds of traditional instruments and modal melodies to which she adds her guitars and vocal harmonies (also unusual for a female vocalist) pulsate quietly in layered rhythms as she sings with compassion about the problems confronting her fellow Africans.

Although her award-winning albums blend folk with contemporary idioms, Traoré puts down her electric guitar in *Desdemona* in favor of a purely acoustic sound that evokes her native Bamana tradition, which she then reconceives. Songs praising young brides and epic warriors are important in Mali, and she presents both classic and sometimes startling new versions here. While Traoré faces what is happening in Africa right now, Sellars remarked that she "retains this depth of sadness ... that feeds your yearning and your sense that the future has to be sought out and achieved." It is this same orientation toward the future, Sellars suggested to me, that motivates Morrison's script: "Toni reimagines and repositions what is frequently told in Western historical sources as a story of failure, and lets you see, actually, the human achievement inside what the world has decided is a failure.... And that was also, needless to say, a Shakespearean project."

Built on the backbone of Morrison's incisive language, *Desdemona* took shape through the fluid rapport between the writer and the composer, who share compatible artistic values. The art of both women is politically ambitious yet personal and lyrical, as they seek to engage us in the complex issues that engage them. Sellars, who traveled between Mali and the United States to work with each artist, called the result a "specifically charged feminine space.... They create a space in their image that is quiet at their center and infinite at the edges."

This space empowers the solo female voice, which shifts in tenor and purpose as it moves between pairs of characters who frequently reside only in Desdemona's memory. The noblewoman opens all but two of the work's ten scenes (and then her mother and servant Emilia fill in for her). Desdemona's dialogue with Barbary—like that between Morrison's text and Traoré's music—functions to expose and transform the wounded identities at the heart of Shakespeare's play. Whereas Othello and Barbary migrate into the mythic enclave of Shakespeare's Venice,[11] Desdemona is transported into an

African imaginary by Morrison and Traoré. "Toni has reconfigured Shakespeare's early present-at-the-creation pictures of colonialism," Sellars underscored. "She updates and reframes the colonialist project and its residue, as does Rokia from an African perspective."

Morrison meditates on the interpenetration of the past and the present in many works. Her research on early America for *A Mercy* (2008), specifically how slavery became associated with race, provided fertile ground for this project. Drawing on African cosmology evokes a circular notion of time flowing backward into an infinite history. Technically, such dynamics disappear in the afterlife, whether in *Beloved* (1987) or in *Desdemona*, since this realm is free of the constraints of time and the expressive limitations time imposes. Nonetheless the past lives on in *Desdemona*, reaffirming an old lesson rooted in ancestor worship in the African context. Desdemona heeds this lesson, for above all, she is here to learn. Morrison also gives Desdemona's teacher, Barbary, a real African name (Sa'ran, or "joy") to challenge the concept that culturally assigned identities fix our doom. Elsewhere Morrison has spoken about naming as a source of power, particularly in African languages where "each thing is separate and different; once you have named it you have power" (LeClair, 126). Thus it is no surprise that Desdemona, too, rejects the miserable destiny implied by her symbolic name from the outset:

> *Desdemona*: My name is Desdemona. The word, Desdemona, means misery. It means ill fated. It means doomed. . . . I am not the meaning of a name I did not choose. (*Desdemona*, 13)[12]

Spelling out the Greek etymology of *dysdaimon*, meaning "ill fated" or "ill starred," Morrison seals Desdemona's dramatic end with a term that Euripides used to characterize the misery of Iphigenia in Tauris. Shakespeare's Italian source drove the same point home by leaving all his characters unnamed except Disdemona, whose ancient Greek root (δυσ + δαίμων) contradicts the concept of *eudaimonia*, or happiness, which Aristotle pronounced the chief good of the ethical life. Correspondingly, Giraldi Cinthio embraced the neoclassical axiom that poetry should instill good mores; thus he warned Italian women to learn from Disdemona's mistake lest they, too, consort with foreigners at their peril.[13]

With Traoré's help, Morrison pushes the naming issue forward into the twenty-first century to the feminist principle of self-definition. Both Morrison's Desdemona and Traoré's Sa'ran raise their voices to revise what others have taught them to believe about their lives. Having been defeated by men, they each struggle to grasp the range and depth of patriarchy's oppressive force. Empowerment can be seductive, especially for the rebellious Desdemona, who falls in love with Othello after he regales her with tales of Amazonian bloodlust:

> *Othello*: There are armies of women who kill men in battles so fierce that the moon itself hides from the ribbons of shed blood.... With male blood they stain their hair and with his bone they sharpen their arrowheads. Whole regimes fall before them. (*Desdemona*, 34)

Initially, Desdemona shares Othello's fascination with Amazon ferocity. The rules of decorum at the Renaissance court had stifled her, reducing her to a pawn in domestic rites of dynastic power, which she flees. "Men made the rules, women followed them," she warns in her opening monologue. "A step away was doom, indeed, and misery without relief" (*Desdemona*, 13).

By contrast, the fabled independence of the heroic Amazons represents an intoxicating antidote: "They fired my mind.... I was captured by love and the prospect of inhabiting a broad original world where I could compete with the Amazons" (*Desdemona*, 36). The ancient women's legendary power helps Desdemona to find her voice and strengthen her capacity to love. Their "broad original" worldview teaches her to break free from her psychological prison. The Amazon myth challenged male authority and the domestic roles assigned to women in its classical formulation, as Morrison recalls by spelling out the Greek etymology of "No-Breast or A-Mazon" (*a-*, no; *mazos/mastos*, breast [*Desdemona*, 34]).

Nonetheless horror tempers Desdemona's fascination with the Amazons in the end, as the narrative shifts to relentless patterns of loss, exploitation, and trauma in modern warfare, which Morrison imagines for Othello. Othello confesses to Desdemona his gang rape with Iago of two withered old women. As a child soldier, he felt driven to rape and kill while high on the "fresh green [coca] leaves" supplied by his captors: "We were potent and indifferent to blood, cries of pain, debasement—to life even our own" (*Desdemona*, 36). His struggle to overcome self-loathing evokes the wars that continue to ravage Africa today. Such powerful emotions can ripple through a wounded society for generations.

Traoré seeks to heal the wounds of a war-torn continent by urging Africans to take pride in their continent and heritage, thus adding her voice to the griots who celebrate Africa's resistance to colonialism in the nineteenth century. Yet even such proud moments are filtered through the painful memory of betrayal by Africans co-opted by European imperialists. Accordingly, Traoré's musical compositions complicate her response to Morrison's layered theme of bloodlust, as together they create a long temporal arc from ancient Greece to colonial and postcolonial Africa.[14]

Together Morrison and Traoré also call attention to the problem of self-definition as it resonates, in particular, for women today. The strife over reproductive rights in the United States, Morrison observes, shows "the absolute requirement of sovereign nations to control, exploit women from the smallest things to the lashing of women who have cell phones." For her part, Traoré speaks poignantly about the performative value of language. "How can you become who you want to be if you don't know who you are?" she asked her Berkeley audience after the American premiere. "How can you live with the expectations that other people have for you and that they're projecting onto you?"[15]

Morrison crafts the dialogue between Desdemona and Sa'ran to illustrate the potential of such questioning to drive change. At times their exchanges may sound didactic to educated Westerners familiar with the discourse of female empowerment. But Traoré remarked on the dialogue's impact for the trio of singers touring with her: "These young women on stage with Toni's text create a symbol of a different situation and the possibility of another era.... It is now possible for women in Africa to make a different choice.... Is a woman free to do what she wants or will she obey her husband all her lifetime?"[16] Noting the difficulty of discussing the "position of women" in Mali, where only a small part of the population is literate (and girls routinely undergo genital mutilation),[17] Traoré found a real image of social change in Morrison's script.

Cross-Cultural Dialogue

Desdemona thus offers a message of hope despite—or perhaps because of—the gravity of the issues it raises. Morrison's engagement with Shakespeare's "Willow Song" shows how she keeps hope alive. Barely more than an abstraction, Desdemona's nurse was merely the bearer of the noblewoman's musical epitaph for Shakespeare, who adapted an iconic lover's lament to unite two unlikely women in death.[18] By contrast, Morrison reaches across the gulf separating Sa'ran and Desdemona by promising them both immortality in her revised "Willow Song," now called "Someone Leans Near":

> *Sa'ran*: "You will never die again."
>   What bliss to know
>   I will never die again.
> *Desdemona*: We will never die again. (*Desdemona*, 49)

Sa'ran ends the new song with the certainty "I will never die again," which Desdemona echoes in the plural "we." An unidentified speaker first made this promise to Sa'ran, and beneath its surface meaning is a deeper message of female empowerment.

> And they will find me there,
>   And they will live,
>   And they will not die again. ("Thunder," 464)

So ends the enigmatic Coptic text "Thunder, Perfect Mind," which Morrison used as the epigraph to her novel *Paradise* (1998). In *Desdemona* she shifts pronouns to personalize the language: "they" becomes "You/I/We will never die again," in effect reinforcing the shared fate of Sa'ran and Desdemona. "Not" becomes "never" to heighten the tone, for Morrison has dried the tears of Shakespeare's Barbary to signal her transformation into the strong and independent-minded Sa'ran.

Scholars have compared the goddess in "Thunder" to other ancient female powers, including the Egyptian goddess Isis and the Jewish Dame Wisdom. Yet the goddess in "Thunder" stands out for her effort to unify opposites in the universe, as when she proclaims:

> For I am the wisdom [of the] Greeks
>   and the knowledge of [the] barbarians...
> I am the one whom they call Life,
>   and you have called Death. ("Thunder," 461)

Her power is felt "not only in women, but also in all people," according to Elaine Pagels. "[Her voice] speaks not only in citizens, but aliens, it says, in the poor and in the rich" (Pagels).

Morrison's subtle allusion in *Desdemona* to a potential unity of opposites underscores her characters' struggle to reach across the racial divide that separates them. "I am black-skinned. You are white-skinned," Sa'ran challenges Desdemona in what has become the work's most-quoted passage. "So you don't know me. Have never known me" (*Desdemona*, 45–46). Desdemona denies that race matters when love is at stake, prompting Sa'ran to call up both versions of "The Willow Song." In between these interludes, the women "clarify" their differences, illustrating that they can indeed listen to each other.

Listening allows Desdemona and Sa'ran to connect in a way that "spans continents and centuries," in Sellars's view, modeling what he calls "a new set of relations ... [based on] radical equality." The meeting between these women, then, symbolizes a much larger dialogue among world cultures, showing how they are enriched when they encounter each other on equal terms. "Shakespeare went out of his way," Sellars added, "to write stories that were all about how intricately wired and cross-woven the world is." He reminded me that there is no more fitting symbol for this exchange than Shakespeare's theater, the Globe.

This message gained special force when the composer's homeland came under siege while *Desdemona* was still being performed in Europe. Traoré reported feeling stunned[19] when northern Mali was seized by armed separatists in January 2012,[20] and then the democratic government in Bamako was ousted, causing international alarm about the future of democracy in Africa.[21] One quarter of Mali's population went hungry as hundreds of thousands were displaced,[22] women were victimized in a rape campaign, children were recruited to fight, and cultural heritage sites were torn asunder.[23] Even music was not spared in an attempt by Islamist militants to destroy communication, social cohesion, and the transmission of values not their own. "We don't want Satan's music," began their religious degree.[24] Although a French-led force wrested power from the insurgents in early 2013, the final outcome remained unclear, particularly in light of the region's strategic importance for both Africa and the West.[25]

In the cross-cultural dialogue imagined by Morrison, Traoré identifies an antidote to intolerance and the very real threat it poses. Noting that "I'm a Muslim, but Sharia isn't my thing" (Morgan), she told the British press that the sensation of being misunderstood is "something I experience everyday. So much misunderstanding between two cultures, two continents because they started their relationship in a very bad way. It's still very complicated between Africa and Western countries" (McNamee).

Traoré developed this awareness while traveling the world as the daughter of a diplomat and part of Mali's elite. Her background has helped her to create a bridge with a Western sensibility by partnering with musical celebrities such as Paul McCartney and the Kronos Quartet, and covering old favorites like Gershwin's "The Man I Love" on *Tchamantché*, which garnered France's equivalent of the Grammy for Best World Album in 2009. Several popular genres, including jazz and R&B, inform her cosmopolitan approach.

In Traoré, then, Morrison has found a compelling partner with whom to examine the roots of our wounded modernity. Morrison crafts her words to stand on their own. But they also anchor the music, serving as the platform from which Traoré launches her passionate response. By transforming Shakespeare's "Willow Song," they invite us to listen for the new sound of women's liberation in their collaboration.

To better disseminate their message, there has been talk of adapting *Desdemona* into a film shot in Mali.

Notes

1. After leaving Vienna, the *Desdemona* project traveled to Brussels and Paris before arriving in the United States in fall 2011 and then returned to Europe, where it was featured during London's Cultural Olympiad in 2012. Wiener Festwochen commissioned the work with Berkeley's Cal Performances, New York's Lincoln Center for the Performing Arts, Théâtre Nanterre-Amandiers, spielzeit'europa / Berliner Festspiele, London's Barbican, London Arts Council, and London 2012 Festival. I delivered a version of this paper at the American Literature Association conference, May 24, 2012, in San Francisco for the Toni Morrison Society panel "Women, Migration, Movement and Mobility in Toni Morrison's Fiction."

2. *Othello*, ed. G. Blakemore Evans, in *The Riverside Shakespeare*; references are to act, scene, and line.

3. I take all comments by Peter Sellars from my program note "Reviving Desdemona and Barbary," which I wrote for the U.S. premiere in Berkeley.

4. Queen Elizabeth issued three statements (two in 1596, one in 1601) authorizing the deportation of "Blackamoors" from her realm. Emily C. Bartels argues that the edicts were not only racially conceived (separating black people from the Crown's "liege people" on the basis of skin color) but also politically motivated. Elizabeth wanted to trade foreigners (including prisoners of war) for English prisoners held primarily by Spain.

5. English views of the Other, whether European Catholics, Muslims, Turks, North Africans, or sub-Saharan Africans, were informed by several discourses, including religion, as well as shifting military and commercial alliances, especially related to the Ottoman and Spanish empires. Any discussion of this context is complex, as demonstrated by the array of theoretical approaches brought to bear on it by scholars.

6. After being captured by Spanish corsairs in 1518, the Islamic scholar known as Leo Africanus (al-Hasan B. Muhammad) was handed over to Pope Leo X (Giovanni de' Medici), whose name he took after being emancipated. In 1526, Africanus completed his *Descrittione dell'Africa*, which the Italian geographer Gian Battista Ramusio published in his own *Navigationi et viaggi* (Venice, 1550). As Croton Black explains, Africanus's manuscript went through several translations, revealing a growing bias against Islam by the time John Pory published the first English edition in 1600 (Black, 272).

7. Philip A. Stadter assesses Herodotus's narrative strategies (83). The weightiness of Morrison's themes distances her from Herodotus. The Hellenic writer appealed to his audience's delight in acts of ingenious deception used by Greek underdogs to defeat tyrants from other lands. On this last point, see Donald Lateiner (231–36).

8. Morrison addressed members of the American Academy in Rome in 2012. She has removed Iago from the stage (though his memory lingers on) to focus on a female perspective, but she also probes the background of Othello, as we ponder what he is like in the play. Shakespeare expanded his thematic and geographic reach through Othello's backstory in the Mediterranean realm, North Africa, and the Levant.

9. As Hegel reaffirmed in his influential *The Philosophy of History* (1837) by describing Africa as a place void of history, memory, and reason. Maghan Keita explores the process of redefining significant areas in Africa, including Egypt, as Asian or non-African (Said's "Orientalizing") since antiquity. Herodotus conflated certain African peoples with Asians or at least drew strong parallels (8, 10).

10. Skype interview with Toni Morrison by Berkeley's Cal Performances, October 28, 2011.

11. Virginia Mason Vaughan explains that Shakespeare played on the Renaissance myth of Venice as a rational commonwealth whose combination of order and freedom promoted prosperity. While praising the Italian city-state, the English still feared its reputation for vice and corruption. Shakespeare drew on several English texts to create his ambivalent portrait of La Serenissima and its Cyprus colony as a context for Othello's and Desdemona's downfall (14–28).

12. Although my analysis is based on performances of *Desdemona*, for the readers' convenience, I cite page numbers in the version published by Oberon (2012).

13. Giraldi Cinthio put the following advice into the mouth of Disdemona: "I am very much afraid that I'll turn out to be an example to young people not to marry against their parents' wishes; and that Italian ladies will learn because of me not to go with a man who is segregated by nature, Heaven, and a way of life from us" (436).

14. In both her instrumentation and song quotations, Traoré recalls the *jeliw* as keepers of West African memory.

15. Morrison's comment is from her Skype interview, which was broadcast while Traoré was interviewed onstage at Berkeley's Cal Performances on October 28, 2011.

16. Remarks by Traoré are from her Berkeley interview on October 28, 2011, and her radio interview with McNamee on June 19, 2012.

17. Trust Law reports that 80 percent of girls and women aged fifteen to forty-nine have undergone this practice in Mali. Maria Caspani, "Mali Singer Pushes Anti-female Cutting Message," September 24, 2012, http://www.trust.org.

18. First Desdemona is paired with Barbary, and later with her servant Emilia, who repeats the willow burden before she too is killed (5.2.254–58). Shakespeare's source was a well-known ayre with lute accompaniment that described a forsaken male lover. Erin Minear explains how Shakespeare develops the musical theme to distinguish Desdemona from Othello. Othello's madness is characterized by unintelligible noise, whereas Desdemona's effort to console him evokes an orderly music of the spheres. His music is audible, but her music is mostly transcendent in keeping with the classical conceit (358–64).

19. "A kind of nightmare started," Traoré later told Tracy Bowden from the Australian Broadcasting Service. "Mali Conflict Prompts Concerns and UN-Led Intervention," *7.30*, January 16, 2013, http://www.abc.net.au/7.30.

20. Local Tuaregs launched the movement to "liberate" northern Mali using arms that many fighters had gained while serving as pro-Gaddafi mercenaries in the Libyan revolution of 2011. Their uprising was supported by Ansar Dine, Al-Qaeda in the Islamic Maghreb (AQIM), and other jihadists who quickly co-opted the movement with the aim of creating a radical Islamic state. Mali's army staged a coup d'état one week before national elections on

March 22, 2012, ostensibly in response to the government's failure to put down the Tuareg rebellion. "Turmoil in the Sahara," *New York Times*, January 18, 2013.

21. Mali had been a democracy since 1991. Although Western powers viewed the military coup as a serious setback for democracy in Africa, the mainstream in Mali initially was not disturbed by it, signaling its divide from the country's elites. The conflict has become a focal point of U.S. and European antiterrorism policies and rhetoric. John Campbell, "Mali Conflict: Three Things You Need to Know," Council on Foreign Relations (CFR), January 16, 2013, YouTube video; Jonathan Masters, "Al-Qaeda in the Islamic Maghreb (AQIM)," CFR, updated January 24, 2013, http://www.cfr.org.

22. By March 2013, the occupation had displaced nearly 500,000 civilians, worsening a food shortage affecting 4.6 million, according to the UN's Office for the Coordination of Humanitarian Affairs (March 25, 2013) and Food and Agricultural Organization (December 2012).

23. A signatory to the Rome Statute, Mali invited the International Criminal Court to launch an investigation in July 2012. Rampant summary executions, deaths by stoning, mutilations, and other cruel acts performed by militant Islamists under the guise of Sharia law were widely publicized and condemned. Mali's army has also been accused of war crimes and torture, and racism has been blamed as one cause of the brutality. Human Rights Watch and Amnesty International reports, "Situation in Mali," paragraphs 92, 94, 96–97, 101, 104, 110–13, 118–23.

24. It continued: "Qur'anic verses must take its place. Sharia demands it." The decree was issued in Gao on August 22, 2012 (Morgan). The censorship was doomed to failure in a society of troubadours and griots where people look to music for direction and spiritual sustenance. In protest Traoré began working on her fifth album, *Beautiful Africa* (2013).

25. France's intervention was controversial, though not entirely unilateral (African partners included Mali, Chad, ECOWAS). French and African troops were welcomed as liberators by northern Malians, and French president François Hollande later received the UNESCO Peace Prize for authorizing the action. Yet France's motives as a former colonial power have been questioned, particularly due to Mali's rich mineral resources. Saeed Shabazz, "Is the French Invasion of Mali Tied to a Colonial War for Uranium?" *Global Research*, January 30, 2013, http://www.finalcall.com.

Works Cited

Amnesty International. "Mali: Civilians at Risk from All Sides of the Conflict." February 1, 2013. http://www.amnesty.org/en/news.
———. "Mali's Worst Human Rights Situation in 50 Years." May 16, 2012. http://www.amnesty.org/en/news.
Bartels, Emily C. "Too Many Blackamoors: Deportation, Discrimination, and Elizabeth I." *Studies in English Literature, 1500–1900* 46, no. 2 (2006): 305–22.
Black, Croton. "Leo Africanus's 'Descrittione dell'Africa' and Its Sixteenth-Century Translation." *Journal of the Warburg and Courtauld Institutes* 65 (2002): 262–72.

Giraldi Cinthio, Giovanbattista. "Decade Three, Story Seven" (A Moorish Captain). *Gli Hecatommithi* (1565). In *Shakespeare and His Sources*, trans. and ed. Joseph Satin, 430–39. New York: Houghton Mifflin, 1966.

Herodotus. *The Histories*. Ed. Carolyn Dewald and trans. Robin Waterfield. New York: Oxford University Press, 2008.

Human Rights Watch. "Mali: Islamists Should Free Child Soldiers." January 15, 2013. http://www.hrw.org/news.

Keita, Maghan. "Africans and Asians: Historiography and the Long View of Global Interaction." *Journal of World History* 16, no. 1 (2005): 1–30.

Kitts, Lenore. "Reviving Desdemona and Barbary." Program note for *Desdemona*, by Toni Morrison and Rokia Traoré. Cal Performances, Berkeley, CA, October 26–29, 2011.

Lateiner, Donald. "Deceptions and Delusions in Herodotus." *Classical Antiquity* 9, no. 2 (1990): 230–46.

LeClair, Thomas. "The Language Must Not Sweat: A Conversation with Toni Morrison." In *Conversations with Toni Morrison*, ed. Danille Taylor-Guthrie, 119–28. Jackson: University Press of Mississippi, 1994.

Littlejohn, David. "So It Wasn't Jealousy after All?" *Wall Street Journal*, November 2, 2011.

McNamee, Anna. "Rokia Traoré discusses her role in *Desdemona*." *The Strand*. BBC World Service. June 19, 2012. http://www.bbc.co.uk/programmes/p00vov3l.

Minear, Erin. "Music and the Crisis of Meaning in *Othello*." *Studies in English Literature, 1500–1900* 49, no. 2 (2009): 355–70.

Morgan, Andy. "Mali: No Rhythm or Reason as Militants Declare War on Music." *Guardian*, October 23, 2012.

Morrison, Toni. *Desdemona*. Lyrics by Rokia Traoré. London: Oberon Books, 2012.

———. "Sellars and Morrison Discuss Collaboration at Rome Prize Ceremony in New York." May 6, 2012. American Academy in Rome, http://www.aarome.org.

Neill, Michael. "Unproper Beds: Race, Adultery, and the Hideous in *Othello*." *Shakespeare Quarterly* 40 (1989): 383–412.

Othello. In *The Riverside Shakespeare*, ed. G. Blakemore Evans, 2nd ed. Boston: Houghton Mifflin, 1997.

Pagels, Elaine. "The Thunder, Perfect Mind." *From Jesus to Christ*. Interview by *Frontline*. PBS. April 1998. http://www.pbs.org/wgbh/pages/frontline/shows/religion/story/pagels.html.

Situation in the Republic of Mali, Case no. ICC-01/12, Article 53(1) Report (January 16, 2013). http://www.icc-cpi.int/en_menus/icc/situations%20and%20cases/situations/icc0112/Documents/SASMaliArticle53_1PublicReportENG16Jan2013.pdf.

Stadter, Philip A. "Thinking about Historians." *American Journal of Philology* 113, no. 1 (1992): 83.

"Thunder, Perfect Mind." In *Women's Religions in the Greco-Roman World: A Sourcebook*, ed. Ross Shepard Kraemer, 456–64. Oxford: Oxford University Press, 2004.

Vaughan, Virginia Mason. *Othello: A Contextual History*. Cambridge: Cambridge University Press, 1994.

AAAYEEE BABO, AAAYEEE BABO, AAAYEEE BABO

(Praise God) (Praise God) (Praise God)

SONIA SANCHEZ

You said one nite on television when
asked if you voted. you said: oh. yes. I remember
all of those people. Fannie Lou Hamer
and others. Beaten. Hurt. Hosed down.
You said: When I vote
it's like a small prayer by the road.

I thought yes. Miss Toni. When i read
you, you become the sermon rinsing
my blood clean and
"vengo en el aire negro como su sonrisa"
(I move in air as black as your smile)

We know so little about migrations.
Of souls crossing oceans. Seas of longing.
we have not always been prepared
for landings in spaces that held
us suspended above our bones.
Paradise. Existed. So they say:

Yo sé, lo sé, yo sé, lo sé, yo sé, lo sé
(I know) (I know it) (I know) (I know it) (I know) (I know it)

In the beginning there wuz we and they
and others we thought
too mournful to be named.
Discussed. Brought before elders.
Even held in contempt. They
were so young in their slaughterings.

In the beginning when memory
was sound. There was
bonesmell. Bloodtear. Whisperscream.
Bodies seeping into each other like
flotsam.
Yo sé- séeeeee, lo sé- séeeeee, yo sé- séeeeee
(I know) (I know it) (I know)

And we arrived carrying flesh
and disguise
Expecting nothing on this shore.
But always searching for
Gusts of life. Sermons.
In the absence of authentic Gods.
New memory.
In our escape from plunder,
In our nesting on agitated land
new memory,
In our fatigue at living
we saw moving toward western
steeples,
mountains cracking through skulls
purple stars
colourless nights
trees praising our innocence
new territories dressing our
limbs in starched bones

In our traveling to weselves
in the building, in the journeyings,

in the killing of women in parlors,
bedrooms, patios, bidettes, to recover our
silverwords to reconnoiter the good amid
the evil. In our traveling to weselves,
to discover our own deaths.
It is rumored that one of the dead tongues
stretched out like a river
rushing wet streams of stone. wings.
skeletons.
Yo sé, lo sé, yo sé- séeeeee
(I know) (I know it) (I know) (know) (know)

In the beginning there was a
conspiracy of blue eyes to iron eyes
and backbone to match.
of palms shrieking with laughter
in convents,
new memory falling into death.

O will we ever know
what is no more with us?
O will weselves ever convalesce
as we ascend into wave after wave of
bloodmilk?
What can we say without blood?

In the beginning there was no end.
In the beginning there was no end.
In the beginning there was no end.

There was she though
"La mujer de todos los pasados"
(Woman in the fullness of time)
Miss Chloe. Spirit tongue.
Miss Toni. Praisetouch.
Miss Morrison. Anointing our eyes
moving us against ice sails,
repelling ice water ghosts
kneeling on razor thin knees
at confession.

Miss Toni Morrison. Woman Spirit.
Spitting teeth
on the wonder of women
recapturing the wings of our
most sacred vowels.
Bringing us into the flesh
of rain and laughter called
Paradise........

Paradise. Existed. So They Sayyyyy
Yo sé, séeeeee, lo sé, séeeeee, yo sé, séeeeee
(I know) (I know it) (I know)

Aaaayeee Babo. Aaaayeee Babo. Aaaayeee Babo.
(Praise God) (Praise God) (Praise God)
for Miss Toni Morrisonsonsonson
....

CONTRIBUTORS

Katherine Clay Bassard is professor and chair of English at Virginia Commonwealth University. She is the author of two books, *Spiritual Interrogations: Culture, Gender and Community in Early African American Women's Writing* (1999) and *Transforming Scriptures: African American Women Writers and the Bible* (2010), as well as numerous articles on African American literature, religion, and black women writers.

Herman Beavers is associate professor of English at the University of Pennsylvania, where he teaches courses in twentieth-century African American literature. He is the author of *Wrestling Angels into Song: The Fictions of Ernest J. Gaines and James A. McPherson* (1995). He is completing a scholarly monograph on jazz and the politics of racial conduct and a new book of poems, *Dreaming the Business of Hurt*.

Claudia Brodsky is professor of comparative literature at Princeton University. She is the author of *The Imposition of Form: Studies in Narrative Representation and Knowledge* (1987), *Lines of Thought: Discourse, Architectonics, and the Origin of Modern Philosophy* (1996), and *In the Place of Language: Literature and the Architecture of the Referent* (2009); coeditor with Toni Morrison of *Birth of a Nation'hood* (1997); and author of several articles and public presentations on Morrison.

Alma Jean Billingslea Brown is professor of English and founding faculty for the African Diaspora and the World program at Spelman College. She is currently president of the Toni Morrison Society and author of *Crossing Borders through Folklore: African American Women's Fiction and Visual Art* (1999), a comparative study of Toni Morrison, Paule Marshall, Faith Ringgold, and Betye Saar.

Davíd Carrasco is the Neil L. Rudenstine Professor of the Study of Latin America at the Harvard Divinity School and the Faculty of Arts and Sciences. He previously was on the faculty at Princeton University, where he collaborated with Toni Morrison on various projects. He is editor in chief of *Oxford Encyclopedia of Mesoamerican Cultures*. His most recent publication is *Aztecs: A Very Short Introduction* (2011).

Marc C. Conner is professor of English and associate provost at Washington and Lee University in Virginia. His books include *The Aesthetics of Toni Morrison: Speaking the Unspeakable* (2000), *Charles Johnson: The Novelist as Philosopher* (2007), and *The Poetry of James Joyce Reconsidered* (2012). He has also published dozens of essays and reviews on American and Irish modernism.

Carolyn C. Denard is founder and board chair of the Toni Morrison Society and currently Dean of the College at Connecticut College. A leading authority on Morrison, Professor Denard has contributed to critical anthologies and essay collections on Morrison's work, and she is editor of *What Moves at the Margin: Selected Non-fiction by Toni Morrison* (2008) and *Toni Morrison: Conversations* (2008), a collection of interviews.

Rita Dove, Commonwealth Professor of English at the University of Virginia, won the 1987 Pulitzer Prize in poetry for *Thomas and Beulah* (1986) and served as U.S. poet laureate from 1993 to 1995. Among her numerous publications are the novel *Through the Ivory Gate* (1992), the drama *The Darker Face of the Earth* (1994), the poetic sequence *Sonata Mulattica* (2009) and *The Penguin Anthology of 20th Century American Poetry* (2011). In 2012 President Barack Obama presented Professor Dove with the National Medal of Arts.

Jan Furman is professor of English at the University of Michigan, Flint. She is also director of the Master of Liberal Studies Program. She has authored *Toni Morrison's Fiction* (1996) and has edited *Slavery in the Clover Bottoms: John McCline's Narrative of His Life in Slavery and during the Civil War* (1998) and *Song of Solomon: A Casebook* (2003). Professor Furman has published scholarly essays on Toni Morrison, Civil War narrative, and slave narrative.

Contributors

Lucille P. Fultz, associate professor emerita in English at Rice University, is the author of *Toni Morrison: Playing with Difference* (2003), winner of the 2005 Toni Morrison Society Book Award. She is also volume editor of *Toni Morrison: Paradise, Love, A Mercy* (2013).

Mar Gallego-Durán is associate professor of American and African American literatures at the University of Huelva, Spain. She is author of *Passing Novels in the Harlem Renaissance* (2003) and coeditor of several essay collections, the most recent of which is *The Dialectics of Diasporic Identification* (2009).

Ann Hostetler is professor of English at Goshen College in Goshen, Indiana. She is the author of one volume of poetry, *Empty Room with Light*, and the editor of *A Cappella: Mennonite Voices in Poetry*. Her interview with Toni Morrison on teaching is included in *Toni Morrison: Conversations*, ed. Carolyn Denard. Among other places, her scholarship has appeared in *PMLA* and her poetry in the *American Scholar*. She is the editor of the *Journal of the Center for Mennonite Writing*.

Lovalerie King is professor of African American studies at Penn State University, where she also directs the Africana Research Center. She is the author of *Race, Theft, and Ethics: Property Matters in African American Literature* (2007) and *The Cambridge Introduction to Zora Neale Hurston* (2008). She has coedited four volumes, most recently *Contemporary African American Literature: The Living Canon* (2013).

Lenore Kitts, a visiting scholar at UC Berkeley, studies how nations cope with traumatic political histories through law and the arts. She is writing a book about Toni Morrison's use of music in her reckoning with slavery. Her publications include related articles and projects on early and late modern Italy.

Claudine Raynaud is professor of English and American studies at the University Paul-Valéry-Montpellier 3. She is author of *Toni Morrison: L'esthétique de la survie* (1996) and numerous articles on black autobiography and has also published in *The Cambridge Companion to Toni Morrison* (2007).

Tessa Roynon teaches American literature at the University of Oxford. She is the author of *Toni Morrison and the Classical Tradition* (2013), *The Cambridge Introduction to Toni Morrison* (2012), and coeditor of the interdisciplinary collection *African Athena: New Agendas* (2011).

Evelyn Jaffe Schreiber is full professor of English at the George Washington University in Washington, DC. Her books include *Subversive Voices: Eroticizing the Other in William Faulkner and Toni Morrison* (2001), winner of the 2003 Toni Morrison Society book prize, and *Race, Trauma, and Home in the Novels of Toni Morrison* (2010), winner of the 2012 Toni Morrison Society book prize.

Sonia Sanchez is currently poet-in-residence at Temple University. She was recipient of the PEN Writing Award in 1969 and the Pew Fellowships in the Arts in 1993. With over a dozen volumes published, Sanchez is best known for her poetry, the latest volume of which is *Morning Haiku* (2010). Her plays are collected and published in *I'm Black When I'm Singing, I'm Blue When I Ain't and Other Plays* (2010).

Adrienne Lanier Seward is professor emerita in English and race and ethnic studies at Colorado College. She is a past president of the Toni Morrison Society and also serves as a member of its executive board. Her current book project is *Race Movies Redux: The Films of Tyler Perry*.

Shirley A. (Holly) Stave is a professor at the Louisiana Scholars' College at Northwestern State University. She is editor of *Contested Intertextualities: Toni Morrison and the Bible* (2006), coeditor of *Toni Morrison's A Mercy: Critical Approaches* (2011), a contributor to the *Cambridge Companion to Toni Morrison* (2007), and the author of numerous essays on the work of Toni Morrison.

Justine Tally is professor of American literature at the University of La Laguna, Tenerife, Spain. She is the author of *Toni Morrison's Beloved: Origins* (2009), *The Story of Jazz: Toni Morrison's Dialogic Imagination* (2001), *Paradise Reconsidered: Toni Morrison's (Hi)stories and Truths* (1999), editor of *The Cambridge Companion to Toni Morrison* (2007), and coeditor with Shirley A. (Holly) Stave of *Toni Morrison's A Mercy: Critical Approaches*.

Valorie Thomas is associate professor of English and Africana Studies at Pomona College. Among her publications are "'Dust to Cleanse Themselves,' a Survivor's Ethos: Diasporic Disidentifications in *Zeitoun*" and "The Break," in Rebecca Walker's *Black Cool: One Thousand Streams of Blackness* (2012). She is completing a book manuscript on African diasporic vertigo.

Cheryl A. Wall, Board of Governors Zora Neale Hurston Professor of English at Rutgers University, is the author of *Worrying the Line: Black Women*

Writers, Lineage, and Literary Tradition (2005) and *Women of the Harlem Renaissance* (1995) and the editor of the *Writings of Zora Neale Hurston* in two volumes published by the Library of America (1995) and *Changing Our Own Words: Essays on Criticism, Theory, and Writing by Black Women* (1989), among other books. She is completing a study titled "The African American Essay: On Freedom and the Will to Adorn."

Philip Weinstein is Alexander Griswold Cummins Professor of English at Swarthmore College. The author of the award-winning *Becoming Faulkner* (2010) and former president of the William Faulkner Society, he has also written another book on Faulkner, a book on modernism, and *What Else But Love? The Ordeal of Race in Faulkner and Morrison* (1996).

Dana A. Williams is professor of African American literature and chair of the Department of English at Howard University. She is the author of *"In the Light of Likeness—Transformed": The Literary Art of Leon Forrest*. She is completing a book-length study of Toni Morrison's editorship at Random House.

INDEX

Adam and Eve, 21–22, 108, 122, 136
Aeschylus, 173–74, 175, 177, 181
aesthetics, xviii, 10, 25, 33, 36, 46, 47, 202–3, 207–8, 211, 212, 214–16
Agamemnon, 173, 175, 177, 178
agape, 119, 121, 122, 123, 124–25, 127, 129
Age of Enlightenment, 20, 22–23, 24, 25–26, 126, 173, 176, 182
African diasporic vertigo, xxii, 194–95, 199, 201–3
alienated existence, 26
Alter, Robert, 120
Apollo, 174, 182
aporia, 33, 34
appropriation, 69, 120, 253n
Athena, 173, 181–82
Atreus, House of, 175

Bacchae, 172, 173, 178–81, 182
Bakhtin, M. M., xvi, 142n, 186
"Battle Hymn of the Republic, The," 174
Baudelaire, Charles, 210, 216
becoming, 8, 11, 12, 13, 14, 120, 156
Beloved, 12–14, 16, 21, 23, 26, 27, 29, 34, 35, 37, 39, 40, 67–68, 107–11, 123, 124–25, 126–27, 133–34, 177–78, 208, 220–21, 253n, 260; Amy, 75, 77, 110, 178; Baby Suggs, xviii, 13, 77, 107–11, 116, 128, 133, 166–67, 169; Beloved, 13, 14, 21, 27, 37, 38, 75, 76, 110, 128, 133, 161, 167, 173, 176, 177; crawling already? baby, 35, 133; Denver, 75, 110, 128, 167–68, 177–78; Halle, 13, 68, 110, 164, 167, 168; Garner, 107, 108; 124 Bluestone Road, 168, 176; Paul D, 13, 22, 68, 69–70, 75, 76, 77, 108, 134, 163–64, 168, 169; Red Heart, 77; schoolteacher, 21, 76–77, 108, 133, 163–66, 168, 169; schoolteacher's nephews, 110, 133–34, 167; Sethe, 13–14, 21, 22, 27, 35–36, 38, 68, 71–78, 107, 108, 109–11, 124, 133, 134, 161, 163, 164, 166–69, 173, 177, 178; Seven-O, 169; Sixo, 13, 163–66, 168, 169; Stamp Paid, 13, 77, 109, 169; Sweet Home, xxi, 107, 108, 163, 164
Benjamin, Walter, 25–26, 28, 207, 209–12, 216n
Bhabha, Homi, 23–24
Bible, xx, 21–22, 119–25, 142n, 211
binary oppositions, 16, 182
birds, 148, 150, 151, 212–13, 236
Black Aesthetic, 42
Black Arts Movement, 42
Black Book, The, Toni Morrison's editorship of, 42, 43

279

black cultural self, 47
black nationalism, xxiii, 221
Blackamoors, 257, 265n
blackness: interpretations of, 61, 86–87, 88, 94, 123, 126, 221, 227; Toni Morrison's conception of, 43, 47
blood, 77–78, 94, 108, 128, 130, 167, 175, 261–62
Blood Bank, 175
Bluest Eye, The, xvii, 9, 15, 20, 33, 34, 54, 57, 61, 119, 125, 126, 128, 196, 213–15, 225; Cholly Breedlove, 8–10, 57, 126–27; Pauline Breedlove, 55–56, 57, 126, 127; Pecola Breedlove, xvii, 8–9, 21, 28, 33, 34, 125, 127–28; the Breedloves, 55, 126; Claudia, 34, 55, 56, 57, 214; critical reception of, xv; Darlene, 8; Frieda, 57; the MacTeers, 55, 196
breaking with tradition, 25
Brown, Sterling A., 44
Butler, Judith, 192, 194, 195, 202
Butler Place, 176

Calchas, 178
Carmichael, Stokely. *See* Ture, Kwame
castration, symbolic, 13
Catholicism, 24, 86, 136
chaos theory. *See* systems theory
Cheng, Anne Anlin, 126
chosen people, 223
Christ, body of, 132, 133, 140
Christianity, 108–10, 113, 114, 116, 117, 182, 200
"City Upon the Hill, The" ("A Model of Christian Charity"), 132–33
civil rights, xx, 46, 96, 98, 100
Civil Rights Movement, 95, 98, 101–2, 103, 175, 180, 240; neighborhoods transformed by, xi–xiii, 93–94, 98, 129
Clearing, the, 108, 111
Clemente Orozco, José, 151–53
Clifton, Lucille, 34
Clytemnestra, 172–73, 174, 177, 178

community, xi, xii, xvi, xx, xxi, 21, 25, 26, 35, 36, 37, 38, 53, 56, 61, 62, 80–81, 84, 85, 88, 89, 95–96, 97, 99, 103, 109–11, 127, 129, 132, 133, 153, 154, 173, 185, 188, 191, 196, 197, 200, 202, 220, 225, 227, 232, 234, 238; disintegration of, 98, 129
corn, 69
creation story, 155
crossroads, 194–95, 199, 202–3

Derrida, Jacques, 192, 241
Descartes, René, 20, 22
Desdemona, 256–60; Amazons, 257, 261; Barbary, the maid, 258, 259, 260, 263; Barbary, the maid, significance of name, 255–57, 266n; Desdemona, xxiv, 261–63; as character in Shakespeare's *Othello*, 257; name of character, 260; Othello, 261; Sa'ran, 260, 262–63
dialectics, 41
dialogics, 12, 189
diaspora, 43
Dionysus, 175, 179, 180
Dionysus in 69, 179, 180
Disallowing, the, 39, 113
disintegration/integration, 95
dominant culture, 82
Douglass, Frederick, 165–66
dreams, 60–61, 86, 87–88, 90, 146, 148–49, 150, 248
Du Bois, W. E. B., 94
Dust Tracks on the Road, 78

Electra, 178
elements of life, xvii
Eliade, Mircea, 26, 29, 149, 151, 156
Ellison, Ralph, 19, 39, 162, 200, 201, 202
Eloe, Florida, 125, 224
entropy, 219, 222, 228n, 229n
epigraphs, 39, 123, 132, 141, 147, 148
eros, 121, 122, 123, 124–25, 127, 129
Eshu, 195, 199–201
ethical turn in Toni Morrison, 26

Index

Eumenides, 173–74, 175, 177, 181–82
Euripides, 178–81
exorcism, 109

Fanon, Franz, 23–24
father, absence of, 112
Faulkner, William, 20
fiction: as archaeology, 164; magico-realist, 192; Western, 14
flying and flight, 168–69, 186, 187, 190; Africans, 168, 170n, 185, 186, 191
folklore, xvi, 154, 191, 192n, 197
"Foreigner's Home, The," 145, 146, 151–52
forgiveness, 103
Foucault, Michel, 134, 142, 192n
framing, 134–35
Franzen, Jonathan, 7, 15
free will, 13
freedom, 70, 98, 149, 168
Freud, Sigmund, 20, 72, 74, 241; psychology, 37
Frost, Robert, xvii
fruit, 102
Frye, Northrup, 119
Fuentes, Carlos, 144
Furies, the, 173, 176–77, 179, 181

García Márquez, Gabriel, 144, 145–46
garden, 68
Garden of Eden, xxi, 107, 117
Garner, Margaret, 35, 161, 177
gender relations, 243–44
gesture, 10, 11, 12
ghost, 33, 37, 74, 109–10, 116, 177
Giraldi Cinthio, Giovanbattista, 256, 260
globalization, 153
God, Old Testament, 107–8, 113, 119
Gothic tradition, 248–49
griot, 189, 258, 261

Habermas, Jürgen, 24–25
hands, 22, 26
Hansberry, William Leo, 44

Heidegger, Martin, 19–20, 24, 30
Herodotus, 265n
hierophany, 29
Holder, Ernest, 101
home, 29, 53, 56, 57, 153
Home, xvii, xviii, xxiii, 21, 62–63, 231–41; Cee (Ycidra), xvi, xvii–xviii, 22, 28, 63, 195–96, 197, 198, 199, 200, 201–2, 232, 235–36, 238, 239–40; Crawford, 62, 196, 202; Dr. Beau, 200; Ethel Fordham, 238; Jerome, 197; Lenore, 197, 200; Lily, 62, 198, 200, 237; Georgia Lotus, xvii, 53, 62–64, 196, 198, 232, 237–38, 239; Reverend Maynard, 197; man in the zoot suit, 198, 199, 240; Mike, 202; Miss Ethel, xvii; Frank Money, xvii–xviii, 21, 22, 62–64, 195–96, 197, 198, 199–201, 202, 231–32, 234–40; Red, 202; Stuff, 202, 238
homelessness, 26, 53
homosexuality, 250–51
Howard Players, 44–45
Howard University, 43–44
Hurston, Zora Neale, 54, 72, 78

Iago, 265n
infanticide, 13–14, 66, 72, 76–77, 133, 164, 173
innocence, 16–17, 108, 123, 129
Invisible Man, 39, 162, 201, 202
Iphigenia, 178

James, William, 233
Jameson, Frederic, 56
Jazz, xvii, 16, 22, 27, 28, 34, 35, 36, 37–39, 40, 58–60, 62, 95–103, 111–13, 134–35, 173, 178, 212–13, 231, 241; the City, 54, 58–60, 62, 134–35; Dorcas, 35, 38, 39, 111, 135, 173, 176, 178; Felice, 35, 38–39, 178; Golden Grey, 111–12; Alice Manfred, 135, 176, 178; True Belle, 112; Wild, 21, 36, 38, 111, 135
Jefferson, Thomas, 159–60, 165–66
Jones, Gayl, 225

jouissance, 70
Joyce, James, 22, 28, 29, 37, 228n

Kahlo, Frieda, 145
K.D., 139, 180
Korean War, 236–37
Kristeva, Julia, 124
Kuhn, Thomas, xvi

Lacan, Jacques, 72, 73, 192n
LaCocque, André, 122–23
Levinas, Emmanuel, 26–27
Libation Bearers, 173, 175, 177, 178
liminality, 196, 200
Lorain, Ohio, 53, 55, 56, 57, 68
love, 121, 122, 124–25, 127, 136, 139
Love, xx, 21, 27, 28, 129, 175, 180, 181–82, 231; Christine, 21, 102, 129, 180, 182; Bill Cosey, 96–103; Cosey's Resort, 96, 97, 98, 99, 101, 102, 103; Heed, 21, 96, 103, 182; Junior, 21; L, 28, 97–98, 100, 101, 103, 175, 181–82; May, 98, 100; Pretty-Fay, 181; Sandler, 99–100, 101; Sooker Bay, 98, 101, 102; Up Beach, 101; Vida, 99, 101, 102

Mackey, Peter Francis, 228n
Malaik, 87–88, 130
Mali, 264
Maltz, Albert, 202
Margaret Garner, 177
master narrative. *See* narrative: master
McAdams, Dan, 233–34
McCarthy, Joseph, 233
memory, 57, 64, 70, 76, 89, 90, 94, 96, 103; autobiographical, 69; bodily, 81, 88; cultural, 82; Mississippi floods, 70; performative, 81; as reenactment, 81, 82; rememory, 66, 71, 73, 133, 141, 168, 169; as repetition, 68; thought pictures, 72–73; traumatic, 66–67, 80
Mercy, A, xxiii–xxiv, 16, 21, 23, 34, 41, 80–81, 82–91, 125, 129–30, 182, 260; *a minha mãe*, 86, 87, 90–91, 249; blacksmith (smith), 21, 83, 86, 87–88, 251; consequences of death, 90; D'Ortega, 83–84, 90–91, 245–46, 247–48, 249; Florens, xvii, 21, 83, 85–88, 91, 129–30, 245, 248, 249, 253n; Lina, 85, 86, 88–89, 90, 249; Scully, 130, 249–51; Complete Sorrow, 89–90; Jacob Vaark, 81, 84–85, 244–48, 249–50; Rebekka Vaark, 84, 85, 89, 90, 244, 247; Virginia, 59, 188, 190, 250; Willard, 249–51
miasma, 172, 174, 176, 177, 178
migration, 134, 138
Milton, John, 21–22, 108
mind-body duality, 114–16
"Model of Christian Charity, A." *See* "City Upon the Hill, The"
modernism, 20, 36–37
modernity, xix, 19, 23, 25; Toni Morrison's understanding of, 20–21
Morrison, Slade, 28
Morrison, Toni: in college theater, 44–47; as editor, 42–43; ethical turn in writing, 26; "Home," 23; master's thesis, 20; "Memory, Creation, and Writing," 48; Nobel Lecture in Literature (1993), 26, 28, 120, 233; Nobel Prize for Literature, xiii, xvi, 44, 211; "The Site of Memory," 67, 70, 74, 78; "Unspeakable Things Unspoken," 179
Morrison trilogy, 35, 107, 132, 173, 174, 175, 177
mother, separation from, 85–86
mother's milk, 76, 110, 128, 167
motherhood, 117, 127–29, 133–34, 138
Mrs Dalloway, 37
mythology, xvi, 110, 181, 224

Nag Hammadi, 27, 39, 117n, 132
narrative: competing, 81; fragmented, 36, 37–38; master, 37; persona, 27; revisionist, 46; voice, 10, 97–98, 101, 112–13
Negro Motorist Green Book, The, 96–97

Nietzsche, Friedrich, 10, 17n, 20, 24, 172
Nora, Pierre, 57, 64

Odysseus, 199
Old Testament, 223. *See also* God, Old Testament
ontology, 24, 29
Oresteia, 173–74, 175, 176–77, 181, 182
Orestes, 173, 178
orphan, 19, 30, 39, 80
Other, the, 7, 8, 13, 27, 68, 75, 82, 86, 91, 246, 250, 265n
outcast, 20, 21, 22, 224

Pallas Athena, 182
Paradise, xvii, 16, 26, 28, 29, 34, 35, 36, 38, 39, 40, 60–62, 110, 113–17, 134, 136, 175, 178–81, 214–15, 220, 227; Arnette, 115, 139, 180; Billie Delia, 176, 181; Zechariah Coffee, 133; comparison with *Tar Baby*, 220–24; the Convent, 38, 114, 115, 129, 134, 137, 138, 139, 179–81, 222, 224, 227; Convent women, 21, 39, 176, 178, 179; Consolata, 39, 40, 114–16, 134, 136–40; Dovey, 114, 138; Nathan Du Pres, 60; 8-rock, 36, 139, 222; Gigi, 180; Lone, 116; Mary Magna, 138, 139; Reverend Misner, 114, 129, 138; Deacon (Deek) Morgan, 114, 116, 134, 136–38, 141, 181, 222–23; Steward Morgan, 114, 138, 222–23; New Fathers, 114, 138, 178, 179; Old Fathers, 114, 138, 140; the Oven, 61, 222–23, 227, 228n; Patricia, the historian, 40; Piedade, 39–40, 116; Ruby, 16, 35, 36, 38, 39, 60–61, 114, 128, 129, 133, 136, 138, 140, 179–81, 221–24; Soane, 114, 134, 141; Sweetie, 35, 138
Paradise Lost, 21–22, 26
patriarchal power, 13, 122–23, 243–51
Patterson, Orlando, 95
Pentheus, 173, 174, 179–80
performativity, 185, 187, 191, 192n, 228n, 262
phantasm, 72–75; three phases of, 72

phantom, 112
philos, 119, 121, 122, 124–25, 127, 129, 139
place as site, 71–72
Playing in the Dark, xvi, 7–8, 11, 82, 252n
postmodernism, 24, 36
Proust, Marcel, 208–9

Radiance of the King, The, 151–52, 153
Random House Publishing Company, 42, 47
rape, 8, 72, 76, 127
reenactment, 88–89
religion, 81–82, 84–85, 107, 110, 144, 148, 149–50, 154
religious motifs, 151
return of the repressed, 37, 40, 66, 75–76
Ricoeur, Paul, 94
Rilke, Rainer Maria, 30
rituals, pagan, 85
Rivera, Diego, 145–46

sacred, the, 24, 29, 144
Said, Edward, 23
Schechner, Richard, 172, 179, 180, 192n
segregation, 96
Sellars, Peter, 256–60, 263, 264, 265n
sexual intercourse and food, 68–70
sexuality, female, 139–40
shamanism, 148, 149
shelter/sheltering, 19, 26, 30, 75
Shulamites, 121–24
silencing, 33, 34
slaves, slavery, 9, 12–14, 16, 22–23, 36–37, 66, 73, 76, 82, 88, 113, 117, 123, 125, 126, 132, 149, 159–69, 186, 243–44
song and singing, 148, 151, 164, 187, 262–63
Song of Solomon, xxi, 9, 10–12, 27, 34–35, 124, 146–51, 155, 174, 176, 178, 185–91, 240–41; Susan Byrd, 190–91; Circe, 176, 187, 189–90; Reverend Cooper, 176; Macon Dead, 21, 34, 35, 150, 187, 188–89; Milkman (Macon, Jr.) Dead, 11, 12, 35, 124, 129, 147, 148–49, 150, 176, 186, 187–91;

Pilate Dead, 10, 12, 27, 35, 148, 150–51, 168, 186, 187–88, 190, 240–41; Guitar, 11–12, 124, 147–48, 149, 150, 174, 175–76; Hagar, 34–35; Hanna, 10; Jake, 187, 189, 190; Porter, 12; Reba, 35; Ryna's Gulch, 187; Seven Days, 11, 175, 176; Virginia Shalimar, 148, 190; Robert Smith, 149; Sugarman, 148, 151, 187, 190; Sweet, 148, 149, 150

Song of Songs, and narrative voice of, 122–23, 125, 127

Souls of Black Folk, The, 94

South, the, 56, 61

Soyinka, Wole, 179

Spivak, Gayatri, 23

storytelling, 26–28, 88, 90, 120, 186, 188, 191, 240–41; as "no-story" and trauma, 66–67

stream of consciousness, 37, 127

subjectivity, 80, 83

Sula, xi–xii, xxi, 9, 10, 13, 34, 57, 125, 127, 153–56, 173, 179; the Bottom, 60, 153–55; Chicken Little, 10, 34; mass suicide in, 155–56; Nel, 10, 34, 125; Eva Peace, 10, 13, 127; Plum Peace, 10, 127; Sula Peace, 9, 10, 21, 22, 34, 125, 129; Shadrack, 9, 10, 21, 154, 155

survival, xx, 10, 13, 14, 16, 27, 57, 59, 63, 64, 66, 67, 80, 81, 83, 85, 86, 89, 90, 91, 95, 108, 116, 164, 168, 187, 196, 200, 221, 227, 233, 238

systems theory, 219–20, 221

Tar Baby, xxiii, 16, 27, 125, 182, 224–27; Cheyenne, 225–26; comparison with *Paradise*, 220–24; Eloe, Florida, 125, 224; Jadine (Jade), 21, 125, 182, 221, 222–23, 224, 225–27; Ondine, 226; Soldier, 225; Son, 125, 129, 182, 221, 224–27; Woman in Yellow, 125

Till, Emmett, 11, 100, 175

Toni Morrison Society, xii–xiii; founding of, xvi; Toni Morrison's participation with, xiii

Trace, Joe, 36, 38, 58, 59, 111, 112, 135, 173, 178

Trace, Violet, 38, 58, 111, 112, 128, 134, 135, 178

transgression, sexual, 68–69

Traoré, Rokia, xxiv, 258–59, 261–62, 264

trauma, 72, 76, 87, 90, 91; Sethe's, 71–75; racial, 148

Trethewey, Natasha, 98, 99, 101

trickster, 194–95, 199–200, 201

Ture, Kwame, 47

Twin, 89

Ulysses, 28, 37, 228n

Underground Railroad, 163

unspeakable, the, 15, 69, 70, 75, 250–51

Van Der Zee, James, 35, 58

veil, 69, 75; pulling back, 67–68

Vietnam War, 179

village values, 58

Vodun, 199

Walker, Madame C. J., 126

Washington Repertory Players, 44–47

water, 29, 64, 70–71, 75, 87–88, 116, 117

Watts Riots, 179

"Willow Song, The," 263, 266n

Winthrop, John, 132–33, 136, 138, 139, 140–41

Woolf, Virginia, 37

women, role of, 84

Wright, Richard, 39

Yoruba-Bantu-Kongo, 194, 197, 199, 200

Žižek, Slavoj, 121

www.ingramcontent.com/pod-product-compliance
Lightning Source LLC
Chambersburg PA
CBHW030335240426

43661CB00052B/1639